PASSING FANCIES in JEWISH AMERICAN LITERATURE and CULTURE

D1529095

JEWISH LITERATURE AND CULTURE

Alvin H. Rosenfeld, editor

PASSING FANCIES in JEWISH AMERICAN LITERATURE and CULTURE

Judith Ruderman

Indiana University Press

This book is a publication of

Indiana University Press
Office of Scholarly Publishing
Herman B Wells Library 350
1320 East 10th Street
Bloomington, Indiana 47405 USA

iupress.indiana.edu

Manufactured in the United States of America

Cataloging information is available from the Library of Congress.
ISBN 978-0-253-03695-7 (hardback)
ISBN 978-0-253-03696-4 (paperback)
ISBN 978-0-253-03699-5 (ebook)

1 2 3 4 5   24 23 22 21 20 19

For my beloved grandchildren

Contents

Acknowledgments

I THANK THE ARTISTS in words or images who created the texts that inspired my work and the many scholars who produced my secondary sources: the literary critics, Judaic studies experts, researchers on race and "passing," sociologists, medical historians, biographers, physicians—the list goes on.

Various friends and family members suggested works relevant to my topic or made other helpful comments: Dorothy Anger, David Birnbaum, Linda Carl, Susan Dyer, Lawrence Etter, John Friedman, Laura Lieber, Eric Meyers, B. J. Purow, Sarah Purow-Ruderman, Marjory Ruderman, and Diane Sasson. They were an important part of this process, personally and professionally, and I am grateful for their interest and input.

Thanks to Dee Mortensen, the humanities editor at Indiana University Press, for being warmly receptive to my initial proposal; Alvin Rosenfeld, the editor of the series of which my book is now a part; and various others at the press, including Paige Rasmussen and Maya Bringe, who responded to my technical questions or cleaned up my errors. My experience from proposal to publication has only reinforced my prior impression of IUP's reputation. I was fortunate that the anonymous readers of my manuscript accepted the task of reviewing it, for they gave my work considerable care and attention and offered invaluable advice as a result. I wish I could thank them in person for their time, energy, knowledge, and intelligence, but here at least I can acknowledge these unnamed scholars for the critical insights that improved this book immeasurably.

At Duke I relied on the IT expertise of Quincy Garbutt, who responded to my computer issues with alacrity and patience. My research and writing were facilitated by the dedicated staff and extensive holdings of the Duke University Library. I so appreciate the assistance of Duke's librarians, especially Jewish Studies specialist Rachel Ariel and literature and theater studies specialist Arianne Hartsell-Gundy, but also those who provided additional needed services, often behind the scenes: Bobbi Earp, Erin Nettifee, Cheryl Thomas, and many more. I am lucky to have access to the breadth and depth of the holdings not only of Duke University but also of the other research libraries in the area and beyond, whose resources I tapped as well. As but one example of the materials available to me, Duke has a complete set of the year's issues of the *Smart Set* that I was looking for—this in spite of the fact that, as Thomas Connolly said of the magazine, in his study of its co-editor George Jean Nathan, "the periodical files . . . have almost completely deteriorated. It is one of the scarcest of magazines."

Finally, I am grateful for the opportunity to have taught at Duke over many years in addition to my administrative posts, and I particularly thank the students in my Duke University seminars on Jewish American literature and culture. Although I had long been interested in this broad subject, it was in these classes that I was able to develop that interest from a "passing fancy" into an actual book. Above and beyond the opportunity to test ideas in a classroom of bright undergraduates, my students' enthusiasm for the authors and issues we discussed increased my own. I hope they got from those classes half of what they gave to me.

PASSING FANCIES IN JEWISH AMERICAN LITERATURE AND CULTURE

1 Jews and Their Complex Identities

"O Brave New World, That Has Such People In't!"

Near the start of Jess Row's 2014 novel, *Your Face in Mine*, the protagonist quotes the above line from Shakespeare's *The Tempest* to an old high school classmate struggling with the loss of his wife and child. They both remember the line, and the play, from their junior year class called "Utopias, Dystopias, and Fantasy Worlds." "Welcome to the rest of your life," Martin Wilkinson exuberantly says to Kelly Thorndike, leaving open for the moment the question of whether Thorndike's life will become a utopia, dystopia, or fantasy world.[1] These are the possibilities that Row's novel explores through the surgical alteration of racial identity in which each character engages, one from white and Jewish to black, the other from Caucasian to Chinese. And these are the possibilities that my study of passing in Jewish American literature and culture will entertain as I examine the various strategies employed over the centuries, mainly by Jews, to facilitate becoming another self.

Although *Your Face in Mine* is science fiction, it is—like much science fiction—not far removed from the reality of current life. Certainly it relates to issues of importance to contemporary readers, such as the fluidity of identity in open societies in modern times, as well as the debated distinction between cultural appreciation and cultural appropriation, or passing versus trespassing. There are many ways to take on an identity to which one aspires and to which, in the eyes of the dominant culture at least, one is not entitled. Much has been written about these ways, especially about how and when black people have crossed the color line to pass as white in nineteenth- and twentieth-century America (a trajectory that Row reverses in his depiction of racial crossing in the twenty-first). A major focus of my study is how Jews have strived to pass into mainstream society by means of tactics ranging from facial surgery and name changes to clothing choices. Consistent with the historical appellation of Jews as a race, there are similarities in the motivations and stratagems for both blacks and Jews in their quest to transform themselves but also differences in the ways they have been able to overcome the obstacles to living as who they think they are and becoming people society says they are not. I also explore the related topics of Jews passing as Christian or black, along with the opposite but complementary trajectory of Christians and blacks passing as Jews. Thus, I hope to fruitfully extend the customary discourse about crossing the color line to include the lines crossing into and out of Jewishness.

The phrase "historical appellation of Jews as a race" is bound to raise eyebrows; since the Holocaust, sensitivity to referencing, much less utilizing, a racial designation is deservedly high. Hitler's categorizing of Jews as a separate race may not have been unique to him or his country and time period, nor was his hierarchical approach to race that ranked Jews as inferior beings; however, Hitler's subsequent step, into a position on Jews as among the parasites (including homosexuals, Gypsies, and others) requiring extermination, had the hellish consequences of which the world at large became fully aware only after the fact. Race theory, social Darwinism, and the eugenics movement all fed into Hitler's "ultimate solution" to the "Jewish question." Although scientific conceptions of racial classifications, originally stemming from eighteenth century German zoology, had been discredited by prominent scientists in England and America shortly after World War I, the racialized notions about human beings that filtered long ago into the popular imagination, and occasionally have reappeared even in scientific investigations, have proved difficult to dislodge.[2] For modern-day Jews, the painful memory of the liquidation of such a large percentage of Europe's Jews on racial grounds is an argument one might understandably make for never using the term *race* again in connection with the Jewish people.

Ethnicity is the term commonly used today with reference to Jews and other groups. But this term is also problematic, as Jonathan Freedman suggests in his parenthetical remark in an essay about negotiating identity, titled "Who's Jewish?," in which he ponders "what it is like to be ethnic (*whatever that means*) in a culture that is obsessed with race."[3] Catherine Rottenberg, in her side-by-side analysis of early twentieth-century fiction by black writers and Jewish writers, differentiates between the terms, arguing that although ethnicity has evolved out of the discourse around race, "'being Jewish' and identifying as 'ethnic' in the United States historically has not interfered with identifying as an American, whereas historically 'being black' has."[4] The problem with this binary even for the particular time and place that Rottenberg has studied—the Progressive era, New York City—is that, as historian Leonard Dinnerstein says, "during the first two decades of the twentieth century racism became a central component in the elixir of American antisemitic sentiments. Indeed, the racial components . . ., always inherent yet mostly hidden, became obvious in the period known as the Progressive era."[5] The differentiation between race and ethnicity is a tenuous distinction in other periods as well, including our own.

Race in its proper contexts is useful for a discussion of Jews and Jewish passing. Jews themselves, in America and abroad, have at times thought of and referred to themselves as a race, and scholars in various fields have also found it instructive to study the ways in which Jews have moved in and out of alignment with blackness.[6] Moreover, the well-known Jewish publication on politics and culture, the *Forward*, has run a series in recent years called "In Jewish Color," pointing up not only the relevance of the subject but also the need to inform the public about it. This is because Africans and African Americans, along with Hispanics and Asians, are increasingly to be counted among the Jewish people. Many such cohorts have existed for centuries, like the Jews of India, China, and Africa; others, like certain branches of the Hebrew Israelites, have more recently been integrated into the fold through rabbinic ordination in traditional seminaries; and still others have become converts. Finally, in spite of the debunking of race as a biological given, the notion of innate racial differences remains salient, as does a purported likeness between blacks and Jews: Philip Roth remarks on that notion and that likeness in his 1986 novel *The Counterlife*, when Maria refers to Jews as a non-white race and Nathan Zuckerman believes that he is "the Moor—in [her family's] eyes—to her Desdemona."[7]

An important aspect of Jewish identity relates race to the geographical classification that since medieval times has been used to differentiate among two broadly defined groups of Jews: those from Spain and environs (Sepharad in medieval Hebrew texts) and those from central Europe (Ashkenaz). The Muslim Moors originated on the Iberian Peninsula, as did the first wave of Sephardic immigrants to England; those Sephardim set the pattern for depictions of Jews in literature and visual art as swarthy—their dark skin, like that of Shakespeare's Moor with his "sooty bosom" and "black face," often betokening to society at large their moral as well as physical flaws.[8] Sephardic Jewry is no more monolithic a term than Arab Muslims, however. After the mass expulsion from Spain and Portugal in 1492, and the anti-Jewish incidents of many decades earlier, Jews from those countries dispersed around the world, adopting different ways of speaking Judeo-Spanish, or Ladino, depending on where they settled. Some of the Jews from the Levant, or eastern Mediterranean, migrated there in this period, but others trace their roots deep into Jewish antiquity. The Greek Jews with ancestries in the Roman Empire are the Romaniots, speaking Greek as their mother tongue.[9] The other Levantine Jews, called Mizrahi (as the Greek Jews are sometimes called as well), are usually subsumed under the classification "Sephardic," like the Romaniots; yet their language is more often Judeo-Arabic and their customs vary among the different countries: an Iraqi Jew is not the same as a Syrian Jew or an Egyptian Jew or a Yemenite Jew. By the same token, the Jews in Iraq differ from the colony of Baghdadi Jews in Calcutta and Mumbai, and that colony developed independently from the two other groups of Indian Jews, the Bene Israel on the Konkan coast and the Cochin Jews on the Arabian Sea.[10] In short, the broad distinction between the Sephardim and the Ashkenazim must not obscure the significant differences among those grouped under the catch-all term Sephardim.

Both Sephardim and Ashkenazim were among the twenty-three Jews who fled Brazil in 1654 for settlement in the United States after the overthrow of the Dutch by the Portuguese; they landed in New Amsterdam (where Governor Peter Stuyvesant was not happy to see them). But the congregation they established—America's first synagogue, Shearith Israel—conducted worship solely in the Sephardic tradition. As Eli Faber says, in his history of the first migration of Jews to America, "Despite the fact that probably as early as the 1720s the majority of Jews in America were Ashkenazic in origin, . . . [t]hroughout the seventeenth and eighteenth centuries the Sephardic rite was the American rite." This rite included such details as the position of the cantor, where morning blessings and major festivals were observed, how chants were worded and babies named, and how the Hebrew language was pronounced. To this day, Shearith Israel, on the Upper West Side of Manhattan, proudly bills itself in a banner on its website as "The Spanish & Portuguese Synagogue."[11]

Although the Sephardim and Ashkenazim in the New World, as in the old, shared a religious heritage and fundamental theology, their differences of class and strictness of religious observance created tensions and clashes that have marked the relations between these branches of Jewish culture for centuries. A prevalent Sephardi attitude toward later cohorts of Jewish immigrants to America was perhaps unintentionally encrypted on a plaque inside the pedestal of the Statue of Liberty, in the excerpt from Emma Lazarus's poem "New Colossus," written in 1883 to raise money for the construction of the pedestal and installed in 1903. The "huddled masses" and "wretched refuse" referred to all immigrants, certainly, but the characterizations seem especially relevant to the approximately two million Yiddish-speaking Ashkenazi Jews who fled their own religious persecution and economic hardship in the Russian Pale of Settlement, most of them becoming part of the vast wave of immigration to America between 1882 and 1924 (including one million Jews in the 1900–1910 decade alone). How ironic, then, that the sheer numbers of these newest Jewish arrivals, joining their earlier-arriving central European brethren—who, having already assimilated, also frequently looked down on them—and thus increasing the proportion of American Jews who were Ashkenazi in origin, would largely push the Sephardim out of the consciousness of the general public and even of Jews themselves. The Ashkenazi culture came to be thought of as *the* Jewish culture in America. As one Jew with a Mizrahi father has put it:

> "American" continues to fall short of representing my cultural identity or even nationality. Even "American Jew" does not fully describe me, because the term conjures up images that reflect only half of me—bagels and lox, Woody Allen,

the Holocaust, *yarmulkes*, and ancestors from Eastern European *shtetls*. People do not seem to realize that "American Jew" also means *chiturni* for dinner, a *hamsa* around the neck to ward off the Evil Eye, a henna party before marriage, and ancestors from Poona, India and Basra, Iraq.[12]

How many Levantine Jews came to the United States in the late nineteenth and early twentieth centuries varies with the source and years: according to one statistic, about twenty-five thousand arrived between 1899 and 1925; another figure is fewer than seventy thousand in the years 1880 to 1925. Whatever the case, both sources call these Jews "a minority within a minority," a very small percentage of the overall influx of Jews in this period of mass migration.[13] Over and above the fact that Ashkenazi Jews even today constitute the majority of American Jews, the wealth of creative output from the mostly Russian Jews in the late nineteenth century and into the twentieth created a body of literature that detailed and quickly came to define Jewish American life in general and the Jewish experience of acculturation in particular. Yiddish newspapers, theater, music, art, humor, food, worship practices—all these and more found their way into mainstream consciousness, from the moment that William Dean Howells asked Abraham Cahan, soon to co-found the daily Yiddish newspaper the *Forverts* (today, as the *Forward*, published daily on line in Yiddish and English versions and monthly as print magazines), to write in English a story that would capture and convey Jewish life at the turn of the century.

From Cahan's "Yekl: A Tale of the New York Ghetto" in 1896 to the post–World War II fiction of the award-winning triumvirate of Saul Bellow, Bernard Malamud, and Philip Roth to the multitude of Ashkenazi Jews writing in the decades since, *Yiddishkeit* and Jewishness have become almost synonymous. Monographs are written about stock figures from old-world Yiddish literature, like the schlemiel, who populate the works of later generations of Jewish writers in America. Literary critics examine themes in Ashkenazi fiction and devote whole books to individual authors. College syllabi for courses in Jewish American literature abound with Ashkenazi writers, not just the well known but the up and coming, and there are multitudes to choose from, enough for many semesters' reading. Rabbinical seminaries in the main train Ashkenazi rabbis. Jewish comedians still tell jokes with Yiddish inflections. Though Levy can be a Sephardic name, it is an Ashkenazi's "real Jewish" rye bread that you don't have to be Jewish to enjoy, in the iconic advertising slogan, and a plate of pastrami on rye with a kosher dill sits on the counter in the Jewish deli, waiting for the surly New York waiter to deliver it.[14] In fact, an entire book rehearses the history of the Jewish delicatessen, called what else but *Pastrami on Rye*. It seems that the only hint of Sephardic culture in widespread currency is the pronunciation of Hebrew found in most American synagogues today, a pronunciation that the state of Israel adopted at its founding—and Hebrew as Israel's everyday language has saddened Yiddishists like Cynthia Ozick, who laments in her 1969 story "Envy; or, Yiddish in America" that "Yiddish was not honored in Tel Aviv or Jerusalem. . . . In the God-given state of Israel they had no use for the language of the bad little interval between Canaan and now."[15]

Of course, the Ashkenazim are hardly culturally monolithic, in spite of a common mother tongue. In addition to the differences between the German Jews who settled in the United States in the mid-nineteenth century and the eastern Europeans arriving a few decades later, there is diversity among the eastern Europeans themselves. Cahan made note of this phenomenon in a passage in "Yekl" in which he describes the Lower East Side of New York City in the 1890s as "one of the most densely populated spots on the face of the earth—a seething human sea fed by streams, streamlets, and rills of immigration flowing from all the Yiddish-speaking centers of Europe. Hardly a block but shelters Jews from every nook and corner of Russia, Poland, Galicia, Hungary, Roumania; Lithuanian Jews, Volhynian Jews, south Russian Jews, Bessarabian Jews . . . in fine, people with all sorts of antecedents, tastes, habits, inclinations, and speaking all sorts of subdialects of the same jargon, . . . not yet fused into one homogeneous whole." This "social cauldron" or "human hodgepodge," as Cahan termed it, produced social, political, and artistic movements that profoundly influenced the adopted country of these immigrants.[16] In sum, there are good reasons for, and abundant treasures in, the rich resources from and about Ashkenazi culture that have come down to us. Yet the resulting Ashkenazi-focused understanding of American Jews has resulted in gaps in Jewish history and storytelling.[17]

Only in recent decades have these gaps begun to be filled by memoirs, histories, and fiction that shed light on experiences left largely in the dark for those with no personal background or professional interest in Sephardic life in America. In Lucette Lagnado's memoir, *The Man in the White Sharkskin Suit: A Jewish Family's Exodus from Old Cairo to the New World* (2007), for instance, we read how her father in Brooklyn would cry, "*Ragaouna Masr!*—Take us back to Cairo!" Jack Marshall, in his own memoir as the child of a Syrian mother and an Iraqi father, *From Baghdad to Brooklyn: Growing up in a Jewish-Arabic Family in Midcentury America* (2005), recapitulates how the differences between being an accepted Jew in the tolerant Muslim environment of former times in the Middle East and being a vulnerable Jew in the isolated shtetls of eastern Europe could result in the Mizrahi Jew feeling exiled in the United States, nostalgic for a lost version of "home," whereas the Ashkenazi Jew was eager to be a "regular Yankee" (to paraphrase Cahan's Jake, né Yekl).[18] Sophie Judah, formerly of the Bene Israel community in India (and now, like many of that community, residing in Israel), remarks in the foreword to her collection of short stories that the Jews in India "for centuries lived in close proximity to both Hindus and Muslims. There has never been a Jewish ghetto or manifestations of anti-Semitism from the local population. This is a concept foreign to Western Jews, for whom it has been a constant presence."[19]

In stories about immigrant Mizrahi Jews in America, passing into the mainstream is accompanied by a desperate hanging on to the foods and customs of life in the Levant, an abiding interest and pride in others who are *de los muestros*, one of us, and a distaste for the Ashkenazim. Gloria De Vidas Kirchheimer's "Goodbye, Evil Eye," in her short story collection of that name from 2000 (a finalist for the National Jewish Book Award), functions almost as a teaching tool for acquainting readers with those Sephardi foods and customs, and that pride and distaste, given the amount of detail on those points along the way; she even takes pains with the backgrounds of her characters to make sure readers understand that Mizrahi Jews come from a variety of countries. This story can be viewed as part of Kirchheimer's mission to rectify the customary one-sided portrayals of "Jewish culture," as well as of a piece with her earlier career as a singer of Ladino music, when her 1958 record on the Folkways label introduced Sephardic compositions to folk singers and their audiences.[20]

Richard Kostelanetz eloquently regrets "the exclusion of Sephardic Jews from histories and generalizations about the American-Jewish experience" in his essay "Sephardic Culture and Me." He lists the titles of many anthologies and sourcebooks that include no Sephardic writers except the occasional token, Emma Lazarus. Using a familiar phrase, he says that Sephardic and Mizrahi Jews "are a minority's minority to the degree that the majority of the minority doesn't often acknowledge their (or our) existence." No wonder his family had a special curse word for the Ashkenazim.[21] An earlier anthology of stories and poetry might have placated Kostelanetz to some degree—*Sephardic-American Voices: Two Hundred Years of Literary Legacy* (1997), edited by the child of Greek and Spanish Jews—but the fact remains that even in 2018, the numbers of Sephardic American primary sources are far distant to those by Ashkenazi writers.

Through the lens of race or ethnicity, whichever term we care to use, Mizrahi Jews are taking to the essay genre in particular to express their concerns and demand recognition. Sigal Samuel, at one time the opinion editor of the *Forward*, edited the aforementioned series "In Jewish Color" in 2015–2016; her own essay titled "I'm a Mizrahi Jew—Do I Count as a Jew of Color?" explored the issue of race by reference to her own history and interviews with others, all of which complicated the answer to her own question. Samuel's grandparents were Hindi- or Arabic-speaking Jews from India, Iraq, and Morocco, and her racial identity is one of constant speculation by others: sometimes she is "read" as white, sometimes as nonwhite. The founder of the organization Jews in ALL Hues told her, "One in two Mizrahi millennials I meet nowadays identifies as a Jew of color." At the same time, a history professor at New York University scolded her because in the context of the United States, she is not a person of color, since Mizrahi Jews never experienced here the state-sanctioned victimization dealt to African Americans or Asians. (The story in Israel, he added, is a different one, and another essay by Samuel relates an example of discriminatory attitudes toward Mizrahi Jews in that country.)[22] Others among her interviewees—from Yemen, Uzbekistan, Israel, and Iran—took issue with the notion that only state-sanctioned discrimination can qualify someone in this country as a person of color. Samuel ultimately decided to count herself as such a person, not only to challenge the Ashkenazi-centric assumption that Jewish equals white, but also to combat her own community's internalized message that Arab—"which is not a race, but is often used as a racial signifier indicating 'brown'"—is a bad identity. She ends by asserting that she is "an Arab Jewish woman of color," thereby claiming a complex, not always understood or sanctioned, Jewish identity.[23]

Loolwa Khazzoom, too, whose father is Iraqi, writes about "the many colors of Jewish women" and dreams for a rethought, retooled rabbinical school curriculum, one that "would teach the halakha [Jewish law] and the traditions of Jewish communities from Argentina to Zimbabwe; texts would include the teachings of the Kes (Jewish priests) of Ethiopia, the Hachamim (sages) of India, and the Kabbalists (mysics) of Spain. Cantorial classes would include the story of the lost tribe of Zimbabwe and the recently converted community in Peru. . . . Staff would include Jewish scholars from China, cantors from Yemen and priests from Ethiopia, and students would reflect Jewish faces from around the world."[24] Khazzoom has edited a collection subtitled *Essays on Identity by Women of North African and Middle Eastern Jewish Heritage* that is designed to give voice to the geographical, racial, cultural, and religious aspirations of these communities. One of these essays is even called "Breaking the Silence." Julie Iny is another of the essayists, with her "Ashkenazi eyes" and skin that conceal the other half of her identity as the child of an Iraqi-Indian father. In Israel, her light skin made her privy to anti-Mizrahi racism. Tellingly, Iny relates her situation to that of blacks in America: "like some culturally assimilated people of color in the United States," she appeared "safe" enough to Ashkenazi Israelis to have them divulge "their racist views about people with whom I shared an ethnic bond. It is perhaps because we are both able to 'pass.'"[25] She actually wishes for the ambiguous skin color that has bystanders of people like Sigal Samuel wondering what those people "are."

Of interest in this context is the restaging of Shakespeare's *Othello* in July 2016, presented by the American Sephardi Federation at the Center for Jewish History in New York, a restaging that not only highlighted the racial content of the play but also gave it a connection to Sephardic culture. As David Serero, the Sephardic actor playing Othello in this production, explained, "I wanted to explore the Moroccan aspects of the play, returning it to Shakespeare's original idea of using the inspiration of Abd el-Ouahed ben Messaoud, who was the ambassador of the Moroccan/English alliance in 1600. Shakespeare was very intrigued by this man—his clothes, costumes, traditions, looks and his darkness." Serero chose to include Arabic music, played on the percussion instrument called a darbuka, and he explained this choice, and his passionate investment in the production, by reference to his cultural background:

> My interpretation of "Othello" is personal, with roots in my own heritage: My dad was born in Morocco and instructed me in the ways of Jewish Moroccan culture. It is a little-known fact that numerous songs in the Arabic song repertoire are Judea Arabic songs by such composers as Salim Halali. . . . I would never have imagined singing those Judeao-Arabic songs (to which I listened during my childhood in Paris) in New York, where the Ashkenazi and Yiddish culture is more prevalent. That alone will make me very emotional onstage. . . . To use Shakespeare in order to showcase that Sephardic culture is a dream come true. Even though times are difficult for Jews in the Arab world, we must not forget that culture of Jews and Arabs at the height of their relationship, especially in Morocco, where King Mohammed V refused to deliver his Jews to Hitler and replied, "If you take my Jews, you'll have to take me first." In playing Othello, I am also paying tribute to this culture and time.[26]

The varieties of Jewish experience detailed above suggest that identification on one or the other side of the Sephardi-Ashkenazi division is sufficient to complicate the use of the term *Jew* as a descriptor of any given person. But we must amplify that complication with the wide and equally complex spectrum of Jewish belief and practice. That is to say, the religious aspect—an individual's interpretation of and adherence to the canonical texts of Judaism, with their prescriptions and proscriptions—obviously must factor into any discussion of Jews and Jewish culture. The German Jewish immigrants in the mid-nineteenth century brought to the United States the modernized, re-formed practice of Judaism known literally as the Reform movement. The eastern European immigrants of later years, if they were not socialists and/or freethinkers, largely adhered strictly at first to their Orthodox heritage from the Old World, following laws of *kashrut* (kosher) as one of the 613 commandments of the Torah; often they found it challenging to maintain this level of observance in the New World, and soon enough, with the second generation especially, a fall off occurred. (The term *Orthodox*, referring to rabbinic Judaism, arose in Europe in the early nineteenth century to distinguish the practitioners from competing philosophies of being Jewish that were stimulated by the Enlightenment.)[27] The Conservative movement began in Germany in reaction to Reform but took root in the United States as a middle way between the other two, a way that would *conserve* traditional practices while permitting some degree of adaptation to the modern world. These are the "big three" denominations in the United States. Reconstructionism, a smaller synagogue-centered movement founded in early twentieth-century America, emphasizes the people-hood of Jews and, like the other branches, has its own seminary training rabbis to lead congregations with this philosophy and its own prayer book for worship.[28] Although these branches contain variations within themselves, from one decade to another and from congregation to congregation, it is the catchall descriptor "Orthodox Jew" that most significantly conceals the complications inherent in that term.[29]

For one, there is Orthodoxy and there is ultra-Orthodoxy. The ultra-Ortho-dox, known in Israel and increasingly in the United States as the Haredim (from the book of Isaiah, those who tremble [before God]), have been described by one scholar as "a minority within a minority within a minority": Jews are a very small fraction of the American population, only a small percentage of Jews are Ortho-dox, and perhaps a third of the Orthodox are Haredi.[30] To the casual passerby on the street, all ultra-Orthodox Jews might appear to be the same, with the men dressed head to toe in black and the women with long skirts and head coverings. Yet diversity is the order of the day even here. On the website Quora, in answer to the question, "What are the sects within ultra-Orthodox Judaism," respondent Gil Yehuda begins his lengthy explanation with this disclaimer: "As it turns out, this question is a bit more complicated than it seems, and would benefit from some sort of 3d model with a Venn diagram, movable timeline, and map."[31] The phrase "a bit" is a classic understatement. For starters there are the Hasidim, followers of one or another eighteenth-century European *rebbe* (rabbi); the best known among these, because they are out and about all over the world, seeking to bring Jews into the observant fold, are the Chabad Lubavitch, but there are many additional subgroups of Hasidim with their own rebbes and customs. Julia Dahl's novel *Invisible City* (2014) does not bother to differentiate; she specifies a borough within a borough, so to speak—residents of the Borough Park neighborhood of the New York City borough of Brooklyn—but makes no tacit distinction between its various Hasidic sects. Dara Horn, too, in *In the Image* (2002), is content to call the religious Jews encountered on an outing simply Hasidic.[32] Among the non-Hasidic in ultra-Orthodox enclaves are the Misnagdim (meaning opposition, in this case to Hasidism), also known as Yeshivish Jews. What all the ultra-Ortho-dox have in common is that, as Nora Rubel puts it, they are "first and foremost Jews living in America, not American Jews."[33]

Other groups with Jewish ties constitute the opposite end of the spectrum from the ultra-Orthodox. Both the Society for Ethical Culture and the Society for Humanistic Judaism were founded by Jews, the former by a rabbi-in-training, Felix Adler, and the latter by Rabbi Sherwin T. Wine. Ethical Culture stresses the moral aspects of living without reference to God or, for that matter, to Jews; Humanistic Judaism is a human-centered rather than theistic approach to Juda-ism, one that identifies with the culture and history of the Jewish people, replaces the word *human* for *God* in Hebrew texts, and allows substitution of a presentation on a secular Jew (such as Albert Einstein) for the traditional Torah portion at a bar or bat mitzvah. In addition, some Jews form their own *havurot*, or fellowships, small groups that may or may not be connected with a synagogue, who gather together for worship, learning, and celebrating life-cycle events. Then, too, many secular Jews belong to no organized synagogue or society and may minimally observe rituals or holidays but consider themselves culturally Jewish. And finally we have the Jews for Jesus, founded in 1973 by a Jewish convert to Christianity who became an ordained Baptist minister; this well-known group is but one iteration of messianic Jews, proselytizing other Jews into accepting Jesus as their Messiah (the obverse of the Lubavitchers, who proselytize Jews to become more Jewishly observant). Although I deem the messianic Jews to have crossed over the bright line separating Jews from Christians, all who so identify cling to a Jewish identity and would claim that my view of who is Jewish is too limited (i.e., that there is no bright line).

Given these many complexities, and the consequent elasticity (some would call it slipperiness) of the term *Jewish*, I have interpreted the term broadly in my study of passing. In this I have followed the lead of the Pew Foundation survey of 2013: as the report states, "the survey illuminates the many different ways in which Americans self-identify as Jewish or partially Jewish, and it therefore provides a sense of how the size of the population varies depending on one's definition of who is a Jew."[34] Certainly the ethics and social justice emphases, or deed-over-creed philosophies, of Ethical Culture and Humanistic Judaism are consistent with some traditional forms of Judaism and with the beliefs of nonpracticing but proud Jews; they are also consistent with the tenets of Unitarian Fellowships and Quaker Meeting Houses (in both of which one customarily finds Jews), not to mention churches of various kinds. Frank Alpine's questioning of Morris Bober's interpretation of Jewishness, in Bernard Malamud's *The Assistant* (1957), pertains in this context. In response to Bober's explanation of Jewish Law as "to do what is right, to be honest, to be good. . . . This is what a Jew believes," Alpine counters, still confused, "I think other religions have those ideas too."[35] In Frank's understanding of Jews, they don't eat ham, they don't do business on Saturday, and they do attend synagogue, but his mentor's interpretation, like the author's, is ethics-centered. And Morris is the kind of Jew that Frank will turn into when he literally becomes the grocer, and a circumcised Jew to boot, at the novel's end.

My major criterion in choosing writers on passing in a Jewish context is how well their works illuminate salient features of the process, whether those passages are by Jews or non-Jews; thus, I am more interested in how the artists describe Jewishness—as faith, practice, culture, race, ethnicity, peoplehood, or community—than in whether someone else would consider them authentically Jewish.

As Cynthia Baker says, in her analysis of the word *Jew*, "ultimately, no one person, group of people, or institution has, or can have, a lock on this deceptively simple but powerful key word."[36] Passing often occurs within and among (as well as out of) the various iterations of Jewish identity, whether from more to less strict observance of Jewish laws and tenets or the other way around, and whether from within or without the customary definitional boundaries of who is a Jew. Some Jews pass out of a category and then return to it, like the Hasidic mother in Dahl's *Invisible City*, who leaves her community, has a baby with a Christian man, and abandons both for more than two decades after disappearing once again back into Hasidism. Some Haredi go "off the *derech* [path]" and must learn to acclimate to the outer, unfamiliar world—to pass as "regular Americans," as it were.[37]

The writers and visual artists I deal with differ significantly with regard to these subjects and their own relationships to Jewish religion, history, and culture. Some are avowedly and proudly Jewish while others barely acknowledge and perhaps even hide their heritage; still others have converted out of their born religion as Jews. A very few, like Thomas Pynchon, are not Jewish at all but are interested in Jews and Jewish culture for one or more reasons, or their works shed light on those about Jews. For some of the artists I discuss, especially the women, other aspects of their identity, like gender or sexual identification, are at least as salient, sometimes more so, than their religion—but gender and religious/cultural issues for female Jews have often been of a piece.

I would underscore that the passing strategies I explore in a Jewish context are not to be understood as strategies, or fancies, of Jews only. Regarding name changes, for one, what can be said about the Jewish immigrants and next generations in the stories I examine can also be said of other ethnicities. As Benzion Kaganoff states, in *A Dictionary of Jewish Names and Their History*, "Democracy equalizes; it tends to bring about a uniformity of language, mores, customs, and personal and family names. A Kohen, a Kovaks, a Kowalsky, and a Koronakis emerge as an ambiguous Cole or amorphous Kay in the American melting pot, and the Jewish, Hungarian, Polish, and Greek origins dissipate in the American experience."[38] Allyson Hobbs has something to add to Kaganoff's list in her discussion of name changes of blacks during Reconstruction, when adopting new names signified not only a fresh start in life but also a rejection of names forced on human chattel during slavery.[39]

Even though many an assimilating or aspiring American of any background adopts a new surname, studies in some years have found the phenomenon to be especially frequent among Jews. For example, although Jews were estimated to constitute only about 6 percent of the almost four million residents of the Los Angeles metropolitan area in 1946–1947, 46 percent of the petitions for name changes that year were by Jews. The researchers contrasted this formidable percentage to the statistics revealing that "racially identified minority groups such as Orientals and Mexicans, who are the objects of prejudice, evidently make little use of the formal name changing device"; they attributed this result in part to the fact that "physical visibility may make ethnically motivated name changing ineffective." For the Jews, in contrast, they postulated that this cohort's "ethnically visible names are perceived by their bearers to hold adverse or objectionable connotations" that can be surmounted by altering a salient marker of identity.[40] Of course, if certain names once hinted at the bearer's religion, nationality, or ethnicity (not that they ever were a perfect indication), this is no longer necessarily the case: through intermarriage, conversion, or the simple passage of time, the local Catholic Church (not to mention the Unitarian Fellowship) may have many a Goldberg and Schwartz in its pews alongside the O'Briens, San Felippos, and Fellinis, and the synagogue may have Zhangs and McNamaras davening with the Silvermans and Cohens. A Lopez may be a Mexican Catholic or a Sephardic Jew (or in the case of Conversos, a bit of both).

But even with the unreliability of names as ethnic identifiers, in at least one present-day town with a small percentage of Jews, the Jewish owner of a bakery looks for a "Jewish name" on the credit card of the purchaser in order to recruit new members to the community. If not a spot-on signifier, it is a start, and the inclination of some to leave a Jewish first or family name intact, or even to reclaim it, is helpful toward that end. That shop owner also seeks to identify fellow Jews on the basis of the "Jewish look." Whether that look involves the shape of the nose, texture of the hair, or color of the skin is information not provided but assumed.[41] The prevalence of such assumptions is supported by research. One sociological examination of "the identifiability of Jews" (titled by that name) centered on testing whether onlookers could correctly judge by appearance alone who is a Jew and who a non-Jew. Incidentally these researchers found that names had "high predictive value" for the judges, especially for the Jewish subjects, and the Jewish judges were most highly attuned to those names. But facial features were the focus, and they turned out to be an important factor in identification; once again, those features remain undescribed in the report. The takeaways from the report are significant: not only that the Jewish participants, all male, "were correctly identified by physiognomy above chance expectation," and that "Jews were taken for non-Jews more frequently than the reverse," but also that the authors presume a higher status to be associated with non-Jews. Given the number of similar studies that preceded on the same subject, cited by the authors, that presumption was clearly too well known to require articulation.[42] Another study, on identifying Jews from photographs, found that the higher the score on antisemitic attitudes, the more likely the onlooker would identify the photo as being of a Jew; this study, too, builds on previous research with the same results.[43] The salient issue in all of the above is that a presumed set of ethnic markers has proven acceptable, even useful, in some situations and counterproductive in others. My study will examine instructive cases of those Jews who have found the name and/or the "look" something to discard, as well as other cases in which it is retained or reclaimed.

Such malleability and mutability hint at identity as performance. Philip Roth shows, especially in *The Counterlife* and *Operation Shylock*, that what is truly essential about an individual's identity is not a race or creed but the imperative to take on alternative selves. Roth plays with this idea when, in *The Counterlife*, he has the secular American Jew Henry Zuckerman become an Orthodox Israeli Jew named Hanoch, and then "reveals" that this Zuckerman transformation is a figment of writer-brother Nathan Zuckerman's imagining, for novelistic purposes. Or is it? Since all of it is a figment of author Philip Roth's imagination, for novelistic purposes, the reader is left with boxes within boxes. Where the "real" Henry/Hanoch is to be found is a puzzle not to be resolved, hard as the reader may try to unpack this novel's "facts." In simplest terms, of course, humans act one way in certain settings and other ways in different situations: the student is not the same with her teacher in the lecture hall as with her peers in the dorm room; the teacher is not the same with his students as with his children. We take on alternative selves and perform identities every day.

With regard to *Jewish* identity, Vikki Bell, in promoting a point made by Jonathan and Daniel Boyarin, remarks: "One's Judaism is not a constant in either an essential or performative sense, but . . . religious and ethnic affiliation can be performed to a greater or lesser extent depending on the context within which 'the Jew' finds him or herself. This is argued not just in the sense of the possibilities of 'passing' as or as not, but also in terms of the places and communities within which one finds oneself and the sense of belonging elicited or desired."[44] Sarah Bunin Benor, in her *Becoming Frum* (observant), analyzes how newcomers to ultra-Orthodoxy learn to perform the roles expected of them by learning the "language" of the culture in the widest sense.[45] For the Orthodox (if I may oversimplify the term and restate Benor's point), performing all the rituals that constitute Orthodox Judaism makes one an Orthodox Jew—in Judith Butler's conception of identity as the "stylized repetition of acts."[46] We can apply the concept of performance to other settings as well. Performing can mean a pretense to achieve the aim of survival in the case of some Jews in the period of the Spanish Inquisition, who nominally converted but practiced their religion in secret; or it can mean upward mobility for Jews in more recent times who changed their names, or listed their religion as Protestant, in order to get a job and get ahead. In counterpoint to finding a more observant Jewish community in which to belong, a Jew might transition to a less observant form, or completely hide a Jewish heritage, or even convert to another religion. Often passing involves a change of physical characteristics to conform to mainstream notions of beauty or a change of clothes to indicate that old-world ways have been put behind. Quite often, passing in whatever direction has exacted a price. Hobbs, in her study of blacks who have passed as white, has commented that "the core issue of passing is not becoming what you pass for, but what you leave behind." She speaks of "the familial dislocations that passing permanently necessitated" and recounts stories of those who would and would not pay the price of such dislocations.[47] In the works I will discuss, passing has likewise involved painful separations in many instances but, at other times, has resulted in fulfilling transformations, occasionally even blessed by the family.

My study concentrates on Jews in the United States beginning with the largest wave of immigration in the late nineteenth century up to contemporary times, though it engages other countries and earlier periods as indicated. As a prime example, the so-called Dirty War in Argentina in the 1970s is the setting for *The Ministry of Special Cases* (2007), by Long Island–born Nathan Englander. This novel is first of all a helpful reminder that the term *Jewish American*, customarily used to define literature by Jews of the United States, is appropriately extended to Jewish literature of the Americas to the south.[48] In addition, the Jews in this work suffer from the same negative stereotyping, antisemitism, and repressive governmental tactics that have marked and still mark the lives of Jews not only in similarly dire circumstances but in their everyday lives in the United States and around the world. The inclusion of Englander is but one example of my "Ashkenazi orientation," to appropriate the term used by Julie Iny in her essay laying bare this bias in all kinds of American Jewish institutions.[49] But if my chapters lean primarily on the abundance of materials about the Ashkenazi experience, I am mindful of the "minority within a minority" and thus include several Sephardic or Mizrahi voices as relevant to my themes. One of the educational services provided by Ashkenazi novelist Dara Horn, in *In the Image*, is that she takes account of Jews from all over the world, those with non-Ashkenazi histories and customs that may be even more foreign to her readers than her descriptions of Orthodox religious practices. Her protagonist's family has taken trips to North Africa and the Middle East, and to the Jewish historical sites in Spain, and another character lectures on the Jewish presence in India and shows slides of "the Jewish communities of Bukhara, Singapore, China, Turkey, Morocco, Ethiopia, Brazil, and Turkmenistan."[50] In these ways, Horn underlines the variety of Jewish backgrounds and experiences, enlarging the geographical range of many readers' conception of what it means to be a Jew.

Dara Horn is one of our contemporary Jewish writers who "take it as a given that they are Jews just as much as they are Americans." The editors of a recent collection of short works by Jewish American writers, including Horn, elaborate on this summative description of the authors in their anthology: each of these stories "looks ahead to new forms of Jewish self-awareness as much as it looks back for history, sustenance, and collective memory."[51] As for the authors I have selected for my study, I deal with some artists who will be household names to readers of this book, others who are less familiar, and still others who may have been popular in their times but are largely forgotten now. In two cases, particular works of fiction are so germane to my topic that they merit their own chapters. Some of these authors deem being Jewish incompatible with being an American, and so underplay or renounce the former identity for the latter, unlike Edelshtein in Ozick's "Envy," who clings to the past and bewails "America the empty bride."[52] Others, like Horn, find no contradiction in the two identities and, in fact, find the marriage between Jew and the United States exceedingly fertile.

For examining Jewish identity in the context of passing the range of pertinent artistic media is quite extensive. As evidence to support my points I engage novels, short stories, memoirs, biographies, feature films, documentaries, Broadway shows, theater criticism, television skits, advertising, songs, paintings, sculpture, comics and graphic narratives. As well, the various artistic expressions I examine are of a piece with the cultural phenomena or trends of their times (and earlier times) by which they were influenced and which they exemplify. Thus, to supplement my close readings of texts, I weave cultural analysis into the discussions of art forms in order to give context to these discussions. Debra Shostak, in her study of Philip Roth subtitled *Countertexts, Counterlives*, has grouped Roth's works thematically rather than chronologically in order to convey how they "converse" with one another.[53] I organize my chapters in the same fashion, in hopes that the authors, art forms, cultural trends, and time periods I explore might "converse" with each other in productive ways.

A word, in conclusion, about why each chapter subtitle is a quotation from Shakespeare. The reasons are severalfold. First, an essay about the ineffective nose jobs in *The Ministry of Special Cases*, combined with the lack of critical attention to this brilliant novel, seemed to me to cry out for "the most unkindest [sic] cut of all," from *Julius Caesar*. (Even Dara Horn alludes to this famous line in *In the Image*, not bothering to elucidate its source.[54]) Rather quickly thereafter, my subtitle for an essay on Thyra Samter Winslow's novelette "A Cycle of Manhattan," with its various name changes, centered inevitably on a play on a familiar line from *Romeo and Juliet*, though the name "Ross" (changed at the last from "Rose") is only problematically sweet. Hamlet's harsh words to Ophelia about changing the face that God had given her were utilized in a 1920 *New York Times* excoriation of the rising popularity of face lifts for women, a fact that prompted its use for my chapter on another kind of facial surgery, the nose job performed on (or repudiated by) Jewish females. Then, since Philip Roth relies heavily on *Julius Caesar* as a central comparison point in *The Human Stain*, I was led into using a line from that play as the subtitle of my chapter on Jews and blacks; the same is the case with the chapter on Jews and gentiles, since Elaine Pollack adopts another line from *Hamlet* for its symbolic resonance in her story "The Bris."

Finally, the black writer in Malamud's *The Tenants* uses Willie Shakespear [*sic*] as one of his pen names, and *King Lear* figures in at the end of the novel, thereby suggesting the subtitle for the conclusion of my study. By that point, locating a few additional appropriate Shakespearean allusions became an imperative. I was drawn into this practice without any grand design at the start, but the foundational role of Shakespeare in the Western canon, the fluidity of identity as one of his common themes, and the applicability of his famous lines to other times and contexts, as suggested by modern authors' adaptations, have made my own usages not only natural but, in some cases (most notably "A Ros[s] by Any Other Name"), almost inescapable.

Notes

1. Row, *Your Face in Mine*, 38.
2. For a discussion of scientific racism see Barkan, *Retreat of Scientific Racism*. Gordon, in *Hitler, Germans and the "Jewish Question,"* explores Hitler's racialism and antisemitism.
3. Jonathan Freedman, "Who's Jewish?," 215 (emphasis added). The editors' introduction to that volume uses the adjective *fuzzy* in describing the term *ethnicity*.
4. Rottenberg, *Performing Americanness*, 4.
5. Dinnerstein, *Antisemitism in America*, 58. To my mind, Rottenberg overstates her case in her parenthetical remark that "Jews, even though they historically were interpellated as off-white, were allowed to identify as white (and this identification did not constitute a transgression nor was it punished), while simultaneously compelled and urged to desire to emulate norms linked to whiteness" (90).
6. See, for examples, Goldstein, *Price of Whiteness*; Brodkin, *How Jews Became White Folks*; and Jacobson, *Whiteness of a Different Color*.
7. Roth, *Counterlife*, 71, 283.
8. One reverend who visited a London synagogue in 1690 said that the Jews he saw "were all very black men, and indistinct in their reasonings as gipsies." William Hogarth's drawings in the next century featured swarthy Jewish men with large noses among other features that identified them as Jews (see Felsenstein, *Anti-Semitic Stereotypes*, 50, 53). Although there was no official Jewish community in England from the Jews' expulsion in 1290 to their readmittance in the mid-seventeenth century, tropes about Jews permeated written and oral discourse in the intervening years, including Shakespeare's *The Merchant of Venice*. I discuss stereotyping of Jews in the British national context in chapter 3 of my book *Race and Identity*.
9. See Stavroulakis, *Jews of Greece*, for a full discussion. Stavroulakis cofounded the Jewish Museum of Greece and was its director for many years.
10. For an informative summary of the three major Jewish colonies of India see Marks, "Jewish Indian Cuisine."
11. Faber, *Time for Planting*, volume one of *Jewish People in America*, 12–13, 58–60. The Shearith Israel website is http://www.shearithisrael.org.
12. Iny, "Ashkenazi Eyes," 82.
13. The first source noted is Polland and Soyer, *Emerging Metropolis*, 226, 280–81. The second is the introduction to Matza, *Sephardic-American Voices*, 6–7. Matza puts the number

of Sephardim in this period as less than 5 percent of the Jewish immigrants. Polland and Soyer discuss the newspapers and aid societies by and for Sephardim in New York City; Matza provides a concise history of the Sephardic presence in the United States from colonial times.

14. The slogan's writer, Judy Protas, was quoted in the *New York Times* obituary at her death in 2014: "'We had a local bread, real Jewish bread, that was sold widely in Brooklyn to Jewish people,' she told The New York Times in 1979. 'What we wanted to do was enlarge its public acceptance. Since New York is so mixed ethnically, we decided to spread the good word that way.' And thus, from Ms. Protas's largely anonymous pen sprang a slogan—'You don't have to be Jewish to love Levy's Real Jewish Rye'—that has far outlived the actual campaign, which began in 1961 and ran through the 1970s" (see Margalit Fox, "Judy Protas, Writer of Slogan for Levy's Real Jewish Rye, Dies at 91," *New York Times*, January 11, 2014, https://www.nytimes.com/2014/01/12/business/judy-protas-writer-of-slogan-for-levys-real -jewish-rye-dies-at-91.html?_r=0). For the delicatessen, see Merwin, *Pastrami on Rye*.

15. Ozick, "Envy," 25. Dr. Sol Goodman, writer and educator, complains about the choice of Hebrew over Yiddish as the official language of Israel in an interview in the documentary *Yiddish, the Mame-Loshn*. Cynthia Baker discusses the connection between the choice of Hebrew by the founding Zionists and Yiddish as a "feminized" language (see *Jew*, 62–63).

16. Cahan, "Yekl," 13–14.

17. The Sephardic Adventures Camp outside Seattle is one strategy by Sephardic Jews in the United States to preserve the traditions of their culture by passing them along to succeeding generations. The camp provides an Orthodox religious experience and immersion in Sephardic culture alongside customary camping activities. See the camp's website for its history and aims: http://www.sephardicadventurecamp.org.

18. Lagnado, *Man in the White Sharkskin Suit*, from back material, 8; Marshall, *From Baghdad to Brooklyn*, 15–16.

19. Judah, *Dropped from Heaven*, x.

20. Kirchheimer, "Goodbye, Evil Eye." See her website: http://www.gkirchheimer.com.

21. Kostelanetz, "Sephardic Culture and Me," 26–27.

22. Samuel, "Racist Israeli Hanukkah Video." See also Iny, "Ashkenazi Eyes," 95.

23. Samuel, "I'm a Mizrahi Jew."

24. Khazzoom, "United Jewish Feminist Front," 179–80.

25. Iny, "Ashkenazi Eyes," 95.

26. Serero, "How to Tell 'Othello' the Sephardic Way," 32.

27. Freedman, *Jew vs. Jew*, 276–77.

28. An old but still useful primer on the differences among these four branches is Rosenthal's *Many Faces of Judaism*.

29. Samuel Freedman discusses the "Orthodox Renaissance" in his chapter "Who Owns Orthodoxy?," in *Jew vs. Jew*, 217–26.

30. Rubel, *Doubting the Devout*, 8. The Pew Report of 2013 gives a variety of figures, depending on how one defines *Jewish*, but Rubel is probably close to the mark when she puts the overall percentage of American Jews in her 2010 book as less than 2 percent and says that about 12 percent of the Jews are Orthodox and about a third of the Orthodox are Haredi.

31. Yehuda, respondent on Quora website.

32. Horn, *In the Image*, 46. Horn spells the word as *Hassidic*; more common spellings are *Hasidic* or *Chasidic*. So too Horn writes *ultraorthodox*; others use *Ultra-Orthodox* or

ultra-Orthodox. When I directly quote an author, I use that author's spellings. Otherwise I employ *Hasidic* and *ultra-Orthodox.*

33. Rubel, *Doubting the Devout*, 137.

34. "Portrait of Jewish Americans," 23.

35. Malamud, *Assistant*, 124.

36. Baker, *Jew*, 10.

37. Memoirs by and articles on the ex-*frum* are common. A recent article in the *New York Times* discusses the difficulties of adjustment (see Brodesser-Akner, "Apostates Anonymous," 36–41).

38. Kaganoff, *Dictionary*, xii.

39. Hobbs, *Chosen Exile*, 27.

40. Broom, Beem, and Harris, "Characteristics of 1,107 Petitioners," 34–35.

41. See Siner, "How I Moved," 7.

42. Savitz and Tomasson, "Identifiability of Jews," 468–75.

43. Scodel and Austrin, "Perception of Jewish Photographs by Non-Jews and Jews," 278–80.

44. Bell, "Performativity and Belonging," 3.

45. Benor, *Becoming Frum.*

46. Bell provides this quotation from Butler's 1993 *Bodies That Matter* in her essay "Mimesis as Cultural Survival," 134.

47. Hobbs, *Chosen Exile*, 18, 155.

48. *The Ministry of Special Cases*, set in South America, is included in my study as a special case because, first, it is by a Jewish American author and, second, it deals instructively with the "Jewish nose" and the nose job. This is not to slight the Canadians, who, like citizens of the United States, are of course North Americans. A collection of essays titled *Key Texts in American Jewish Culture* contains an essay on Mordecai Richler's *The Apprenticeship of Duddy Kravitz*, a Canadian novel that performs some of the same functions as Philip Roth's "Goodbye, Columbus," which was published in the *Paris Review* in the same year (1959). See Dellheim, "Is It Good for the Jews?," 57–74.

49. Iny, "Ashkenazi Eyes," 93.

50. Horn, *In the Image*, 16, 24, 25.

51. Aarons, Patt, and Shechner, introduction *New Diaspora*, 5, 2.

52. Ozick, "Envy," 57.

53. Shostak, *Philip Roth*, vii.

54. Horn, *In the Image*, 207.

2   The "Jewish Nose" and the Nose Job in Nathan Englander's *The Ministry of Special Cases*

"The Most Unkindest Cut of All"

In HIS FIRST novel, published in 2007, Nathan Englander utilizes big noses and the medical procedure to reduce their size as a primary vehicle for exploring the Jew's place in a particular country and time—Argentina in the 1970s—but also, by extension, in all countries and times. His central plot device and symbol in this work, the nose job, is best understood in a historical context, for identifying a certain (deformed) shape of nose as a signifier for "the Jew" has its origins in Europe and the distant past, hardening into race theory in the mid-nineteenth century in the United States as elsewhere. Ordinary citizens and artists alike readily appropriated this particular racial marker, among others, for use in characterizing and usually denigrating the Jewish Other. As but one example, in 1874 the prominent American writer Oliver Wendell Holmes Sr. published a poem, "At the Pantomime," that relates the narrator's initial horror at having "Hebrews" squeezed in next to him at the theater, identified in part by their noses: "The beak that crowned the bistred face / Betrayed the mould of Abraham's race, . . . / The hook-nosed kite of carrion clothes."[1]

Englander is not the only modern American novelist to overtly make the connection between this putative Jewish racial identifier and surgery to change the shape of the nose. The debut novel *V.* (1963), by Thomas Pynchon, for instance, links rhinoplasty and the negative view of the Jewish nose when Rachel Owlglass pays for her roommate's surgical procedure but expresses unhappiness about Esther Harvitz's decision to have it. As Pynchon writes, "It disgusted Rachel, her theory being that it was not for cosmetic reasons these girls got operated on so much as that the hook nose is traditionally the sign of the Jew and the retroussé nose the sign of the WASP or white Anglo-Saxon Protestant in the movies and advertisements."[2] Indeed, Pynchon describes the operation itself in such gruesome detail over several pages in chapter 4, subtitled "In which Esther gets a nose job," that a reader, too, might experience disgust of a visceral sort (and perhaps vow consequently never to go under the scalpel). More than half a century after *V.*, Jesse Row published his own first novel, *Your Face in Mine*, about so-called racial reassignment surgery in the new age. The plastic surgeon at the center of the novel, musing about his profession, states: "It all begins with the Jewish nose. In the Western world at least. The nose that looks like a sail. A hatchet. Shylock's nose. An aggressive nose, a nose that intrudes, a nose that *takes*."[3] As noted in the author's first acknowledgment at the end of the book, Row has read his Sander Gilman, the most eminent and prolific analyst of "the Jew's body" (the title of one of Gilman's many disquisitions on the subject) and of the human quest for the embodied beautiful.[4]

Gilman, in several of his works on racialized body images, discusses the rise of aesthetic surgery in mid-nineteenth-century western Europe and addresses the nose job as a means of circumventing (while capitulating to) the racial notions of the day. As but one example of such notions, he quotes the author of *Notes on Noses* (1848), who not only described the shape of the "Jewish, or Hawknose" but linked it to specific characteristics, especially the "considerable Shrewdness in worldly matters" that enabled the accumulation of profit.[5] (Hence the "hook-nosed kite" of Holmes's "At the Pantomime.") Jay Geller and Sara Lipton, in their respective essays "(G)nos(e)ology: The Cultural Construction of the Other" and "The Invention of the Jewish Nose," provide additional historical insight by reca-pitulating the changing ideas about the markers of a Jew. Geller relates that before the seventeenth century, depictions of Jews in Europe showed them with certain accoutrements like tall hats and money bags; later, Jews began to be identified by physical features like beards. A growing reliance on physical markers hardened into a trust in physiognomy to reveal inner as well as outer differences among peoples. Lipton moves further back in time, dating the invention of the "Jewish nose" to the late thirteenth century, when the "range of features assigned to Jews consolidated into one fairly narrowly construed, simultaneously grotesque and naturalistic face." By 1776, the Swiss writer and theologian John Caspar Lavater had advanced a "science" based on physical markers, and as a result of this influ-ential work, as Geller puts it, "physiognomic verities became commonplace." Although Jewish noses obviously do not have a universal appearance, a particu-lar shape has been "stereotyped and caricatured in Western society as a 'Jewish nose' and selected as a symbol that differentiates Jews from non-Jews," in the words of sociologist Frances Macgregor.[6]

Another late eighteenth-century commentator, Dutch anatomist Petrus Camper, ascribed meaning to the measurement of the nasal index (defined as the line between the forehead and the upper lip, passing through the nose) in relation to the facial angle (the nasal index intersecting with a horizontal line from the jaw). Camper precisely defined the aesthetically beautiful face as that in which an angle of one hundred degrees to the horizontal is created by the facial line. More than a century after Camper delineated the angle of the perfect nose, the self-designated beauty expert (and cosmetic surgeon) Henry Schireson wrote that "the American ideal [nose] now is an angle of 28.5 degrees—thus giving the nose a saucy tilt one degree higher than that of the Venus de Milo."[7]

When observable or assumed physiognomic differences reified into ideology, the relationship of nose to face came to distinguish the different races, with the African closest to the ape and the Jew closer to the African or "Mongol" than to the European.[8] Purported interbreeding of Jews with Africans accounted in nineteenth-century ethnology (among Jewish ethnologists as well as Christian) for the Jews' physiognomy, including the shape of the nose. To quote a portion of a description of Jews by British race theorist Robert Knox, in his *Races of Man* (1854): "A large, massive, club-shaped, hooked nose, three or four times larger than suits the face—these are features which stamp the African character of the Jew, his muzzle-shaped mouth and face removing him from certain other races. . . . Thus it is that the Jewish face can never [be], and never is, beautiful."[9] Even into the next century, one American author, a minister and professor from North Carolina, published a study in 1910—*The Jew as Negro*—whose thesis, in Eric Goldstein's summary, was "that ancient Jews had thoroughly mixed with neighboring African peoples, leaving little significant difference between the Jewish and Negro types."[10] The word "impartial" in the subtitle of this work, *Being a Study of the Jewish Ancestry from an Impartial Standpoint*, strikes us today as ironic if not downright outrageous, but at the time, Reverend Abernathy surely believed in his academic objectivity. Along with skin color and hair texture, among other features, the nose was seen as a defining Jewish and hence inferior characteristic, yet so assertive—as Row's character puts it, "an aggressive nose, a nose that intrudes"—that even interbreeding with those of putative *superior* stock could not diminish the Jewish appearance of the offspring. Just as a drop of "black blood" would effectively stain a person as black, so too it was supposed that a Jewish nose would indelibly mark one as Jewish; as one antisemite remarked in the 1920s, "Jewishness is like a concentrated dye: a minute quantity suffices to give a specific character . . . to an incomparably greater mass."[11]

If interbreeding was thought to be incapable of diminishing differences and assimilating the Jew, conversion was no more effective in enabling passing. Gilman repeats a remark by Heinrich Heine about the "long nose which is a type of uniform, by which the King-God Jehova [sic] recognizes his old retainers, even if they had deserted" (as Heine himself had done).[12] Making a similar point, in discussing the German philosopher Walter Benjamin in the context of racist ideas about the alleged Jewish stench (the *foetor Judaicus*), Geller briefly mentions the Jewish nose itself. "The nose is a sign of the Jew that, until the development of the rhinoplasty, no assimilation could remove," he comments, and he quotes Moses Hess's *Rome and Jerusalem* (1862) on the point that "the German 'objects less to the Jews' peculiar beliefs than to their peculiar noses. . . . Jewish noses cannot be reformed.'"[13] Geller does not comment on the triple sense of this last word: along with redemption, which is the obvious meaning in the sentence, "reformed" suggests the inadequacy of the Reform Jewish movement, begun in Germany and taking many practices from German Protestantism (calling rabbis reverend and holding services largely in the vernacular, for example), in making German Jews less of an Other, and finally the re-formation that modern rhinoplasty would soon afford.

Sander Gilman has often related the story of Dr. Jacques Joseph, who invented the modern technique for the nose job. An assimilated German Jew (born Jakob Joseph), Joseph proudly bore dueling scars on his face as a sign of his bravery and integration into the German dueling societies, whereas the surgical procedure he invented, which is still used today, is conducted within the nasal cavity and thus leaves no visible scars. Trained as an orthopedic surgeon, Joseph was dismissed from his practice when he undertook a cosmetic (rather than restorative) operation on a child's ears. Hearing of this event, a man came to the doctor to ask for a corrective procedure for his nose, whose size and shape had brought him only misery; after the successful rhinoplasty in 1898, Joseph reported to the Berlin Medical Society that he had cured his patient in both a physical and a psychological sense. The patient was not necessarily Jewish, for dissatisfaction with one's nose in the nineteenth century could as likely be felt by an Irish man or woman, since stereotypes about the "Irish nose"—read, pug nose—also predominated, associating this shape, too, with negative characteristics.[14] Gilman nonetheless remarks: "It is unclear whether Joseph's first patient was Jewish, but the depiction of his psychological sense of social isolation due to the form of his nose certainly mirrors the meaning associated with anti-Semitic bias at the fin de siècle. It is clear, however, that Joseph's initial clientele was heavily Jewish and that he regularly reduced 'Jewish noses' to 'gentile contours.'"[15]

When Frances Macgregor interviewed rhinoplasty patients in New York and published her results three quarters of a century after Joseph's first rhinoplasty in Berlin, she found that both Jewish and non-Jewish patients referred to the "Jewish nose" and their desire to obliterate it. Macgregor divided her subjects into two groups, one of which she designated the "Changers" because their surgeries were predominantly motivated by "ethnocultural considerations and group stereotyping." Fifty-nine percent of the forty-six patients in this group were Jewish, and all wanted to "look like an American." (For the Jews this often meant having the stereotypical Irish bob.)[16] A Jewish eighteen-year-old would-be model looked to the pages of the fashion magazines for the turned-up nose she would need and justified her surgery on the basis of the discrimination she faced in the industry "because I have a Jewish nose." But the nineteen non-Jews in this group also had issues with identity, and that identity was in many cases the one they were merely presumed to have on the basis of the shape of their noses. Often they were firm in their assertion that it wasn't being taken for a Jew that bothered them; it was the fact that they weren't being "taken for an American," and/or they just wanted "to look better." Others merely stated their problem without elaboration: "People always think I'm Jewish." Macgregor sums up the motivations of the "changers" as a whole: "By changing [the nose] these patients hoped to erase their marginality, merge into the larger culture, and thereby gain acceptance."[17]

Macgregor's summary statement about the impetus of these patients toward surgery sums up as well the plots of much Jewish American fiction since the nineteenth century, in which the Jewish immigrants and their descendants seek to shed old-world habits, customs, and appearances, the better to fit in as Americans. Bernard Malamud's short story "The Jewbird" is but one illustration of this phenomenon: in this surrealistic tale, a talking black bird who says his name is Schwartz, and who speaks with a Yiddish inflection, flies in the window of apartment dweller Harry Cohen and arouses such antipathy in Cohen that he eventually flings the bird to his death. The bird's very kindness to Cohen's son, tutoring him so that his grades improve, only infuriates Cohen, not only because Schwartz is in this sense a better father than Cohen, but more importantly because Schwartz in his accent and other qualities represents a legacy that Cohen eschews for himself and his child. Schwartz is, we might say, "too Jewish": among such signs as the bird's name, accent, and proclivity for herring is his protuberant beak. Philip Hanson provides a relevant ornithological sidelight in his discussion of identity in Malamud's story, pointing to the "unpleasant ethnic connotations" of Harry Cohen's denigration of the talking bird's "big snoot." By referring to the real-life nicknames of big-snooted birds, Hanson in a way grounds Malamud's flight of fancy:

> The unabridged Webster's Third New International Dictionary includes entries for "Jewbird" and "jew [sic] crow." "Jewbird" is a slang name for the ani of the Southern US and South America. The nickname is applied "for its conspicuous beak." "Jew Crow" is slang for the English chough, a bird closely related to the raven. Similarly the dictionary remarks of the chough that the bird is "probably so called for its prominent beak." The pejorative slang names for these birds come out of a tradition of ethnic stereotyping and slurring, a tradition in which Cohen participates. His actions suggest a consequence of assimilation that Malamud finds unpleasant . . . a forgetting of where one came from.[18]

In Englander's novel, the stereotypical Jewish nose takes on a central role in a wider symbolic and geographical context than that in Malamud's short story. Not surprisingly, as with Jess Row, Englander looked to Sander Gilman's work and acknowledges it at the end.

The Ministry of Special Cases received several enthusiastic appraisals when it first came out.[19] However, precious little attention by literary critics and reviewers has since been paid to this important work. Indeed, it is telling that in 2012, the *New York Times* Book Review discussion of the second of Englander's two short story collections went so far as to totally omit the fact that Englander had ever produced a novel at all.[20] This omission is perhaps the unkindest cut that the novel has received, though it is by no means the only one. My response to that oversight, and to the paucity of critical attention, is to elaborate on a key feature of this rich and relevant work: the nose job.

References to the nose appear with regularity in *The Ministry of Special Cases*, but the most memorable are the rhinoplasties that the Poznans receive in lieu of cash payment for Kaddish Poznan's clandestine work in removing tombstone traces of a plastic surgeon's unsavory parentage. Opinion of this motif has itself proven to be an unkind cut. Of the early reviews of the novel, at least two specifically pointed to these nose jobs as a serious flaw in the work. Wyatt Mason in the *New Yorker* faulted Englander for the "bathos" of this element of the novel— "the nose joke comes off as more Catskills than Gogol"—and considered it a prime example of the novel's tonal infelicities because Englander "consistently undercuts seriousness with shtick." Ruth Franklin in the *New Republic* took a similar tack, arguing that the shifts in tone between tragedy and comedy undermine the novel's effect: "If things happen to [the characters] that are bizarrely unreal, then empathy is disrupted, and it never really recovers." Franklin entitled her review "Kaddish's Nose" only to highlight her judgment that this prominent aspect of the characters and the work they inhabit constitutes the ruination of the novel's promise.[21]

Some other early reviews, in contrast, noted the symbolic resonance of the nose job, but none devoted space to it.[22] Within literary criticism, only one essay, by Gustavo Sánchez Canales, actually centers on *The Ministry of Special Cases* (in contrast to the number of analyses of Englander's short stories), and Canales's is the only article to highlight the significance of the nose job in the context of the novel's themes.[23] Yet, like Gogol's *The Nose*, Englander's novel actually places so much emphasis on this particular facial feature that it almost seems a separate character; indeed, the Jewish nose is as conspicuous in this work as it is on the faces of all three Poznan family members. Showing the extent to which contemporary American Jewish novelists are branching out of familiar (usually US) territory, Englander uses the nose not merely to foreground a putative physiognomic trait of "the Jew" but also to put Jewishness itself in the framework of Argentinian culture and politics both before and during the Dirty War. William Deresiewicz, reviewing *The Ministry of Special Cases* for the *Nation* in the month of its release, made the curious assertion that Pato "is not arrested because he's Jewish, he's arrested because he's a leftist, and Kaddish and Lillian are not stymied in their pitiable efforts to retrieve him because they're Jewish either."[24] Both statements are off the mark, in light of historical evidence to the contrary. *The Ministry of Special Cases* refers often to the predicament of the Jews and, in that sense, could actually have been subtitled with the name of one of Pato Poznan's books: *Reflections on the Jewish Question.*[25]

Frank Graziano, in *Divine Violence: Spectacle, Psychosexuality, & Radical Christianity in the Argentine "Dirty War,"* details the foci and modus operandi of both the military junta that overthrew the Perón government in March 1976 and the takeover government headed by General Jorge Rafael Videla. In the discourse that pervaded and animated this movement, leaders emphasized inculcating the values of Western (i.e., noncommunist) and Christian civilization and eliminating anything and anyone seen to oppose that process.[26] Students, labor unionists, and Jews were prime targets for interrogation, torture, and "disappearance"—the three categories overlapped. Though constituting less than 1 percent of Argentina's population during this time, Jews made up more than 12 percent of the victims.[27] In Englander's novel, Dr. Mazursky mentions this disproportionality when he says of the kidnapped, "Too many are blameless. And too many are Jews" (146). Englander linked the tactics of the Dirty War to the nose job when he remarked in a 2007 interview that to "disappear" a person is not only to deny him or her a future but "to reach in and undo the past . . . to make [the "disappeared"] not-ever. . . . It is a way of fracturing the seeming unbreakable link between future and past." (He includes the same idea, phrased almost identically, in the novel itself [303].) Commenting in that interview a bit later on the role of plastic surgery in the novel, Englander did not repeat the word *fracturing*, a word appropriate for a nose job, but instead made the same point with *broken*: "The altering of identity through surgery is another way that the continuum [between past and future] gets broken."[28]

One other historical phenomenon in Argentina is relevant to Jewish culture and to the novel's emphasis on the nose. In addition to the Dirty War, prostitution and crime in Buenos Aires in the late nineteenth and early twentieth centuries figure into Englander's portrayal of his protagonist, Kaddish Poznan, and Poznan's acquiescence to a nose job. For decades, the city drew hundreds of pimps and prostitutes from eastern Europe, where they had suffered poverty and pogroms, because conditions were favorable in Argentina: As Edward Bristow says, in his study of the white slave trade, "Everything was arranged for high profits: the imbalance of numbers between males and females; the Latin cultural toleration for prostitutes, thorough police and political corruption, weak laws and new shipping routes." Before the turn of the century, the number of pimps constituted 10 to 20 percent of the Jewish population of Buenos Aires, a population that numbered about one thousand Jews altogether. In 1911, records indicate that 80 percent of the city's prostitutes were Jewish. Not surprisingly, the respectable Jewish community exhibited a range of responses to their disreputable coreligionists, including a refusal to associate with them. In fact, this strategy served as inspiration to New York Jews, who, in 1909, urged "communal ostracism, as

it is being adopted by our people in Buenos Aires. There they excluded the traf-
fickers from the synagogue, from the services of the shocket [kosher slaughterer],
and finally even from the cemetery. . . . Let us do the same here. Let us push them
out from our midst, till they go and band themselves together, to stand forth in
the eyes of all as a community of lepers." By 1914, the "unclean ones" in Buenos
Aires (as they were always termed by the established Argentinian Jews) had of
necessity formed their own synagogue and cemetery.[29]

After providing details of Kaddish's upbringing and status as one of the
"unclean," Englander picks up the story with Kaddish's employment by prominent Jewish families to obliterate the names of their unrespectable ancestors
from the gravestones on the un-kosher side of the Jewish cemetery. That is, they
employ him to fracture the link between past, present, and future. When the
political climate is uncertain, the "clean" ones must seek at all costs to keep the
attention of the powers-that-be away from them, and one way to do that is to
disassociate themselves from any other than model citizens (defined not only
as those engaged in legitimate businesses but also as those who close their eyes,
ears, mouths, and memories to what is going on around them). Kaddish Poznan
is doubly marginalized: as a Jew and a *hijo de puta*, the son of a whore, he is an
outcast in the eyes of both the Argentinian majority and the Jewish establishment. Only someone like him could be hired for, and undertake, such a demean-
ing, even sacrilegious, job.

When Kaddish steals out in the middle of the night with his sack of tools, he
and his son, Pato, stumble across a dead body in the cemetery; Kaddish immediately identifies that boy as a Christian because "such a nose as this God hasn't set
on a Jewish face in 2,000 years" (12). He not only leaves the body there but also
rationalizes his lack of concern by telling Pato that the murder is simply a result
of the government "cleaning up" revolutionaries in the process of securing a better life for all citizens—a belief shared by many Argentinians at the time, who
shrugged off the arrests and disappearances with a "that's what happens" (que va
ser) or "it must have been because of something" (por algo habrá sido).[30] Referring
to Pato and his friends, and to a facial feature that is an encoded term for "Jew,"
Kaddish issues the warning that life will be safe "for those who don't make trouble and keep their big noses clean" (14). Englander in fact highlights the size of
Pato's nose: Pato enters the bathroom nose first (96); the hole in his friend's mat-
tress is, for Pato, "somewhere to stick his nose" (245); Kaddish thinks the baker
could remember Pato by the shape of his nose (205); and Lillian describes Pato to
the girl released in her custody as having a "huge, big nose" (227). In Kaddish's
naive belief that keeping such a nose clean will forestall trouble, Kaddish is the
child and his nineteen-year-old son, the father.

The size of Kaddish's own nose matches that of his son. The plastic surgeon
Mazursky, in characterizing Kaddish's nose as "horrendous," "monstrous," and

"a big fin of a kosher nose" (30, 68), spouts the stereotypical disparagement of the so-called Jewish nose along with the aesthetician's repugnance for lack of proportion.[31] The doctor must state this view forcefully in order to obtain Kaddish's agreement to substitute plastic surgery for the hefty sum he is owed, but Kaddish needs little special pleading after being told his "deformity" is the reason he can't sleep (and, not incidentally, the reason he is ugly). With his nose job, Kaddish loses "his most defining characteristic" (77). But even after the nose job, Mazursky lets Kaddish into his house "for the nose" (315)—again figuring Kaddish not as a whole man but rather in terms of one physical feature, which the doctor, with his skills, has "fixed," made into "the only perfect thing" (317).

This confluence of "Jewish noses," operations to "correct" them, and the social isolation before (and even after) such operations lends special significance to *The Ministry of Special Cases*. In Englander's novel, getting the nose reduced to "gentile contours" may make Kaddish better looking by the standards of insiders and wannabe insiders (like Mazursky), but it is not enough to make him an insider. He cannot pass as one; he is inauthentic. Englander suggests as much by having Kaddish stare in the doctor's examination room at the masks that Mazursky has brought back from his travels (63), a scene that symbolically equates plastic surgery with attempting to hide one's true identity.[32] The irony is that, disaffected with his religion and his Jewish cohorts as he may be, Kaddish does not at first intentionally try to pass; he merely is making the best of what he sees as a bad situation: Mazursky's inability to pay Poznan for his cemetery "cleanup" in any way but a surgical procedure for Kaddish and wife Lillian. Kaddish's initial reason for the surgery derives from his take-what-you-can philosophy, the philosophy of a man who from birth has never been given much from life (with the sole exceptions of Lillian and their child). Thus, he cuts a deal—"a Kaddish-cut deal" as only he can cut (140)—to have his nose cut and Lillian's too in the bargain. But the remark from Mazursky that his surgical skills "can liberate the man trapped within the Jew" (70) must resonate, for Kaddish will soon mouth similar sentiments to Pato: "We look different and this is our chance to look better than everyone else. We can, with this, fit in" (73)—a passing fancy, indeed, and one that not even the wealthy, assimilated Mazursky holds. The only passing that will be done among the major characters in this novel is that of Pato, who will be cut from the records of his existence—"disappeared"—and most assuredly murdered.

Ultimately the nose job has the effect only of further distancing Poznan from his rebellious son, first emotionally and then literally. *The Ministry of Special Cases* presents an instructive difference from Philip Roth's "Goodbye, Columbus" in terms of the motivation for and outcome of the nose job. Mr. Patimkin retains his nose with its bump but funds his daughter's surgery so that she can conform to American (that is, gentile) standards of beauty and hence become more mainstream and successful (and in so doing, exemplify his own "making it"). In Englander's treatment, Pato Poznan wants to keep his big nose—the sign of his Jewish identity—and, unlike his father's new nose, it remains as one of his defining features.[33] Pato lambastes his father for even entertaining the notion of a nose bob: "It's enough what this government forces on us already; we don't need to volunteer to make ourselves look the same" (72). One is reminded in this context of Dorothy Parker's droll comment about Fanny Brice, the famous vaudevillian who underwent a rhinoplasty in defiance of the wishes of the impresario Flo Ziegfeld: Parker said that Brice "had cut off her nose to spite her race."[34] This is one element in Pato's view of both parents' rhinoplasties.[35]

Pato has lost part of his finger while struggling with his father in the cemetery, for chiseling off Jews' names—a kind of "cleaning up"—is not what he wants to be doing, even though his father has more than once promised him a cut of the deal (51, 73). The only cut that Pato gets from his labors is a body cut. Regarding Pato's fingertip, Englander writes that "this was how sons were born to fathers, from ribs and hands, from parts taken and shared" (56). When Kaddish later tosses the fingertip into the ash tray in the hospital, the severing of the finger marks that between father and son as well. And so it is with Kaddish's nose job, though in that case it is Kaddish's "tip" that is thrown in the trash after surgical removal. When Pato later cries out to his father about not wanting to be made to look the same, he waves his partially amputated finger, stating that he has already lost too much; he is not about to sacrifice his nose too. These seemingly disparate events are thereby symbolically united.

Indeed, Englander constantly draws attention to removals, some undertaken by desperate individuals for the sake of preservation and some by the military junta for the purpose of destruction. The nose job is to be seen in the context of the Poznans' activities: getting cuts of the deal; chiseling Jewish names from gravestone and clipping threads from the Torah curtain ("facelift[s] for the family name," as Kaddish puts it, using a term to which a plastic surgeon can relate [32]); Kaddish's burning of Pato's incriminating books, address books, class photos, record albums, diaries, and letters; Lillian's surreptitious snatching of the General's contact information from her boss's Rolodex; and her chipping away of ice in the freezer to dislodge ransom money or funds for a steel door. Most significantly, the nose job's alteration of identity connects to the government's confiscation of books, its expunging of official records—birth certificates, diplomas, and the like—that testify to a person's existence, its plucking of babies from one set of parents in order to deliver them to another (producing in Lillian "the same kind of disorientation she'd felt when she first saw her new nose" [108]), and, in the ultimate removal, its "disappearings" of adults (168). Wyatt Mason, in his *New Yorker* review, noted the importance of the novel's "disturbing erasures," but in failing to credit the nose job with having anything to do with "this morally fraught subject," he missed a connection as plain as the nose on his face.[36]

According to Dr. Schireson, one of America's first plastic surgeons, who studied under Jacques Joseph, "The perfect nose is the one that is rarely or never noticed."[37] Being "fixed" from one perspective can mean being made better, even "perfect"—that is, being made to fit in by becoming inconspicuous, as impossible to locate as the keyhole on the new door purchased by Lillian for safety's sake. But being "fixed" can also mean being neutered, hence rendered ineffectual, as well as being put in a fix, a mess. After Pato goes missing, his friend Rafa says to Kaddish and Lillian, "Pato told us you guys had yourself fixed, that you'd gotten yourself neutered and spayed" (159). Having their noses bobbed to become more good-looking (more Aryan) has not made Kaddish and Lillian fit in better, much less ensured the safety of their son; to the contrary, try as they might, they are as ineffectual at getting their son back as the expensive steel door was in keeping him in (or the goons out). Their nose jobs play a role in the guilt they experience for their failure. When they go to the police station to see if the authorities have their child, the policeman, upon looking at the photograph of Pato and then at his parents' faces, says that by the looks of their noses, Pato can't be their child: "This kid didn't come from either of you." Kaddish's cry in response to the offi-cer—"'It's not my nose,' Kaddish yelled, referring to his own"—is futile, evoking a sarcastic rejoinder at the opposite pole from the reality of the situation: "At least you can be thankful for that" (132).

Lillian's nose job, performed by one of Mazursky's students as his first such operation, not surprisingly goes awry—literally. The fact that her nose slides off her face ("broken free," as Kaddish says, with no sense of irony [140]) may come across as shtick to some readers, but it is symbolically essential, not to mention emotionally resonant. Her nose has been disappeared just like her son:

> "Every time they look," she said [to Kaddish], "when they see his picture—when they see both faces—already they don't believe. . . . The first time I ever enjoyed my own reflection was after Pato was born. For a parent, from then on, when I looked in the mirror I saw myself and I saw him. We were the same, Kaddish. A son and a twin. Now he's gone from the mirror too. It is like mur-der, this nose."
> "You can still see Pato in the mirror."
> "I can't," she said. . . . "I can't find my own face in there anymore; how am I supposed to find his? My son is gone, and the one way I had him, that is gone too. . . . I want my big nose back, Kaddish. I want to see Pato when I look in the mirror. Go find me my old nose." (140–41)

Lillian's loss of a twin flashes the reader back to Kaddish's operation, when Mazursky told Lillian that a "rhinoplasty like this is as serious as detaching Siamese twins. There is a chance . . . that we may lose one of them after separation"

(76). The surgeon's flip remark comes all too true: first Lillian's own nose is lost, and then her Siamese twin of a son disappears.

Mazursky will restore Lillian's nose, but only to the standard of beauty he had achieved with Kaddish's, which is the majority standard or, as Pato puts it, "the horror of a nation with one acceptable nose" (81).[38] Like the Catholic priest Lillian engages in the hunt for Pato, she now has something resembling a "perfect triangle of a nose" (259). When Kaddish and Lillian intrude on the General's home in order to argue for assistance, the General's wife comments to Lillian, having seen her both before and after the nose job, that Lillian now looks "more Argentine in some way" (187), which (as Lillian well understands) is a snide remark about her ethnicity, because to this woman and her cohort, a Jew cannot be a true Argentine—they are mutually exclusive terms. When Mazursky "fixes" the student's botched job by creating his standard-issue beautiful nose instead of restoring the old nose that Lillian wants back (152), he shows no understanding of what Lillian means by "fixing": she cannot in the least be "thankful for that" because Pato *is* Lillian's old nose, her twin, and without it she is without him and without herself. Her son is not free, and she will never be free from looking for him.[39] One is reminded again of the connection between Pato's lost finger and a parent's nose job, because Lillian had asked her son, after the doctor stitched up his fingertip, "Will it be fine? . . . Will it be perfect?" and Pato had responded, "What's perfect?" (57). "Perfect" and "fixing" are relative terms. Schireson, referring to the psychic scars inflicted by a misshapen nose, wrote in 1938 that "the nose is an unemotional feature, unlike the eyes or mouth. It screams only when it is wrong"; but Lillian's nose "screams" when "right."[40] ("I want it wrong. Wrong in the old way, big in the old way," she cries to Kaddish [141]). Mazursky may have gotten out of his debt to Kaddish by paying through the nose (as he says, utilizing a familiar expression in a literal way [68]), but Lillian is now paying through hers in a figurative but equally real way. This woman who has undergone the unkind cuts of *two* nose jobs has delivered the unkindest cut to her beloved son: she believes that with her resemblance to him chiseled away, she has aided in cutting him out of her life and, God forbid, his own. "'Murder,' Lillian said, her old nose gone, Pato missing from the mirror. 'To change a face it is murder'" (172).

Like Gogol's nose, Lillian's takes on a significance detached (appropriately in her case) from a mere facial feature, as she pokes into the affairs of every bureaucrat, Jewish or otherwise: "My own little junta—me and my nose. The pair of us broken, going around and spreading dread" (158).[41] She is defiant and determined when the priest asks her why Jews insist on living where they are not wanted; sarcastically, she responds, "Do you think the generals turn their own selves pink trying to breathe while we suck all the air up with our giant collective Jewish nose?" (283). It is irrelevant that her nose, and her husband's, are now as "Argentine" and as technically functional as any Catholic's. Her husband's Jewish nose had literally impeded *his* breathing, but metaphorically, the Jewish nose remains as a marker whether fixed or not. And it is the Jews (among other undesirables) who cannot breathe in this atmosphere of dread. As Lillian puts it, "I know that when there's death in the air the Jew is more susceptible, more likely to catch it" (246).

When Lillian presses the head of the Jewish community to be more aggressive in finding their missing children, Feigenblum fittingly responds in terms of the nose, in that familiar saying: "Why cut off our noses, Mrs. Poznan, only to spite our face?" (245). In other words, making a fuss will only bring the authorities down harder on the Jews. Englander stays true to the actual situation in Argentina at the time, for the official Jewish mouthpiece in the country, the Delegation of Argentine Jewish Associations (DAIA), founded in the mid-1930s, was loath to make waves and went along with the regime out of fear and self-preservation. As Paul Katz relates, in his study of the DAIA's position during the Dirty War, this organization "responded to regime pressure by further excluding Jews the regime deemed 'subversive' from the very community DAIA claimed to represent. In particular, DAIA offered support to an anti-Semitic regime by combating charges of official anti-Semitism in Argentina and internationally, sidelining human rights advocates and marginalizing Jewish *desaparecidos* and their relatives."[42] In contrast to Pato's room, which Kaddish has stripped of mementos that could implicate other innocents, Feigenblum's office is stuffed with proud trophies: "honors and accolades, the statuettes and Judaic symbols that those in power procure. . . . [and] photos of Feigenblum and personages of import" (239). Fullness and emptiness are thus contrasted in their emotional as well as physical senses. With the power accorded to him by the state, Feigenblum disappears Pato yet again by refusing to add his name to the list of missing children, a list sanctioned by the government and woefully underreported. Bringing "her beautiful new nose right up to the glass," behind which hangs the official list of missing Jewish children (243), Lillian is impotent to get Pato included in it. She knows that if it were Feigenblum's son who were missing, "he'd be back in a day" (246). Actually, the president of the DAIA from 1976 to 1980 did have to count his own son among the disappeared, at which point he enlisted all possible contacts in the Argentine and US governments to get him released—"the only *desaparecido* successfully freed from a clandestine Dirty War detention center by a Jewish organization," as Katz informs.[43] In Englander's novel, the Jewish establishment (here called the United Jewish Congregations) had already closed ranks against the Poznans because of Kaddish's unsavory past, effectively disappearing the parents as well as the child. As Kaddish reflects, they had "kept him on the other side of the wall his whole life" (234).

Will Blythe, reviewing *The Ministry of Special Cases* in the *New York Times*, faulted the novel for being "mythological" rather than realistic, and for "soften[ing] the ragged edge of history too much; the Dirty War becomes a stage set for explorations of identity."[44] He attributed this "softening" to Englander's youth, though Englander was thirty-seven at the time of the novel's publication and hardly a youth. Blythe's cutting remark about softening history is not only unkind; it strains credulity. For in this novel, the crimes of the Dirty War, the silence of "model citizens" in the face of them, and the relentless but fruitless attempts of the main characters to find their disappeared son are about as brutal as they can be. Englander performed his own surgery while writing the novel, deciding not to use the "ten bazillion Dirty War facts" he had gathered, making "painful cuts" as he went along. Yet by concentrating on the case of one fictional family, the author has portrayed every sordid aspect of that period in Argentina's history in graphic detail: the public roundups and violent kidnappings by plainclothes security men, the disappearance and often the murder of anyone considered to be a subversive, the removal of information from the records, the dropping of bodies into the La Plata River, the stealing of babies from mothers' wombs and arms so that they can be raised by generals and other officials as their own, the frustration and agony of the parents as they seek in vain for information on their loved ones. These details, and Pato himself, stand out in startling vividness in spite of the regime's attempts to "disappear" them, just as the names on the Torah curtain in the synagogue of the unclean ones remain in stark relief because they are unfaded underneath the threads that Kaddish has painstakingly removed.

Blythe may hold on to a sentimentalized belief that "the more Kaddish fails the more we love him" and that the affection of the family "endures through every disaster," but this is wishful thinking.[45] We grow weary of Kaddish's failed schemes, even as we understand why he undertakes them and sympathize with his guilt; with Lillian, we lament, "There's no deal [he touches] that doesn't sour. A thousand nose jobs and each would fall" (182). Kaddish is not exactly the lovable schlemiel of much Yiddish and Jewish American literature, the kind of loser-as-winner discussed by Ruth Wisse in her classic *The Schlemiel as Modern Hero*.[46] He might more accurately be disparaged with the term *schmegegge*: a loser-as-loser. The strain of circumstances strains our "love" for him, and more to the point, it strains Lillian's as well; as not infrequently happens in such cases, the loss of their child fractures the marriage. Saying the mourner's prayer for his son as no father, not even one named Kaddish, should have to do, Kaddish accepts his son's death, as well as Lillian's consequent expulsion of her husband from the home, and moves alone to Israel—a fact noted obliquely, in passing (120), and undoubtedly facilitated by the threats of the General's wife against his life after his botched attempt to ransom her father's bones in exchange for money to finance Lillian's fruitless bribes. Lillian, in contrast, remains in Buenos Aires, refusing to give up hope for her son's return. Englander has prepared the reader for the last scene in the novel, with its poignant final image repeated previously at key moments throughout the work: Lillian siting in her wingback chair facing the window, waiting for her son to turn the corner. If there were a sequel to this novel, and a hundred sequels after that, Lillian would still be waiting. Or she would be marching with the Mothers of the Plaza before the Pink Palace (a phenomenon Englander does not include in the novel), demanding information on their children as they do to this day, every Thursday. If that final image of Lillian's steadfast and lonely vigil does not break one's heart (as Lillian's is broken [137]), then one either has the "ice-cold heart" of the General's wife (335) or has had the heart surgically removed.

Meanwhile, as Englander said in an interview at the book's publication, the "greatest tragedy is also funny."[47] Wyatt Mason's notion that Englander "consistently undercuts seriousness with shtick" is itself an undercutting of Englander's intention and achievement. The nose jobs, those literal surgical procedures in *The Ministry of Special Cases*, constitute a primary and essential component of the novel's black humor—the only kind of humor that could simultaneously capture the surrealistic horror of the situation and provide the reader, and even occasionally the participants, some small relief from it.

Notes

1. Jacobson, in *Whiteness of a Different Color*, quotes a portion of this poem (182). I strongly disagree with Jacobson's characterization of it as a "philo-Semitic paean." Although by the end of the poem Holmes recognizes the Israelites as the progenitors of Jesus Christ, the poem remains to my mind thoroughly antisemitic. The lines that follow the "hook-nosed kite," after all, are "The snaky usurer, him that crawls / And cheats beneath the golden balls / Moses and Levi, all the horde, / Spawn of the race that slew its Lord." "Bistred" means pigmented with a brown coloring, and a kite is a cheater in financial matters. The poem may be found at the Accuracy Project website (http://www.accuracyproject.org/t-Holmes-AtthePantomime.html).

2. Pynchon, *V.*, 45.

3. Row, *Your Face in Mine*, 331.

4. Among his source materials, Row acknowledges Gilman's *Creating Beauty*, but Gilman also discusses the "Jewish nose" in several other works, among them *Jew's Body*; "Jewish Nose"; *Picturing Health and Illness*; and *Making the Body Beautiful*. Englander in his own acknowledgments lists this last text as one of his resources.

5. Gilman mentions this work in *Creating Beauty*, 74, and *Making the Body Beautiful*, 120.

6. Geller, "(G)nos(e)ology," 247. On these points Geller references the work of Gilman as well as that of Dennis Showalter in the 1980s and Eduard Fuchs's 1920s study of caricatures of Jews. See also Lipton, "Invention of the Jewish Nose," and Macgregor, *Transformation and Identity*, 89. Lipton refers to the Jewish nose throughout *Dark Mirror*, her full-length study of missals, psalters, caskets, sculptures, altar pieces, stained-glass windows, and other works that were created and displayed throughout the Middle Ages. See especially the chapter "The

Jew's Face" (169–200), which discusses the reification of the "Jew's nose" in the context of the rise of interest in nature and the human body in the first half of the thirteenth century.

7. Schireson, *As Others See You*, 70–71. Apparently Schireson created these measurements from a composite of the cover girls in Sunday supplements and on magazine covers (see Haiken, *Venus Envy*, 10).

8. Gilman, *Picturing Health and Illness*, 83.

9. Quoted in Jacobson, *Whiteness of a Different Color*, 180.

10. Goldstein, *Price of Whiteness*, 43.

11. Gilman, "Jewish Nose," 371–74. The quotation is on 374. Many resources are available on stereotypes about Jewish physical characteristics as reflected in works of fiction across cultures, especially in Europe and the United States. As but one example, I explore in *Race and Identity* how notions about the Jewish nose and other racial characteristics play out in the writings of D. H. Lawrence, comparing Lawrence's treatment of these tropes to his adaptation of those about Gypsies and Native Americans.

12. Heinrich Heine, *Werke*, cited in Gilman, *Creating Beauty*, 81, and "The Jewish Nose," 377.

13. Geller, "Aromatics of Jewish Difference," 238–39. The two-page section is cleverly entitled "Cutting Off One's Nose to Spite One's Faith." Geller also cites this passage from Hess in his earlier, more extensive disquisition on the Jewish nose, "(G)nos(e)ology" (249). Gilman, too, quotes from Moses Hess in "Jewish Nose" (380) and *Creating Beauty* (72).

14. Gilman devotes separate segments of his *Making the Body Beautiful* to Jewish and Irish noses; see, too, his brief discussion of the Irish nose in *Picturing Health and Illness* (83) and in *Jew's Body* (185). In *Making the Body Beautiful*, Gilman also remarks that the "racial nose is, of course, not only a 'Jewish' nose. The too-long nose is read in other cultures as racially marked and, therefore, the source of unhappiness. In Mexico, over the past few decades, there has been an explosion in the number of rhinoplasties, as wealthier Mexicans seek to obscure their Indian ancestry" (198).

15. Gilman, *Jew's Body*, 185–87; repeated in *Making the Body Beautiful*, 154.

16. There is a certain irony in the fact that the "Irish nose" was desirable for Jews because the Irish immigrants, "vilified as a 'simian race'" and of questionable whiteness, fared worse than the Jews during most of the nineteenth century (see the comments on the Irish by Goldstein, *Price of Whiteness*, 18).

17. Macgregor, *Transformation and Identity*, 88–92, 96. Macgregor interviewed New Yorkers who sought rhinoplasties in the years 1946–1954.

18. Hanson, "Horror and Ethnic Identity in 'The Jewbird,'" 365.

19. Examples of laudatory reviews include those by Peter Terzian and Drew Nellins.

20. Schiff, "Camp Stories," 1, 9.

21. Mason, "Disappearances"; Franklin, "Kaddish's Nose." Allegra Goodman, in her review, merely implies that the motif of the nose job seems "forced" (36).

22. Jeremy Treglown, in concluding his review, notes the "bleak symbolic resonance" of the nose job; Franklin terms it "one of the novel's leitmotifs." Shifra Goldenberg, in "What's in a Name," unfavorably contrasts Englander's first novel with his first volume of short stories and comments that the whole incident of the nose job should have been a short story because "its richness is nearly forgotten when the whole of Englander's novel is considered."

23. Canales, "'Benevolent Self Was a Disgrace beyond Measure.'" See 63–69 for Canales's references to the nose job. The essay, a perceptive exploration of the importance of memory in Jewish continuity, is one of only two sustained critical approaches to Englander's novel

published to date. The other, "'Making One Story'?" by Lisa Propst, examines Englander's novel and Jonathan Safran Foer's *Everything Is Illuminated* in terms of their "forms of reconciliation" but makes no mention of the nose job. Goldenstein's "Every Individual Should Feel *As If*" devotes only a little over a page to Englander's novel but does relate the nose job to the effacement of the past (see 73–75).

24. Deresiewicz, "Imaginary Jew."

25. Englander, *Ministry of Special Cases*, 93. Subsequent references in the text to this novel are to this edition.

26. Graziano, *Divine Violence*, 25–33.

27. Go-I, "Jews Targeted in Argentina's Dirty War." My thanks to Jenna Greenspan, Duke University class of 2015, for providing this resource and the work of Paul Katz (see below) in her term paper on "Crimes of Silence in Argentina's Dirty War," written for my seminar on Jewish American literature in the fall of 2014.

28. Englander, interview 2 with Drew Nellins.

29. Information in this paragraph on prostitution in Buenos Aires is from Bristow, *Prostitution and Prejudice*, 111, 115–16, 118, 219, 223–24. Englander also acknowledges this resource. For a synopsis of a documentary that explores sex trafficking in Argentina in this period, see Brown, "Raquel: A Marked Woman," 60. Sholom Aleichem's 1909 story "The Man from Buenos Aires" hints at but never pinpoints the shady enterprise of the businessman formerly from Latvia, now living in Buenos Aires, a city he describes as "a cesspool. Hell on earth. But a heavenly hell. That is, hell for some and heaven for others. . . . I'm a kind of middleman, what you might call a jobber. That is, I provide a commodity that everyone knows about but no one ever talks about" (see 170–71). The strong suggestion is that this well-dressed man on the train in eastern Europe is engaged in the business of prostitution, especially given that he says he is traveling to Soshmakin to find a Jewish girl to bring back to Buenos Aires.

30. Quoted in Katz, "New 'Normal,'" 382–83.

31. "A nose too sharply hooked," said Schireson, when writing of the "Jewish nose" (90), "is always a disturbance on esthetic grounds."

32. During and after World War I, however, when surgeries to correct soldiers' facial deformities caused by trench warfare could not achieve the desired results, the British and French sometimes hired artists to create full or partial "portrait masks" to create a psychologically and socially acceptable face. Such masks, like the surgeries themselves, were seen at the time as reconstructive rather than cosmetic (see Haiken, *Venus Envy*, 35–36).

33. Pato's insistence on keeping his nose is reminiscent of the statement by a young American male of Pato's age who did have the operation but resented the necessity for doing so: as he told Frances Macgregor, "I have had my nose changed due purely to the fact that I live in a society where there are conventional forms to follow." He capitulated to cultural norms because, as he said, "The pressure to conform and the discrimination is too great" (see Macgregor, *Transformation and Identity*, 91). This patient is probably the same as the one Macgregor elaborates on later in the chapter, in "the case of David Stein" (105–12, see especially 109). Haiken has recorded that the plastic surgeon Jacob Daley, who tried to discourage prospective patients from having their noses bobbed to conform to society's standards of beauty, was interviewed by *Time* magazine in 1945; the reporter noted that the doctor had "kept his own magnificently large, arched, craggy and overhanging neb" (*Venus Envy*, 220–21). Daley was Jewish, though Haiken doesn't say so (perhaps it is to be understood

by the shape of his nose). Nathan Englander has also retained a nose that can be described in the same way as Daley's.

34. Quoted in Gilman, *Making the Body Beautiful*, 205 (no source given). Parker, née Rothschild, was herself half-Jewish but did not identify Jewishly. Schireson was Fanny Brice's surgeon, though in his 1938 book on plastic surgery he makes no mention of her name when detailing the case. Indeed, a before-and-after photo included in a set of such photos, after page 322, is captioned "Famous Irish American comedienne with 'Jewish nose,'" though the woman is clearly Fanny Brice (see Schireson, *As Others See You*, 86–88). Barbra Streisand, who played Fanny Brice in *Funny Girl* and whose Jewish identity is the context for Neal Gabler's biography, had Stephen Sondheim revise the lyrics of "I'm Still Here" for her 1994 concert in Madison Square Garden to include the line "I kept my nose to spite my face" (see Gabler, *Barbra Streisand*, 213).

35. I see Goldenstein's point in maintaining that Pato rejects his father's new nose on ideological rather than Jewish grounds. The text supports her view in Pato's impassioned urging of his father to reject the Jews who have rejected him (52) (see Goldenstein, "Every Individual Should Feel *As If*," 74). Nonetheless, it seems to me that the weight of the novel taken as a whole equates maintaining a putative Jewish physiognomy with an unwillingness to renounce a Jewish identity.

36. Canales, in contrast, points to the nose job as "another instance of the motif of obliteration" (63).

37. Schireson, *As Others See You*, 66. Joseph changed his Jewish-sounding name when he studied medicine in Berlin and Leipzig, among other efforts to mask his heritage (see Gilman, *Jew's Body*, 181, and *Making the Body Beautiful*, 122).

38. Gilman, in *Creating Beauty*, 19–20, cites a 1996 *Wall Street Journal* article headlined "Argentina Is a Land of Many Faces, Fixed by Plastic Surgeons," about the rise in number of nose jobs and liposuctions in that country; Gilman quotes an Argentinian psychiatrist who remarked that beauty is valued in the country because "working hard and being a good citizen won't get you anywhere." Englander puts a different spin on the rhinoplasty (and the "good citizen") in his novel set twenty years earlier, but the notions of what defines an acceptable look, how a culture determines it, and the lengths to which some will go to achieve it are the same.

39. Lillian's old nose is never restored, but the development of DNA technology in recent years has resulted in the restoration of some children's links with their true past and the reconnections to some of those mothers who have marched in protest for years in the Plaza de Mayo.

40. Schireson, *As Others See You*, 78.

41. Gilman, in *Creating Beauty*, 98, remarks parenthetically on Gogol's story (1836), stating that it reflects "the meaning that the nose has as a sign of disease and difference in Russian culture." Gilman does not elaborate, but the disease to which he refers may well be syphilis, which in the congenital form may collapse the nose and did indeed inspire dread in many cultures. Gilman addresses syphilis, and the anxiety it provoked, in *Creating Beauty* as well as in his other studies.

42. Katz, "New 'Normal,'" 368. Katz attempts a nuanced approach to this issue, treating it as "a case study of the means by which exclusionary violence co-opts civil institutions and empowers repressive regimes, and of the complex liabilities this co-option generates" (369). He provides examples of the "limited concessions" that DAIA lobbied for, including the

release of jailed journalist Jacobo Timerman, but also its later renunciation of Timerman and its continual denunciation of Jewish human rights activists like Rabbi Marshall Meyer (see 377–79). According to the Duke University curator of the Marshall Meyer papers, Englander interviewed Meyer's widow, Miriam, when writing this novel (personal conversation with Patrick Stawski, November 5, 2015).

43. Katz, "New 'Normal,'" 376.

44. Blythe, "Innocents Lost."

45. I believe the opposite tack is also untrue: Shifra Goldenberg's remark that "Englander fails to bring us close enough to the couple to elicit our empathy." Goldenberg, "What's in a Name.".

46. Wisse, *Schlemiel as Modern Hero*.

47. The Englander quotations in this paragraph and the previous one are from the author's interview with Drew Nellins.

3 Jewish American Women and the Nose Job

"God Hath Given You One Face, and You Make Yourself Another"

IN 1920, IN the very earliest years of the professionalization of plastic surgery, the *New York Times* appropriated Hamlet's accusation to Ophelia in its editorial decrying the new trend toward face-lifts.[1] Decades later, with the rising acceptability, even popularity, of cosmetic surgery, Hamlet's diatribe was turned on its head in reference to another aspect of female appearance: the shape of the nose. In Myrna Blyth's 1975 novel, *Cousin Suzanne*, Suzanne's mother tries to allay her daughter's concern about her nose by saying, "It's the nose God gave you," which prompts this immediate rejoinder from Suzanne: "To hell with *that*." After a pause, the ever pragmatic and status-conscious mother comes up with the solution du jour: "So you'll have it fixed."[2] And so Suzanne does.

Not incidentally, for more than two decades *Cousin Suzanne*'s author was the editor in chief of *Ladies' Home Journal*, a prime purveyor of notions about beauty for body and home, and, relatedly, of advertising for cosmetic surgery. It was during her reign as editor, starting in the early 1980s, that the number of articles on cosmetic surgery began to rise exponentially, in *Ladies' Home Journal* as well as in the other magazines geared toward the "ladies."[3] In fact, making another face for oneself through cosmetic surgery, and specifically by means of a nose job, has for many decades been a frequent topic in American culture, especially as the procedure pertains to Jewish women like Cousin Suzanne. Even in recent collections of essays by young feminist writers about body image, and even when the authors write about their refusal to undergo nose jobs, those authors and the milieus of which they write are invariably Jewish.[4]

It is instructive to compare their topic with a work written by a Christian woman from an overtly Christian perspective. Although this writer's very personal recounting and rebuttal of society's emphasis on women's looks is subtitled *Springing Free from Skinny Jeans, Nose Jobs, Highlights and Stilettos*, in fact the author mentions nose jobs only once, with a two-word sentence in reference to Japanese women having surgery to make their eyes look more European. "Noses too," she adds.[5] Indubitably and inevitably, in spite of the fact that people of different backgrounds and origins opt for rhinoplasties, the nose job is primarily an issue for and about the Jew. Indeed, according to Elizabeth Haiken, in her comprehensive study of plastic surgery, the "first group of Americans to undertake surgical alteration of ethnic features in any numbers were . . . Jews who did not like their noses."[6]

In the preface to *The Jewish Woman in America*, coauthored by Charlotte Baum, Paula Hyman, and Sonya Michel and published in 1976, the authors remark that Sonya, as an adolescent, was "urged to have her nose 'fixed' and her hair straightened in order to improve her marriage prospects and, incidentally, to look more gentile."[7] Haiken remarks in passing that in American society at large, the notion of home in the twentieth century had evolved from the Victorian norm as a site for production to the modern ideal of leisure and display, shared by a heterosexual couple in a companionate marriage. "This development [says Haiken] strengthened the prevailing conviction that in the marriage market, a woman's face was her currency."[8] An early cosmetic surgeon, Gustav Tieck, finally felt comfortable enough with acceptance of his profession, and the results of his work, to admit in 1920 that over the past twelve years, he had operated on more than one thousand noses. Tieck did not say what proportion of these operations were performed on women—though of the seven before-and-after gender-identifiable photographs in his report, six are of women—much less on Jewish women, but he did note: "Young women of marriageable age, particularly, feel keenly the disadvantage of distorted features. If the surgeon can . . . improve facial appearance in such cases, he is ministering to a legitimate and important demand, worthy of his best efforts."[9] The ubiquity of rhinoplasty for success in the marriage market, especially during the early to middle twentieth century but continuing to a lesser extent today, is reflected not only on the faces of actual Jewish girls but also in a wide variety of media: fiction and film; memoirs, comics, and graphic novels; television sketches and songs; art installations and documentaries; medical journals, histories, and sociological studies. In short, the trend toward having the "Jewish" nose bobbed has constituted a cultural phenomenon that has evoked analysis, satire, and lament, often simultaneously.

Immigrant and second-generation Jewish writers in America, both male and female, often depicted Jewish women wishing to appear less Jewish, precisely in order to attract Jewish men. As Baum, Hyman, and Michel recount, in connecting the Jewish nose with medical advances designed to "fix" it, "Jewish women who did not 'naturally' look gentile often became displeased with their appearances, a phenomenon which was at least partially responsible for the rapid growth of plastic surgery in the late twenties. In her memoir, *My Sister Goldie* [1968], Sara Sandberg recalls one young plastic surgeon who made the rounds of Jewish resorts looking for potential patients. . . . Sandberg also recalls how her sister tried to convince her to have her nose 'fixed.'" Edward Dahlberg, in his 1963 autobiography *Because I Was Flesh*, confesses to having "doted on the short up-turned gentile nose" and been embarrassed by having a mother "with a nose that was a social misfortune." Samuel Ornitz, in *Bride of the Sabbath* (1951), depicts a Jewish male's repugnance for a woman's Jewish features, especially her "too-aquiline Jewish nose." Tellingly, Ornitz goes on to say, "Now, usually a nose is Jewish only to Jewish eyes or to a Gentile when he knows one is a Jew. Were Becky French, say, he would admire her aristocratic Gallic nose."[10] The final sentence reveals the cultural relativity of standards of beauty, along with the negative associations of the specifically "Jewish" nose. In other circumstances, an aquiline nose would be considered an asset, but on the Jewish female face it is "too-aquiline."

Once plastic surgeons developed the means to remedy problematic noses, and as they increasingly incorporated cosmetic procedures into their repertoire, the designations "distorted," "disfigured," and "deformed," among others, became umbrella terms for a variety of physical features not according with commonly accepted standards of beauty. Referring to the new prominence of the mental health issue popularly termed the "inferiority complex" as a bona fide impetus toward cosmetic surgery, Haiken relates that "by the late 1930s, words like 'deformity' had come to connote any and every physical attribute that might spark the feelings of inferiority that would threaten an individual's chances for social and economic security and success."[11] Deborah Sullivan, in her analysis of women's magazine articles about cosmetic surgery, notes the frequent reference to such surgery as "a cure for genetic 'deformities,' even though [as she says] the attributes labeled as deformities fall well within the normal range of physical variation or age-related changes."[12] A New York self-described "aesthetic" surgeon practicing today, B. Aviva Preminger, relates that Jacques Joseph coined his own term to explain why patients came to him for nose jobs: "antidysplasia—the feeling of being disfigured and aversion to such disfigurement and its emotional and material consequences."[13] In recent times, too, some plastic surgery texts refer specifically to the "Jewish nose," and a 1996 manual details its corrective procedure: "a classic rhinoplasty with lowering of the dorsum, narrowing of the bony pyramid, refinement and elevation of the excessively long hanging tip."[14] Here, "refinement" and "elevation" may be seen to connote aesthetic and even (if inadvertent) behavioral qualities as well as referring to positions of the surgeon's knife.

Sociologist Frances Cooke Macgregor was a pioneer in addressing the twin subjects of beauty as a social phenomenon and cosmetic surgery as a means of correcting "ugliness." In her study *Transformation and Identity: The Face and Plastic Surgery* (1974), she exhibits the objectivity of the scientist but also uses the particular terminology shared by surgeons like Tieck and those interviewed for the magazine articles. For example, she discusses "the Jewish nose" in a chapter titled "Living with a Deviant Face"—surely signifying only deviance from the norms of the particular place and time, but an off-putting word nonetheless—and she uses the phrase "facially deformed" as a catchall term that includes not only war injury, harelip, and facial paralysis but also a high forehead, a receding chin, and a Jewish nose. That said, Macgregor helpfully reinforces the cultural relativity to which Samuel Ornitz had earlier alluded and adds an observation about attributes presumed to accompany this physical feature: "In a milieu where racial or religious prejudice prevails, a large convex nose, the Jewish stereotype, may automatically assign to its possessor all the physical, mental, emotional, and moral characteristics with which that group is supposedly endowed."[15]

A factor supporting one commentator's view of Thomas Pynchon as "our most Judaical WASP" is that in *V.*, he acknowledges the significance of the nose job for a woman's happy outcome in her quest for a mate.[16] Although Rachel Owlglass recognizes that the need for this operation is the result of an age-old negative stereotype, she nonetheless capitulates to it in her desire to help out Esther Harvitz. She pays a (Jewish) plastic surgeon for her (Jewish) roommate's rhinoplasty because "four months from now would be June; this meant many pretty girls who felt they would be perfectly marriageable were it not for their ugly nose could now go husband-hunting at the various resorts all with uniform septa."[17] If Sara Sandberg is correct, then these girls may have first found their plastic surgeon at such resorts. Pynchon no doubt took his cue from novels of the 1950s and from the rhinoplasties of the Jewish girls he knew on Long Island. Rachel, after all, is in many ways a classic "Jewish American Princess" (often shortened to its even more offensive acronym JAP), from the north shore of Long Island, who leads a privileged existence with golfing, "Negro" maids, and the other accoutrements of the lifestyle.

Herman Wouk's 1955 *Marjorie Morningstar* is considered by many to be the first depiction in American literature of the so-called JAP, defined by her ostentatious manner of dress and opulent life style; yet, although Marjorie's indulgent parents do attempt to give her the best of everything, making up for what they did not themselves enjoy as immigrants from eastern Europe, the author does not say that Marjorie has had a nose job—only that she has "a fine little nose" (noted right away on the second page).[18] Another young woman in the novel, however—conveniently and perhaps significantly also named Marjorie—was once unattractive, but as Noel Airman explains, "She's had her nose fixed . . . and she's really quite pleasant-looking."[19] This conversation occurs, not coincidentally, at the woman's lavish engagement party, the unspoken assumption being that her nose job has enhanced her marriageability.

In the early 1960s, Andy Warhol produced several iterations of a work that he called *Before and After*. The drawing is a split view of a woman's head in profile, the left side of the canvas portraying the woman before a nose job and the right side showing the results of the operation. Except for the difference between a large droopy nose and a smaller up-tilted one, the two sides of the canvas displayed at the Whitney Museum of American Art in New York seem exactly the same, and yet the woman appears anxious and unhappy on the before side, and serenely contented after—uplifted emotionally as well as physically. The version of this work at the Metropolitan Museum of Art more obviously shows a down-turned mouth on the left and an upturned one on the right, and other iterations of this artwork also highlight the improvement in looks and mood afforded by a nose job. The origin of the work, as described on the Metropolitan Museum's website, is noteworthy: "Warhol based this composition on a small advertisement for a plastic surgeon that ran in the National Enquirer in early April 1961, which he had enlarged and projected in order to trace it onto the surface of the canvas—a precursor to the silkscreen technique he pioneered the following year. The work was first exhibited in the window of Bonwit Teller, the Fifth-Avenue department store, in early April 1961 as part of a display that included five other early paintings by the artist."[20]

That Warhol saw such an advertisement in a newspaper is not surprising. It was common in the twentieth century for practitioners to utilize a variety of venues for recruiting customers: not only magazines but also newspapers, phone directories, and department stores. Haiken reproduces a page from the Manhattan Yellow Pages of 1952 with three ads, two of which trumpet nose reshaping in their headlines and feature before and after profiles of the nose job, profiles that resemble Warhol's artwork.[21] How fitting that Warhol's *Before and After* was exhibited in an upscale Manhattan department store (no longer in existence) that purveyed high-end apparel. By displaying modern artists like Warhol and Salvador Dalí, Bonwit Teller branded itself as a sophisticated destination for the discriminating shopper of means; additionally, Warhol's canvas in that window advertised that plastic surgery, along with Bonwit Teller merchandise, was an avenue to becoming stylish and beautiful and, hence, marriageable. The doctor's office and the department store were thus twin meccas for a woman's success in being fitted out and fitting in. Making this marriage of convenience even more overt, in 1972 Gimbels department store began to sponsor well-attended public lectures by cosmetic surgeons, thereby starting a trend.[22] In "Goodbye, Columbus" (1959), written in the same postwar era when Jews were making it in America, Mrs. Patimkin complains about Brenda's expensive buying habits—"You don't have to go to Bonwit's, young lady"—and Neil Klugman lists both the nose job and this department store in his accounting of prizes to be won as a result of his "acquisitiveness" in pursuing not only Brenda but also her privileged lifestyle: "gold dinnerware, sporting-goods trees, nectarines, garbage disposals, bumpless noses, Patimkin Sink, Bonwit Teller—."[23]

Elizabeth Haiken has characterized surgery such as Brenda's as lying "at the nexus of medicine and consumer culture."[24] Certainly a new nose and new clothes could be portrayed as complementary evidence of improved self-esteem. A 1940 *Good Housekeeping* story revealed as much when it related how a woman with a "big nose" and "dowdy dress" in the cosmetic surgeon's waiting room was transformed into a fashion plate after her rhinoplasty: "The same girl—but how hard to recognize! A saucy hat perched back of her brand-new pompadour, her dress was trim, her bearing confident. Everything about her bespoke a touching new-born vanity. . . . This miracle had followed a brief five days in the hospital, where skilled surgical hands had trimmed down her nose to pleasant proportions."[25] In fact, greater transformations than an enhanced fashion sense could be effected by a rhinoplasty: Cousin Suzanne's attitude is so improved by her obtaining a new nose that in addition to looking "exquisite" when dressed up she even gets higher grades on class assignments and does better than expected on the college boards![26]

With the link between appearance and attitude, cosmetic surgery came into its own when self-help books, lectures, and institutes became popular, all engaged in the campaign to improve an American's ability to "win friends and influence people" (the title of Dale Carnegie's 1936 best seller)—to sell oneself by means of a confident, outgoing personality that overcomes or masks the inferiority complex, a term so familiar by this time that the popular press called it by its initials, IC. One cultural historian counted the attributes touted in these personality-driven guides and pinpointed the most celebrated descriptions: magnetic, fascinating, stunning, attractive, glowing, dominant, forceful, and energetic. Although many of the guides were geared toward businessmen, women were also targets, urged to compete in the romance market. Like a Dale Carnegie course or a self-help guide, a nose job could turn one into a confident extrovert, ready to face the world and influence others.[27]

Riv-Ellen Prell discusses the "Jewish American Princess"—and, not unexpectedly, Brenda Patimkin's nose job—in the context of middle-class consumerism. Prell characterizes the JAP as excessively fixated on the adornment of her body, enabled by "middle class affluence and dependent on the male as producer." She situates the rise of the stereotype in post–World War II economic security among the white middle class in general, with consequent moves to the suburbs, and the experiences and expectations of the next generation that stood in contrast to those the parents had known during the Depression and wartime. Samuel Freedman provides some statistics: "Between 1940 and 1957, the share of Jews in white-collar jobs soared from 10 percent to 55 percent. One-third of the American Jewish population moved from cities to suburbs in the twenty-year period after World War II."[28] Consumer items were now available in abundance in the United States, along with the means to procure them. Prell does not deal with *Cousin Suzanne* in her analysis, but Suzanne's princess lifestyle in 1950s Hewlett, New York, one of the upscale "Five Towns" on the north shore of Long

Island, bears on this point even more extensively, elaborating on the fact that, as the novel records, "most of the women of the area [the towns of Woodmere, Cedarhurst, and Hewlett are specified] had two abiding concerns: decorating themselves, decorating their homes."[29] Bendel's, Bloomingdale's, and Saks, if not Bonwit Teller, loom large in this novel. Roth's Neil Klugman, in his ambivalent pursuit of Brenda Patimkin and *her* well-appointed home and affluent lifestyle in suburbia (Short Hills, New Jersey, in the novella), recognizes the artificiality of that world—including Brenda's nose.[30] One cosmetic surgeon has metaphorically linked home and face in his remark that "plastic surgeons are, after all, exterior decorators (perhaps the psychiatrists are the 'interior decorators' of medicine)."[31]

Prell reflects on the circumstances that caused the Jewish woman to become the butt of jokes and scathing assessment by the 1970s: "*Goodbye, Columbus* provided the outline of a set of relations that would generate the American Jewish humor of the 1970s. . . . The consumer culture generated an unceasing and insatiable set of demands. American Jewish men, inheritors of a long tradition of 'overdemanding wife' jokes, translated the frustrations of their class and epoch into the Jewish woman, whose body became a surface reflecting affluence, purchased at a high price." The economy was weakening by then, the nature of work had changed, and middle-class women were more frequently leaving the domestic realm to fulfill themselves professionally and to earn the second income necessary for keeping up the lifestyle. Prell concludes, "As Jewish women, supported by the larger feminist movement, abandoned their role as 'Jewish mothers,' fundamentally defined as self-sacrificing, they were portrayed more frequently as 'princesses.'"[32]

Prell's essay centers on male responses to the adorned female Jewish body, but she includes two female comics in her analysis: Joan Rivers and Gilda Radner. Especially pertinent in the linking of the nose job to consumerism are the lyrics from a *Saturday Night Live* skit from February 1980 in which Gilda Radner, as "Rhonda Weiss," performed a commercial for "Jewess Jeans":

> She's got a lifestyle that's uniquely hers,
> Europe, Nassau, wholesale furs . . . .
> She shops the sales for designer clothes
> She's got designer nails and a designer nose.
> She's an American princess and a disco queen.
> She's the Jewess in Jewish jeans.[33]

This milieu of designer adornments, including noses, is skewered by feminist comic book cofounder Aline Kominsky-Crumb, "perhaps the first female autobiographer to work in the graphic novel genre," as Stephen Tabachnick comments, who "portrays herself as the stereotypical Jew who seems to embody all the traits ascribed to Jews by the popular media and pokes fun at both herself and the stereotype when doing so."[34] Hillary Chute recounts Kominsky-Crumb's background as Aline Ricky Goldsmith, raised in the affluent Long Island suburb of Woodmere (one of the Five Towns) in the 1950s, and quotes the artist herself on her early life "in an upper middle class ghetto, surrounded by ostentatious materialism and rabid upward striving. . . . To say that I never fit into this world of 'post war jerks' is an understatement . . . but such intense alienation has provided me with years of comic-tragic material."[35]

Chute observes that Kominsky-Crumb, like the other "graphic women" the author discusses in her study of that name, "debunks traditional expectations for representations of women's bodies"; her focus is on the artist's in-your-face presentations of genitalia and sexual trauma and does not include another, literal in-your-face representation: the Jewish nose.[36] But Kominsky-Crumb presented her own (self) portrait when she dealt with the subject of rhinoplasty in her 1989 autobiographical comic called "Nose Job." Originally published in issue 15 of *Wimmen's Comix*, and then forming part of a chapter of Kominsky-Crumb's memoir of 2007, *Need More Love*, the narrative opens with Aline recalling a song she saw in *Mad* magazine with the line "She used to be a freak, til [sic] they overhauled her beak." Kominsky-Crumb does not give the details of that particular song, but she is clearly referring to a recording by the Dellwoods called "She Got a Nose Job," one of the tunes on the 45 rpm record *Mad Twists Rock 'n' Roll* that was included as an actual playable record in *Mad* magazine's Fifth Worst Annual in 1962. The lyrics, voiced from a male perspective, emphasize the relationship between a "turned up" nose and a suitable romantic partner:

> Nose job (now she's the prettiest gal in town).
> Nose job (now she's the prettiest gal in town).
> She got a nose job, she got a nose job.
> It's now turned up instead of hanging down.
> She got a nose job, she got a nose job,
> And now she's the prettiest gal in town.
> She never had a boy to walk her home
> She never had a boy who cared.
> But now she's never left alone
> Since she had her shnozz repaired.
> She got a nose job, she got a nose job.
> It's now turned up instead of hanging down.
> She got a nose job, she got a nose job,
> And now she's the prettiest gal in town.
> She never had no one to taste her kiss.
> Her future looked mighty bleak.

Now she's on every guy's list
Since she overhauled her beak.
She got a nose job, she got a nose job.
It's now turned up instead of hanging down.
She got a nose job, she got a nose job,
And now she's the prettiest gal in town.
Well I know someday I'm gonna marry her
'Cause I love her, yes I do.
And the kids we have, we know for sure
They're gonna all get nose jobs, too.
She got a nose job, she got a nose job.
It's now turned up instead of hanging down.
She got a nose job, she got a nose job,
And now she's the prettiest gal in town.
Now she's the prettiest gal in town (nose job) . . .
Now she's the prettiest gal in town (nose job) . . .
Now she's the prettiest gal in town (nose job) . . .[37]

Kominsky-Crumb—like the real-life Sonya Michel (coauthor of *The Jewish Woman in America*) and the fictional Esther Harvitz, Marjorie Morningstar, Suzanne Goldfarb (from *Cousin Suzanne*), and Brenda Patimkin—"grew up with cosmetic surgery all around," as she writes of her Long Island environment of 1962 in "Nose Job"; she labels the number of Jewish girls in junior high school getting nose jobs a "disturbing epidemic." The same characterization was made by a Manhattan psychiatrist in 1956, when he remarked in the *Psychiatric Quarterly* that "the writer [referring to himself] was particularly stimulated to work along this line when he became aware that an *epidemic of plastic surgery* is going on among teen-agers wanting to correct prominent 'Semitic' (Armenoid) noses— often forced to such operations by their parents or the example of a beautified friend."[38] Even twenty years beyond this psychiatrist's diagnosis, in the Hewlett, Long Island, of *Cousin Suzanne*, "after every Christmas or Easter vacation girls returned to high school with two black eyes and Band-Aids over the bridges of their lumps of newly bobbed noses."[39]

Defiantly, Aline Kominsky-Crumb became the only one of her friends to avoid this surgery, running away from home in order to resist the pressure by her parents and returning to finish high school only when they relented. Her rebellion against plastic surgery, and the standard of beauty it represents and achieves, does not obviate the fact that the persona pictured in this comic considers herself ugly. In a parenthetical but central remark she notes, "(No, we Jews are not a cute race!)," referring not only to the "prominent noses" but also to the "oily skin & frizzy hair." An attractive woman in photographs and real life,

Kominsky-Crumb has chosen to picture herself in her work throughout her career in decidedly unattractive, sometimes grotesque ways; by this means, she has emphasized not only society's notions of beauty, and not only a defiant rebellion against according with them, but also, and for many females most saliently, a woman's diminished self-esteem for *not* according with them.[40] Kominsky-Crumb simultaneously flaunts and flouts the ways of looking at the Jewish body. As Hillary Chute says, paraphrasing Art Spiegelman, comics can be "discomfiting in how [they] can play with and against visual stereotypes."[41] The caricaturist form of "Nose Job" encourages both an exaggeratedly unattractive self-portrait of the "before" Aline (that is, the real and always Aline) and an imagined but rejected "after" Aline, the latter glowing with a straight nose, straight hair, wide smile, and sparkly eyes and, not incidentally, sporting a lovely and feminine dress as well.[42] Sander Gilman comments on Kominsky-Crumb's refusal to undergo a nose job that by looking like folk singers Joan Baez or Buffy St. Marie, after new styles of appearance for women were socially acceptable, "one could look as 'beat' as one wanted as long as one did not look 'Jewish.' . . . The hidden meaning [of Kominsky-Crumb's tale] is that it is alright [*sic*] to look Jewish as long as you are visible as anything but a Jew." The alteration of the nose through rhinoplasty, that is, "is a potential need, even if it is rejected."[43]

On this point, the remembrances of another feminist, Melanie Kaye/Kantrowitz, are germane. Close in age to Kominsky-Crumb, from Brooklyn rather than Long Island, this writer inhabited the same nose-obsessed culture as Kominsky-Crumb and countless other young Jewish girls of her era and beyond: "When I was growing up in Flatbush . . . every girl with a certain kind of nose—sometimes named explicitly as a Jewish nose, sometimes only as 'too big'—wanted a nose job, and if her parents could pay for it, often she got one. . . . What was wrong with the original nose, the Jewish one? Noses were discussed ardently in Flatbush, this or that friend looking forward to her day of transformation." The significant difference lies in the fact that Melanie's nose was un-Jewish: "My aunts lavished on me the following exquisite praise: *look at her, a nose like a shiksa* (gentile woman). This hurt my feelings. Before I knew what a *shiksa* was, I knew I wasn't it. And with that fabulous integrity of children, I wanted to look like who I was. But later I learned my nose's value, and would tell gentiles this story so they'd notice my nose." Kaye/Kantrowitz reaches the obvious conclusion: "A Jewish nose . . . identifies its owner as a Jew. Nose jobs are performed so that a Jewish woman does not look like a Jew."[44] Of course there are practical reasons that a woman, especially in the era of college admissions quotas, might not wish to look like a Jew. Eric Goldstein, in his book on Jews, race, and American identity, briefly remarks on the internalization of negative opinions about Jewish physical traits, taking note of a female student's statement about applying to Vassar in the 1920s; in his paraphrase, these women "assiduously avoided profile shots when posing for their application photos, hoping to hide their noses." The ostensible reason is that such a profile did not accord with society's notion of beauty, but I suspect that a "Jewish nose" (along with a "Jewish name") might also diminish one's chance of acceptance into the college of one's choice.[45]

It is interesting but not unanticipated that although Jewish novelist Meg Wolitzer, in her 2008 novel, *The Ten-Year Nap*, deals with all sorts of female body issues, her physical descriptions of her main female characters are actually quite limited with a singular exception: the nose of the one decidedly Jewish woman. Roberta Sokolov, in the author's first, if inadvertent, clue to that character's ethnicity, "was not someone to whom men were often instantaneously attracted"; soon we are told that "her nose was clearly too bluntly large for her face, though more than one sympathetic female friend had told her that she possessed a sort of soulful, Semitic look." Even in the closing pages of the novel, when the four primary characters are no longer gathering in the Golden Horn Restaurant, the waiter remembers them as "the ordinary-looking brown-haired one . . . ; the very tall and pretty blonde one . . .; the slightly thick-built one with the nose; and the Asian one." Earlier, in South Dakota, where Roberta has gone to drive a teenager to an abortion clinic, the girl asks her point-blank if she is Jewish. "It bothered Roberta slightly whenever this subject came up, because, really, the person who mentioned it was always at least indirectly referring to Roberta's nose, which was too big for the dimensions of her face." Nonetheless, Sokolov proudly responds, "A hundred percent"; she is happy to have enlarged this sheltered teen's sphere by becoming the girl's "first Jew."[46]

In contrast, Diane Noomin, co-creator with Kominsky-Crumb of the feminist comic *Twisted Sisters*, created an autobiographical persona, DiDi Glitz, in *Glitz-2-Go*; in one of the stories in this collection focused on suburban Long Island Jews, DiDi's friend has a nose job and liposuction—"finding ways to get away from being Jewish," as Tabachnick interprets one theme of "Life in the Bagel Belt."[47] Noomin also created "The Agony and the Ecstasy of a *Shayna Madel* [beautiful girl]: The Epitome of a Perfectly Pretty Jewish Girl," a *Wimmen's Comix* publication of 1973. On the cover, in a simulated board game, a girl transforms herself from plain to pretty by means of cosmetic surgery, almost reaching the square marked "Marry a Doctor—Jump 10 Spaces." Reminiscences in an April 1, 1962, diary entry, replete with Yiddish words and intonations, have the mother complaining: "Why cantchew be normal like Teri? Enuff with the moping always in your room! Go have some fun arready!" The daughter defiantly and despondently responds, "Well, I could get a nose job but what's the use . . . I still have pimples on my ass!"[48] As with "thick-built" Roberta Sokolov, this girl's nose is not the only deficiency of her Jewish female body.

In both his essay "The Jewish Nose: Are Jews White? Or, the History of the Nose Job" and his later cultural history of plastic surgery *Making the Body Beautiful*, in the chapter titled "The Racial Nose," Gilman references Kominsky-Crumb's

"Nose Job" (and, more briefly, Warhol's *Before and After*).[49] Although, to be sure, he does not dwell on the gender issues involved in the zeal for rhinoplasties—as Ann Pellegrini has commented, in his "path-breaking studies of race, gender, and Jewishness, Gilman has framed his arguments through and around the Jewish male"[50]—Gilman does remark that gender as well as race became an important factor in the mid-twentieth-century spate of nose jobs.[51] He might have mentioned a question asked in the second panel of Kominsky-Crumb's graphic memoir: "Why do boys get to keep their noses?" Perhaps in homage, Tahneer Oksman chose to entitle her recent study of Jewish female identity in graphic memoirs with a close approximation of Kominsky-Crumb's question: *How Come Boys Get to Keep Their Noses?* She opted for this title in spite of the fact that, as she says in her introduction, most of the autobiographical cartoonists she analyzes "have moved on, at least somewhat," from what we find in Kominsky-Crumb: "a fixation with the Jewish nose as a symbol for the marginalized female Jewish self."[52] The word *somewhat* seems to me the operative one with regard to Jewish females and their noses.

Reasons for this difference between "boys" and "girls" have been supplied over the decades, with consistency. In the 1930s, the plastic surgeon Jerome Webster remarked to one male would-be patient that a woman would have more reason than a man to undergo a rhinoplasty because "a man is judged more by what he does than what he looks like." In the early 1960s, in a discussion by religious leaders of the morality of cosmetic surgery—a discussion initiated by the American Society of Facial Plastic Surgeons—Rabbi Immanuel Jakobovits opined that the only reason a man should have cosmetic surgery was economic, but a woman's surgery would be justified to better her marriage prospects or her relationship with her husband.[53] One can hardly imagine a Jewish female of any era writing of her "Jewish nose" the way Gary Shteyngart's protagonist in *Absurdistan*, for example, fondly if ironically describes his "pretty Jewish beak that brings to mind the most distinguished breed of parrot."[54] Kominsky-Crumb pairs beak and freak, after all.

Artist Deborah Kass did feature Barbra Streisand's profile in sixteen versions, but it took a male artist, Dennis Kardon, to celebrate the "Jewish nose" (in its variety) in his "49 Jewish Noses," cast from actual Jews' faces and exhibited as part of *Too Jewish, Challenging Traditional Identities* at the Jewish Museum in 1996, in a section of the display called "Re-Considering the Ethnic Body."[55] Sander Gilman remarks of this piece, "Kardon reproduces healthy, functioning Jewish noses, noses that mark the ethnic differences of the American Jew. Kardon is constrained to do this, as the association of ethnic-specific cosmetic surgery still haunts the daily life of American Jews."[56] Those American Jews are disproportionately female, however. In Shteyngart's novel, in the foreign country of Absurdistan, where one's nationality is always questioned, the hotel manager remarks of himself and his visitor, "'It is clear to both of us who we are,' . . . bowing his muscular nose toward my equally prominent proboscis."[57] The racial nose distinguishes men as well as women, but men do not undergo this "ethnic-specific cosmetic surgery" nearly as often as women do. In 2017, three-quarters of the rhinoplasties performed in the United States were on women, a fairly consistent percentage.[58] True, Brenda Patimkin's brother, Ron, is having his nose fixed soon, as Brenda has already done, because both inherited the "bumpy" nose of their father, but this is the exception that proves the rule.[59] More representative is an episode of the television show *Finding Your Roots* that aired on March 9, 2016, in which the actor Dustin Hoffman related that when his parents moved from Chicago to Los Angeles so that his father could try to make it as a director, his mother had her nose bobbed "to un-Jewish herself" (as Dustin phrased it); in contrast, photos clearly show that Harry Hoffman and his two sons each left a "prominent proboscis" intact. In spite of the fact that the father was avowedly atheist, and the household was not Jewishly observant, the men could remain as Jews literally on the face of it, whereas the mother felt the need to make herself over to get on in Hollywood.

One celebrated woman did achieve success in the entertainment world while defying society's pressure to conform to standard notions of beauty. As an eighteen-year-old, Barbra Streisand flirted with having a nose job "to change the tilt . . . and take off a little bit," she is quoted as saying. Two years later, on opening night at the Coconut Grove in Hollywood in 1963, she joked self-deprecatingly, "If I'd known the place was going to be so crowded, I'd have had my nose fixed." Jokes made about herself, by herself, were a kind of defense mechanism; after all, Streisand had been the subject of much taunting as a grade schooler, called "big beak" and "cross-eyes," along with *Mieskeit* (Yiddish for ugliness) by her classmates. Her stepfather compounded the problem at home, comparing his biological daughter to Barbra with the phrase "Beauty and the Beast." As a fourteen-year-old, Streisand covered her face when a camera turned her way at a party, and an early boyfriend recounted that the sixteen-year-old girl "thought she was ugly, with her nose and all." Her nose completely turned off other would-be boyfriends. Surely she was sensitive to the fact that there was much commentary behind her back in addition to the remarks made to her face. In her acting class at New York's Theatre Studio, one of many acting schools in Manhattan at this time, some in the class likened her nose to an anteater's snout; casting agents and nightclub managers were quick to discount her because of her nose, among other physical characteristics. Her first agent, among others, told her more than once to get her nose fixed, and the owner of *Variety* wrote in his influential show business magazine that Streisand should consider a "schnoz bob." Even after she began to reach acclaim as a singer, Barbra questioned, "Do you think anyone could ever love this face?" Her costar in the Broadway version of *Funny Girl*, a lover-turned-rival, knew just how to try to trip her up when, in the midst of their love scenes on stage, he would whisper the word "nose" in her ear.[60]

Yet the shortening that Streisand made was not to her nose but to her name when she early on eliminated the second *a* in Barbara, her given name. The Streisand nose, often displayed in profile, was itself profiled in the media: either tamely described in magazines as "aquiline" (*New Yorker*) or, in other, less charitable cases, as "the nose of an eagle" (*Saturday Evening Post*) or a "nose like a witch" (*Life*). Elizabeth Haiken relates that in the early 1960s, when Streisand first came to public attention, "almost all of the many articles about her in these early years (more than twenty ran in national magazines in 1963 and 1964 alone) mention her nose."[61] Even in 1969, when the Friars paid tribute to Streisand as entertainer of the year, only the second female to be accorded that honor since the club's founding in 1904, the comic Joe E. Lewis could not resist a gentle jab when he wrote for the souvenir program, "*Time* magazine ran her nose on the cover, and *Newsweek* ran the rest of her." Biographer James Spada remarks about the significance of Barbra's rise, achieved in spite of her looks: "The allure of Barbra's glitzy success was especially inspiring to youngsters who didn't fit into the WASP mold of cheerleader or captain of the football team. If she could turn homely into exotic and a prominent 'schnoz' into a classic profile, and make the cover of *Vogue* in the bargain, maybe they could too."[62] Spada's comment is an optimistic suggestion that these inspired teenagers could, in fact, love their own faces, even if Barbra herself had her doubts about her own.

Deborah Kass, born a decade after Streisand, in 1952, and raised on Long Island, was one admirer of Streisand's nose and the decision to leave it alone; she commented, "Barbra was the first Hollywood star I could identify with. I loved Marilyn Monroe, I loved Clark Gable, but I didn't know what I was missing until I saw Barbra—someone who looked like everyone I knew. She was someone who understood the power of her difference and who wasn't easily absorbed into a male narrative. She was completely aspirational."[63] In her *Warhol Project*, Kass paid homage to both Warhol and Streisand by painting those sixteen Streisands in the manner of Warhol's Jackie canvases (in which Kennedy, in contrast to Streisand, sports the nose then in fashion, small and slightly pug), and Kass paired Warhol's *Before and After* with a movie still of Cinderella and the glass slipper in her 2013 *Before and Happily Ever After* retrospective, exhibited at the Andy Warhol Museum. In the final analysis, however, Streisand's refusal to alter her appearance did not as a rule inspire Jewish teenage girls, or their parents, to follow her example in refusing a rhinoplasty, in spite of the supposition of biographer James Spada that Streisand, being ahead of her time, "would change many people's attitudes about what constituted female beauty."[64] Haiken quotes a New York teenager who said to a *Newsweek* reporter in 1966, "Streisand? . . . That's her look. Would you believe it on anyone else?"[65] As writer Ophira Edut put it decades later, "We Jewesses get the message early: It's better to be Barbie than Barbra Streisand."[66]

A notable exception to the reluctance to follow Streisand's example is Lea Michele, actress and singer from her earliest years (in such Broadway shows as *Les Misérables, Ragtime, Fiddler on the Roof,* and *Spring Awakening*) but perhaps best known for her role in the television series *Glee,* which aired for six years (2009–2015). In her book *Brunette Ambition*—part memoir, cookbook, and guide to fashion, fitness and beauty—Michele features Barbra Streisand as a "Role Model" in a chapter of that name, as well as in a vignette entitled "The Day I Met Barbra." Three photos of Streisand are included and serve to reinforce the Streisand look. Michele, herself the child of a Mizrahi father and Italian mother, notes that she was cast in *Fiddler on the Roof* because, "while I wasn't fully Jewish, I was the most Jewish-looking girl in the business"; in case the reader has not discerned that this remark is a covert reference to her nose, Michele later recounts how casting directors "frequently told me that I wasn't pretty enough for TV, that I was too ethnic to ever be mainstream. One manager told me that as soon as I got my period and was, accordingly, old enough for plastic surgery, I should get my nose done immediately." The advice obviously has rankled. With regard to her many successes, Michele in effect thumbs her nose while presenting "a big fat middle finger" to that manager who advised a nose job.[67]

In her memoir, Michele does not mention a relevant 2011 episode of *Glee.* When the glee club co-captain accidentally breaks the nose of Michele's Jewish character, Rachel Berry, her doctor recommends a rhinoplasty. Rachel tells her friends that she wants a nose job to look "less Hebraic," and she considers modeling a new nose after that of a girl with traditionally defined beauty. The two girls then sing the duet "I Feel Pretty/Unpretty," which represents through its combination of actual songs the opposing self-perceptions of the girls. Ultimately, Rachel decides against having surgery, convinced by a club member's question, "Do you want to disappoint Barbra?" Rachel admits, "Of course not. She's my idol."[68] Fittingly, this episode also featured Duck Sauce's song "Barbra Streisand." And the Duck Sauce album containing that tune adapted one of Streisand's own album covers, replacing her photo (and that of Barry Gibb) with duck beaks, no doubt to emphasize a refusal to "overhaul [the] beak," as the Dellwoods' lyric has it.

As for Streisand herself, it was inevitable that she would play the role of Fanny Brice in the 1964 Broadway show and the 1968 biopic *Funny Girl* (a film pinpointed by Lea Michele as influential) at age twenty-one and twenty-five, respectively. By the time of the show, Barbra and Fanny "had been conflated into one image," as William Mann puts it.[69] First there was the voice, which reminded Barbra's roommate in 1960 of Fanny Brice. ("Who's Fanny Brice?" the eighteen-year-old Barbra asked.[70]) Too, Streisand's rise to stardom from a difficult childhood in a Brooklyn housing project was similar to Brice's background. And then there was that nose. When Mary Martin was considered for the role of Fanny, and expressed an interest, Stephen Sondheim said to producer Ray Stark (married to Fanny Brice's daughter), "You've gotta have a *Jewish* girl! And if she's not Jewish she at least has to have a nose!"[71] Although Brice underwent a rhinoplasty, she started out in vaudeville with her original nose, one that she fairly quickly believed would hinder her career and thus needed fixing. Flouting Florenz Ziegfeld's objections, the star came to well-known plastic surgeon Henry Schireson for the operation because, as the doctor later related, she thought her nose limited her to playing "Jewish types." Schireson was proud of his work; referring to his results, he noted that people "now speak of [Brice's] beauty—instead of her funny nose."[72]

Although Streisand did not get a nose job to remain true to this aspect of Brice's life (just one of the many ways in which the show and movie veer from the facts), both portrayals—Broadway show and film—do emphasize the nose and its relationship to mainstream standards of beauty. Within the first two minutes of the movie, for example, Brice's mother refers to her daughter's nose in her song of motherly pride: "Is a nose with deviation / Such a crime against the nation?" Indeed, the film could just as well have been entitled *Funny Face*, given all the references to Brice's inferiority about her "deviant" looks, except for the fact that a 1957 movie starring Audrey Hepburn—with her classically beautiful face, no less—already bore that title. Fanny doesn't have "an American beauty nose," and she is very self-conscious about it. In several ensuing scenes, a self-perceived ugliness is tacitly assumed by the filmmakers, and hence the audience, to refer to the nose (and, less importantly, to the skinny legs as well). The tone of the movie is, as Lester Friedman describes it in his study of Jewish images in American films, a "careful mixture of self-mockery and self-confidence." It may well be true, as Friedman asserts, that *Funny Girl* marks "a turning point in the cinematic portrayal of Jews, one that shows Jewishness as something to be proud of. . . . Here, for once, is the Jewish performer being Jewish, instead of hiding behind a neutral name or twisting his/her features out of shape to conform to a standard of WASP beauty."[73] However, if Brice as portrayed by Streisand does not twist her features out of shape for the sake of conformity, she is nonetheless insecure about her looks.

As evidence, in one scene Flo Ziegfeld insists that Fanny sing in the final extravaganza about "the most beautiful brides in the world"; he needs someone with a big voice to close the show, he states. Although the implication of that insistence is that her nose would not detract from the message, Fanny cannot see herself among the beautiful women (much less the beautiful *marrying* women), and thus she creates a self-parody instead of adhering to the script. After a bevy of gorgeous Ziegfeld Girls parade in scanty costumes, surrounded by mirrors so they are multiplied in number, Fanny galumphs onto the stage as a very pregnant bride (pillow stuffed under her gown) and pokes fun at herself while looking into her handheld mirror. She cannot play it straight, so to speak, only huge and ugly.

After the show, she justifies her straying from the script by telling the furious Ziegfeld that she needed to have the audience laugh with her, not at her.

As for Streisand's love interest in the film, the handsome Egyptian actor Omar Sharif who plays the gambler Nicky Arnstein, Fanny tells him that he must know many gorgeous girls, so "this should be a change" to romance Fanny Brice. After they marry, Streisand's song of joy, "Sadie, Married Lady," contains the telling lyric, "The groom was prettier than the bride." (In real life, Nicky Arnstein was not so "pretty," sporting his own prominent nose.) When Fanny gets pregnant for real, and they have baby Frances, Brice insists that Frances is pretty and makes her husband repeat it. Later, when Frances is a little older, Fanny says to Nick, "She's gorgeous, and getting to look just like you. Who says I'm not lucky." In one of the final scenes of the film, when Arnstein ends the marriage, Fanny tearfully says to him, "You made me feel beautiful for a very long time." Arnstein replies, "You *are* beautiful" and then leaves the scene and the marriage. But this is too little too late—the weight of the film has been on Fanny's nose (often shown in the famous Streisand profile) and on the opposite of beauty that is represented by that nose. Whether their real-life child, Frances Brice, actually inherited her parents' ethnic nose, and whether Fanny insisted that her daughter, too, get a nose job, is not clear. But it would not be surprising.[74]

Pressure from the parents, often the mother, to have a nose job is a common lament in Jewish women's narratives. Kominsky-Crumb's mother was adamant that Aline needed a nose job in order to get a husband and unrelentingly nagged Aline to get the operation. Lisa Jervis, in her essay "My Jewish Nose," relates that "from adolescence on, I've had a standing offer from my mother to get a nose job." Her mother had had one herself, at the age of sixteen, undergoing a "compulsory . . . rite of passage" for girls of her generation, and Lisa's father remarks that he would not have gone out with the mother if not for it.[75] Virginia Blum begins her very personal study of cosmetic surgery with an anecdote about her own "mother problem": her mother, without consulting her, made an appointment for her to see a doctor whose rhinoplasty on a neighbor had created a nose that Blum's mother admired; and in the doctor's office, the mother did all the talking about what she wanted for her teenage daughter's outcome. Noting that the "adolescent girl, especially, enters the world tentatively and waits for it to say yes or no to her face and body," Blum recounts the feelings of inadequacy that she felt when the world, in the form of her mother and doctor, said no to her nose.[76] Thomas Pynchon's *V.* also remarks on the mother's influence, when Rachel Owlglass complains to the plastic surgeon (deliberately named Schoenmaker, or "pretty maker") that he alters his female patients inside as well as externally, so that they in turn will make sure their daughters go under the knife: "What kind of Jewish mother do they make, they are the kind who make a girl get a nose job even if she doesn't want one." Plastic surgeons cannot magically transmit the mother's acquired characteristic of a new nose to her daughter, of course, but, says Rachel, they "pass along an attitude" that will achieve the same result.[77]

The mother's role in advocating for a daughter's rhinoplasty is most clearly articulated in the documentary *My Nose*, created by yet another Long Island Jewish woman who was a teenager in the 1970s, Gayle Kirschenbaum. Kirschenbaum conceived her project as both a thirteen-minute short and a feature film and described *My Nose* this way when raising money for the production: "What do you do when you think you look good and your mother is convinced what you need more than anything else is a nose job? *My Nose* is a personal documentary that will explore my mother's preoccupation with my nose and what drives people into the plastic surgeon's office." Because of the pressure from Kirschenbaum's mother for her to have a nose job, and the conflict-ridden mother-daughter relationship of which this pressure was a symptom, Kirshenbaum retitled her feature film *Look at Us Now, Mother!* Moreover, on the basis of the positive response to her short film, she developed *Transforming Difficult Relationships*, self-described in the third person as "a humorous, insightful seminar in which Gayle draws on her experience of building a healthy relationship with her mother out of a difficult one. In it, she discusses 'The Seven Healing Tools' for how to turn negatives into positives and revitalize relationships." Her mother is a full partner in these projects and gets equal billing on the feature film.[78] Mother and daughter have not only reached a rapprochement about Gayle's unfixed "Jewish nose"; they have also made capital out of it.

For other teenagers, as we have seen, the nose job was de rigueur. The actress Lisa Kudrow provides a further example. Kudrow was raised in Southern California, another mecca for the rhinoplasty by so-called Valley Girls, a term often used as a veiled reference to the West Coast versions of Jewish American Princesses.[79] (Los Angeles by the 1950s was the second-largest Jewish community in the United States, its population of Jews more than tripling between 1930 and 1950.)[80] Kudrow revealed in *Allure* magazine in 2002, when she was thirty-nine years old, that she had had a nose job when she was sixteen. Referring to her former "hook nose," she stated, "But I'm not even sure I love how that turned out. I think plastic surgery looks weird—like plastic surgery." However, with a different perspective on the matter, she referred eleven years later to how the nose job had transformed her life as a teenager, calling the operation "life altering": "I went from, in my mind, hideous, to not hideous. . . . I did it the summer before going to a new high school. So there were plenty of people who wouldn't know how hideous I looked before. That was a good, good, good change."[81] Another perspective is provided by essayist Julie Iny, who was "ostracized and taunted because of [her] 'big Jew nose,' despite the large Jewish student population" in her West Los Angeles junior high school in the mid- to late 1980s. Speaking of herself in the third person, Iny writes that "this little Jewish girl hated to look at herself in the mirror and asked to change her nose." She adds, looking back in

2003: "I feel tenderness toward that little girl and the decision she made, but at the same time I feel shame. And then frustration: There was no language, no public discourse to foster pride and acceptance of my Jewish body. Little Jewish girls like me, harassed because of our Semitic features, were—and still are—forced to seek individual relief rather than communal support." Whether Iny inherited that "big Jew nose" from her Ashkenazi mother or Mizrahi father we do not know. The telltale ethnic feature could have come from either side. But we do know that her parents did not like their daughter's desire for a nose job, and "made sure that the doctor knew [she] was Jewish and told him not to make any radical changes."[82]

In November 2015, the *Forward* published a full-page opinion piece about a new Amazon-produced television show set in a Jewish country club in New Jersey in 1985—a country club like that of Brenda Patimkin's family in "Goodbye, Columbus" and Cousin Suzanne's in the novel of that name. (Literary worth aside, in many respects Blyth's Aileen from the Bronx, envying the lifestyle of Suzanne from north shore Long Island, is reminiscent of Roth's Neil from Newark, aspiring, if temporarily, to Brenda's lifestyle in Short Hills.) The author of the *Forward* piece, Elissa Strauss, reviews the show with an eye toward "the prurient male gaze," as her headline announces, and complains about the failure to explore women's experiences: "I wanted to learn so much more about these characters [among them, the "sultry princess" and the "eager-to-please pretty girl"] that have been flattened into stereotypes for much too long now." Strauss says nothing about rhinoplasties in her review, but she doesn't need to: the accompanying photograph is of three attractive teenage girls in bikinis, lounging at the country club pool, each girl with a white bandaged nose raised toward the sun.[83]

In more recent years, retaining the ethnic nose has become a more acceptable option than in the 1950s–1980s. Lea Michele, born in 1986, took up that option: her memoir advises the presumably female reader, "Don't try to make yourself look like everyone else,"[84] and she happily comments that the television industry "has changed a lot [since she first started out]—there's a lot more diversity in terms of who gets to be a leading lady—and I think that shows like *Glee* really put that trend in motion."[85] Certainly *Glee*, in its successful run, celebrated diversity of all kinds, including that of the nose. The episode that aired on April 26, 2011, was called "Born This Way" and featured the song of that title (a cover of the Lady Gaga song); the performers wore tee shirts flaunting the various differences they were born with. Midway into the performance, having made the decision to retain her "Hebraic nose," Rachel Berry makes a splashy entrance and unveils her tee shirt with the word *NOSE*. Like the others, she has decided she is "beautiful in [her] own way."[86] I am reminded of a character's reaction to Esther's "before" portrait in Pynchon's *V*.: "Look at it, the nose. . . .Why does she want to get that changed. With the nose she is a human being."[87]

Another television show, *Seinfeld*, had already taken up the topic two decades earlier than *Glee*. In the episode of November 20, 1991, entitled "The Nose Job," Kramer casually remarks that Jerry's new girlfriend, Audrey, who is present in the scene, just needs a nose job to be pretty. He has no clue why that suggestion would be perceived as offensive even by the men (who nevertheless don't say anything) much less as hurtful by Audrey or horrifying by Elaine.[88] Elaine's outraged reaction is a Seinfeld-esque version of Lillian Poznan's recoiling against the idea of offering her friend Frida a free nose job, in Englander's *The Ministry of Special Cases*; as Lillian puts it, "I'm not offering my friend a nose job. . . . It's insulting."[89] The audience for *Heeb*, a magazine from 2001 to 2010 and now available as a web-only version, is described on the website as unaffiliated young Jews who "feel little connection with organized Jewish life, but search for ways to express their Jewish identities that are relevant and meaningful to their lifestyle." As noted by Eric Goldstein, *Heeb* "regularly celebrates Jewish physical distinctiveness, with articles on the 'Jewfro' hairstyle and a photo exposé on the 'crazy curls, shapely schnozzes and hefty hips' of the 'Jewess.'"[90]

It is gratifying that *Heeb* is praising Jewish females' "shapely schnozzes." What a change in attitude a shift in adjective from "beaked" to "shapely" seems to mark. How different the situation is from that recounted by Virginia Blum, for example, in whose family a nose job was necessary if the daughter would find a successful Jewish man to marry: "It was our own cultural and ethnic 'brothers' for whom we were being redesigned in the conventional WASP image. It was as though circulating among us was a tacit agreement that Jewish men prefer gentile looks superimposed on originally Jewish bodies."[91] If times change, and some women are not willing to alter their looks to please a man, they may no longer be willing to pin their hopes on a *Jewish* catch, notwithstanding that male's presumed change of heart and perspective. Ophira Edut, as it turns out, chose Barbra over Barbie after all, relating in her memoir how and why she refused the requisite "covert spring-break appointment with the rhinoplastician": "Why bother changing when we can find a goy-boy who worships us, 'Jewish' looks and all?"[92] In 1970s television, the Jewish Rhoda Morgenstern (Valerie Harper was actually a non-Jewish Italian), who began as a character on *The Mary Tyler Moore Show*, marries a Roman Catholic on her own show, *Rhoda*. As David Zurawik says, in his study of Jewish characters on prime-time television, "non-Jewish masculinity is depicted [in *Rhoda*] as superior to Jewish masculinity."[93] But even if a woman does opt for a nose job, a Jewish husband may no longer be the end all and be all. Myrna Blyth's novel bears up that point, for Suzanne refuses "three nice Jewish doctors" (one of whom—with thinning hair and a rounded belly who "had learned the secret of perpetual, respectable middle age"—she jilts on their wedding day) and gets married twice to powerful non-Jewish men, respectively named Johnny Poparossa ("a Mafioso soldier") and Nicho Anapoulis (a rich Greek tycoon with his own island, purchased as a wedding present for his bride). Even perennially second-fiddle Aileen eventually takes a page from cousin Suzanne's playbook and ends up charming an oil-rich sheik in Kuwait—a "happy ending" as a gossip columnist concludes on the last page of the novel, with nary a Jewish husband or nose job for her in sight.[94]

All that said, no matter whether the field of prospective partners or friends or colleges has widened for the Jewish woman of recent times, the nose job remains a requested procedure. The aesthetic surgeon Beth Preminger, in her summary essay on the Jewish nose and plastic surgery in a volume on Jews and American popular culture, cites a Harvard coed interviewed for a 2000 issue of the *Harvard Crimson*: after undergoing a rhinoplasty to refine her Jewish look, she was "more accepted in the Harvard social scene." Preminger includes another remark from the Harvard article: "During my four years at a New York suburban high school, I knew at least 30 girls who had nose jobs, all of whom were Jewish." If, as Preminger concludes, the nose job for Jewish girls is "here to stay," she ought to know, because she offers the procedure as part of her practice, featured just below the face-lift as one of the surgeries she performs on the face.[95] And I find it significant that the editors of this reference book on Jews and American popular culture considered it necessary to include an essay on the Jewish nose and plastic surgery in the first place.

Neal Gabler's biography of Barbra Streisand, subtitled *Redefining Beauty, Femininity, and Power,* seems to me to overstate the case when this author asserts, as James Spada did before him, that Streisand "helped redefine femininity and beauty," "managed to change the entire definition of beauty," and is a "standard bearer for a new conception of beauty." True, he is taking one cue from influential feminist Gloria Steinem, who said in 1966, even before the release of the film *Funny Girl,* that "Barbra Streisand has changed the bland, pug-nosed American ideal, probably forever." Gabler adds the definitive: "Forever." He also quotes a female writer for that film, who said that Streisand had "made life a lot better for a lot of homely girls." Gabler comments, "especially, presumably, Jewish ones." But the fact remains that although the ethnic look is in vogue these days, and nose jobs resulting in standardized pug noses are out, the rhinoplasty itself is still a sought-after option for "homely" girls (the characterization still obtains) and maybe even "especially, presumably" for "Jewish ones."[96]

Surely Kathy Davis is correct in cautioning against ignoring specific time periods and cultural conditions when discussing the Jewish nose job. She has rightly noted that the "alterations that Jacques Josef [*sic*] performed on 'assimilated' Jews in the context of European anti-Semitism in the early twentieth century had a different meaning than the ubiquitous nose jobs performed on Jewish teenagers in the early sixties in the United States under the motto: 'You had your bat mitzvah, and you got your nose done.'"[97] I would add to Davis's inventory the "surgical interventions" performed surreptitiously on the most Semitic of Polish Jews' noses by doctors helping them to escape detection by the Nazis in 1940s Warsaw, as recorded by Diane Ackerman in *The Zookeeper's Wife*.[98] These various refinements of the work of God and heredity are not equivalent, to be sure, but they do have in common the felt need to look other than how one was born, to make for oneself another face—to look less Jewish, more Aryan, and hence more attractive. Surely a woman may be a feminist and still opt for a nose job. But Virginia Blum's contextualization of her own rhinoplasty is apt: "The story of my household is like that of many Jewish American families whose assimilation is symbolized through physical appearance. . . . Certain kinds of noses speak Jewishness. I have heard too many people say that he or she 'looks' Jewish on the basis of the size of a nose. Jews assimilating into a largely gentile culture thus strip from our features the traces of our ethnicity."[99]

One of those many Jewish American families was surely that of writer Hortense Calisher, whose early story "Old Stock"—which the author stated was autobiographical—less overtly, but just as dramatically, relays Blum's point about the "Jewish look." In this story, the assimilated and haughty German Jewish mother, Mrs. Elkin, looks down on "other Jews whose gross features, voices, manners offended her sense of gentility all the more out of her resentful fear that she might be identified with them." These are aspects of "what she hated in her own race." The presence of "those people" with Yiddish accents at a farmhouse she and her daughter are occupying for the summer just proves to her that the place is in a decline, but when her friend Miss Onderdonk, not knowing that her confidante is Jewish, also attributes the decline to the owner's taking in Jews, Mrs. Elkin after a long hesitation says, "I thought you knew that we were—Hebrews." Pointing to Hester, Mrs. Elkin's teenage daughter, Miss Onderdonk remarks, "The girl here has the look, maybe. But not you. . . . Does you credit. . . . Had your reasons, maybe. . . . Ain't no Jew, though. Good blood shows, any day." As the Elkins leave, "Miss Onderdonk's voice, with its little, cut-off chicken laugh, traveled down to [Hester] from the steps: 'Can't say it didn't cross my mind, though, that the girl does have the look.'" What Mrs. Elkins takes away from the incident is not that her daughter might have been wounded by this exchange but rather how "silly" it was that Miss Onderdonk didn't believe she herself was Jewish: "It certainly was funny . . . the way she kept *insisting*."[100] The mother is actually quite proud that she does not have "the look," that she can pass as a Christian. This reader is left wondering, if the story did not end there, how long would it take for the mother to insist that her daughter get a nose job?

It is true that an ethnic "look" does not have to be Jewish. In fact, Lea Michele's nose could have been deemed Italian rather than Jewish. Her Catholic mother is the former Edith Porcelli, and her Jewish father, Mark Sarfati, is of Turkish and Greek ancestry—either or both of these parents could have passed along this prominent feature. But the ethnicity that Michele would *have* to play as Rachel in *Glee* is Jewish, because the Jewish nose, not the Italian nose, is the familiar marker. Frances Macgregor found, in her study of "transformation" through facial plastic surgery, that almost all of the patients in the second cohort seeking rhinoplasties were non-Jewish and almost half of these were Italians, but they desired a nose job not because they were identified as being part of a particular group, as with the Jews, but rather because they were teased about their ugly nose: they wanted it "fixed" rather than "changed," to use Macgregor's distinction.

Other ethnicities have obtained nose jobs for the same reason as the Jews have: not so much to eliminate an unattractive feature, per se, as to camouflage an ethnic identity, though the two factors are associated. In Macgregor's study, a patient in the first group, the "changers," wanted her broad, flat nose fixed because, as the woman said, "I don't find it advantageous to have decisive Negro features. The less you look like a Negro, the less you have to fight. I would pass for anything just so long as I am not taken for a Negro. With a straight nose I could . . . pose as an Indian, Egyptian, or even a Balinese." Given that this woman was an aspiring model, we may take the word "pose" in two senses. Another so-called changer would have been happy with a Balinese nose; she had her Filipino father's flat nose, which made her appear uncomfortably "oriental."[101] These non-Jewish ethnic patients were a very small percentage of those in the study accessed by Macgregor for her 1973 book. Statistics over time from the American Society for Plastic Surgery reveal the larger picture. In 2017, only 6 percent of rhinoplasties were performed on African Americans, 4 percent on Asian Americans, and 10 percent on Hispanics. Caucasians accounted for 75 percent of these procedures (the unspecified Other counting for the remaining 5 percent).

The nose job was third in the top five of the twenty-three cosmetic surgical procedures listed for both 2016 and 2017 (after breast augmentation and liposuction). Yet it is instructional to see not only that the number of total rhinoplasties in 2017 was lower by 44 percent from the year 2000 but also that the number of women undergoing this procedure was lower by 30 percent from that year.[102] We cannot know what percentage of the rhinoplasties performed by board-certified plastic surgeons during those sixteen years was on Jewish women in particular, or on Jewish men for that matter. We do not know whether the reduction in numbers over that span was a result of acceptance of ethnic appearances in general, by society and the individuals in it. One can only hope that if this trend continues, it remains nourished by a climate of multiculturalism and openness to difference. However, although rhinoplasties were down 2 percent in 2017 from the prior year, the *increase* of 2 percent from 2015 to 2016 is perhaps a reminder that such a climate is not a given. In a scenario that many in America have never thought possible in the twenty-first century, but that no longer seems thoroughly improbable, the numbers of nose jobs requested by ethnic minorities could conceivably rise even more if "the look" once again becomes an unwelcome facial signpost.

Notes

1. Cited in Haiken, *Venus Envy*, 41, from the newspaper for August 4, 1920, 17:4 and August 6, 1920, 8:4. Two 1920s-era short stories by the popular writer Fannie Hurst center on the deleterious influence of the face-lift: "Forty-Five" and "The Smirk." See Kroeger, *Fannie*, 84, 128.

2. Blyth, *Cousin Suzanne*, 47.

3. The narrator of *Cousin Suzanne*, Aileen, was recently "the managing editor of a magazine for teenage girls" called *Modern Teen, the With-It Magazine* (2). Although geared toward a younger audience than *Ladies' Home Journal*, Aileen's magazine would be similar in catering to girls' desires to look beautiful and fit in. Cousin Suzanne had been a model for that teen rag. Sullivan explores "cosmetic surgery in women's magazines," the subtitle of a chapter of her book *Cosmetic Surgery* (155–86). We find *Ladies' Home Journal* in Anzia Yezierska's story "Where Lovers Dream," published in 1920 in her collection *Hungry Hearts*, when a young doctor-in-training tries to Americanize his ghetto girlfriend by buying her copies of this magazine (see Schoen, *Anzia Yezierska*, 22). Blyth, now in her late seventies and a vice president at AARP, has somewhat disingenuously taken an about-face, criticizing the women's magazine industry for foisting onto American females the notion that they are not good enough as they are (see her *Spin Sisters*).

4. See, for example, Jervis, "My Jewish Nose," 62–67, and Edut, "Bubbe Got Back," 24–30. Interestingly, Jewish women in early-mid medieval art were portrayed without the caricatured nose so often attributed to Jewish men at the time, although written sources readily attributed negative characteristics to Jewish women. It was not until the turn of the fifteenth century, at the close of the Middle Ages, that the Jewish woman begins to be portrayed with the characteristic features of the Jewish man, including the beaked nose (see Lipton, *Dark Mirror*, 202–37).

5. Starbuck, *Unsqueezed*, 16.

6. Haiken, *Venus Envy*, 184.

7. Baum, Hyman, and Michel, *Jewish Woman in America*, x.

8. Haiken, *Venus Envy*, 39.

9. Tieck, "New Intranasal Procedures," 117.

10. These works are cited in Baum, Hyman, and Michel, *Jewish Woman in America*, 224–25. The authors do not provide page numbers for their references.

11. Haiken, *Venus Envy*, 122–23. It was not only cosmetic surgery that the inferiority complex sold; the 1931 *Ladies' Home Journal* ad reproduced in Haiken, *Venus Envy*, 120, uses this psychological term to sell Lux soap to women for washing their "lovely frocks."

12. Sullivan, *Cosmetic Surgery*, 165.

13. Jacques Joseph, *Rhinoplasty and Facial Plastic Surgery*, n.p., cited in Preminger, "Plastic Surgery, Aesthetics, and Medical Professionalism."

14. F. V. Nicolle, *Aesthetic Rhinoplasty*, n.p., cited in Preminger, "'Jewish Nose' and Plastic Surgery," 2161.

15. Macgregor, *Transformation and Identity*, 76–77. In Roth's *Counterlife*, 39, Nathan Zuckerman's cousin Essie links the nose to a purported Jewish trait, cheapness, when she sardonically remarks that "in Israel you hear the best anti-Semitic jokes" and relates a riddle told by a Tel Aviv taxi driver: "Why do Jews have big noses? . . . Because the air is free."

16. Lippman, "Pynchonicity." One cannot overemphasize the extent to which *V.* is a "Jewish" novel, though written by a non-Jew. Slang Yiddish predominates—the protagonist, Benny Profane, who has a Jewish mother, is called a *schlemiel* and a *schlimazel* numerous times, for example—and other Jews pop up here and there in the panoply of characters.

17. Pynchon, *V.*, 45.

18. Wouk, *Marjorie Morningstar*, 2.

19. Ibid., 269. In *Jewish Woman in America*, Baum, Hyman, and Michel seem to have an ambivalent take on Marjorie Morningstar as the so-called JAP. On the one hand, they include her in that category, in which the "spoiled and materialistic, self-centered and assertive" woman "cares for no one but herself" and "manipulates the world for her own selfish ends." But they mitigate their assessment of her a few pages later: "While Marjorie Morningstar is regarded by many to be the first 'real' Jewish American Princess, she is essentially presented as a positive character whose missteps along the proper female path symbolize Wouk's perception of modernizing American ways as an affront to sustaining traditional values" (see 237, 238, 252). I read the novel as more complicated and less "traditional," and others share this view. See, for example, Bolton-Fasman, "Original Jewish Princess and I," 46, which lauds the many feminist aspects of the novel. In addition, one finds the stereotypical JAP in works published decades before Wouk's and Roth's. Winslow's "Cycle of Manhattan" provides an especially vivid example. In a version of the stereotype appropriate for the immigrant generation, the mother in Yezierska's 1925 novel, *Bread Givers* (244), calls her daughter a princess when she sees her in the new clothes purchased for a career in teaching. And for an example of a wife as a JAP, Michael Gold's *Jews without Money* (217–19) offers up the materialistic, ostentatious Mrs. Cohen, "the typical wife of a Jewish *nouveau riche*."

20. *Before and After*, The Met, http://www.metmuseum.org/art/collection/search/490117.

21. Haiken, *Venus Envy*, 79. A 1937 issue of *Popular Science Monthly*, in its two-page photographic essay titled "New Noses in 40 Minutes," also depicted a before-and-after photo of a woman who had her typically Jewish nose corrected; though the nose is not labeled as such, it does not need to be. The accompanying text, it should be noted, minimizes the risks and pain and maximizes the drama of the transformation (see Haiken, *Venus Envy*, 124–25).

22. Ibid., 154, 296.

23. Roth, "Goodbye, Columbus," 26, 100.

24. Haiken, *Venus Envy*, 296, 12.

25. Murrin, "New Nose in a Week," 82–83, cited in Haiken, *Venus Envy*, 129. Certainly a familiar technique of purveyors of beauty potions and lotions, as well as of surgeries, is to increase the discrepancy between "before" and "after" pictures, whether with a sour expression turned into a happy face or dowdy attire transformed to stylish fashion.

26. Blyth, *Cousin Suzanne*, 55. Virginia Blum's interviews with plastic surgeons show the extent to which these doctors see the positive effect of bodily interventions on patients' attitudes and feelings of self-worth. As but one example, a rhinoplasty transformed a withdrawn teenager with a nose that didn't "fit her" into the president of her class who is popular with the boys (see Blum, *Flesh Wounds*, 104).

27. This paragraph is indebted to Susan Cain's *Quiet*, chapter 1, "The Rise of the 'Mighty Likeable Fellow': How Extroversion Became the Cultural Ideal" (19–32). The cultural historian to whom Cain refers is Warren Susman. Cain does not deal with cosmetic surgery, but her description of the cultural milieu in the first decades of the twentieth century provides further background for my discussion of the nose job. Laura Browder addresses the popularity of "success manuals" in the 1910s and 1920s in relation to the rags-to-riches American ideal and the deconstruction of that ideal in such immigrant autobiographies and novels as those by Yezierska and Abraham Cahan (see Browder, *Slippery Characters*, chap. 5, especially 162–65).

28. Freedman, *Jew vs. Jew*, 40.

29. Blyth, *Cousin Suzanne*, 42.

30. Prell, "Why Jewish Princesses Don't Sweat," 339–54. Prell discusses other novels about Jewish women of the 1970s in which body alteration, including of the nose, is considered a must, such as Gail Parent's *Sheila Levine Is Dead and Living in New York* (1972) and Louise Rose Blecher's *The Launching of Barbara Fabrikant* (1974) (see Prell, "Cinderellas Who (Almost) Never Become Princesses," 129).

31. Robert M. Goldwyn, *Operative Note: Collected Editorials*, 44, quoted in Blum, *Flesh Wounds*, 58.

32. Prell, "Why Jewish Princesses Don't Sweat," 343–54. The quotations are on 353–54.

33. *Saturday Night Live* transcripts, season 5, episode 11, http://snltranscripts. jt.org/79/79kjewess.phtml.

34. Tabachnick, *Quest for Jewish Belief and Identity*, 157. Chute, in *Graphic Women*, eschews the "perhaps," declaring Kominsky-Crumb "the originator . . . of women's autobiographical comics" (30).

35. In Diane Noomin, *Twisted Sisters*, 139, quoted in Chute, *Graphic Women*, 33–34.

36. Chute, *Graphic Women*, 44. Tabachnick, *Quest for Jewish Belief and Identity*, 179, merely remarks that Kominsky-Crumb is "obsessed with the size of her nose."

37. The recording can be heard on YouTube: https://www.youtube.com /watch?v=eCuiN2JnjpE.

38. Meerlo, "Fate of One's Face," 31, italics in the original, quoted in Haiken, *Venus Envy*, 195, without either the damning italics or the notation about the influence of the parents and peers. In *Transformation and Identity*, Macgregor defines *Armenoid* as a term used by physical anthropologists to describe a nose "characterized by considerable length and height, convexity of profile, a depressed tip with a downward sloping septum, and thick, flared alae or wings" (89). She cites a significantly titled work of 1947, Ernest A. Hooten's *Up from the Ape*.

39. Blyth, *Cousin Suzanne*, 47.

40. See Oksman's *How Come Boys Get to Keep Their Noses?* for a photograph of Kominsky-Crumb as a teenager (31), a remark by the artist herself that she was "pretty cute at that time, but I portrayed myself as a hideous monster" (32), a 2005 self-portrait (36), and Oksman's statement on how the artist looks in person (26).

41. Chute, *Graphic Women*, 12.

42. Originally published in *Wimmen's Comix*, no. 15, titled *Little Girls* and subtitled *Case Histories in Child Psychology*, the three panels of "Nose Job" may be found on the web: http://www.adambaumgoldgallery.com/KominskyCrumb_Aline/Nose_Job1WB.jpg;

http://www.adambaumgoldgallery.com/KominskyCrumb_Aline/Nose_Job2WB.jpg; http://www.adambaumgoldgallery.com/KominskyCrumb_Aline/Nose_Job3WB.jpg.

43. Gilman, "The Jewish Nose," 394, repeated in *Making the Body Beautiful*, 198.

44. Kaye/Kantrowitz, "Jews in the U.S.," 123.

45. Goldstein, *Price of Whiteness*, 177–78.

46. Wolitzer, *Ten-Year Nap*, 140, 141, 350, 163.

47. Tabachnick, *Quest for Jewish Belief and Identity*, 171.

48. Noomin, "Agony and the Ecstasy of a *Shayna Madel*."

49. Gilman, "Jewish Nose," 393–94; Gilman, *Making the Body Beautiful*, 196–98. Gilman repeats his remarks once again in a later essay, "R. B. Kitaj's 'Good Bad' Diasporism," 191–92. Here he also mentions Adam Rolston's "Nose Job" (1991), Cynthia Madanzky's "Rhino," and Deborah Kass's take on Andy Warhol, "Jewish Jackie" (1992), with its multiple images of Barbra Streisand in profile.

50. Pellegrini, "Whiteface Performances," 109–10.

51. Gilman notes as well, in *Jew's Body* (188), how Sigmund Freud's collaborator, Wilhelm Fliess, operated on the nose to cure sexual dysfunction, since the tissue of the nose and of the genitalia were thought to relate to each other. Of the 156 cases he recorded, only 12 were men; Gilman comments that "what Fliess managed to do . . . was to convert a quality of race into an attribute of gender." Joseph Skibell utilizes Fliess's theories, and Dr. Fliess himself as a character, in his novel *A Curable Romantic*, set in early twentieth-century Vienna. The protagonist's lady love, a patient of Freud's, puts her hopes in "Dr. Fliess's revolutionary new cures. 'If my problems are nasal in origin, as he maintains, he'll be able to cure me with one quick surgery'" (94). References to Wilhelm Fliess are scattered throughout the novel, as if the author, like his protagonist, "couldn't get Dr. Fliess's damned nose out of [his] brain!" (54).

52. Oksman, *How Come Boys Get to Keep Their Noses?*, 2. The cover of Oksman's book is a riff on the third page of Lauren Weinstein's 2006 graphic memoir "Diana," in *Girl Stories*. In this panel, although the caption reads, in part, "I have a bigger nose," the caption covers the nose. (See Oksman, *How Come Boys Get to Keep Their Noses?*, 160, for a reproduction of Weinstein's panel.) Likewise, Oksman's cover design puts the book's title over the nose. The absence of the nose can have several meanings, which Oksman discusses on 158–63 in reference to the nose, both present and absent, of the Jewish female in this particular work by Weinstein. I would note that the cover of the paperback edition of Englander's *The Ministry of Special Cases* also puts the title over the nose—indeed, over the entire face—to make the graphic point about being "disappeared."

53. Dr. Webster's statement is quoted by Haiken, *Venus Envy*, 107; she references the 1961 discussion by religious leaders on 163–64. In her summary, only the Jewish authority, the rabbi, mentions the difference between men and women with regard to a justification for cosmetic surgery.

54. Shteyngart, *Absurdistan*, 3. Interestingly, in "Yekl" (3), Cahan notes early on the exceptionalism of his protagonist's nose: "decidedly not Jewish." (In combination with Jake's other "strongly Semitic features," however, even this nose "seemed to join the Mosaic faith.")

55. This work may be seen at http://www.denniskardon.com/noses.php?s=noses.

56. Gilman, "R. B. Kitaj's 'Good Bad' Diasporism," 191.

57. Shteyngart, *Absurdistan*, 125.

58. The 2017 figure relates to the 218,924 rhinoplasties performed that year by surgeons certified by the American Board of Plastic Surgery. ("Ethnicity" statistics in this report do not include Jews.) The records of plastic surgeon Jerome Webster show that between about 1930 and 1950, almost three-quarters of the four hundred people who came to this doctor because of their noses were women (see Haiken, *Venus Envy*, 187). Although Frances Macgregor, in her study of eighty-nine New Yorkers who requested a rhinoplasty between 1946 and 1954, found that almost half were men, this is not the norm. See Macgregor, *Transformation and Identity*," 82–83, and American Society of Plastic Surgeons, "Plastic Surgery Statistics Report 2017," https://www.plasticsurgery.org/news/plastic-surgery-statistics/.

59. Roth, "Goodbye, Columbus," 13.

60. Details in this paragraph are from Spada's *Streisand: Her Life* and Mann's *Hello, Gorgeous: Becoming Barbra Streisand*. That Streisand wished, if briefly, for a nose job is from Mann (64); her remark at the Coconut Grove is quoted by Mann as a caption to a photo included in a bank of glossy photographs after 118, and Spada quotes it as well (129). The anteater's snout is also from Mann (11). "Big beak," etc., comes from Spada (16); the stepfather's invidious comparison is on 28. Spada reports on Barbra's turning her face from the camera on 31, and her self-perception as ugly on 50. For the nose turning off potential casting agents and boyfriends, see Spada, *Streisand: Her Life*, 56, 58, 75. For the urgings of others for Streisand to have her nose fixed, see Mann, *Hello, Gorgeous*, 90, and Spada, *Streisand: Her Life*, 80, 88. Barbra's wondering if anyone could love her face is quoted by Spada (83); he quotes the teenage Streisand calling herself *Mieskeit* on 84 but also notes, on 492, that in the 1990s, when she was a superstar in her fifties, Streisand used the same word to describe her teenage self to a huge and admiring Las Vegas audience in the MGM Grand—by that time, she could look back with some affection (and self-mockery) to her insecure, face-hating young self. Spada talks about the devious whisperings of her erstwhile lover, Sydney Chaplin, on 156.

61. Haiken, *Venus Envy*, 196–97.

62. Spada, *Streisand: Her Life*, 236, provides the remark by Joe E. Lewis; Spada's commentary about the allure to teenagers is on 166. In contrast to Lewis's tone, the review of *A Star Is Born* for *New York* magazine in 1976, by critic John Simon, was a venomous commentary on Streisand's nose: "O, for the gift of Rostand's Cyrano to evoke the vastness of that nose alone as it cleaves the giant screen from east to west, bisects it from north to south. It zigzags across our horizon like a bolt of fleshly lightning, it towers like a juggernaut made of meat" (quoted in Spada, *Streisand: Her Life*, 366).

63. Quoted in Wolff, "Warhol Warhol Everywhere." Bloom discusses Deborah Kass in *Jewish Identities in American Feminist Art*, 110–14.

64. Spada, *Streisand: Her Life*, 75.

65. Haiken, *Venus Envy*, 198, citing *Newsweek* for May 30, 1966, 91–92.

66. Edut, "Bubbe Got Back," 27.

67. Michele, *Brunette Ambition*, 23, 187, 191.

68. The episode is referenced in Zeveloff, "Cut to Fit," 27. Zeveloff does not say that Lea Michele, the actress who played Rachel Berry, is half Jewish, but she does note that like Streisand, Michele refused her manager's advice to get a nose job. The cover of this issue of the *Forward* features Zeveloff's essay and contains a photograph montage called "Face Off" in the familiar before-and-after style of the 1950s advertisements and the Andy Warhol adaptation.

69. Mann, *Hello, Gorgeous*, caption on photograph between 310 and 311.

70. Spada, *Streisand: Her Life*, 61.

71. Quoted Spada, *Streisand: Her Life*, 138; see 149 for the similarities in background.

72. Schireson, *As Others See You*, 86–88. By the standards of the surgical profession in his day and ours, Schireson was a quack with a record of professional and financial malfeasance a mile long, but somehow, he maintained standing with the public. Haiken details his history (*Venus Envy*, 81–87).

73. Friedman, *Jewish Image in American Film*, 186, 184.

74. A photo of Frances Brice Stark, included in a bank of photos after 310 of the Mann biography, shows her with a bumpless, aquiline nose.

75. Jervis, "My Jewish Nose," 63.

76. Blum, *Flesh Wounds*, 1–2, 9, 6.

77. Pynchon, *V.*, 48. Schoenmaker and Esther, his patient, are actually having an affair and he wants to do more work on her: "If I can bring out the beautiful girl inside you, the idea of Esther, as I have done already with your face . . . ." Esther responds, "It isn't me you love . . . . You want to change me into something I'm not" (see 294, 296).

78. Information on the seminar is found on http://gaylekirschenbaum.com/. In these productions, Kirschenbaum displays an affectionate if critical attitude toward the nagging of a stereotypical Jewish mother; she utilizes the same materials that Jewish male comedians and authors have exploited for their jokes and their novels but with a more understanding perspective.

79. Belzer discusses the Valley Girl stereotype in reference to Monica Lewinsky (and herself), "On Being a Jewish Feminist Valley Girl," 181–88. Belzer got a nose job in her West Coast Valley Girl days but became a feminist on the East Coast; now she is "a young Jewish leader whose Jewish nose has been altered" (187). Feminism and nose jobs are no longer irreconcilable. In Virginia Blum's words, "We need to transcend feminist criticisms of body practices that can wind up being as shaming as the physical imperfections that drove us to beautify in the first place—as though some of us are superior to the cultural machinery while others desperately fling ourselves across the tracks of cultural desire" (63). Of course, here Blum begs the question of what constitutes a "physical imperfection."

80. See Phillips, "Not Quite White," 77, 84.

81. The *Allure* interview is cited by Susman, "Here's what the cast of 'Friends' were up to this week." Kudrow's remark about the "life-altering" rhinoplasty is cited by Eggenberger, "I Got 'Life-Altering' Nose Job at Age 16, Was 'Hideous' Before."

82. Iny, "Ashkenazi Eyes," 91.

83. Strauss, "Prurient Male Gaze Is Alive and Well in 'Red Oaks,'" 23.

84. Michele, *Brunette Ambition*, 166.

85. Ibid., 188.

86. The performance of "Born This Way" may be seen on YouTube: https://www.youtube.com/watch?v=15QAgfoDNPg

87. Pynchon, *V.*, 50.

88. The pertinent clip can be found on YouTube: https://www.youtube.com/watch?v=dPrpGCcFtt4

89. Englander, *Ministry of Special Cases*, 73.

90. The target audience is described on the website's About page: http://heebmagazine.com/about. The quotation from *Heeb* refers to "Jewess," *Heeb* 3 (Spring 2003): 40–51, and is found in Goldstein, *Price of Whiteness*, 235.

91. Blum, *Flesh Wounds*, 10.

92. Edut, "Bubbe Got Back," 27, 26.

93. Zurawik, *Jews of Prime Time*, 182. Much of Zurawik's book is devoted to Jewish-Christian intermarriage in television shows.

94. Blyth, *Cousin Suzanne*, 111, 4, 227, 242.

95. See Dr. Preminger's website: http://premingermd.com/rhinoplasty. She cites the *Harvard Crimson* of October 10, 2000, in "The Jew and the Nose," 225.

96. Gabler, *Barbra Streisand*, 8, 116, 117, 157.

97. Davis, *Dubious Equalities and Embodied Differences*, 98–99.

98. As reported by Ackerman, *Zookeeper's Wife*, 221–22.

99. Blum, *Flesh Wounds*, 5.

100. Calisher, "Old Stock," 263, 264, 270, 272–75. Calisher states in her preface to this collection that the Elkins family are her relations, and "Hester was certainly me" (ix–x).

101. Macgregor, *Transformation and Identity*, 92. The author also notes that after World War II, "Japanese women, influenced by American GIs and Western films," began to undergo surgery on their noses and eyes "in order to approximate more nearly the Occidental ideal" (see 98n29).

102. American Society of Plastic Surgeons, "Plastic Surgery Statistics Report 2017."

4   Renaming as a Strategy for Passing in Thyra Samter Winslow's "A Cycle of Manhattan"

"A Ros[s] by Any Other Name"

Jewish tradition places utmost importance on names, dating as far back as the creation of the Hebrew Bible and the various oral and written commentaries on it. According to biblical exegesis by Rabbi Eliezer ha-Kappar in the earliest centuries of the Common Era, the Israelites in the land of Egypt performed four mitzvoth before receiving the Torah at Sinai and without being commanded by God; one of these four was refusing to change their names.[1] Centuries afterward, in the newfound freedom of the United States, many Jews of their own accord did just the opposite, in order to acclimate to a new land. Jewish American fiction writers have played with and on this theme ever since. A prime example is Thyra Samter Winslow's story "A Cycle of Manhattan," in which a family arriving in New York in the late nineteenth century as the Rosenheimers changes its name over the ensuing decades to signify, and bolster, its assimilation and prosperity: first to Rosenheim, then to Rosen, then to Rose, and finally to Ross. As one of the upwardly mobile children puts it, when urging the final change: "Rose is so—so peculiar. . . . Any one could tell it had been something else, Rosen or worse. . . . Let's change it to Ross. That's not distinctive but it isn't queer or foreign."[2] For this family, a Ross by any other name would not only *not* smell as sweet, it would, like a protuberant nose, also give them away.

The name of the author herself does not "give her away" as a Jew. Born into a Jewish family in small-town Arkansas in the mid-1890s (the exact year is in question), Winslow became a journalist, drama critic, writer for film and television, and author of much prose fiction as well as a weight reduction guide and articles on beauty. She married twice, to non-Jewish men both times, and converted to Roman Catholicism in her final decline (having been visited often in the hospital by both a Christian Scientist and a Catholic, who competed for her allegiance). Most of Winslow's writings, like her name, also mask her origins. For that reason, "A Cycle of Manhattan" stands out among the other stories in Winslow's 1923 collection, *Picture Frames*. It is by far the longest at thirty-five thousand words (seventy-seven pages), and the only one about Jews.[3] The rest of the stories center largely on lonely young women from the Midwest or New York who despair of their meaningless existences and who hunger for something grander— more romantic, adventurous, and satisfying than their humdrum lives with boring fiancés or husbands ("Mamie Carpenter," "Amy's Story," "Indian Summer," "A Love Affair," "Corinna and Her Man," "The End of Anna")—or on lonely old women lamenting their stressful lives with ungrateful adult children ("Grandma," "Birthday"). Of the eleven stories in the collection, six are even titled with the name of the female protagonist or, in one case, her relationship (grandma). In reality, although that grandma may have the designation of an elder, and the title of her own story, she is not even given a name; she is defined only by her role. In "Grandma," the protagonist literalizes T. S. Eliot's dictum that the journey, not the arrival, matters, for when she travels by train to spend four months with each child, only then and only to strangers on the train can she pretend that her life is fulfilling: the story ends with the sad statements, "Grandma was just a little, tired, lonely old lady again. Another of Grandma's romantic journeys was over" (49). In "Birthday," we find another unnamed grandmother, to whom the narrator often refers as "old lady." Like the seventy-three-year-old grandma in the previous story, this "Gramma" lives with and, even at age eighty-two, daily serves children who take her for granted. In general, any momentary triumphs in Winslow's stories in this collection are canceled by ultimate dashed hopes, with a concomitant begrudged settling for things as they are (or, in Anna's case, a suicidal way out).

Winslow presents yet another grandmother in her story dealing explicitly with the Jewish experience of assimilation in America. This grandmother in the collection has a name, at least a surname—Mrs. Feinberg—but when addressed by outsiders she is sometimes called Mrs. Rosenheimer, as if she were an appendage of her son-in-law. "A Cycle of Manhattan" revolves around the Rosenheimers and their relentless climb into the bourgeoisie to such a degree that every character in the story, and every setting, becomes subsumed by this upward striving; thus, the grandmother—whose first name we never learn—must become a Rosenheimer too. And yet, she is the moral touchstone of the story, a Rosenheimer antagonist as it were, in ways that continue to resonate long after she dies and steps out of the picture frame. In taking this view, I am arguing against the opinion of one of the very few literary critics to have written on this work, Susan Koppelman, who states that there "is not a single member of the Rosenheimer family . . . for whom a reader can feel genuine affection. . . . Winslow wrote 'A Cycle of Manhattan' as if none of the characters had any dignity or depth."[4] I believe this critic has overlooked the subtlety of the story in her distaste for its portrait of Jews on the make.

And Jews on the make abound in this work, to be sure. If the weight of the endings of the stories in *Picture Frames* is on resigned settling for the status quo,

"A Cycle of Manhattan" breaks with that pattern. True, its conclusion can be viewed ironically, with Manning Ross, now a self-declared artist, returning to the exact apartment the family members had lived in when they were poor and struggling to succeed in America (hence the cycle of the title). But now that apartment has become a chic studio, as if it had shed its old-world identity in the process of becoming as upwardly mobile as the Rosses themselves. Here we have another journey or set of journeys—not from small town to big city, as in so many of the other stories in Winslow's collection, but from Lithuania to America and then to various addresses in New York City and beyond. Names are of the utmost importance in this journey, not merely the family members' first and last names, but also the streets they live on. In one case, in a neat conflation, a street with a nice Scottish name is even adopted by a character as a replacement for his first name.

Appropriately enough, given the theme, the work first appeared as the lead story and only "novelette" in the March 1919 issue of the literary magazine the *Smart Set*, coedited by George Jean Nathan and H. L. Mencken.[5] The *Smart Set* bragged in its subtitles for the year that it was "A Magazine of Cleverness," and it pictured glamorous, well-dressed women on all the 1919 monthly covers, women who look not unlike the increasingly fashionable Rosses in Winslow's story.[6] (On the March cover, the woman in furs could be none other than Carolyn Ross herself.) During the years of Nathan and Mencken's editorship (1914–1923), the magazine published the likes of James Joyce, F. Scott Fitzgerald, Aldous Huxley, and Edna St. Vincent Millay, to name only some of the authors admired by readers of today, but it is fair to say that the other contributors of fiction and poetry in the March 1919 issue are, like Winslow, now unknown to most. Winslow was one of the editors' favorites. In the first eight months of the 1919 publication of the *Smart Set*, Winslow had stories in five of them (January, February, March, April, and July), including a second novelette, "Caged." George Jean Nathan was a great mentor to the young Winslow and suggested the titles of many of her works. For his part, H. L. Mencken must have seen in Winslow's fictional piece a capsule reinforcement of his own exploration of American names, as set forth in his monumental study of the American language first published the same year as Winslow's novelette and revised with addenda in succeeding decades. At least some editions of his study contain an explicit reference to "A Cycle of Manhattan" and the Rosenheimers' name changes.[7]

In fact, Mencken's now classic work provides a gloss on, and backgrounding for, Winslow's largely forgotten story. In *The American Language: An Inquiry into the Development of English in the United States*, Mencken notes, "Changes in surnames go on in all countries, and at all times. They are effected largely by transliteration or translation."[8] By attributing such changes to an abrasion of unfamiliar names to those more accommodating to the new land—he mentions as one example that "the Jewish *Jonases* have joined the tribe of *Jones*"

(579)—Mencken gets at (though he does not mention) a common practice of immigration officials at Castle Garden and Ellis Island to arbitrarily make an unfamiliar, often unpronounceable, name more acceptable to American ears. In his lengthy disquisition on immigrants' surname changes, in his chapter "Proper Names in America," Mencken waxes most prolix (595–601) on the subject of the *Jewish* immigrants, whom he terms "the most willing to change their names." With his primary focus on Ashkenazi Jews, he details how this willingness was not American-born but had its roots in Russia, whether to avoid conscription into the czar's army, to sound more Russian and hence gentrified, or, if the bearer was a communist, to adopt an alias that would throw the police off one's trail. He also explains that willingness by reference to the fact that Jewish family names were adopted late in eastern Europe: "It was not until 1782 that the Jews of Austria were compelled to assume surnames, and not until 1812 and 1813 that those of Prussia and Bavaria, respectively, had to follow" (597–98). At times, the authorities inflicted names on Jews that were intended to humiliate or embarrass, but if a bribe were perhaps forthcoming, a Jew could assume a pleasant-sounding surname of his own choosing.[9]

With an example straight from Winslow's story, Mencken asserts that in contrast to other cultures, the Jews might change their names in order to "prettify" traditional names, "whereby the names in *Rosen-* become *Rose* or *Ross*" (begging the question of why shorter should equal prettier per se). Mencken also comments that the first generation of immigrants and their native-born children seek to hide their Jewishness by changing their names so as to avoid "all the disadvantages that go with their foreignness and their Jewishness," adding a footnote that, in true Mencken fashion, acknowledges the pressures of antisemitism but also questions the Jews' somewhat "dubious" attribution of the causes (596).

After dealing with surnames, Mencken devotes several pages to the given names of Jews, remarking on the ancient precedents: "the Jewish exiles brought back many names from the Babylonian captivity, and Moses himself apparently bore an Egyptian name" (634). He notes, it seems with some bemusement, "Of late the Jews have taken to naming their sons *John, Thomas, Mark, James* and *Paul*, not to mention *Kenneth, Clifton, Lionel, Tracy* and *Vernon....* Jewish given names are being rapidly assimilated to the general American stock, including the stock of fancy names. *Shirley* is now probably more common among Jewish girls than among Christians" (635). Mencken's commentary on Jewish naming practices sets Winslow's story in a much larger cultural context than the typical reader of a magazine geared toward the "smart set" might understand; her story, in turn, breathes life into the myriad facts and statistics found in Mencken's tome.

At every critical point in "A Cycle of Manhattan," the author puts name changes front and center. At the parents' move to America with their four children, the Rosenheimers' six-year-old son, named Isaac, is "almost immediately" called Ike, and one-year-old Emanuel becomes Mannie (98). The oldest, Yetta, will transmogrify to Yvette "suddenly" when she reaches eighteen because "the crowd she was going with thought Yetta an awful name, old-fashioned and foreign" (131). Yetta at only the age of thirteen had been the person to suggest a family name change from Rosenheimer to Rosenheim, when they were moving from MacDougal Street to a better address on East Seventy-Seventh. Rosenheim is the name that duly appears above the letter box in the tenement entrance hall, written in large letters by the father. Indeed, Winslow symbolically ties the family's dwelling places to its evolving surname throughout her story by referencing the letter box at each new place and the ever-truncating name it bears.[10]

When Ike is twelve, and bullied by a boy who taunts him with "Ikey Rosenheim, Ikey Rosenheim," he lashes out at his family: "You make me sick, naming me Ike. You might have known. This family has terrible names. No wonder people make fun of us" (118–19). In the 1940s, A. A. Roback's *Dictionary of International Slurs* defined *Ikey* as low slang for a Jew and a pawnbroker, from the name Isaac; perhaps the fact that it is a near rhyme with another low slang term for a Jew, *kike*, also plays a role in its use and its offensiveness, though Roback does not say so.[11] In any case, Ike wants to be called Harold, but his mother reminds him that he must keep the letter *I* since he was named after his grandfather Isaac. And so he does, becoming Irving.

In his discussion of Jewish given names, Mencken states that the same first letter is usually retained when changes are made, but he does not explain why this is (634). Winslow, however, provides the explanation even before Ike flirts with the name Harold, when the final child, Dorothy, is born in 1897 to the Rosenheimers: "There was a great discussion, then, about names. Before this, a baby had always been named after some dead ancestor or relative without much ado. It was best to name a child after a relative, but according to custom, if the name didn't quite suit, you took the initial instead. By some process of reasoning, this was supposed to be naming the child 'after' the honoured relative." As Alfred J. Kolatch elaborates in "The History and Development of Personal Names," which serves as the appendix to his dictionary of English and Hebrew names, naming a Jewish child after a relative is custom rather than law, and in various periods throughout Jewish history the practice was either condoned or condemned. For Ashkenazi Jews, perpetuating the memory of a deceased relative is the norm; Sephardic Jews, "less superstitious," have been much more inclined to name children after living relatives, even, on occasion, parents. Kolatch relates that when Jewish families in modern times adopted both a Hebrew and a secular name for their children instead of bestowing a single Hebrew name as in the past, the practice eventually led to the desire for "a 'modern' or 'fancy' (secular) name for the child."[12] This is precisely the situation we see in "A Cycle of Manhattan." Because the newest child in Winslow's Ashkenazi family is "an American baby" who "seemed, in some way, to make the family more American," the parents want something fancier than Dora, after a deceased great-grandmother, and decide on the "stylish" name of Dorothy (108), which at least preserves the first initial.

This family considers itself forward- rather than backward-looking. The father's career trajectory within the garment industry has at this point taken him from pants cutter to foreman to half owner of the Acme Pants Company, Men's and Boy's Pants (and will eventually take him to part owner of the Rex Suit Company, advertising their ready-made suits in the popular weeklies). He signs his joint partnership for the company with an assumed middle initial, on the supposition that he "ought" to have a middle name since it is American to own one. Now he is Abraham G. Rosenheim, a name that Irving happily writes above the letter box. As the business prospers and expands, and at Yetta's instigation when she is sixteen and not yet Yvette, the family relocates again. The neighborhood on East Seventy-Seventh, after all, "was filling up with terrible people, straight from the Ghetto—or the old country—and bringing foreign habits with them" (122), and so the Rosenheims escape to Sixth Avenue in the Bronx, where they shed yet another syllable along with the father's Hebraic first name: "One of the startling changes of the new régime was the name above the letter-box. A simple and chaste A. G. Rosen was announced in Irving's most careful writing. Rosenheim explained that, at the factory, every one called him Rosen for short and it might make it confusing to keep the old name. The family hailed Rosen joyfully. Surely they were real Americans, now" (125). But surely they are not yet "real" Americans, for no sooner do they arrive at a destination than it seems inadequately "American." The Bronx becomes to them as unfashionable as the previous addresses, and fifteen-year-old Carrie urges a move to Harlem, where the apartments and the schools are better and certainly more "stylish." Now going to a private school ("the only kind of school suitable for rich girls"), Carrie objects to her "cheap" name and changes it to Carolyn. The new apartment on West 116th Street is also expensive, in a grand, ornamented building with an elevator no less; the furniture is described in detail, and the family's delight with its new environment is magnified by and through those possessions. The family now has its first maid, and it seems to them imperative to effect yet another name change: from Rosen to Rose. Like noses, names can be shortened and in the process un-Judaicized. As well, the G as a middle initial for the papa has been replaced by a new middle name, Lincoln, for what could transform one into a real American better than a name change to Abraham Lincoln, an American hero. And what name could be more symbolically, more proudly, associated with freedom from bondage as the family throws off its shackles of old-world persecution and new-world poverty.

Up until this point in the story the family has associated mainly with Jewish people, keeping company with those of equal social status and striving after the company of those on the rung above. The Roses do not deny their heritage, and they do not seem on the surface to want to avoid, by their name changes, "all the disadvantages that go with their foreignness and their Jewishness," as Mencken says of such changes. Whatever their name du jour, the Roses' upward mobility combined with their practice of associating with their own people exemplifies how Jews of the period, in the words of historian Eric Goldstein, "attempted to satisfy their dual impulses for integration and distinctiveness."[13] But the family's ambivalence toward Jews and Jewish culture becomes manifest in their appreciation of the youngest child, Dorothy, now twelve years of age: "Although the family kept always with their own race and declared, on all possible occasions, their great pride in it and their aversion to associating with those of other faiths, the thing that delighted them most about Dorothy was, for some unexplainable reason, that every one said 'she looked like a Gentile.' Mrs. Rose would repeat it to her friends, that people had said, 'you'd never guess it—just like a Gentile that child looks.' Her friends agreed and there was nothing in their minds but cordial congratulation over the fact" (141). Perhaps that "unexplainable reason" is actually explainable on the basis of a face without that proverbial Jewish nose; the family's delight—its greatest delight—in that child's appearance is the same reaction Mrs. Elkins experiences in Hortense Calisher's "Old Stock," when told *she* doesn't look Jewish. There is something in the minds of the Rose friends, all right, but it is hidden from friends and family alike, if not from the reader.

With such admiration, expressed in racial terms, and the hidden message it carries about inferiority, it is no wonder that Dorothy not only changes her name to Dorothea but develops both a full-scale dislike of those Jews she considers vulgar and a concomitant interest in associating with the gentiles she resembles physically. She is more detached, or detaching, from her people than are her siblings. One of her brothers may be "proud to associate with 'outsiders,' liked to think he looked and spoke and acted like one of them. But he would never have married a Gentile." Her sister Carolyn "liked best the people of her own race, but she preferred them with American or English accents, appearance and accomplishments" (158–59). Dorothea, on the other hand, "went with 'outsiders'" (163) and knows that "the men she liked didn't belong to her race" (167–68). The question of whether she will marry a man like Hamilton Fournier is left open, but the author suggests that given her tradition of getting everything she wants, and her rationalization that she is "proud of her race," Dorothea will surmount her parents' reaction and "keep on having" whatever it is that she wants, even if what she wants is a non-Jewish husband. Indeed, we are told that Mr. Ross (most recently Mr. Rose) "was getting accustomed to Dorothea's friends, unbelievers though they were" (171). Some of these friends may be non-Orthodox or, heaven forbid, atheists, but increasingly the friends surely include gentiles. Marriage to a gentile is one passing strategy that the author leaves to the reader's imagination, but it almost seems a next step, considering what we have seen of the family's evolution.[14]

Since upward mobility is an impulse not to be denied, the family moves yet again, to Riverside Drive and an even grander building with a uniformed door man and a *mirrored* elevator. Again the ornate furnishings are described in correspondingly ornate detail. Along with the furnishings the apartment sports additional human acquisitions: cook, housekeeper, chauffeur and a part-time washer-woman. Not surprisingly, with this move up the ladder the family adopts another name change. The fancy digs do not have a letter box, but the elevator man writes down the names of the new occupants, so he can remember them, listing the father as A. Lincoln Ross and thereby revealing that the family has once more removed traces of Jewishness. Son Emanuel, always called Mannie (which "isn't a name at all," he complains), registers at Columbia University as Manning Ross (150), and Irving, a lawyer for his father's business, becomes Irwin (157): now all the children, and the father, have new first and last names. The mother, whose given name of Minnie is mentioned early in the story, and who retains that name throughout, seems nonetheless to be content with being known as Mrs. A. Lincoln Ross; she is identified with her husband, just as her mother had been called by her son-in-law's name when he was Rosenheimer.

The family eventually moves up to a five-story house on East Sixty-Fifth Street off Fifth Avenue and acquires a Long Island country home as well—both residences are decorated tastefully by interior designers from Madison Avenue, without the ornate furnishings typical of the nouveau riche but, rather, with understated (yet costly) accoutrements described in similarly understated language. There is one final move to be made before the story ends, however. Manning had dabbled briefly with college life at Columbia and then Harvard (more exclusive than Columbia), but having gone to art school for a year or so, he now needs a studio. (Of course he will retain his allowance and refresh himself when needed at his parents' two homes, even though they belong to the bourgeoisie he disparages.) Manning finds his studio in a remodeled building a block from Washington Square in the Village and describes his apartment animatedly to his parents: "No elevator, real Bohemia, three flights up, uncarpeted stairs." He proclaims to his family that this is "the way to live! None of your middle-class fripperies. Plain living, high thinking–this is the life!" (172–73). Ironically, unbeknownst to him, this is the same plain apartment from which his parents began their American journey decades earlier. The nameplate now bears the name Manning Cuyler Ross—"I'm so glad I took Cuyler for a middle name last year," he exclaims—along with the word *masks*. With this one word, presumably Manning's artistic métier, the author succinctly and cunningly raises the specter of inauthentic identity, similar to Nathan Englander's use of Dr. Mazursky's masks in *The Ministry of Special Cases*.

Winslow injects other Jewish families with similar trajectories into the story, no doubt to indicate that the Rosenheimers' aspirations and acquisitions are part of a larger cultural trend. Mr. Rosenheimer's distant cousin Abramson, an already-acclimated immigrant after twelve years in America, becomes the Rosenheimer guide and partner when the Rosenheimers arrive in the New World. The Abramsons, too, shed the past gradually, eliminating letters from their surname to become Abrams and later Adams; the sons of Abra(ha)m, through this evolutionary name change, are in effect disinherited from their forebears. Sam Adams also changes his first name to the street they had lived on, MacDougal, because he thinks it sounds better (certainly not Jewish), even though his family, like the Rosses, has abandoned the street itself for ever-tonier addresses. Winslow in this instance most directly shows the linkage between one's address and one's sense of identity. The Adams and Ross families unite in another kind of partnership when Yvette marries MacDougal, settling into "a new and elaborate apartment in Central Park West" (144). Meanwhile, the author casually notes the Americanization of other families' names: Moskowski becomes Moss, and Grabinski transforms to Graham.

This process of assimilation via name changes is reminiscent of the situation in Europe in the nineteenth century, as Mencken pointed out. Benzion Kaganoff relates, in his history of Jewish names, that the "Prussian edict of March 11, 1812, emancipated the Jews but made emancipation conditional upon the adoption of family names within six months. The names chosen were subject to approval by the authorities." Whether in the Prussian kingdom or the Russian empire, one important reason for commanding the adoption of surnames was to "Westernize, 'civilize,' and assimilate the Jew." More, to "many an 'enlightened' Jew, the adoption of a family name looked to be one more asset in the struggle to secure equal rights and integrate oneself in the Gentile world." A century later in the United States, a self-determined family name change was seen by many to accomplish the same goal. What should not escape notice in an analysis of name changing as a form of assimilation, in "A Cycle of Manhattan" as elsewhere, is how atypical the United States was and is in the ease with which one may change a name, and how few restrictions there are in the selection of a new name. In the 1930s and '40s, Nazi Germany forbade the changing of names and commanded the reassertion of some names that had already been changed; in that era, France and Norway also issued edicts about Jewish nomenclature. Just as in earlier centuries, then, Jews continued to face restrictions in name choices.[15] In contrast, the very freedom that Jews in Europe sought in the golden land of America, to determine their own addresses and livelihoods, was also available in the selection of their names.

Mencken's implication that where names are concerned, shorter is prettier, is borne out, it appears, by Kaganoff's statistic that "almost half the Jews who change their names in America each year are content with shortening." The Rosenheimers in Winslow's story do shorten, more than once, but this family is also part of the almost 60 percent who transform to a name not recognizably Jewish.[16] Ironically, the family's name in its final iteration is the same as that of a noted University of Wisconsin sociologist of Winslow's time who adhered to the prevalent eugenicist and racist notions; this Ross was one of several influential authors whose antisemitic rhetoric about the influx of eastern European Jews reinforced long-standing views of Jews in general. As Leonard Dinnerstein relates, in his study of antisemitism in America, "In Ross' mind Jews were rightly excluded from elite resorts, schools, and private associations not because of bigotry or religion but because of 'certain ways and manners.'"[17] This phrase comes from Ross's essay "The Hebrews of Eastern Europe in America," published only five years before Winslow's story appeared in the *Smart Set*. Whether Winslow deliberately took a dig at the family by opting for this particular surname is a matter for speculation.

In her introduction to a collection of stories by Fannie Hurst, Susan Koppelman remarks that many immigrants to America wished to change their names in order "take advantage of the greater opportunities of all kinds available to those who are most 'like' members of the dominant culture"; in addition, "they thought of their history as that of a wandering people, a history of successive assimilations, and knew full well that there already had been successive name changes. They may, in fact, have seen the overarching 'fact' of their tradition as change, adaptation for the sake of survival." Koppelman's take on these reasons for name changes, as well as for other adaptations, cannot be argued, yet I must draw the line at her statement that Hurst's "'The Gold in Fish' is perhaps the most important presentation of this phenomenon in American literature."[18] There is no doubt that Hurst's story had more lasting effects than Winslow's: it was made into both a play (*It Is to Laugh*, 1927) and a movie (*The Younger Generation*, 1928), the latter directed by none other than Frank Capra.[19] But where name changes are concerned, in my estimation "A Cycle of Manhattan" is a more important presentation than Hurst's story, because it is both more expansive and more incisive.

Koppelman compares the two stories in an essay published a few years before her Hurst edition, but she provides only a summary of Winslow's story, in a little more than a page. She considers that work "an extended exploration of a bad joke," "a bad story" that "shames the people it purports to represent. Winslow provides no context for the feelings and choices of the characters and she perpetuates stereotypes." Koppelman further asserts that "Hurst's story has a moral center," whereas Winslow's is a work of "capricious, social-climbing buffoonery."[20] Although I fully understand the source of Koppelman's disfavor, she has left out the "moral center" in her assessment of "A Cycle of Manhattan" by failing to pay attention to the role of the grandmother. If the paterfamilias, Mr. Rosenheimer/

Rosenheim/Rosen/Rose, had permitted yet another name shortening after the final iteration of Ross, and another after that, the name would have disappeared completely, and with it the family. This is what happens with the grandmother, whose given name is unknown, and whose surname disappears soon after the story begins. Midway through the "cycle" she dies, but nonetheless she remains a trenchant character. Her story is as important as her family's, for she is the embodiment of the erasures they have found necessary to make.

Interestingly, when the family members first step off the boat from steerage, we are told that they number seven "if you count Mrs. Feinberg" (97). The grandmother is hardly to be counted in the story of the Rosenheimer family, for she is a throwback to the old country and old country ways and will soon become superannuated. At the start, however, she trembles with excitement at entering their first apartment and exclaims that "this is fine—this is the way to live" (101)—a sentiment to be echoed years later by the grandson in her arms whom she now affectionately calls Mannischen, when he grows up to become Manning and unknowingly occupies the very same dwelling. Grandma's significant role in setting up house is emphasized: "There wasn't much money and it had to be spent very carefully, but each article meant exploring, looking and haggling. Grandma took the lead in buying—didn't Grandma always do such things? . . . Didn't she take care of the children and do more than her share of the housework?" (102). Winslow devotes a good deal of space to Grandma's utility not only in shopping and child care but also in scrubbing floors and constructing furniture from boxes. The *if* in "if you count Mrs. Feinberg" thereby takes on an ironic meaning, since the family could not function as well—and chooses not to—without her. The word *Grandma* begins several sentences, even if she is working in tandem with her daughter: another, more subtle way that her lead role is highlighted. This initial period of immigration ends with the declaration: "Grandma and Mr. and Mrs. Rosenheimer, looking at the children and at their two big rooms—all their own and so nicely furnished—could hardly imagine anything finer" (103).

At fifty-seven years of age, though "spry," Grandma shows herself to be less flexible emotionally than she is physically, for she is unwilling or unable to adapt fully to her new surroundings. While the second and third generations are learning English, "only Grandma showed no desire to learn the ways of the new country. She didn't mind picking up a little English, of course. . . . It didn't hurt to know something about the language. But as for reading—well, Yiddish was good enough for her" (105). When, after a year in America, her daughter discards the *sheidel* (wig) worn by Orthodox Jewish married women and tries to persuade her mother to do the same, Grandma demurs; to her, this is one of the "things you couldn't do decently, even in a new country" (106). Stylishness, so important to Mrs. Rosenheimer, holds no significance for Grandma. And when the first American-born child arrives, it is the grandmother who wants her to be named after her own mother, though again she loses out to the family's notion of stylishness as captured in the American-sounding name of Dorothy. Later, it is she who literally wails at the notion that Ike might become Harold and thus contravene religious custom.

A pivotal moment comes when Mrs. Rosenheimer tires of the two-room flat on MacDougal Street and advocates for a move to a better neighborhood. Their home, "which had looked so grand, was old and ugly, too, when compared with those of other people," the narrator says, inside the head of Minnie Rosenheimer. "Of course Grandma liked it, but, after all, Grandma was old-fashioned. Mrs. Rosenheimer discovered, almost in one breath, that her mother belonged to a passing generation, and didn't keep up with the times—that she, herself, really had charge of the household" (110). Grandma belongs to a "passing generation" only because she has become outdated in her family's eyes; her family has become a passing generation in another sense, as they shed their Jewish names and customs. From this point on, Minnie takes the lead, starting with the search for new housing, when she "act[s] as spokesman" and finds a four-room flat on East Seventy-Seventh Street.

Grandma adjusts to the new place over time, and she still does all the cooking ("of course") and bosses the children (115). Now sixty-two years old, she remains constantly busy, but because she doesn't feel as comfortable in the shops as she had on MacDougal Street, presumably because more English is spoken in them, her daughter takes over the marketing. Once again Minnie tries to convince her mother to give up her wig, and once again Grandma refuses: "She couldn't yield everything to the customs of the unbelievers. She even muttered things about 'forgetting your own people'" (116). Grandma is mentioned less and less as the family is occupied with financial achievements and rising status. At the next move, to the Bronx, they accede to Grandma's wish for a big kitchen as long as she is the primary cook. Meanwhile, in the grand seven-room flat, Grandma shares "a tiny cubicle" with Dorothy (124).

In the Bronx, Grandma at age sixty-five is isolated in a fourth-floor walkup several blocks from her Yiddish-speaking friends. She is "just a trifle bewildered. . . . She didn't seem to fit in." Life is not unpleasant, to be sure, with the finer furnishings and nicer clothes. And she is of utility in the running of the household: she still prepares the meals and does housework, which she enjoys, and the burden of heavy scrubbing is relieved by the welcome part-time washer woman. However, Grandma's position as respected elder is gradually undermined, even by the five children she helps to raise and cleans up after: "The children, growing up, were developing unexpected opinions of their own that didn't agree with her ideas. They called her old-fashioned and giggled at her advice" (127). The children are similarly disrespectful toward their mother, whose loud voice, heavy accent, and occasional reversion to Yiddish draw their reprimands; having internalized

Christian American norms of speech, they must disavow and distance themselves from any behavior that so overtly expresses Jewishness.

The next apartment, on West 116th Street in Harlem, is another move up for the family, but although Grandma can use the elevator to get out in ways she couldn't in the Bronx, she cannot walk all that well any more. And with a full-time maid to do the cooking and cleaning, there isn't much for Grandma to contribute in the house: "She had thought that life meant service and now there was nothing to do." People on the street stare at her sheidel, which embarrasses her, and they find it hard to understand her Yiddish-inflected English (135). Worse, even her grandchildren "frown at her attempts at conversation." So when company is in the home, Grandma usually stays in her room. True, Irving brings her candy, and Yvette sings for her, but a beautiful home and new clothes cannot fill the void at the center of her life. "Grandma knew she ought to be awfully happy. Yet there seemed to be something—missing" (136). That something is a sense of self and of having a meaningful place in the world. Grandma is gradually being "disappeared," not in the Pato Poznan sense of total physical obliteration, but certainly in a very real emotional sense.

Grandma's tensions with her daughter are surely typical of households in which a grandmother is taken in after the death of her husband and finds herself in conflict with the female head of the household, the daughter, over who is in charge and whose ways of operating will hold sway. Karen Brodkin, in the introduction to her study of Jews in America, describes just such a situation in the three-generation household of her own youth: her mother was "in rebellion against my grandmother's control and her version of domesticity. . . . [It was] a mother-daughter struggle over turf and household decision making as well as the meaning of being a Jewish woman."[21] In "A Cycle of Manhattan," Winslow puts her emphasis squarely on the changing definitions not only of Jewish womanhood but also of homes themselves for a family that opts for and quickly adopts the cultural values of America.

While they are living on Riverside Drive, in 1909, Grandma dies at the age of seventy-two. She seems "quite content to die, and though the family was fond of her, her going did not cause any undue emotion." Her daughter's last words on the subject constitute the final mention of Grandma in the story and reveal at the same time how the family members justify much of their behavior on the basis of money and status: "It ain't as though Mamma ain't had everything money could buy these last years. A grand life she's had, nothing to do and her own room and all. . . . It's good we was able to give it to her. She was a good woman but now she's gone and I can say I ain't got nothing to reproach myself for" (142). This Grandma is but one of the overworked, underappreciated grandmothers in *Picture Frames*, for in these collected stories, old age tends to bring exploitation on the one hand and condescension on the other. Perhaps Winslow felt this to be true of the United States in general. And since her own maternal grandmother lived with the family, one may venture that she drew to some extent on her own circumstances.[22] Grandmothers feature prominently in stories outside this collection as well: "Her Own Room," in *Century*, 1921; "The Odd Old Lady," in the *New Yorker*, 1927; "Matt," in the *Chicago Tribune*, 1930. As Richard Winegard puts it in his doctoral dissertation on Winslow, "All work hard, ask for little, and accept what is given in silence. All are in some way outcasts in the family group, tolerated but not accepted."[23] Clearly the grandmother is a stock figure in Winslow's fiction, one of several character types on which Winslow relied over and over again in her more than two hundred stories. But in "A Cycle of Manhattan," Winslow shows herself capable of providing a nuanced portrait of family dynamics, along with an opening out to include the issue (and price) of adaptation to a new country.

"A Cycle of Manhattan" was well known and praised in its day, included, for example, in the Modern Library's volume *An Anthology of Famous American Stories*, edited in 1936 by Angus Burrell and Bennett Cerf and reissued several times thereafter. In this collection, unlike the first publication in the *Smart Set*, Winslow keeps good company with the famous likes of Hawthorne, Poe, Melville, and Twain; James, Wharton, and Dreiser; and Hemingway, Fitzgerald, and Faulkner, among many other familiar names.[24] "A Cycle of Manhattan" exemplifies what Burrell and Cerf say about her fiction in general, in their biographical notes: "Her work is for the most part impersonal, detached; she records faithfully and lets the facts speak for themselves. Mrs. Winslow's outlook is one of trenchant irony."[25] This mode of writing fits with the remembrances of those who knew her as a young woman in small-town Arkansas; as Winegard remarks, his interviewees recalled that she "had an acerbic wit and was never loath to use it against the gentiles who excluded her or even against members of the Jewish community."[26] Certainly this story expresses the author's bemusement bordering on scorn for upwardly mobile Jews (though the fullest picture of her, as provided by Winegard, suggests that she was status conscious and upwardly mobile herself), and its out-of-proportion length in *Picture Frames*, when compared to the other stories in the collection with similar themes in Christian settings, suggests a particular dissatisfaction with the culture into which she was born and which she left behind. Whether there is a connection between this dissatisfaction, not to mention her eventual conversion, and her exclusion by gentiles in the Arkansas community of her youth can only be pondered, not demonstrated. Nonetheless, along with the shallow, materialistic, and self-absorbed Jews in "A Cycle of Manhattan," Winslow presents a sympathetic Jewish grandmother, deracinated in the New World, clinging to the customs that give her life meaning, and offering for the reader an alternative way of thinking about what constitutes a fulfilled existence.

Notes

1. I thank rabbi emeritus John Friedman of Judea Reform Congregation in Durham, North Carolina, for this information. The other three mitzvoth were remaining chaste, refraining from gossip, and not changing their language.

2. Winslow, *Picture Frames*, 149–50. Subsequent references in the text to the stories in this collection are to this edition.

3. The family members in "Birthday" seem to have traditionally Jewish first names— among them, Minnie and Herman—but since they are making a centerpiece for the Church Circle sale, and using candles left over from the Christmas tree, it is doubtful that Winslow means for them to be taken as Jews, or at least practicing Jews.

4. Koppelman, "Naming of Katz," 237, 239. Charlotte Baum, Paula Hyman, and Sonya Michel refer to "A Cycle of Manhattan" sporadically in *Jewish Woman in America*, but their concern is with gender issues; they do not touch on names, the grandmother, or any of the other subjects with which my chapter deals.

5. Koppelman notes in "Naming of Katz" (249) that she could find no evidence of periodical publication of the story, but Winegard's 1971 dissertation on Winslow provides the requisite information: it first appeared in the *Smart Set* 58, no. 3 (March 1919), 3–35.

6. Other subtitles in other years included the equally pretentious "The Aristocrat among Magazines," "For Minds That Are Not Primitive," and "The Only Magazine with a European Air" (see Connolly, *George Jean Nathan*, 82).

7. See http://www.bartleby.com/185/48.html for chapter 10 of the edition published in 1921, which, in footnote 32, references Winslow's story as the source of these particular changes. The edition that I have used for my discussion of Mencken does not credit Winslow.

8. Mencken, *American Language*, 578. Subsequent references in the text to this work are to this edition.

9. Mencken's dates do not always accord with those in Kaganoff's dictionary. Kaganoff's work centers on the subject of naming practices among Jews over millennia, among the Sephardim as well as the Ashkenazim, and understandably goes into much more detail than Mencken's disquisitions on the same subject. Regarding the matter of officials granting offensive names if money was not forthcoming, I would note that Professor Seymour Mauskopf of Duke University has had a distinguished career as a historian in spite of being literally labeled a "mouse head."

10. Interestingly, the practice of changing surnames when one moved was common among medieval Ashkenazi Jews, in great part because at that time the first name was deemed more important than the family name. Other circumstances also led to a variety of surnames for the same individual (see Kaganoff, *Dictionary*, 18–19). As Kaganoff remarks, "This disorganized state of affairs as regards Jewish family names created great difficulties for government authorities, and so, when the German states undertook to 'emancipate' the Jews at the turn of the eighteenth and nineteenth centuries, they made an effort to regularize Jewish family names by requiring them to adopt fixed and permanent ones." The situation in medieval and later times was different for Sephardic Jews in Mediterranean lands, where their numbers in the cities and integration with their Arab neighbors afforded the impetus and ability to adopt fixed surnames. Kaganoff explores Sephardic family naming practices on 12–15.

11. Roback, *Dictionary of International Slurs*, 40, 51.

12. Kolatch, *Name Dictionary*, 319–20, 323. Mencken does not comment on the fact that Sephardic Jews do not feel bound to name a child after someone who is deceased; although he does not ignore the Sephardim in his discussions, he concentrates on the Ashkenazim. See Kaganoff, *Dictionary* (98–99), for a discussion of the differences in this particular naming practice between Sephardim and Ashkenazim. Winslow's focus is solely on the mass immigration of eastern European Jews starting in the late nineteenth century.

13. Goldstein, *Price of Whiteness*, 102.

14. In 1908, when Dorothea was eleven years old and called Dorothy, New York's Jews intermarried at a rate of 1.17 percent. By 1916–1918, when Dorothea was between nineteen and twenty-one, the rate for American Jews as a whole had grown to 4.50 percent. These statistics are from Goldstein, *Price of Whiteness*, 98, 263n49.

15. Kaganoff, *Dictionary*, 22, 66–67.

16. Ibid., 70–72.

17. Dinnerstein, *Antisemitism in America*, 65. Dinnerstein devotes several pages to this writer's published analyses of Jews. Ross was also dismissive of other immigrant groups, since the massive influx raised fears of foreigners in general.

18. Koppelman, "Introduction: Rediscovering Fannie Hurst," xix.

19. Kroeger, *Fannie*, 140–41, 150.

20. Koppelman, "Naming of Katz," 244.

21. Brodkin, *How Jews Became White Folks*, 16–17.

22. Winegard, *Thyra Samter Winslow*, 2. This source is the most extensive biographical accounting of Winslow to date.

23. Ibid., 87–88.

24. Winegard comments that the story was generally considered by reviewers of *Picture Frames* to be the best in the volume, that Edna Ferber thought it should have been a novel, and that Winslow adapted the story for a stage play in collaboration with Arthur Richman, though he could find no indication that it was ever produced. (Winslow claimed that it had been.) After the story's first appearance in the *Smart Set*, Winslow attempted to sell it to the movies but withdrew it from consideration once she decided to include it in *Picture Frames* (see Winegard, *Thyra Samter Winslow*, 16–17, 23). She would later write several screenplays for Hollywood.

25. Burrell and Cerf, *Anthology of Famous American Stories*, 1331.

26. Winegard, *Thyra Samter Winslow*, 6.

5 Renaming and Reclaiming
"To Thine Own Self Be True"

Isaac Asimov, reflecting on his first name in "Seven Steps to Grand Master," relates how in the mid-1920s a well-meaning neighbor in Brooklyn, where his family had settled after emigrating from Russia, advised his mother that the name Isaac was a stigma, a term understood as a giveaway to his Jewishness. When the mother asked what she should call her son instead, the neighbor responded, "Call him Oiving" (which Asimov "translates" from the Yiddishized English to Irving, "a grand old aristocratic English family name"). Even at his tender age of four or five, according to Asimov, he would not permit such a name change: "What I thought was that I *was* Isaac and if I were called anything else, I wouldn't be me." He concludes, "Had I accepted Oiving, it would have proved every bit as stigmatic as Isaac, for so many Jewish mothers had sought escape for their young hopefuls in that direction that Oiving became as Jewish as Isaac and without the biblical cachet of the latter name."[1] "A Cycle of Manhattan" illustrates Asimov's point, when Isaac becomes Ike, who becomes Irving and finally, in the last step to gentrification, Irwin.

The practice of renaming is of long Jewish tradition. Name changes are actually quite common and meaningful in the Hebrew Bible, as noted by Alfred Kolatch in the supplementary materials to his dictionary. Kolatch remarks that the significance of naming throughout biblical history is emphasized in *renaming*, as when Abram becomes Abraham; Sarai, Sarah; and Jacob, Israel, among numerous other examples. Such changes, says Kolatch, "were made to honor or glorify a person's newly acquired position or to predict the role of the individual in the future." Abram, for instance, means exalted father, whereas Abraham means father of a mighty nation or father of a multitude; the addition of the Hebrew letter *H*, the symbol of God, indicates that this first Hebrew has accepted one God and thus will spawn a people with the same credo.[2]

Another kind of renaming is found in the long-standing superstition, in Sephardic and Ashkenazi traditions, that an ill person must have a name change so that the Angel of Death will not be able to find him or her. Lucette Lagnado, in her memoir of her half-Syrian, half-Egyptian family, opens her chapter "The Essence of a Name" with the cryptic statement, "Your name is your destiny. Change your name, the mystics say, and you will avert even the most terrible fate." At her birth in Egypt in the mid-1950s, four years after the death of her newborn sister, her family was at a loss for a given name: "Names were critically important in determining a person's fortunes, yet because of the shadow cast by the death of my sister, deciding what to call me had turned into a high-stakes game of chance." Lagnado expands on why she remained unnamed for days:

> Legend had it that hundreds of years back, my ancestor, Rabbi Laniado of Aleppo, stricken with a fatal malady, had glimpsed the Angel of Death lurking by his bedside. Since his doctors were powerless to save him, he took matters into his own hands—he changed his name and instructed his family to proclaim he was no longer Rabbi Laniado. The stratagem worked like a charm. He tricked the Angel of Death into leaving his room, and survived to a ripe old age.
>
> Yes, a name could do that—it could quite literally mean the difference between life and death.

After much deliberation, this baby is named not after a relative, as is the custom, but for the pretty teacher of her older brother in his French school: Lucette. "'Ça lui portera bonheur, Inshallah [God willing],' my mother remarked; It will bring her good luck.'"[3]

In an Ashkenazi context, the same practice of evading the Angel of Death through a name change is delineated in a book for young readers by Sydney Taylor, author of the popular *All-of-a-Kind Family* series written between 1951 and 1978. Born in 1904, Taylor, unlike Thyra Samter Winslow, had warm feelings about growing up Jewish, in her case as the child of eastern European immigrants on the Lower East Side of New York. Each of the five short works of fiction in her series stems from the autobiographical impulse to recapture the pleasures of a childhood in a big family that joyfully and religiously celebrated all the Jewish holidays; each of these works carefully explains not only the holidays but also a variety of Jewish religious rituals and practices, thereby serving as a kind of primer on Jewish culture for young readers of all backgrounds from the 1950s until today. In the final book in the series, *Ella of All-of-a-Kind Family*, the youngest child and only son, Charlie, falls down a gas main while playing with his friends and is seriously injured. Taylor duly informs the reader about Jewish renaming practices:

> "Uncle Hyman came to see me today," Papa remarked. "He keeps begging me to speak to the rabbi about changing Charlie's name."
> "Changing Charlie's name?" repeated Ella.
> "Yes. It's an old, old Jewish ritual that goes back hundreds of years. It is done at a time like this, when a person is very sick."
> "I've heard something about it somewhere, Papa. But why is it done? What's its purpose?"

"I have a book which explains better than I can." Papa looked question-
ingly at Mama. "Will it upset you if I read to Ella about it?"

Mama shook her head. So Papa went to his room and came back with an old
volume in his hand. He rifled through the yellowed pages. "Here it is. It's written
in Hebrew but I'll translate it for you." Adjusting his glasses, he began to read.

"'It is believed that when the Angel of Death comes for a person, he
calls him by name. When they do this, the loved ones are saying, *Go away,
Angel of Death. The one lying here is not the one you seek. He is someone
else bearing a different name. Whatever fate you may have in store for that
other one, you cannot apply to this one.*

"'Sometimes the new name is chosen by opening a Bible at random
and picking out a name which may appear on that page. But more often,
one is chosen which has a meaning. For example, Haim or Haya, which
means life—or Hezekiah, meaning May God give strength—or Raphael,
meaning May God heal. This new name is added to the sick one's name.

"'The change is then discussed with the rabbi, who announces it in
the synagogue. A special prayer is recited, part of which reads, *Just as his
name has been changed, so may the evil decree passed on him be changed—
from justice to mercy—from sickness to complete recovery.*'"

"The whole thing sounds so strange, Papa. It's like something out of the
Middle Ages."

"It is a ceremony that still goes on, Ella. Of course we know that our fate
lies in the hands of the Almighty—not in ours. But it is a last desperate hope—
like a prayer we offer up to God. Surely, Ella, prayer can never hurt, can it?"[4]

And so Charlie is renamed Charles-Irving, and, this being a work for young readers, all ends well: the Angel of Death is fooled, and the boy recovers fully, even to
the extent of reclaiming the name Charlie.

Of course, name changes of Jews have been common in the United States for
reasons other than the one described by either Lucette Lagnado or Sydney Taylor.
It strains the reader's credulity when, in Eileen Pollack's story "The Bris," the son's
reaction upon learning in his forties that his father is not technically Jewish is to
ask, "What kind of Jew is named James Sloan?"[5] All kinds of Jews, as we know,
are named James Sloan—perhaps the family was Slovinsky or Slovowitz in the old
country; a name change to something less apparently Jewish could occur at any
point in the transition to the golden land, starting from arrival at Castle Garden
or Ellis Island, when an immigration officer simplified an unpronounceable surname. Newly arrived settlers might take it on themselves to abandon an old-world
name for something perceived to be more elegant. A tenement denizen in Michael
Gold's *Jews without Money*, Mottke the vest maker, pokes fun at immigrant Jews
who effect such changes: "If his name is Garlic in the old country, here he thinks
it refined to call himself Mr. Onions."[6]

In his study of Jewish names and their histories, Benzion Kaganoff remarked
at the time of publication in 1977 that roughly 80 percent of the applications to

state courts for name changes were placed by Jews; he estimated that about 160,000 Jews modified or substituted their names annually.[7] "A Cycle of Manhattan" gives evidence that changes might be made for a utilitarian purpose, not just "elegance," per se: In the 1920s, Manning Cuyler Ross undoubtedly got into Columbia more easily with that name than if he had retained Emmanuel Rosen-heimer. At this time, as Eric Goldstein relates, college administrators and students alike argued that the character of their institutions was being threatened by an influx of Jews. He reproduces as one piece of evidence a 1923 sign posted by students at New York University with the warning (under the Hebrew characters spelling *kosher*), "Strictly Kosher—Must not APPLY HERE. SCURVY KIKES ARE NOT WANTED At New York University / if they knew their place they would not be here / Make New York University a White Man's College."[8] According to historian Leonard Dinnerstein, Harvard University president A. Lawrence Lowell was so concerned that the percentage of Jews in Harvard had escalated from 6 percent in 1908 to 22 percent in 1922 that with support from alumni and present members of the Harvard community, he publicly announced a limitation on matriculation by Jews into the school. His example spurred similar actions by other institutions, among them Columbia, Princeton, Yale, and Cornell, to mention only a few among many.[9] Criteria for admissions to Columbia were instituted to weed out Jews after Jewish enrollment at the school reached 40 percent in 1919 and were effective in doing so: within two years, that percentage had been reduced by half.[10] Karen Brodkin remarks that "Columbia's quota against Jews was well known in my parents' community."[11] No wonder, as Allyson Hobbs comments in her study of racial passing, that in the early twentieth century, "Jewish applicants changed their names to outmaneuver discriminatory admissions policies that limited enrollments at prestigious universities."[12]

In addition to passing one's way into university, perhaps the desire for an appropriate stage name has been the motivation for change, whether the notion of "appropriate" involves a shortening, an "Americanization," an ethnic erasure, or some combination. The jazz musician Artie Shaw, for example, born in 1910 as Arthur Jacob Arshawsky, wrote of his adopted name, "Doesn't *sound* very 'foreign.' Certainly doesn't sound much like a Jewish kid, either, does it?"[13] Or perhaps one wants simply to be accepted as a friend by non-Jews. Frances Cooke Macgregor recounts the case of one of the rhinoplasty patients she interviewed, who changed his name from Schulberger to Steelman when he left the army after World War II. Macgregor quotes him as explaining, "It was my first act when I left the army because of the fun made of my name. My problem is discrimination. I want an opportunity to make the kind of friends I want." Macgregor adds, "The kind of friends he wanted were Gentiles."[14]

In the 1920s, noted industrialist and antisemite Henry Ford denigrated the Jewish practice of name changing for just this reason. Goldstein reports that

Ford, in his series on the "international Jew" in the *Dearborn Independent*, "drew attention to the practice . . ., exposing it as another means by which Jews tried to blend in to the American mainstream while retaining their racial solidarity." The newspaper singled out prominent attorney Louis Marshall for using an assumed "Anglo-Saxon" name and working to undermine the principle of America as a "Christian nation."[15] Madison Grant's *The Passing of the Great Race* (1916)—termed by Dinnerstein "the most celebrated racist tract of the Progressive era"—included name changing in the litany of complaints about "the swarms of Polish Jews" who, like other unsavory immigrants, "adopt the language of the native American; they wear his clothes; they steal his name, and they are beginning to take his women, but they seldom adopt his religion or understand his ideals." In the late nineteenth century, too, in a statement that undercuts Winslow's Moskowski becoming Moss and Grabinski Graham, the editor of the *New York Sun* scornfully observed, "Thousands of *skys* . . . were being made over into Gordons, without dropping their old *sky* characteristics or taking on manners and accents belonging to their new name."[16]

Another Jew named Marshall would never have come to Henry Ford's notice, since he was merely a hardworking immigrant born in Baghdad in 1888 and living in Brooklyn in the 1930s. That immigrant, Albert Marshall, produced a son, Jack, whose memoir, *From Baghdad to Brooklyn: Growing Up in a Jewish-Arabic Family in Midcentury America*, provides information on name changes as well as much else about the assimilation experience for Mizrahi Jews. In a section of chapter 17 called "What's in a Name," Jack Marshall explains, "Like many European immigrants who felt the need to reconfigure their family names, deconstructing, flattening, or cropping their native 'inskie,' 'heimer,' or witz' to proper Anglo-American size, in order to 'blend in,' my father tailored his Arabic family name to the social norms of his adopted country." Although Kaganoff states that of "the various waves of Jewish immigration to America, the Sephardic Jews steadfastly stuck to their traditional Spanish and Portuguese names (Lopez, Touro, Seixas)," the decision was clearly different for this Mizrahi Jew from Iraq, centuries later.[17] More, the original Arabic family name, *Mah'aal*, was conveniently close to what Henry Ford called an "Anglo-Saxon" name to make the change almost seamless. But most importantly, as his son puts it, "the Anglicized 'Marshall' was used as a badge of safe conduct through the new world of the European mercantile class; much like raising your country's flag in treacherous times to avert suspicion, or daubing a cross on your door at news of an approaching pogrom." For the son as well as the father (and for this family as for Winslow's Ashkenazi family with "heimer" at the end of its original name), an adopted surname is a passing device; as Jack says, "I soon came to feel that in not attaching to me a socially defining identity, this freed me from automatically being assumed a member of any particular ethnic group. If a name could be a cipher, 'Marshall' was as close to being a vacancy as I could imagine."[18]

Freedom versus vacancy: two sides of the coin for interpreting a name change that obscures origins. "A Cycle of Manhattan" reveals both sides, and many other works of fiction also explore this dichotomy. In Fannie Hurst's 1925 story "The Gold in Fish," for one, Morris Goldfish insists on changing the family's name from Goldfish to Fish (and, not incidentally, his first name from Morris to Maurice). When his sister asks why he did not choose to shorten the name Goldfish to Gold instead of to Fish, the brother has a ready answer: "Because Gold is a common and obviously modified name. Everybody has done it that way. Look in the telephone and you'll see fifty Golds to one Fish."[19] Joseph Heller's 1979 novel, *Good as Gold*, plays on this point. In Heller's take on the name Gold, the protagonist, Bruce Gold, with his aspirations toward social status, wishes that he were not Jewish and curries favor with non-Jewish figures like Pugh Biddle Conover. The bigot Conover will give Gold his comeuppance by coyly but deliberately calling him by many clearly Jewish versions of the name Gold: Goldberg, Goldfarb, Finegold, Goldstaub, Goldsmith, Goldstein, and Goldfedder, not to mention the bizarre and insulting substitutes of Goldenrod, Goldilocks, Golddust, Shapiro, Neiman Marcus, Kaminski, Hymie, Manishevitz, Lehman Brothers, Schwartz, Wise, Abie, Rappaport, Ikey-Kikey, Felix Mendelssohn, Silver, Brass—and, in one breath, Goldman, Sachs, Bache, Halsey, Stuart. The frequent connection of Jews with money in this list is another deliberate poke in the eye.

One Gold thus becomes fifty variations in Heller's novel. As I have commented in an earlier study of Joseph Heller, "The strong implication, of course, is that what Conover and Newsome [another gentile figure, a Washington insider to whom Bruce toadies] refer to as 'you people' is a composite of interchangeable parts." As Heller states in an epigraph to his novel (crediting Bernard Malamud), "If you ever forget you are a Jew, a Gentile will remind you."[20] Conover's permutations of Gold's name through Silver to Brass make the author's additional point: that his protagonist's upward mobility devalues him in "a reverse of the alchemical reaction to which Gold aspires," as I have put it. The weight of the novel suggests devaluation in the reader's eyes as well as Conover's. The various Gold siblings may be flawed to one degree or another, but most of the older ones at least are good-hearted individuals, with love for family and religion. Only the California sister, Joannie, who prefers to be called Toni, is akin to Bruce in shallowness. Not coincidentally, she and her husband, Mr. Fink (shortened from Finkleman), belong to several temples for "civic" rather than spiritual purposes; indeed, one of the reasons they changed their name is to "forget we're Jewish."[21]

The Fishes in "The Gold in Fish"—like the Rosses in "A Cycle of Manhattan," the Finks in *Good as Gold*, and the Marshalls in *From Baghdad to Brooklyn*—change their names for "business and social reasons": "Goldfish" is "a liability and not an asset." As the self-christened Maurice puts it, "Morris Goldfish and Maurice Fish are two different human beings. . . . Certain walks of life are closed to Morris Goldfish that I, as Maurice Fish, propose to enter" (256–57). To enter these walks of life, Maurice has engraved calling cards made for the family, with the new, more acceptable name (259). His wife, Irma, sums up: "Maurice and I refuse to continue to be ridiculous because of a name" (258). Although, as Susan Koppelman notes, the removal of Gold from the surname Goldfish is "no longer a secure cover for being a Jew," this is something the Fishes will have to discover for themselves.[22] Predictably, Irma, by means of a rhinoplasty, has also attended to what she would consider a ridiculous, certainly ugly, face, making her nose as suitably sculpted as her name (257). The shortening of the name by the family, however, makes Birdie feel "amputated" (261), a graphic image reminiscent for the reader of *The Ministry of Special Cases* of Pato's loss of a finger and loss of a life, as well as of the nose jobs that Kaddish and Lillian undergo. At the close of Hurst's story, Birdie throws the name Goldfish back at her brother and returns to the family's old home in the Bronx, with her now-widowed mother in tow; the story ends with the simple declaration, "Birdie and her mother. Going home" (281). Although the ending seems rather facile, it does mark a reclaiming of identity, for the mother if not for Birdie (because Birdie never lost it).

A lengthening rather than shortening of a name is the symbolically central plot point in Laura Z. Hobson's *Gentleman's Agreement* (1947). Here, the gentile writer Phil Green, who publishes using his "ritzy"-sounding middle name, Schuyler, transforms himself into a Jew in order to experience antisemitism firsthand; he makes this transformation in part by eliminating his middle name and taking on Philip Greenberg.[23] (His secretary, not knowing his secret, tells him that it's a good thing his name is Phil because a name like Irving or Saul would be a dead giveaway if he were writing to hotels to reserve a room [100].) In a scene reminiscent of several in "A Cycle of Manhattan," but opposite in intent, Green prints the name CAPT. J. GREENBERG in bold caps above the name Green on his letter box in the apartment building, in order to stake a claim, as it were. This is his "calling card," in effect, an advertisement of identity. Immediately the building's superintendent tries to erase that name, because Jews are not allowed as tenants in the building—though the man does not state that fact openly, saying only, "It's the rules. Not in these three houses. The broker should of explained, that is, excuse me, if you *are*" (117–18). It infuriates Green that a veteran who fought for the United States, as he and his friend Dave (a bona fide Jew) had done, should be denied access to housing based solely on religion presumed on the basis of a name. At the same time, the more familiar pattern emerges, as his secretary, Elaine Wales, reveals her own secret when she believes her boss to be Jewish: a Jew herself, she has changed her name from Estelle Walovsky in order to get the job, which had been denied to her twice on the basis of her name (100). It seems that the Human Resources Department of the avowedly liberal magazine editor was engaging in practices he did not know about, which he puts a stop to as soon as he learns of them. These prejudicial hiring practices were as familiar to Jews as they were to blacks before the passage of fair practice labor laws.[24]

In works of fiction written by both Jews and non-Jews, it is common for Jewish characters like Estelle Walovsky to abandon their Jewish-sounding names. In addition to the ones already discussed, Werner Sollors, in footnotes to his analysis of black-to-white passing, incidentally provides a few more, including Anzia Yezierska's *Salome of the Tenements* (1923), Samuel Ornitz's *Bride of the Sabbath* (1951), and Mary McCarthy's *The Group* (1954).[25] Scores more could round out this list, but arguably one of the most clearly symbolic name changes of all is found in Bernard Malamud's "The Lady of the Lake" (1958). In this story, a department store floorwalker named Henry Levin sets off for Europe and a new life, "tired of the past—tired of the limitations it had imposed upon him." Significantly, once he lands in new territory he begins to call himself by a new name: Henry R. Freeman.[26] Immediately the narrator also calls him "Freeman," as if to reinforce the ease with which a man can reinvent himself and erase his history. Our Mr. Freeman will soon become unsettled, however, when a beautiful Italian woman he has just met asks him if he is, perhaps, Jewish. "Freeman suppressed a groan. Though secretly shocked by the question, it was not, in a way, unexpected. Yet he did not look Jewish, could pass as not—had. So without batting an eyelash, he said, no, he wasn't." The narrator repeats Freeman's puzzlement on the basis of the fact that "he absolutely did not look Jewish," thereby emphasizing the all-too-familiar notion that there is a certain "Jewish look" (which Freeman is happy not to possess). Ultimately Freeman puts the issue to the back of his mind, since his "ancient history" is not anything to bother about (227–28).

On his second visit to Isabella del Dongo, on the island that he believes to belong to her, Isabella gives him a tour of the palazzo. Freeman is shocked to learn that the paintings in the gallery, and the statuary outside, are for the most part mere copies of famous artists, and he regrets that he "couldn't tell the fake from the real" (233). Authenticity and its opposite are the twin poles around which the story revolves. Intermittently during their several meetings, Isabella gives Freeman tests to determine his true identity, first by asking him outright if he is Jewish, second by using the pretense of having a moonlight swim so that she can see whether he is circumcised, and third, by asking him whether a mountain formation looks like a menorah or a Virgin's crown. Freeman believes that he has passed all tests.

> However, the worry that troubled him most was the lie he had told her, that he wasn't a Jew. He could, of course, confess, say she knew Levin, not Freeman ... but that might ruin it all, since it was quite clear she wanted nothing to do with a Jew. . . . Or he might admit nothing and let her, more or less, find out after she had lived awhile in the States and seen it was no crime to be Jewish; that a man's past, was, it could safely be said, expendable. . . . Another solution might

be one he had thought of often: to change his name (he had considered Le Vin but preferred Freeman) and forget he had ever been born Jewish.[27] (235)

What bothers Freeman the most is the act of lying itself, "not so much the denial of being Jewish—what had it brought him but headaches, inferiorities, unhappy memories?" (236).

Ironically, Freeman is dismayed to eventually learn from Isabella that her family are not the island's wealthy owners but merely the poor caretakers of the palace; she has been pretending all along, in order to get to America. Her real name is not even del Dongo (just as Henry's is not Freeman). After her confession, Freeman asserts disingenuously that he, for one, is not hiding anything, which elicits her enigmatic response, "That's what I was afraid of" (238). On Freeman's final visit to the island, after he has determined to win her in spite of her circumstances, she asks him the same question she had posed at their first meeting: "Are you a Jew?" Again he tries to pass as a Christian: "How many no's make never?" Isabella then reveals—literally, by uncovering her bluish tattooed numbers—that she had hoped he *was* Jewish, because she had been sent to Buchenwald by the fascists when she was a girl. "I can't marry you," she says ruefully. "We are Jews. My past is meaningful to me. I treasure what I suffered for" (240). Wishing to be a free man, Malamud's protagonist discovers, when it is too late, that others will reject him precisely because they do not wish to free themselves from their past and, by implication, from Jewish history and peoplehood. The past is not expendable to all Jews. Freeman's concept of suffering because of his religion—his headaches and insecurities—proves shallow in light of the reality of *her* suffering. Fittingly, in the last line of the story, Isabella the real woman has disappeared, and Freeman is left embracing only the statuary that, like him, is a fake. He is given no time to finish the admission, "Listen, I—I am—" (240). It is too late for him to reclaim his identity as a Jew, to become Levin again.

Malamud's portrait of a self-denying Jew, especially poignant coming so soon after the full disclosure of the atrocities of the Holocaust, hints at the "headaches, insecurities, and unhappy memories" of life all too common in an openly antisemitic time in the United States. However, Levin's discarding of his Jewish name, if common among assimilating or assimilated Americans, has a counterpart in the opposite strategy: the taking back of an identity marker. The writer and activist Melanie Kaye/Kantrowitz—she of the shiksa nose—recounts the reclaiming of her patronymic in her unusual last name. Her father had changed his name from Kantrowitz to Kaye before her birth, "pressured by the exigencies of being a Jew in the forties, even in New York. 'It was easier,' he'd explain, 'people always called me Mr. K. anyway, they couldn't pronounce or remember it.'" (This excuse is reminiscent of Mr. Rosenheimer's in Winslow's story, when he shortens his name to Rosen.) Kaye/Kantrowitz wryly comments, "(But when have you heard of a Gloucester, a Leicester, a McLoughlin changing his name)."[28] Clearly, the father was trying to avoid the indignities that often besieged a Jew in the 1940s. After her father died, however, Kaye/Kantrowitz took back his birth name and, with it, his identity as a Jew and hers as well, using the unusual punctuation of a slash to indicate that she is either/or and both. In works of fiction, too, names that have been relinquished do not necessarily land in the trash heap of history; they are available for reclamation as an important component of selfhood. Two novels of more than a half century apart illustrate this kind of salvage operation: Jo Sinclair's *Wasteland* (1946) and Dara Horn's *In the Image* (2002).

Wasteland

The name Jo Sinclair, I would note at the start, is a pen name; the author was born Ruth Seid, the child of Russian immigrants. Harper Brothers, the publisher of *Wasteland*, awarded Sinclair a $1,000 prize for the best novel by an unknown writer, and the work continues to be the most familiar of her four novels, although she is largely still unknown to the general reader today. In *Wasteland*, Jacob Braunowitz's name change to John Brown constitutes *the* point of emphasis. No one at the newspaper where he works knows he is Jewish: "His name wasn't Jewish; he didn't look like a Jew, either. Why mention it? Why make a point of it?" (28). Alienated from his parents, especially his father, Brown is emancipated (but, as he will later come to understand, also deracinated): "He was alone. Like he didn't have a country, or a home, or a family—or even a name. He didn't want that man's name anyway! He'd make his own name."[29] Complementing naming as a central motif in this novel is the Jewish holiday of Passover. Brown feels the lure of his family home on that occasion, but at the same time, he has for five years refused participation in the ritual of the seder, at which the story of the Exodus from Egypt is told, and when the youngest child at the table asks the Four Questions. This is when he feels his Jewishness "in the bone and in the flesh, something one could not cut out of himself, or run away from" (65). Yet he does feel cut off: "(You aren't his son, or his name, so how can you ask the questions, how can you say father to him, so who are you anyway?). . . . Nameless. Whatever name he had was a lie." (66) He confesses to his psychiatrist that equating Jews with his father, he is ashamed to be a Jew and "[doesn't] want to be one" (67).

John Brown's sister Debby is the person who has advised him to see a psychiatrist, her own in particular: "He's a doctor, he knows how to name things" (11). The novel's inner monologues as well as the spoken dialogues become part of the conversations between Brown and his doctor. The fact that this psychiatrist is never named only centers attention on his patient's name, emphasizing its importance; on several occasions, the same word, *anonymous*, is used to describe both the doctor and John Brown, but the sense of the word differs for each man:

the doctor's identity is not at stake here, but that of the man who attains anonymity through a misnomer is very much at stake. In the same way that the reader is privy to the thoughts of the main character, so too the author has us look over the shoulder of the psychiatrist, as it were, by presenting us with his notes on the sessions with Brown. The psychiatrist writes of his patient, whom he labels "S" (another name change and cover for true identity): "Further need for identity in S is seen in changing his name. Besides being typically Jewish, that name was given him by father and mother who were never parents to him. The religion of his ancestors is a parenthood, and his parents definitely have failed him. . . . S has felt nameless for some time, began a long time ago the search which has not yet ended—for name, for identity. . . . Yet, through the years, he has not been able to cast off the house. The 'house' is birth, people, family ties" (116). Bit by bit the doctor begins to name the things that John Brown has been unwilling to name, meaning unwilling to face: his birth name and his sister's lesbianism. The first time the doctor calls his patient Jake, Brown feels it as "a terrific, fisted blow" and stammers "after a long pause" that his name is John and that no one save his parents has called him Jake in eighteen years. The doctor says, "It would be good to get used to your own name, wouldn't it? Do you dislike the name itself? Aside from any of the things to which it seems to tie you?" Jake isn't sure, but yet it is "even, in a tiny odd way, a relief to have the moment here." And he repeats the name, as if getting used to it (119).

Passover and the character's name are inextricably linked. Although Jake complains about the seder, and hasn't attended one in years, the doctor diagnoses that at "the same time, S is unable to leave these traditions in his mind, even after he has left them physically, because he feels a strong, groping urge for roots, for the stable cultural, racial, social roots of a people" (180). The pictures in Jake's mind have a bearing on the pictures he creates in his job as a photographer. The psychiatrist writes in his notes that his patient "has tried to keep from these pictures any 'stigma' of family, Jews, self. He has tried to keep these photographs 'untainted,' untouched by the emotions which have tortured him. Yet their great talent, their sensitiveness and art, lie in the fact that into these pictures have seeped his hunger and shame, his tormented family relationships, his 'name'" (222). Putting the word *name* in quotation marks makes it clear that something far larger than a mere name is at issue; a name is a stand-in in this novel for a relationship with one's past—to the family and to the culture of which the family for generations has been a part. The photographs, after psychiatric treatment, become a true record of what the artist sees, both objectively and subjectively. When the doctor uses the word *morgue* in the following remark, he refers literally to the newspaper term for a reference file, but the reader also understands the figurative meaning: the death of identity that his patient had suffered for so long: "S has begun to take his pictures out of the dark corner of the morgue, has shown them to D [Debby] (person of authority, symbol of the world). S has begun to take pictures of his family, made the first attempt to include his family (religious origin, name, self) in his creative self" (223). The novel ends with another Passover seder, with Jake not only present but asking the Four Questions as the youngest son, fully invested. He even takes photographs of the elaborately set table, with "the shine and shimmer of the glasses, the rich look of the wine." The captions he considers are JEWISH HOLIDAY, TWENTIETH CENTURY, or THEY KEEP FAITH IN AMERICA, TOO (317). The reader might adapt the ritual questioning and ask, Why is this night different from all other seder nights? But the weight of the novel makes the answer an easy one: because Jake has seen a psychiatrist and gotten straight with his family, himself, and the world.

The Passover seder is a time of rebirth, as well as a ritual observance of the Exodus from Egypt. As the doctor has said, Passover holds out the promise of "spring and hope" (59), which in this case is hope for regeneration of the wasteland that has been the life of John Brown. The holiday always occurs around the time of the protagonist's birthday; now acknowledging the name Jake instead of John or Jack, Sinclair's protagonist enlists in the Army Signal Corps on his actual birthday, as if this thirty-five-year-old man-child were being born again, into true manhood. Perhaps it is merely coincidental that Sinclair has chosen eighteen as the number of years since her protagonist was last called Jake by everyone, but it is fortuitously symbolic in any case because eighteen is a lucky number in Jewish tradition: in the system of Gematria or numerology, eighteen translates into the word *chai*, or "alive."

How different the take on the Jewish family, Jewish identity, and even the efficacy of self-knowledge through psychiatry is Jo Sinclair's novel from another on similar themes, Philip Roth's *Portnoy's Complaint* (1969). Unlike Alex Portnoy's sessions with his own psychiatrist, who merely begins to address his patient's "complaint" in the final (punch)line of Roth's satiric work—"So [*said the doctor*]. Now vee may perhaps to begin. Yes?"—John Brown's complaint about being a Jew has been addressed throughout the course of Sinclair's work and neatly resolved by the end.[30] Among other developments, Jake can now use the term *sister* for Roz (304) and ask his nephew Bernie not to use the word *nigger* (294). Most significantly, he has taken back the name Jake (if not yet Braunowitz): "All of a sudden I like Jake again" (313). Many contemporary readers will find the conclusion overly tidy, especially because the novel as a whole is very much of the Pollyanna mode in the sense of we-are-of-one blood; indeed, the Red Cross scene of giving blood for the troops overseas literalizes the emphasis on brotherhood, of feeling at one with all elements of society, especially the outsiders like "Negroes": "It's like giving your blood against any kind of segregation there is in the world," says Debby (282). Although the resolution seems pat when viewed with cynical eyes, the novel's hope for regeneration of the wasteland is understandable, since

Sinclair set the story during World War II and published it only a year after war's end. It may be too late for Malamud's anti-hero to reconnect with his history, but Sinclair optimistically offers the final words for Jake, as "with all his heart" he takes on his role and reads, "Wherefore is this night distinguished from all other nights? . . ." (321). In those three concluding dots, supplied by the author, lies the tentative hope, even expectation, that there is more to come.

Indeed, *Wasteland* is all about continuity, encapsulated in the "ancient, ageless" repetition of the story of the Exodus at the seder. Jake tells the doctor about the "meaningful moment" when the youngest son feels himself "in the shadow of history, in the thousands of years of Jews" who stand behind him, and that ahead of him, generations of sons yet unborn will be carrying on the tradition (53–54). This sense of tradition—the long history of Judaism as a religion, and Jewishness as a culture—is exactly what animates all the writings of Dara Horn. Horn, who has a doctorate in comparative literature from Harvard, with a concentration in Yiddish and Hebrew, is the author of five novels—the first appeared when she was twenty-five—along with short stories and essays; she was named one of Granta's "Best Young American Novelists" and has won two National Jewish Book Awards and the Edward Lewis Wallant Award, among several other honors. Except for her third novel, *All Other Nights* (the title taken from the ritual Four Questions at the seder), her novels are nonlinear and proceed by a process of starting in present day and then digging ever deeper into the past in order to uncover origins, secrets, and explanations. Her fourth novel, *A Guide for the Perplexed* (2013), in this sense perfectly replicates her typical philosophical and literary approach to her writing. A layered work, like *In the Image* (her first novel), *The World to Come* (her second), and her most recent, *Eternal Life* (2018), *A Guide for the Perplexed* is partly about the layers of history in the Geniza (storeroom) of Cairo, an ancient treasure trove of thousands of documents from the medieval period, discovered and brought to light by Solomon Schechter in the nineteenth century. Digging down to uncover a personal and cultural past is the essential element of any work by Dara Horn, but *In the Image* is a particularly fruitful work for investigating Jewish naming, renaming, and reclaiming.

In the Image

Benzion Kaganoff utilized for his history of Jewish naming practices the research of a sociologist who had studied Scandinavian immigrants in the United States. That research, in Kaganoff's summary, showed that in this particular immigrant population, the second generation tended to "slough off everything which is foreign and likely to prove an obstacle" to adjustment to the new environment. But the third generation, "already quite secure in their Americanism," is open to a recovery operation: "What the sons of immigrants wish to forget, the grandchildren wish to remember." In his application of this research to the Jewish experience, Kaganoff concluded, "It may well be that the new emphasis on ethnicity and the abandonment of the traditional melting-pot concept will become operative among the younger generation of Jews in their attitude toward changing their family names."[31] Dara Horn brings this concept to life in *In the Image*, which centers on the motif of recovery—though of first names rather than family names.

The novel revolves around two intersecting characters, the young girl Leora (no last name given) and the old man Bill Landsmann, grandfather of Leora's best friend, Naomi, who has recently died in a car accident. Early in the work, Landsmann invites Leora to a slide show of his travels to remote Jewish sites around the world: "We are both interested in Jewish history," he persuades.[32] The author herself is also intensely interested in the subject, as evidenced, for example, in the lengthy disquisitions in this work on Benedict Spinoza and the Prague Cemetery (not to mention the instruction on numerous other elements of Jewish history and culture in her other novels). More to the point, the plot revolves around the reclamation of lost items. The issue of leaving something behind is broached immediately, because the grandfather calls Leora after her first visit to his home to tell her that she has left her sweater and needs to come again to retrieve it (23). The same thing happens after subsequent visits, until Leora realizes that the old man is surreptitiously taking her possessions (sweater, hat, wallet, gloves) so she will return and, in a sense, allow him to reclaim his lost granddaughter (25). In this novel the symbols are, we might say, overdetermined: the glove, for instance, is what Naomi drops and bends to retrieve when she is struck by the car; Leora later finds a lost glove on the road and wonders if "somehow, in some alternative life, all the lost gloves in the world might be reunited with their owners" (32). The reader soon sees that the glove is a stand-in for the artifacts of Jewish history and that the entire novel is a salvage operation.

Chapter 2, titled "In the Valley of Discarded Names," begins to spell out these connections. At the East Mountain Zoo that Leora and her boyfriend, Jason, often visit, the Hasidic Jews on holiday are named Shloymie, Mendie, Gitl, Freydl, and the like—names that modern, assimilated Jews like the parents of Leora and Jason decidedly do not give their children. But the chapter branches out from discarded names to discarded items of worship. The old man in the nursing home where Jason does community service rather puzzlingly enjoins Jason to become a deep-sea diver rather than a soccer player. He soon reveals that when he first came over from eastern Europe, the other Jews threw their tefillin overboard as the ship entered the New York Harbor, anxious to shed their orthodoxy in the belief that "tefillin were something for the Old World, and here in New York they didn't need them anymore" (52). Mr. Rosenthal wants Jason to become a deep-sea diver to retrieve them. Not knowing much about his Jewish heritage, Jason asks Leora what tefillin are, thereby giving Dara Horn another opportunity to provide a lesson in Jewish practice: tefillin are a set of two little black boxes, each containing the central creed of Judaism, the Shema, and connected to leather straps. Orthodox Jewish men affix one box to their arm and one to their forehead to pray each morning, in accordance with the commandment in the Shema (53). Later in the novel, the author shows an Orthodox Jew laying tefillin, to bring the concept to life (254).

After Jason sustains injuries precluding a career as a soccer player, his teammates begin to forget him: "Even people slip out of their minds like things dropped over the deck of an ocean liner." Jason sinks "into the depths"—the author retains the water image while referring to depression—but is "rescued" (55). He becomes friends with classmates named Moyshie, Avi, Shmulie, and Yossie and soon enough transmogrifies into Yehudah (56, 65). Later the novel returns to Yehudah's story, and Horn treats Jason's religious transformation with sympathy—as a valid alternative to what she has called "the anemic element of the way I grew up in a community where it was like, here's Jewish history: There was a shtetl, and there was a Holocaust, and now there's Israel."[33] But at this pivotal point in the novel, when Jason becomes Yehudah, she returns to the subject of names, providing a flashback to an incident in the life of seven-year-old Leora. When her mother found a composition that she herself had written in the first grade, Leora insisted that the essay could not be by her mother because the last name was different. Importantly, Leora was a "conservation-minded child . . . who never allow[ed] her parents to throw anything of hers away," and so she asked who was now using her mother's old name (66). She wondered what happens to those discarded names: "Perhaps there was a place somewhere where all the unused names were gathered, a giant dried-out dessert valley where the names, shriveled and lifeless, lay at the bottom." The author continues:

> As the years passed, Leora met more married women, more immigrants. . . . Slowly there gathered in the Valley of Discarded Names hundreds, even thousands more: Rogarshevsky thrown away in favor of Rosenthal, Rosenthal thrown away in favor of Ross. Ross tossed out for Steinberg (a marriage). Steinberg cast away for O'Brien (a second marriage). Liu discarded for Lou. Anand Gupta for Andrew Gordon. Natalya for Natalie. Wilhelm for Bill. Jesus for Jeff. All those names discarded, only written, not spoken, like the name in the corner of her mother's composition, sitting at the bottom of the valley like untouched bones. . . . Leora knew that Yehudah was a dried-out name, one that Jason had found at the bottom of the valley and that he wanted to speak back to life. (67)

This is the culmination of the chapter, and everything beforehand has led up to it. Lost gloves betoken discarded tefillin and cast-off names, which in turn betoken a Jewish history that cries out for rescuing.

Bill Landsmann can be seen as a stand-in for Dara Horn. Just as his travels and their images on his slides rescue the diversity of Jewish culture around the globe, so too does Horn in this novel and her other works rescue Jewish history for the untutored reader. She takes us back in time to Bill Landsmann's own history, as a boy named Wilhelm in his native Vienna, transformed into Willem in the Netherlands to which his father migrates between the wars. She tells of Willem's fear of being seen as circumcised in the bathroom of the Rijksmuseum in Amsterdam, since the sign out front had read, "No Dogs or Jews Allowed." She notes the enormity of what was lost in the Holocaust: "a language, a literature" (71). And she relates the conditions of sweatshop labor in New York, labor undergone by Bill's grandmother Leah, whose painful story Bill never knew. In fact, in escaping New York for a return to Austria after her husband dies in a fire, Leah throws two things overboard: the tefillin that her father had given her to be repaired in their old town, and "her story," reinventing herself with the fictitious family name of Landsman: "Landsman (or as the government registers would later spell it, Landsmann), a name common enough so that no one would question it, but also a word that had meant so much to her family in America and now meant nothing to her—literally, a word for a person who came from the same place as you, from the same hometown." (161)

Apart from Bill Landsmann, no major character save one has a specified family name in this novel: not Leora or her postcollege love, Jake. The only other surname is that of the man Leah is forbidden to marry because he is a Cohen; by strict Jewish law a Cohen may not marry a divorced woman, no matter that Leah extricated herself immediately from her abusive first husband and never consummated the marriage. Horn needs to provide this name as a plot device, because it explains the succeeding events. Leah and Aaron Cohen in fact do defy her parents by secretly marrying, and she is pregnant with Bill Landsmann's father when she hurriedly leaves for Europe after Aaron dies in a fire. This is when she makes up her new name and new identity. The surname Landsmann is mentioned five times on the novel's very first page, as if to emphasize the notion of a community of Jews (a meaning of the name that Horn withholds until halfway through). What birth name Leora's mother gave up at her wedding is as unknown as her married name (Leora's family name). Leora finds Jake's last name on the conference website, after she listens to his lecture on Spinoza in Amsterdam, but the reader is not told that name (130). And when Willem's father wants to write to his aunts, in order to leave Amsterdam, the narrator notes only the absence of their last names (228). The only name that is important in and to this novel is Landsmann, betokening a person from one's own territory and hence a kin.

All those names "discarded, only written, not spoken . . . sitting at the bottom of the valley like untouched bones" (67) will be filled with life again, as in the story of Ezekiel in the valley of dry bones that Jake explains to Leora (128).

Tefillin have been dredged up from the New York Harbor in a clean-up operation and have found their way to a store of antiques and curiosities called Random Accessories, where Leora stumbles on them while writing a feature story on a skull garnering attention as a missing link. When Jake, as a token of his affection, sends her one of the tefillin, he encloses a note from Ezekiel, chapter 37, verses 13–14: "As I opened your graves, O my people, and brought you up out of them, I shall put my spirit in you and you shall live." (132). Tefillin and names, missing links to the past, are rescued in the course of this novel. So, too, in the literal flood of a hurricane at the novel's conclusion, are a treasured dollhouse, a diamond engagement ring, and pictures from Naomi Landsmann's childhood— the latter saved in advance by Bill's supposedly demented wife, who has rescued them before they were lost by sending them to Naomi's brother in California. The night before Leora is to marry Jake, she dreams that she has become a deep-sea diver and has visited the city lying beneath New York City, under the ocean, "a city made up entirely of things that the people in the world above have forgotten, all that they have decided, deliberately or otherwise, to cast into the ocean" (272). Dara Horn is the ultimate deep-sea diver, recovering aspects of Jewish culture that we may have forgotten or never known, and, in the opposite image, breathing life into dry facts as if they were reanimated bones.

Leora's mother had playfully asked Jake, when he could not produce the name of the predicted hurricane, "Are you one of those people who's bad with names?" (236). Dara Horn, in contrast, is really, really good with names. One of the most interesting parts of *In the Image* is the intricate Landsmann family tree that follows the novel as a kind of afterword. Horn clearly labored over it with love, and the reader who attends carefully to its many branches will find that it "speaks" volumes about names. Least important is the fact that Leora's beloved Jake is actually related to Bill Landsmann, through the line of a brother of Bill Landsmann's grandfather Aaron, the only one of Aaron's siblings who survives the cholera epidemic of 1895 (a relationship hinted at by Jake, when he tells Leora that as a child his mother had told him about a great-uncle trapped on an apartment's top floor and killed in a house fire [171]). Most important are the first names of those on the tree; no surnames are listed. In the generation of Bill's great-grandparents, the names are biblical: Aaron and Miriam, Jacob and Deborah. Leah's generation is replete with Yiddish names—Malka, Sheyna, Gitl, Pessya and the like—along with the familiar names from the Bible, and two on this line change their names when moving to America: Moyshe becomes Morton and Freydl, Frances. The children and grandchildren of Aaron's surviving sibling, Hayyim, stay in Europe (except for Jake's grandmother, who winds up in Holland) and die in the Holocaust with their Yiddish names intact; those of Leah's siblings who migrate to America adopt the practice of Uncle Morton and Aunt Frances in choosing modern, trendy names like Charlotte and Gloria for their offspring.

The names in this part of the family tree change with the fashions in succeeding generations, and thus we find the expected Jill, Sandra, Debbie, Jennifer, and so forth. However, one person down Leah's line eventually marries an Israeli, or so the name Yael would indicate, and their children, born in 2001 and 2002, are named Tamar and Eitan. And lo and behold, Sandra and Brian name their children Sheyna, Gitl, Pessya, Malka, and Hayyim—in another of Horn's abundant coincidences in this novel, these happen to be the exact names of Aaron's siblings at the start of the other line of ancestry. As well, Ann and Neil beget Daniel, Ilana, Shira, and Ari. For a while, a given name could mark a person as from a particular generation, but as Kaganoff has noted, "Styles in name selection continue to change, with every decade or so producing new favorites. Sometimes only a few names survive to be used again in the next generation. At other times a name which has not been used for a number of generations will suddenly become popular and begin to reappear." Names are cultural artifacts, and as such "can serve as clues for deciphering the cultural patterns of Jewish history: from them we can determine whether people's sentiments inclined toward religious separateness or assimilation or Jewish nationalism . . . . And names also reveal something about the political and economic situations of Jews through the centuries."[34] In other words, a name is not a Random Accessory.

Jake tells Leora that he became a historian in order to recover lost things, the things that go underground but never really disappear (173). Through her interest in uncovering aspects of Jewish history that are lost to many readers, and her extensive research skills honed in her pursuit of her doctoral degree, Dara Horn has produced texts that illuminate as well as entertain. Brought up in the same New Jersey town as Philip Roth's Brenda Patimkin, Horn is not only very different from Brenda but also very different from Brenda's creator in her aims and achievements. Saul Austerlitz related, after publication of *A Guide to the Perplexed*, that Horn said she "appreciates the Jewish writers of a preceding generation—'they created an audience for Jewish literature in English'—but feels no particular affinity for their work: 'They were writing a story not any more familiar to me than Junot Diaz talking about Dominican immigrants in Paterson.'"[35]

Horn is one of the best representatives of the contemporary Jewish fiction writer without ambivalence about religion and culture. In the conversation included at the back of the Norton paperback of *In the Image*, she remarks, "I wanted to create a different style for American Jewish literature, one more connected to the Jewish literary tradition of constant reference to ancient text" (unnumbered, penultimate page). The connection came easily to her, as a Jew. As she characterized Judaism, in an essay in the *New York Times*, it is

> a religion unusually friendly to writers. Memory as an article of faith often comes naturally to writers, who by temperament are likely to be diarists and record-keepers, forever searching past events for elusive patterns—and forever

believing that such patterns are to be found. In his essay "The Art of Fiction," Henry James provided many a future writing instructor with a handy opening-day quote: "Try to be one of the people on whom nothing is lost!" For Jewish writers, this advice is almost unnecessary. When you are surrounded by those who honestly believe that the past endlessly repeats—people who name you after your dead ancestors, reread the same book every year, and earnestly inform you that you yourself once stood at Sinai—you are already living in the past, so you don't have to try that hard to be one of those people. . . .

Writers and believers live their lives haunted by the same question: What happens to our days once they disappear? The objective fact is that each day that passes is lost forever, as forbidden to us as the dead. But prayer and fiction offer a different answer. Those lost days still live among us, written in each person's hand, turned into stories.[36]

It is through the reclaiming of names in her first novel that Horn showed the importance that she would place in succeeding works on educating her reading public about the rich heritage of Jewish thought and practice. *In the Image* announces the mission of this Jewish American novelist to tell stories that revive lost days with honor and gratitude.[37]

In the use of naming as a prime motif, Horn bears what might seem like a surprising kinship to an early twentieth-century writer, Anzia Yezierska, best known for her 1925 novel *Bread Givers*, in which the female protagonist seems to want nothing more than to break away from Jewish orthodoxy. Yezierska herself had a tortured relationship to what she regarded as the patriarchal precepts and practices of Orthodox Judaism; her burning aim, like that of the tefillin discarders, was to become a real American. And yet she took pains to reclaim her old-world name some years after being renamed Hattie Mayer when the family came to America. Even more, in one of her unpublished manuscripts, the Jewish female narrator tells of changing her name in order to get a job and then adds, "The day I gave up my Jewish name, I ceased to be myself. I ceased to exist. A person who cuts himself off from his people cuts himself off from the roots of his being, he becomes a shell, a cipher, a spiritual suicide."[38] The word *cipher* is an echo of Isaac Asimov's term, repeated as well by Jack Marshall in his own memoir many decades later. Of course, not every Jew who camouflages an ethnic identity with a new name feels "cut off from the roots of his being," but for many who have maintained, claimed, or reclaimed a first or last name that does serve as an ethnic marker, Asimov's remark resonates: "If I were called anything else, I wouldn't be me."

Notes

1. Asimov, "Seven Steps to Grand Master," 20–21, quoted Koppelman, "Naming of Katz," 232–33.

2. Kolatch, *Name Dictionary*, 314.
3. Lagnado, *Man in the White Sharkskin Suit*, 86, 89.
4. Taylor, *Ella of All-of-a-Kind Family*, 99–100. For background on this practice, see Kaganoff, *Dictionary of Jewish Names*, 101–3.Taylor has been compared to Louisa May Alcott and Laura Ingalls Wilder in writing warmly of close family ties in an earlier era. Although her works do not enjoy the same renown as those of Alcott and Ingalls, they are certainly in circulation today. A non-Jewish mother told me about this series, which her daughter thoroughly enjoys, and the copies in my public library are continually checked out and, by their tattered appearance, well read. Taylor's series on family life in the early twentieth century is as nostalgic a remembrance of things past as such television shows of the era as *I Remember Mama*, about a Norwegian American family in 1910 San Francisco.
5. Pollack, "Bris," 93.
6. Gold, *Jews without Money*, 22.
7. Kaganoff, *Dictionary of Jewish Names*, 69.
8. Goldstein, *Price of Whiteness*, 127, 129.
9. Dinnerstein, *Antisemitism in America*, 84–86.
10. Marcus, "'May Jews Go to College?,'" 138. Marcus elaborates on the situation at Harvard and other schools in the 1920s and 1930s and connects college discriminatory practices to an overall anxiety about Jewish "infiltration" and threats to America's identity as revealed in works by Ernest Hemingway, F. Scott Fitzgerald, and Willa Cather.
11. Brodkin, in *How Jews Became White Folks* (30–32), also provides information on discrimination against Jews in higher education. Her remark about Columbia University's quota is on 32.
12. Hobbs, *Chosen Exile*, 20.
13. *Trouble with Cinderella*, 92, quoted Dreisinger, *Near Black*, 111.
14. Macgregor, *Transformation and Identity*, 99.
15. Goldstein, *Price of Whiteness*, 126. The reference is to *The International Jew: The World's Foremost Problem*. Henry Ford's diatribes against Jews were influential not only on his American readership: as Adolph Hitler told a *Detroit News* reporter, "I regard Henry Ford as my inspiration" (quoted Dinnerstein, *Antisemitism in America*, 83, from Albert Lee, *Henry Ford and the Jews*). Philip Roth's *Plot against America* deals extensively with antisemitism in the United States in the 1940s; it refers to Ford and Father Coughlin's Christian Front (264–65).
16. Dinnerstein, *Antisemitism in America*, 66, 67, 36.
17. In Turkey, for example, family names were not even compulsory until 1935 (Kaganoff, *Dictionary of Jewish Names*, 69, 12).
18. Marshall, *From Baghdad to Brooklyn*, 155–57.
19. Hurst, "Gold in Fish," 262. Subsequent references in the text to this story are to this edition.
20. The line, from Malamud's story "Black Is My Favorite Color" is actually, "If you ever forget you are a Jew a goy will remind you" (80).
21. Heller, *Good as Gold*, 365–76, 83. My self-reference is from *Joseph Heller* (159). See my chapter "What to Do with 'A Jew Like That': Defining Joseph Heller as a Jewish-American Writer," 135–66.
22. Koppelman, "Naming of Katz," 235.
23. Hobson, *Gentleman's Agreement*, 13. Subsequent references in the text to this novel are to this edition.

24. Arthur Miller deals more extensively with this issue in his 1945 novel *Focus*, in which the protagonist is a discriminatory hiring manager—and in which it is assumed that a Miss Kapp, whose name "must be Kapinsky or something," is not the company's "type of person" (see *Focus*, 17). Dinnerstein comments (154–56) that postwar employment discrimination was addressed with legislation that instituted fair labor practices, starting with the Ives-Quinn bill of 1945, but real change was slow to happen. On African Americans passing to gain employment, see Hobbs, *Chosen Exile*, 152.

25. Sollors, *Neither Black nor White Yet Both*, 493nn5–6.

26. Malamud, "Lady of the Lake," 221. Subsequent references in the text to this story are to this edition. Malamud's is not the only work in the United States in which a change of name to some variant of "free man" is salient. An early example is "A Providential Match," by Abraham Cahan, an 1895 translation, with changes, from an earlier version published in Yiddish. In the English version, Mottke Arbel changes his name to Robert Friedman upon arrival in America from Russia. Like Malamud's Henry Levin, Arbel's name change and freedom do not lead to a marriage with the girl of his dreams. The ultimate disappointment of assimilationist strategies like name changing is a constant theme in Cahan's fiction.

27. An interesting commentary on the name Levin as changed to Le Vin is provided by Kaganoff in *Dictionary of Jewish Names* (72). Speaking of name changes, Kaganoff remarks, "Often the changed name loses its distinction when too many co-religionists use it. Levin, a Russian name (cf. *Anna Karénina* by Leo Tolstoy), can be seen as an illustration. Russian Jews were quick to note the easy transition from Levi or Levy to Levin. Soon there were so many Jews using the name that every Levin or Lewin was taken for a Jew. But the name was then given a French twist, in Le Vine, La Vine, Levigne, and even Lhévinne." Malamud's Levin, illustrating this phenomenon, toys with a Frenchified Le Vin.

28. Kaye/Kantrowitz, "Jews in the U.S," 129.

29. Sinclair, *Wasteland*, 65. Subsequent references in the text to this novel are to this edition.

30. Roth, *Portnoy's Complaint*, 274.

31. Kaganoff, *Dictionary of Jewish Names*, 76.

32. Horn, *In the Image*, 17. Subsequent references in the text to this novel are to this edition.

33. Austerlitz, "The Hidden One."

34. Kaganoff, 62, 40. I find my own family history in the list of names that Kaganoff provides to illustrate the changing fashions in naming among Jews in America (62–63). Bessie, Ida, Fannie, and Pearl, to cite just a few common names for female immigrants, are names found in my own grandparents' generation; my mother and her first cousin were both named Harriet, popular for a child of those immigrants; and there I am as Judy in the next generation—not Judith, which I now much prefer, but Judy, which was all the rage at that time, before the arrival of the next crop of favorites: Cindy, Jennifer, Stacey, and the like. And so it goes.

35. In this interview, Horn is also somewhat dismissive of her contemporaries (she names Michael Chabon and Nicole Krauss) who write what she thinks of as sentimentalized versions of Yiddish old-world culture—a position she satirizes in her short story "Shtetl World."

36. Horn, "Articles of Faith."

37. In this context of recovering names, I would mention Julie Orringer's novel *The Invisible Bridge*, about the fate of Hungarian Jews in Nazi occupation, a work referenced

in the Aarons, Patt, and Shechner introduction to *New Diaspora*, 7–8. After the war, the survivors read the thousands of names of their dead on the wall outside the synagogue, and Orringer devotes a very long paragraph to listing scores of these names. As the editors comment, Orringer's novel "is a contemporary kaddish, a Yizkor Book, a chronicle of remembrance" (8). Orringer thus provides another example of naming as reclaiming and of a Jewish author's investment in the Holocaust and Jewish history in general.

38. Interestingly, in a reference to an ethnic marker as obvious at one time as a name— before the rise of cosmetic surgery to alter a "Jewish nose," that is—this unpublished manuscript is titled "We Can Change Our Moses but Not Our Noses" (see Schoen, *Anzia Yezierska*, 7, 129n12).

6 Jews and Gentiles Becoming the Other

"Neither a Borrower nor a Lender Be"

Antisemitism in America

Highlights of the Jewish experience of antisemitism over the course of American history provide useful background for my exploration of Jews and Christians crossing the line into each other's territories. This history begins in the mid-seventeenth century, when a contingent of twenty-three Jews from Brazil landed in New Amsterdam and Governor Peter Stuyvesant allowed them to remain only under pressure from the Dutch West India Company; his disdain for Jews exceeded even that for Quakers and Lutherans. Henry Roth would give the governor an ironic nod in *Call It Sleep* (1934), when he affixed the name *Peter Stuyvesant* to the steamer that brings Albert Schearl's family from steerage to Ellis Island in 1907. Albert finds many obstacles to making it in America, but in Roth's emphasis the man's psychological problems are largely the cause. However, as Leonard Dinnerstein details in his compendious study of antisemitism in the United States, negative attitudes toward Jews have always been a determinative factor in the American Jewish experience, existing alongside the country's valuation of opportunity and freedom. That is, for centuries Jews have lived with and worked around the tension between "deeply ingrained and culturally accepted Christian teachings" and the foundational principle that America is the land of liberty for all (provided one is white).[1]

Governor Stuyvesant's grudging admittance of the Jews was followed by restrictions on jobs, trade, worship, and voting, not only in New Amsterdam but also throughout the colonies. These restrictions were not uniformly enforced, and eventually the Jews in this period gained more acceptance. But as Dinnerstein writes, "The mixed condition of tolerance, ambivalence, and rejection Jews experienced in the colonies was to persist throughout American history" (11).

All during the nineteenth century, students learned from the more than 150 million copies of the popular McGuffey readers that the United States was a Christian country. And in a variety of texts—schoolbooks, nursery rhymes, and children's books among them—"the Jew" was portrayed in a negative light (18–19).

These intertwined lessons were absorbed early, in public school and the home as well as at church. Even in today's religiously and culturally diverse America, the view of the United States as a Christian (Protestant) nation stubbornly persists. Though *Judeo-* is tacked as a prefix onto *Christian*, the reference is clearly to the "Old Testament" predecessor and precursor of Christianity.

In 1840, Jews constituted less than 1 percent of the American population: perhaps fifteen thousand Jews. By 1845, that figure had risen to approximately forty thousand, as central European Jews began to migrate to this country; and by the time of the Civil War, Jews numbered one hundred fifty thousand. In the mid-1800s, German immigrants were urged by prominent rabbis to avoid bringing attention to themselves, utilizing such strategies as diversifying their occupations and making their modes of worship more in tune (literally, in the case of organs in temples) with those of Christian America (26); yet nativism grew and even surged in the 1850s, as anxieties about slavery put the country in crisis mode. Overt antisemitism increased in tandem, including accusations against Jews of using Christian blood for ritual purposes (the "blood libel") and physical attacks on individual Jews and Jewish institutions. "To be sure," notes Dinnerstein, "American antisemitism was on a much lesser scale than Jews had known in Europe, and with no legislative restrictions or governmental support for opposition to them, Jews maneuvered around the bigotry." Some of the additional maneuvers adopted for keeping one's Jewish head down, familiar in earlier generations and common in later ones too, were living and socially interacting with fellow Jews, hiding one's heritage, and changing one's name (29).

The Civil War and its aftermath made the Jews' position in America even more tenuous, and thus Dinnerstein entitles his chapter on the years 1865–1900 "The Emergence of an Antisemitic Society." As Jews both increased in number and achieved financial successes, popular magazines in the United States, as in other countries, portrayed the Jew with stereotypical facial features and habits. Devout Christians agitated to institutionalize Christian doctrine; devotees of the Sabbath Crusade, for example, wanted a Sunday day of rest written into legislation. The reverend Dwight L. Moody held revivals around the country urging the conversion of Jews to Christianity (38). Immigration restrictions were called for, to halt the influx of various undesirables and to reserve the United States for the "real" Americans—those of Anglo-Saxon heritage.[2] In 1879, the American Society for the Suppression of the Jews, formed by members of the elite of the Gilded Age, met with around one hundred in attendance. Said one leader, owner of an exclusive, restricted hotel in Coney Island, "If this is such a free country, why can't we be free of the Jews?" The group adopted resolutions for themselves prefiguring the fiats hardened by Hitler into law for his regime years later: no election of Jews to public office, no attending theaters producing works by Jewish composers or acted by Jews, no buying or reading books authored by Jews, and the list goes on (40). Although this society was short-lived, barring Jews from clubs, resorts, and private schools ensued.

The practice of constraining Jews from vacation spots and other venues picked up dramatically in the 1920s, fomented in part by Henry Ford's diatribes in his *Dearborn Independent* and no doubt influenced as well by the Red Scare after World War I, when charges of radicalism and socialism were added to those of race and religion already leveled against Jews. (This is when the ardent communist writer born Itzok [Isaac] Granich, who first published under the less Jewish name Irwin Granich, legally neutralized his name to Michael Gold.) Signs and newspaper advertisements for resorts were often quite explicit: "A hotel exclusively for Gentiles," for example, or "Adverse to association with Hebrews." Restrictive housing covenants were levied against Jews and other minorities: owners of apartment houses could legally prohibit "Catholics, Jews, and dogs" until the Supreme Court outlawed such covenants in 1948. Jews founded their own clubs and resorts as a result of these discriminatory practices and managed to find housing in cities and suburbs; often when the Jews moved in, the gentiles fled (92–94).

Accessing jobs was equally problematic. University employment, for one, was as difficult for Jews to obtain as college admission. Jewish faculty members at colleges and universities numbered fewer than one hundred in the 1920s, and the recommendation letters of some distinguished professors who did find positions contained endorsements damning with faint praise: "has none of the offensive traits which people associate with his race"; "by temperament and spirit . . . measure[s] up to the whitest Gentile I know"; "is a Jew, though not the kind to which one takes exception"; "one of the few men of Jewish descent who does not get on your nerves and really behaves like a gentile to a satisfactory degree." Employment outside of academia was also discriminatory, whether overtly so or cloaked, and the list of businesses engaging in such practices was extensive. One factory owner summed up the situation rather neatly, if convolutedly: "We try to have only white American Christians in our factory regardless of religion." Even the personnel department of a company whose major shareholder was a Jew—Sears, Roebuck—would not hire Jews in the 1920s (88–89, 103).

In the 1930s, the Depression and the rise of Hitler exacerbated Jewish scapegoating here as abroad. More than one hundred antisemitic organizations were founded in the United States between 1933 and 1941 (only about five such associations having been created in all of American history previously), and several looked to Hitler for inspiration. Even President Roosevelt's heritage was questioned because of his Jewish cabinet appointments and his "Jew Deal"—surely there must be Rosenthals or Rosenbergs in his background (109–12). In fact, when the president passed away, one college professor commented, "The best damned thing that ever happened to America was when that Jew in the White House,

Rosenfeld, died" (136). (The only "Jewish name" with Rosen in it that seemingly was not attributed to the president was Rosenheimer.) As influential as Henry Ford had been on American attitudes in the 1920s, with his scurrilous newspaper accusations against Jews, Father Charles Coughlin matched him in the 1930s with his radio broadcasts, whose influence extended into the 1940s. Even members of Congress openly praised Father Coughlin and voiced similar antisemitic sentiments: as but one example, John Rankin of Mississippi attributed the push toward war in 1941 to an international conspiracy of Jews, insisted that all Jews were communists, openly used words like "kike" and "nigger," and in other ways voiced the prejudices of many elected officials *and* ordinary citizens (135–36). During World War II, surveys of high school students and factory workers revealed that Jews were second only to "Negroes" as the most undesirable group for roommates or neighbors. Those reporting criticism of Jews heard in ordinary conversations rose from 46 percent in 1940 to 64 percent in 1946 (131–32). Even the American military provided antisemitic materials to the soldiers and overlooked antisemitic actions by chaplains and other personnel.[3]

After the war, antisemitism abated, at least openly and blatantly, among the general populace. By 1951, the percentage reporting that they overheard criticism of Jews had dropped to 16 percent, and with some ups and downs, that figure fell to 12 percent in 1959. By 1950, 69 percent had no objection to a Jewish neighbor, and by 1954 the figure had risen to 80 percent. Only a quarter of resorts had restrictions against Jewish patronage by 1957, and within five years the practice had all but disappeared (157–58). Factors reducing discrimination against Jews after World War II include, among others, the revelation of Hitler's atrocities, the resolve of returning servicemen and women to decrease discrimination at home, exposés of prejudice in mainstream films and magazine articles along with more academic publications, and a general postwar optimism about opportunities in the United States. President Truman made a statement about American priorities by setting up panels and commissions to address racism and bigotry in employment, education, and other arenas; by ending racial segregation in the military; and by proposing a civil rights bill in 1948 (151–52). Civil rights groups of all stripes gained more clout to fight discrimination. With all this progress, the 1950s encouraged hopefulness on the part of all American groups who had suffered so grievously from prejudices against them.

However, fifty-seven antisemitic organizations remained in 1950, and in the 1950s and 1960s, several publications continued to blame Jews for the world's ills. In 1955, Will Herberg, in *Protestant, Catholic and Jew: An Essay in American Religious Sociology*, remarked that many Americans were, in fact, antisemitic but refrained from acting on it since it was no longer respectable to do so. Squelched antisemitic attitudes could and did come above ground and gain expression in action on many occasions. Dinnerstein remarks of an upsurge of antisemitic acts in New York in 1959–1960 that "this kind of recurrent vandalism, waxing and waning periodically without any particular rhyme or reason, serves as a constant reminder of the unpredictability of aggressive antisemitic incidents." If overt antisemitism went "out of fashion, accompanied in many cases by a sense of bad conscience," it nonetheless "remained as a generally unexpressed undercurrent that surfaced at unexpected moments in different parts of the United States" (157–58, 163, 165).

Dinnerstein's 1998 study ends on an optimistic note, with certainty that anti-semitism would continue to decline "in potency" in succeeding years (170). In certain respects his optimism has borne fruit, but his own evidence reveals that from time to time, and especially in moments of instability, undercurrents of antisemitism will surface in spite of this country's lip service to cultural plural-ism. And so it is today. If in the 1930s many believed that "Jew bankers run the government," as one woman wrote to President Roosevelt (109), similar charges have been leveled against President Trump's administration. So far these charges are expressed by right-wingers and white nationalists, who fault the president for having an inner circle of Jewish advisors who are leading the country away from Trump's campaign promise of America First. No one has as yet imputed Jewish heritage to our forty-fifth president—no Trumpstein or Trumpberg is alleged to (dis)grace the family tree—but as an article in the *Forward* headlined, "'Alt-Right Sees 'Jewish Coup' in Trump Policy Flips."[4] Even more troubling than words is the rise in anti-Jewish incidents of violence and vandalism in the past couple of years. In the present climate of intolerance, when rebutting prejudice is often scorned as "political correctness," continued progress on racial, religious, and gender issues is disturbingly in question.

With regard to prejudice against Jews, Jonathan Judaken informs that the term *antisemitism*, coined in 1879 by Wilhelm Marr, has a racial basis, from the philological and anthropological distinction between Aryans and Semites. He rejects its supposed opposite term, *philosemitism*, because it likewise implies that Jews are a group with a particular essence or set of characteristics, in this case to be admired. Dinnerstein points to the liberal Protestant weekly the *Christian Century* as evidence of how easily Christians' supposedly philosemitic defenses of Jews could devolve into blaming Jews for bringing on discrimination by their own behaviors and calling for Jews to convert (109–10). As Judaken illustrates, even those whom he characterizes by his awkward preferred term, *anti-antisem-ites*, "can become entangled within the nefarious stereotyping in their efforts to oppose [antisemitism]." That is to say, anti-antisemitism is as complex though "less ideologically charged" than philosemitism.[5] With these ideas and this his-tory as background, I turn now to fictional and real-life situations in which, for differing reasons, gentiles and Jews aspire to become the other and hence "borrow" each other's identities.

The Gentile as Jew

In act 1 of *Hamlet*, in the well-known words of my chapter's subtitle, Polonius advises his son, Laertes, that monetary exchanges in the form of loans and debts might well result in the loss of friendship and thus are to be avoided. Eileen Pollack's story "The Bris" (first published in 2006) owes much to Polonius's admonition, which this author adapts, one might say subverts, to reinforce her point about generosity as a necessary component of love. Pollack's highly original, contemporary take on the passing narrative not only serves as a fitting introduction to the subject of gentiles and Jews trading places but also commands examination on its own merits. Previously included in *Best American Short Stories* in 2007, the work was reissued in the collection *The New Diaspora: The Changing Landscape of American Fiction*. As the editors of this anthology explain, they have chosen "to introduce new writers and recognize those whose work has been relatively neglected." Identity issues remain central in the changing landscape traversed by these authors, but they often take a different form: "ironized, detached from the traditional anxieties about acceptance and exposure."[6] Pollack's story is a prime example.

"The Bris" centers on the secret of a beloved father and his extraordinary request of his son to help him complete a passage long overdue. In this tender story, *passing* is used in both senses: the father, James Sloan, who is about to pass (to die) in his eighties, reveals that he is actually a gentile passing as a Jew (an Orthodox Jew, to boot). "Not only am I not an Orthodox Jew, I am not a Jew of any kind," he admits in extremis, and Marcus is understandably dumbfounded: "This isn't making sense. All these years and, what, you've only been pretending to be a Jew?"[7] As if this revelation were not destabilizing enough for his adult son, who now has to reconcile a long held perception of his father's identity with the truth of that identity, the father asks that the son facilitate an unorthodox—to say the least—late-in-the-day circumcision.

How did this astonishing situation come to pass? World War II had given the father a way out of his strict Baptist upbringing in Texas; he felt somehow at home with Jews in the army and, afterward, in New York. Pretending to be Jewish was not something he took on deliberately: "He hadn't taken the job at Lieberman's [a Catskill hotel] with the intention of passing as a Jew. It was just that once he got there, everyone assumed he was one" (89). He had wanted to convert but was afraid to be circumcised, and Marcus phrases his realization about why he had never seen his father naked in terms of another kind of passing, with reference to an I. B. Singer story and perhaps the Streisand film adaptation: "The realization that his father's obsessive modesty had been a deliberate sham made Marcus feel as foolish as a shtetl wife who's just learned that she's been a dupe of a Yentl-like deceiver, so ignorant of the facts of life she couldn't figure out that her 'husband' was a woman dressed up as a man" (89). Now that the father is about to die, he is insistent on being circumcised so that he can be buried in an Orthodox cemetery next to his beloved wife (who knew of his secret); otherwise the ritual bathers of his corpse would of course discover his foreskin and block the burial. Marcus— who has been to a bris only twice and was too squeamish to watch the cutting both times—feels incapable of honoring his father's request.

Pollack weaves into her story an important motif of repaying debts, playing with the contrast between a cash nexus and connections forged by love. Marcus has always prided himself on his independence, including from a father who has done everything for him and to whom the debt has always seemed too large to repay: "Marcus felt like a gambler who could never repay his bookie. Better to . . . run away, start a new life, put your debts behind you" (91). But now the father calls in the chits, as it were. When the son flies to Florida for what must surely be the last visit, he is instructed to find a certified *mohel* (ritual circumciser) to perform the circumcision and to convince the father's rabbi, Dobrinsky, to sign an Orthodox certificate of conversion. As the plot line so far would indicate, the search for a solution to James Sloan's problem—which he has foisted onto his son—is rather madcap, like something from the Marx Brothers movies the two had always enjoyed together.

Marcus Sloan's quest is not an easy one. For one, Rabbi Dobrinsky, who the father said would be on board, balks at doing what is asked of him: "I have known your father nine years. . . . We discuss politics and theology. More than that, we are friends. So don't you think it's a shock, all of a sudden he tells me he's not a Jew? Against non-Jews I have nothing. But against non-Jewish friends who pretend to be Jewish. . . . Pardon me if I do not believe that the reward for so many years of deceit should be an easy deathbed conversion" (96–97). But the rabbi can be "bought," as it turns out: a stickler for rules, he bends them—or suggests he will—if Marcus will fill in for a doubles tennis match. Then the rabbi changes the rules, stipulating how many games Marcus and his elderly, feeble partner have to win before the rabbi will consider the request. When Marcus's return serve hits the rabbi in the eye, Dobrinsky reneges: "This is the Almighty's way of reminding me what happens to those who turn a blind eye to deception. . . . I can't be party to more betrayals" (99). That the rabbi has betrayed his friend, and Marcus, by going back on his bargain not once but twice seems not to have occurred to him.

Marcus's next task is to find a doctor who will perform a circumcision on a man who is not just elderly but actually dying. He locates a potential prospect in the pediatrician Dr. Schiffler. An accountant by trade, Marcus and his lawyer ex-wife had always been precise, allocating equal labors and equal shares of household expenses in the marriage. Now Marcus must operate outside his comfort zone:

> Marcus related his quandary [to the doctor], although even as he spoke he wondered what kind of madman would be telling such a tale. Usually, when he entered a doctor's office, it was in his capacity as an accountant. . . . Now Marcus was the *shnorrer* [beggar].
> It wasn't a position he favored. In high school, they'd read a play in which Marcus had found a line that encapsulated his own philosophy: *Neither a borrower nor a lender be.* Yet here he was, begging favors from everyone he met. Only the fact that he was begging these favors on his father's behalf lent the begging some nobility. (101)

Dr. Schiffler refuses to perform the procedure, but Marcus, on his way out of the office, steals from the nurses' station the tools he will soon need: bandages, gauze, letterhead, and a lollipop. This taking is part of an incipient plan for the giving. Now Marcus will be the one to tell a lie, that the rabbi *and* the doctor are on board.

When James Sloan is returned to his condo from the hospital, to die at home as he wishes, Marcus is "unable to think of anything except how much he owed this man and how little he could do to pay him back" (105). So again he looks for a mohel, and the one whom he finds in an outdated directory is reminiscent of Malamud's otherworldly marriage broker Pinye Salzman in "The Magic Barrel"; that is, he seems almost like a figure conjured up out of need, living in a rundown section of town in a cottage "laden with . . . the odor of salted fish" (106). When the man refuses Marcus's generous sum—all the money that Marcus has left—Marcus has an epiphany: he has no need of a specialist; *he* will become the mohel, if an ersatz one. Having gotten his father drunk on Manischewitz wine (what else?), Marcus exposes his father's genitals, gives several twists and turns, applies the gauze and bandages, and tells his father another lie, that the rite has been performed (108). Though the author does not use the word, she makes it clear that this is a mitzvah, usually defined as a good deed but more technically a commandment (just as performing a circumcision on the eighth day of a boy's birth is a commandment for Jews). Surely Pollack is referencing, and rewriting, the story of Noah and his son Ham, who saw his father naked after Noah was in a drunken stupor from imbibing too much wine. In Genesis, Noah curses Ham and his descendants, the Canaanites. James Sloan, in contrast, is comforted by the deed he believes has been done (in the author's powerful expression, he savors the bliss), and when he mistakenly praises Dr. Schiffler for performing the circumcision—"See. This is how a real Jew behaves" (109)—the reader understands that the real Jew here, other than James, is Marcus. It is insignificant that, at first glance, Marcus thinks that the "penis as a whole was nothing like Marcus's own.... *How can you be my father? How can I be your son?*" (108). Marcus becomes like his father in the generosity of the act, in giving what is asked of him, no matter how difficult the labors—in making sure the father has his bris, complete with a lollipop. Sweet indeed.

Marcus even symbolically *becomes* his father when James asks him for one more favor: immersion in the *mikveh* (ritual bath) that is de rigueur at such a passage. Swaddling his helpless father and carrying him to the nearest lagoon, Marcus tenderly bathes him "the way a parent bathes a child." Since a faux circumcision has been performed, the entire charade will of course soon be discovered, and the father will not be interred in the Ahavath Yisroel Orthodox cemetery after all; in a time to come, Marcus will go so far as to disinter his mother and her parents so that they can be buried with James. But all this is beyond the conclusion of the story. For now, as Marcus stands in sludge and Rabbi Dobrinsky, a latecomer in more ways than one, recites Hebrew prayers, Marcus's thoughts re-echo the story's theme and signal the lesson that Marcus has learned about being a "lender":

> Oh Pop. . . . *you were such a generous man. Why did you stop a few millimeters short of doing all you could?* Because even if a person was asked to cut off his foreskin, or, for that matter, his entire cock, he needed to give and give and give, no matter how frightened the giving made him, no matter how much it hurt.
>
> Marcus raised his face to the star-drenched sky, and . . . composed his own prayer of thanks for having been allowed to repay even a small part of the debt he owed his father. Although really, it didn't make much sense to keep track of such matters, any more than it made sense to measure what the sun and stars gave a person as opposed to what that person gave to the sun and stars. (110)

Pollack had earlier included a brief scene in which Marcus drives by a homeless man selling newspapers that nobody wants because begging has been outlawed; the fact that even beggars have to sell something, engaging in a cash transaction that is quid pro quo, causes Marcus to think, "These days, no one was allowed to give anything away for free, not even charity" (94). I have saved for last, in this discussion of "The Bris," one more important character in this story: Marcus's girlfriend, Vicki, who, unlike the ex-wife, is happy to give, give, and give again without keeping track or expecting something in return. Marcus has vacillated about marrying her and having children with her, but the lessons from his father have him imagining bathing his children with her, as he is now bathing his father at the story's conclusion. He has heeded another deathbed commandment from his Pop: "'Marry her!' his father whispered hoarsely. 'Marry that girl today!'" (104). And why not? "It struck him that his marriage, like most of his friends' marriages, had failed because each member of the couple had been so wary about being asked to give more than his or her fair share. What he loved about Vicki was her generosity. . . . She assumed that Marcus was as generous as she was, and her love and good opinion kindled in his heart a desire to give" (101). Having given in to that desire, he is ready to take the next step. "The Bris" revolves around a bizarre set of circumstances and comic absurdities, detailed almost mythically (the quest, the impossible challenges) yet relatable on a realistically human level. More, a story that seems to poke fun at orthodox religion is actually quite religious, for it is a homily about "the nobility of begging" and the nobility of giving and, not incidentally, about a dying father's request (and trust) of his son and a son's love for his father. It is also, in the words of the editors of *The New Diaspora*, "a classic identity-as-quandary fable upended, the Gentile in search of acceptance and self-validation now desiring to be a Jew."[8]

The twin motifs of a gentile passing as a Jew and the need for a proper bris by a mohel appear in another story in the same collection as Pollack's: "Electricity" (1993), by Francine Prose. Prose employs these motifs quite differently, however. In her version of the passing story, Sam, at age fifty-seven, undergoes a religious transformation and becomes frum as a member of a Hasidic sect in Brooklyn. When his daughter, Anita, asks him about the time they missed attending a relative's bar mitzvah years before, Sam laughingly responds, "Anyhow, we didn't miss anything. Simon was bar-mizvahed in the Reform temple. The church." To this man, who used to turn off all the lights to save money on the family's electric bill, the light bulb of true religion went off one day, and in effect, he became electrified.

Sam's first words upon meeting his months-old grandson for the first time are a question—"Has he been circumcised?"—and he immediately insists that Bertie, who was in fact circumcised in the hospital, have another rite in the home, performed properly by a mohel. To this once-Reform Jew, Reform Jews are hardly Jews at all—the implication of the word "church," of course, is that they are little more than gentiles pretending to be Jews. Sam's wife feels his transformation as an abandonment, akin to that experienced by their daughter, whose husband has just left her and their baby for another woman; Edna can only wish that her own husband return to his "normal self." But that is where the similarity ends, for in the long run this is not a story about abandonment but rather about connection. Notwithstanding the daughter's initial skepticism about her father's being "born again," the story does not in fact denigrate the Hasidic way of life; to the contrary, it shows the strength and vibrancy of that movement, and its attractive qualities to Anita herself, who feels an electric pull to her father at the story's end. (Whether Anita will make that passage herself is unknown and not truly important.) Incidentally, the story also reveals the underlying reason why some Hasidim set up shop all over the world to proselytize to Jews, a situation to which Prose briefly alludes: not only the Reform Jews in Prose's story, but by extension all non-Orthodox Jews, are inauthentic Jews, almost like gentiles passing as Jews.[9]

Both "Bris" and "Electricity" are varieties of the gentile-to-Jew passing narrative, notwithstanding the irony that Sam was already a Jew—though in his post-"conversion" estimation, a pretend Jew. Certainly Prose's story, like Pollack's, illustrates, albeit in a very different way, the search for "acceptance and self-validation" as a religious Jew. An intriguing autobiographical work of an earlier period, Leah Morton's *I Am an American—and a Jew* (1926) may also be regarded as a passing narrative by a gentile posing as a Jew, in spite of the fact that through the decades it has not only been accepted as an accurate record in the main of the author's Jewish life but has also been featured in literary studies, course syllabi, and the general readership as a sterling representation of the tensions between ethnic and national identities. According to the memoir by Thomas Stern, the author's son, however, "Leah Morton"—a pseudonym for Elizabeth Stern—was masquerading as a Jew. In fact, the son's investigation for the sake of setting the facts straight, and hence finding his own identity, shares key features with family histories by later writers James McBride and Danzy Senna, to be discussed in the next chapter. Central among these features is a parent's hidden identity, overlaid and disguised with the patina of self-invention.

The gradual evolution from the wholesale acceptance of the Elizabeth Stern story to its problematizing in the 1990s has not resulted in surety but, rather, in reimagining *I Am an American—and a Jew* as an example of the kind of work Laura Browder calls ethnic impersonation. In the early to middle years of that decade, two collections on American literature included Stern in the context of Jewish American writers. The 1991 anthology *Writing Our Lives: Autobiographies of American Jews, 1890–1990* contains an excerpt from Stern's best seller and, in a preface, details Stern's history and asserts her importance as a woman able to negotiate a treaty between being Jewish and being American. The 1995 *Oxford Companion to Women's Writing in the United States*, in the section on Jewish American writing, begins tentatively to question the authenticity of the narrative; the editors state that the memoir combines "autobiographical material with fictional episodes" and note that "Stern's own background is murky: Ellen Umansky, who edited *I Am an American—and a Jew*, believes Stern may have been Christian by birth but adopted by a Jewish family." Yet a few pages later in this compendium, the description of Stern seems again to assume, or at least imply, that she was a Jew, one who "reject[ed] Jewish orthodoxy and traditional feminine roles in favor of assimilation. . . . Her narrative is complicated, however, when she encounters anti-Semitism and when she feels the powerful yearning to be back within the stable structures of her former life."[10]

By the 2000 publication of Laura Browder's study of ethnic impersonators, Elizabeth Stern's "murky" life had come into sharper relief because of her son's accounting of it. Thomas Stern had published his own memoir in 1988, entitled *Secret Family*, which asserted that his mother was actually the illegitimate child of a Welsh Baptist mother and a German Lutheran father. Browder recounts how, according to the son's findings, Stern was raised in the foster home of a Jewish couple for a decade, from 1907 to 1917, but eventually returned to the home of her mother. Her marriage to another illegitimate child likewise raised in a Jewish foster environment allowed both husband and wife to take on Jewish identities when it was convenient for them, but neither was a convert to Judaism. Indeed, Stern's identity was particularly fluid, according to her son, as quoted by Browder. In addition to saying that she was Elizabeth Levin, daughter of a rabbi, she "often boasted that she was the daughter of a prosperous German merchant, Chris Limburg [the actual name of her Christian father]. And often she boasted that she was a Morgan, the offspring of 'important people' in Pittsburgh, who were Welsh or English. Sometimes Elizabeth admitted that the Morgans were coal miners, even though that lowered her status."[11]

The accuracy of Thomas Stern's accounting of his mother's shifting identities, and of her eventual decision to pass as a Jew, cannot be verified in full because Elizabeth Stern destroyed the body of evidence. Ellen Umansky's introduction to the 1986 edition of *I Am an American—and a Jew* presented Stern and her husband as Jewish, in great part because they were married by a prominent Orthodox rabbi in Pittsburgh, as revealed in a copy of their 1911 marriage certificate. But Umansky's essay on Stern in 1993 takes into account the letter she had received from Thomas Stern the year before, along with her further communications with him and her own research to try to verify his claims about the facts of his mother's life and identity. Umansky was not able to find conclusive answers to this riddle, only "scattered pieces of information," hence the "murkiness" to which the editors of the *Oxford Companion* allude, but she does refer in this essay to *I am an American—and a Jew* not as a memoir but as a work of fiction with autobiographical elements. She remarks that if Thomas Stern's "story of his family's origins—a story that apparently took him thirteen years of research to unravel—is even half true, it sheds new light on Elizabeth Stern's representation of Jewish women in her two 'Jewish' novels: *My Mother and I* and *I Am an American—and a Jew*. It also sheds new light . . . on Elizabeth's self-representation as a Jewish immigrant, born into a family of devoutly religious Eastern European Jews."[12] Laura Browder's discussion of Elizabeth Stern explores possible motives for Stern's self-representation as a Jew and even for that Orthodox ceremony, yet ultimately what is most salient is the fact that, in defiance of her son's protestations that she "shouldn't publish that book! It isn't true! It twists our family! It makes us what we are not," Elizabeth "screamed, 'I have to publish my book! It makes me what I want to be.'"[13]

Probably the best-known gentile-to-Jew passing story in American literature is *Gentleman's Agreement* by Laura Z. Hobson, a Jewish woman born Laura Zametkin, daughter of a cofounder of the *Forward* and raised in a nonreligious, socialist environment. A 1944 letter to Hobson from noted journalist Dorothy Thompson, in which Thompson stated that antisemitism cannot be erased because the majority of Americans "don't like the race as a whole," no doubt strengthened Hobson's resolve to offer an education and a corrective to the American public.[14] A post–World War II phenomenon, the novel laid bare the rampant if sometimes genteel antisemitism of the times just as John Howard Griffin's *Black Like Me* would later expose for the general public the anti-black sentiment in the 1950s. Hobson's best-selling novel was immediately made into a feature film starring Gregory Peck and Celeste Holm; extremely successful, it won three Academy Awards and was nominated for eight. Both versions follow reporter Phil Green as he masquerades as a Jew and sets about experiencing antisemitism firsthand in order to create a series of essays for a popular magazine.

John Minify, Green's editor at *Smith's Weekly*, believes (correctly) that anti-semitism in America is rising among the general populace and thereby merits an exposé. But even before Green comes up with his idea for approaching the subject, his sister is displeased that he has decided to take on the assignment at all. One of the "smart set" in tony Grosse Pointe, Michigan, Belle uses the expression "Jew us down" and Phil does not even register it, being, as he later puts it, tone-deaf.[15] Soon his hearing starts to sharpen to insults that non-Jews let slide: a cab driver's disparagement of "rich Jews" (39), a congressman's reference on the House floor to a columnist as "the little kike" (52), popular novels' portrayals of Jews in nega-tive stereotypes (55). Finally he comes up with an idea he cannot "pass up": the idea to pass *as* (63–64). He and Minify plan out the campaign for Phil, posing as a Jew, to uncover antisemitism in the many arenas known to possess it: "Clubs, resorts, apartment leases, social life. Interviews for jobs, applications to medical schools. Perhaps some trips to 'trouble spots' that came into the news" (73).

Because he doesn't "look Jewish, sound Jewish" (64)—meaning, no doubt, that he doesn't have a prominent nose, or speak with a pronounced New York or Yid-dish-inflected accent, or use Yiddish terms—Phil Green is able to play double agent so he can pick up anti-Jewish remarks that would not be delivered directly to a Jew. The novel plays with stereotypes and, some might say, indulges them as well. Phil Green's nose is "straight," though Hobson immediately has him remember that his Jewish childhood friend, Dave, also has a straight nose. Another Jewish character in the novel, Joe Lieberman, has a "beaked nose," but the narrator is quick to clar-ify that this nose is what one finds on "the face of a Jew in a Nazi cartoon" (122). Yet Baz Dreisinger, writing of the film version of *Gentleman's Agreement*, comments that the film pays only "lip service to the idea that Jews are physically no different" from non-Jews. Agreeing with a 1948 review of the film in *Commentary*, Dreisinger points to the facts that both Miss Wales, the secretary, and Dave Goldman, the friend, "look quite different" from everyone else, the former with a bigger nose and the latter with a shorter stature and curlier hair than the Christian characters.[16]

I concur with Dreisinger's insistence that the film has it both ways in asserting that Jews are both not different and different; I also find confusions on this point. Perhaps June Havoc was chosen for the role of Elaine Wales, née Estelle Walovsky, because she had a prominent nose, though she was not in fact Jewish, and perhaps the Jewish actor John Garfield was chosen to play Dave precisely because he looked stereotypically Jewish as well, in his own way. In the novel, however, Dave is "tall and lanky" like Phil (64), and Miss Wales is described only as "intelligent, quick, interested" (94) when she first arrives on the scene; later, her physical qualities are emphasized: blond hair and pale skin, high cheekbones that "made her seem Scandinavian, Slavic, something foreign and interesting" (99). After Miss Wales reveals herself to him as a Jew, he still sees her as the "Nordic type; the Aryan type" (191) because of her looks—thereby reinforcing Green's original thought that he could pass a Jew because Jews don't all look the same. Indeed, in these qualities she does resemble the actress who played her on screen, who was in fact of Scandinavian heritage.

Even in the novel, the issue of what a Jew "really" looks like is problematized. Miss Wales uses the word *kike* to refer to the "wrong" kind of Jew, prompting Green to ruminate on the various possible reasons for what some today would call Jewish self-hatred and what Hobson in this novel refers to as "an unconscious longing, hidden and desperate, to be gentile and have the 'right' to call Jews kikes." Green realizes that the fact that neither of them looks "especially Jewish" makes them "O.K. Jews; they were 'white' Jews" (155). In this context, I note the remark by one of Frances Cooke Macgregor's interviewees in her study of cosmetic surgery recipients, who said he wanted a rhinoplasty because if his nose was altered, "then I can show them [gentiles] by my behavior that there are nice Jews. I'll be a 'goodwill ambassador. I can prove to people that I'm not only a 'white man' but a 'white Jew.'"[17] So there is a typical Jewish look, after all, and it is not white. To be sure, some Jews may be tall and have straight noses, but in that regard they don't look "especially Jewish." Joe Lieberman's "beaked face" in Hobson's novel is specifically noted by the narrator later on as an objective fact, not just a Nazi caricature as had been qualified earlier. Although one cannot gainsay Professor Lieberman's argument that his looks fit "perfectly the Syrian or Turkish or Egyptian type—there's not even such a thing, anthropologically, as the Jewish type" (212), the fact remains that the "beaked face" has historically been negatively associated with the Jew.

In addition, a person's speech might be another giveaway to an essentialized Jewish attribute. Miss Wales, after all, has "the curious New York speech that [Phil] is not yet used to, plus some extra oddities that intrigued his ear" (99); examples of her pronunciations are provided, and one might surmise, when later learning of her true "race," that her speech is a coded expression of that race, even if the facial features are not. Hobson also gives an example of the kind of race joke that Phil feels comfortable with as long as it is told by Anne Dettrey, the woman's editor at the magazine, and her crowd, because a name, a nose shape, or a religion are of no matter at their gatherings (122). There is supposedly "no cruelty" in that milieu, in a joke about a high-class man getting the wrong phone connection and asking for "Breckston, old chap, Lord Harrowbridge Turnbridge Pethbright, y'know," only to have the answer come back: "Oi! Hev *you* got the wrung numbair!" (123). Somehow the Jew in this joke can't be any Jew but, rather, one with a long beard and wearing a black skullcap, as he is described. My point in mentioning this joke is not to imply that race and religion are off limits in joke telling but instead to point up the necessity for Jewish dialect (among other attributes) in this joke to identify the unintended recipient of the call as a Jew and to create the humor.

Other identifiers are tacitly assumed to refer to Jews. Green understands the code words voiced by one Christian doctor about a Jewish physician: "not given to overcharging and running visits out, the way some do" (96). The various remarks of this kind, taken one by one, seem like "no big things. No yellow armband, no marked park bench, no Gestapo. Just here a flick and there another. Each unimportant. . . . But day by day the little thump of insult. Day by day the tapping on the nerves, the delicate assault on the proud stuff of a man's identity" (97). Anyone sucked in to the Jew's orbit risks getting tarred with the same insults. Word inevitably reaches a midwesterner in Belle King's circle, Jefferson Brown, that the Jew who writes under the name Schuyler Green is none other than Belle's brother; he pieces together the relationship in conversation with one of Green's coworkers, who has gone to Detroit to work on a story about the auto workers' strike. Initially astounded that Dick King's wife is a "yid," who most probably changed her name from Bella, Brown realizes that in order to belong to "the Grosse Pointe smart set, clubs, all that," she has been "passing." He experiences such infiltration into these Christian enclaves as "a sudden stink." Notwithstanding the tasty irony that the antisemitic Belle King is now a Jew-by-association (certainly not by choice), we are again confronted with the notion of a particular Jewish appearance: Brown says, "Yellow underneath, all of them. They'll do it every time if they can get away with it. . . . Bella doesn't look Jewish. Does [her brother]?" Believing Schuyler Green to be Jewish, his coworker manages to find a small, nebulous feature of Green's face that supposedly has a Jewish cast: "There's that Jewish something when he smiles, around the mouth" (158). This coworker sees himself as resistant to antisemitic talk and actions, but he has already spoken of Green as "pushy the way they all are" and "touchy" as well (157). The entire conversation is related by the narrator rather than experienced directly by Green; in being behind Green's back, so to speak, the conversation stands in for the many other stereotype-ridden exchanges that he does not hear.

Bit by bit, by means of his passing as a Jew, Phil Green comes to identify with the Jew. So when he tells his son, Tommy, to tell his friends that his dad is "partly

Jewish" (164), that remark is true in some emotional sense. And when, after eight weeks gathering his information as a pretend Jew, he tells Tommy that the game they have both been playing is over, he terms the game Identification (270). The novel bears a similarity to *Black Like Me*, termed by Laura Browder a "spiritual autobiography" (214); as Griffin relates, "Because I was a Negro for six weeks, I remained partly Negro or perhaps essentially Negro."[18] Phil Green, for his part, was a Jew for two weeks longer. His pretense was supposed to last for six months, but like a pharmaceutical trial that is discontinued after a short period of time because the drug's efficacy is quickly discovered, the results of Green's investigation into American antisemitism are only too evident after a few short weeks. The novel and film of *Gentleman's Agreement* surely had some degree of positive effect in conveying the message Hobson wished the public to receive. Elliot Cohen, reviewing the movie for *Commentary*, called it "a moving, thought-provoking film, which dramatically brings home the question of antisemitism to precisely those people whose insight is most needed—decent, average Americans." Yet in contrast to this optimistic assumption that antisemitism had been "brought home" to the doorstep of Mr. and Mrs. Average American, the message seems to have been repudiated by some and, for others, garbled in transmission: one person commented on the film that since Jewish bankers control all of America's monies, antisemitism couldn't possibly exist, and a stagehand on the set said that the moral was that one should never be rude to a Jew because he might, in fact, be a gentile.[19]

Another novel of the period, Arthur Miller's *Focus* (1945), also sought to convey the extent and impact of antisemitism in mid-1940s American society. The story turns on the ironic fact that an antisemitic hiring manager at an antisemitic firm becomes the target of antisemitism himself when he purchases a pair of spectacles to more accurately identify any Jewish applicant trying to pass as a Christian. Matthew Frye Jacobson, in his chapter on "Looking Jewish, Seeing Jews," devotes detailed attention to Miller's novel and is more admiring of the plot than I am, deeming it "whimsical" and "a creation of wry genius."[20] Although I appreciate the irony, I am not persuaded that putting on a pair of glasses makes a person suddenly look Jewish—not only to those around him but to himself as well. At one point the character considers showing his baptismal certificate to attest to his Christianity, but so powerful is his so-called Jewish appearance that "no proof, no documents, no words [could change] the shape of a face he himself suspected." My hesitation about the critical plot device notwithstanding, the symbolism of the novel's title does work for me: the physical and psychological effects of antisemitism come into focus when one is perceived to be a Jew and thus discriminated against. For example, the protagonist is refused a room in a hotel at which he had been welcomed before—being turned away from this place with its "restricted clientele" is the equivalent to letting others "make a Jew out of you," as his wife complains.[21]

Miller calls his protagonist Mr. Newman, a name that implies how an anti-semite might turn over a new leaf after losing jobs, being turned away from restricted hotels, and becoming the target of the Christian Front, all on the basis of being mistaken for a Jew. In effect, Newman's experiences eventually make him a new man, not in the sense that his antagonists would have it, but in the sense that, to quote Jacobson, he passes into being "an honorary Jew . . . a newly minted social Jew and a newly converted racial liberal."[22] Newman ultimately if symbolically proves the validity of a Jewish character's claim in the novel "that Newman was strictly a Jewish name" (76).Thus, his name is the inverse in meaning to that of Malamud's Henry Levin, the Jew who wanted to be a Freeman—a man free from being Jewish. Instead, Newman actually exemplifies Malamud's dictum that "all men are Jews, except they don't know it," by which Malamud meant that all humans at some point will meet the historical fate of suffering.[23] As for the "proof" of identity that a baptismal certificate would confer, a persuasive counterargument is offered by Henry Louis Gates Jr. in an essay on Anatole Broyard: on the question of a rightful identity, Gates remarks that "to pass is a sin against authenticity, and 'authenticity' is among the founding lies of the modern age." Documents such as birth certificates constitute our identity but they are not "signs of an independently existing identity."[24] In becoming in effect a "Finkel-stein"—the name of the Jewish owner of the candy shop on the corner—Newman achieves his wish to "break away the categories of people and change them so that it would not be important to them what tribe they sprang from, even though in his life it had been of the highest importance" (217).

The Jew as Gentile

In "Electricity," as I have argued, the father considers Reform Jews to be almost like gentiles masquerading as Jews, with their temples that in his estimation would more accurately be called churches. The opposite direction might also apply: to the Orthodox, especially in the mid- to late nineteenth century, when Reform Judaism arose in Germany as a modernization of Jewish practice and then flowered in the United States, Reform Jews were (and are, to some of the ultra-Orthodox today) Jews passing as gentiles.[25] After all, among the typical Protestant practices adopted by the new movement in both Germany and America, the early Reform rabbis were called reverend, religious school was held on Sundays, services were conducted largely in the vernacular, and paid Christian choirs provided the music to organ accompaniment. I will return to the subject of Reform Judaism in my final chapter; suffice it to say here that after World War II and the Holocaust, the pendulum of classical Reform in the United States began to swing away from such assimilatory approaches—not least because of the discovery that no matter how modernized and adaptive the religious practices of many of Germany's Jews, and no matter how loyally they had fought in World War I, they were still annihilated, as Jews.

In Francine Prose's story, if the "temples" even in postwar America are still "churches," at least metaphorically speaking, Joseph Heller takes it one step further. At the conclusion of *Gentleman's Agreement*, we find that Phil Green's series of articles is being turned into a book—in effect, the book we have just read. So, too, Heller's Bruce Gold is writing a book on the Jewish experience in America—the book we are simultaneously reading, called *Good as Gold*—and his California sister, Joannie, provides what could be considered the next stop on the route to passing as gentile: "If you want to know what my Jewish experience is, I can tell you," she says to her brother. "It's trying not to be. We play golf now, get drunk, take tennis lessons, and have divorces, just like normal Christian Americans." But in a far different take on playing Christian, her sister Rose, sixty years old, remembers how hard it was to find a job when she first started out: "A lot of the ads had lines that no Jews should apply," she tells her younger siblings, so eventually she decided to lie to the agencies and say she was Protestant. "I didn't even know what Protestant was but I knew it was good. They all knew I was lying, with my looks, but they didn't really care. At least they could send me out."[26] Many other Jewish American job seekers who did not "look Jewish" also lied about their religion in order to get a job. A letter of 1933 to the advice column featured for six decades in the *Forward*, "Bintel Brief" (Bundle of Letters), expressed a mother's anguish that her daughter had to resort to such a subterfuge:

> Our daughter graduated from college with high honors, but this did not help her find a job. She could not find work for a long time, but two months ago she got a very good job in an insurance company, and she brings home a check for thirty-five dollars every week. We should be satisfied, yet our world is turned upside down since she got the job.
>
> My husband is very upset, because in order to get the job my daughter had to give her religion as Episcopalian. If they had known she was Jewish they wouldn't have hired her. She doesn't have typically Jewish features, and from her appearance she can be taken for a Christian. One of my sons says she also had to get a recommendation from a priest, because lately many Jewish girls say they are Christians in order to get a job. The priest's recommendation is the only way to assure the boss that he is not being fooled.[27]

These passing stories lend an added dimension to the situation of Miss Wales, whose looks and name change alone were enough to secure her a position at the magazine that was not inclined to offer jobs to Jews.

In Michael Gold's *Jews without Money*, Mendel, one of the bums in Mikey's Allen Street neighborhood early in the century, does more than get a tattoo and eat pork and ham, practices traditionally forbidden to Jews; he actually commits the "supreme sin" by making the rounds of the Bowery missions and getting baptized in return for money, food, clothes, jobs, and even "a chance to learn the cornet." Mrs. Gold is horrified to hear of this, but Mendel insists that he has remained a true Jew:

> This is just a way of making a living [he explains]; I am out of work, so why should I starve? Those Christians, a black year on them, are so crazy to have Jews baptized they even pay for it. So what do I do—I fool them. I let them sprinkle their water on me—and all the time, under my breath, I am cursing them. I am saying, to hell with your idol! To hell with your holy water! When they are through, I take my potatoes and go—but I am the same Mendel still, a Jew among Jews!

Because of his subterfuge, he insists, his fraudulently acquired potatoes are actually "Jewish potatoes." Even Katie Gold, along with everyone else in the neighborhood, cannot help but admire the flamboyant shape-shifter: for it "was amusing to Jews that Mendel could fool Americans with his tricks. It was flattering to Jews to know that he often passed himself off as a real American, yet talked Yiddish and was loyal to his race."[28] Clearly, a "real American" is a Christian American to these Lower East Side denizens in the immigrant generation, not to mention in the view of many Christian Americans in all generations of our country's history.

A more profound passing as a Christian occurs, of course, when born Jews deny their heritage even to the point of bone fide conversion. In *Gentleman's Agreement*, two of Phil Green's coworkers deride a new fiction serial in their magazine that portrays "countesses and young dukes and American society folk." They argue that the author must be "half psychotic inside" from a quarter century of hiding the fact that he is Jewish "just so he can be the snob he really is—the best clubs, the *Social Register*, the whole routine" (208–9). This brief mention of a secret Jew could well describe a man whose similar story is instructive and hence worth elaborating: George Jean Nathan (1882–1958), coeditor with H. L. Mencken of the *Smart Set*, mentor to Thyra Samter Winslow, influential New York theater critic, and man-about-town.

In the same March 1919 issue of the *Smart Set* that featured Winslow's "A Cycle of Manhattan," Nathan commented on the play *A Gentile Wife* in a review that is eye-opening to readers of our times because of its utter candor about the critic's disdainful attitude toward Jews. *A Gentile Wife* ran for only thirty-one performances, between December 1918 and January 1919. Nathan praised this "first play by a youngster" as "the most significant and promising drama given the American stage by a native writer in a number of years" but remarked on the inevitability of its failure

> in the largely Roman-nosed popular theater of New York by virtue of its abstention from the customary box-office whimsy of laying the vaseline to Jewry in

sufficiently large and oozy gobs. Since the average New York audience is usually made up for the most part of Jews, such a play stands mighty little chance
of financial success unless it brings down its big curtain on a rosy piece of verbal fireworks in which Jesus Christ, Disraeli and Jacob Schiff are proclaimed
as belonging to the same race, and unless it brings down its final curtain with
the discovery that not Milton Rosenbaum, but the low Patrick McCarthy, was
the man who actually stole the money. Any variation of the theme is bound to
offend the tender sensibilities of the theatergoing Anglo-Oriental.

Nathan's rococo writing style and his coy circumlocution about noses do not in
any way mitigate the antisemitic message: that the Jews have too much audience
power in the theater, voting with their feet against a play that portrays their kind
in a negative light. More, Nathan goes on to suggest that newspaper reviews are
influenced by the Jewish department store magnates: "an enthusiastic record of a
play that handles the racial question without thick gloves would not be likely to
drive crazy with joy the Messrs. Gimbel, Altman, Saks, Stern, Greenhut, Abraham & Straus, and the rest of the full-page advertisers." Nathan's final coup de
grace is to malign the "Mosaic managerial departments" of the theaters, who
balk at a play like *A Gentile Wife* but permit what Christians might easily view as
profane stage or screen portrayals of *their* religion.[29]

Such statements might help to explain why that same issue of the *Smart
Set* featured Winslow's portrait of vulgar, nouveau riche Jews: the attitudes of
the two writers were akin. In actuality, George Jean Nathan, like Winslow, was
of "oriental" heritage. That is, he was born to parents who were practicing Jews
and, in his case, pillars of the Fort Wayne, Indiana, Jewish community, though
his mother eventually converted to Catholicism, as Nathan and Winslow would
do as well, shortly before their deaths. Thomas Connolly's full-length study of
Nathan details the ways in which this "quintessential urban sophisticate" did his
best to conceal his Jewish background. "He lived in dread of 'exposure,'" Connolly relates, "[obfuscating] his family background. . . . He repeatedly refused to
discuss his Jewishness." Mencken, no lover of Jews himself, "sneered at Nathan's
background, and slurred him without hesitation in his posthumously published
memoirs." In those memoirs, Mencken related how, in the proof stage of their
twin faux biographies, Nathan had insisted on the removal of the sentence "One
of us is a baptized man," since they were *both* to be assumed to be Christian.
Mencken also commented, in a bit of armchair psychoanalysis, about Nathan's
squiring of starlets and other beauties; employing the term for the personality
deficit popularized in Mencken's time, he diagnosed that "a typically Jewish inferiority complex is in him, and it gives him great satisfaction to have some eminent (or even notorious) fair one under his arm."[30] Perhaps Mencken's remark
that Nathan was a "social pusher" rather than the more familiar term "social
climber" was itself a reference to the stereotype of Jews as pushy.

In the Nathan collection at Cornell University, his alma mater, there are very few personal traces, though the collection does contain a record of his membership in the Penguin Island Country Club, of which he was proud enough to retain proof. The director and drama critic Harold Clurman, though not a classmate at Cornell, remarked in his own memoirs of Nathan's secret self: "At Cornell Nathan had been a flashy undergraduate, a foppish playboy with pretensions to continental sophistication, which he never quite abandoned. . . . All of this was an evasion, a mask to hide something in his background that might cast doubt on the validity of his snobbishness and his aristocratic stance. One day acting on a hunch, I asked Sinclair Lewis whether Nathan was Jewish. 'Only a hundred per cent,' Lewis answered." Other documents provide further details of Nathan's Jewishness. A letter of October 1938 from Mencken to publisher Alfred Knopf recounts information from the actress Lillian Gish, with whom Nathan had been romantically linked. According to Gish, as retold by Mencken, Nathan "gave her his word that he had no Jewish blood." Yet when Nathan wanted to make a move to a Park Avenue apartment, he asked Gish to make those arrangements for him, a fact that Mencken attributes to the house's restriction against Jews. As Mencken wrote to Knopf, "The agent would not rent to Gish when he found out it was for Nathan. The agent refused to believe that Nathan wasn't Jewish, even on Gish's word that G. J. N. had so sworn." Lillian Gish possessed more than a modicum of antisemitism herself, and the rumors that Nathan was actually Jewish may well have scotched their relationship; at any rate, Mencken said that Gish told him "she believed [Nathan] was going downhill professionally . . . [and] that the influence of the Jews in the theatre is fast becoming intolerable."[31] If she had Nathan in mind in this last remark, it is quite ironic in light of Nathan's own views on the subject, as revealed in his theater review in the March 1919 issue of the *Smart Set*.

The only extant direct documentation of Nathan's personal views on his Jewish background is found in correspondence with Isaac Goldberg, who was working on a biography of Nathan in the mid-1920s. Housed in Goldberg's papers in the New York Public Library, this series of letters from Nathan to Goldberg contains only one that is handwritten, and quite lengthy besides. Connolly provides all of the requisite portions, but the following are the most salient and interesting parts:

> I [Nathan] indicated the deletion of the Jewish allusion for a simple reason. The common practice of arbitrarily discerning biological and psychological influences in the Jew because he is a Jew seem absurd and objectionable to me. . . . Whenever I read this or that about a man because of a Jewish strain in his blood, it makes me sick. Heine was no more Heine because he was a Jew— though the thing has been emphasized *ad nauseam*—than Swinburne was because he was a Christian. . . . It is always the Jew himself who insists upon such things, the more observing goys have in the main given up the practice.

Nathan concludes, "Let us have done with such business. It makes the Jew a self-conscious and silly figure, and he should not be one. The next time I read in your writings of Spinoza, say, that he was a Jew, I shall take the first train to Boston and kick you in the pantaloons." It appears that Goldberg, himself a Jew and no doubt the intended object of the barb that "it is always the Jew" (though Mencken also made such assumptions), pushed back on the elimination of any reference to Nathan's heritage, for in a follow-up letter, this one dictated rather than hand-written, Nathan insisted, "I have no more to say about the Jewish matter, save to protest strongly against it on the ground I have already indicated. Why all the race consciousness? The sooner all Jews forget it, the better it will be."[32] Nathan's insistence held sway, because in the published work by Goldberg we find no reference to religion save the notion that his subject was a "complete agnostic, and views all clergymen with a sardonic eye."[33] Goldberg's chapter 2, on Nathan's forebears and upbringing, is devoid of any mention of Jews.

Allyson Hobbs, writing of blacks passing as white in *A Chosen Exile*, makes this analogy: "Just as Americans might feel more self-conscious about their national identity in a foreign country, those [African Americans] who decided to pass described similar pangs of nostalgia for lost origins."[34] Seemingly George Jean Nathan, whether comfortable or at times discomfited in his adopted Christian country, had no such nostalgia. Several factors may account for his lifelong obfuscation of his Jewish heritage and his late conversion to Catholicism. His father had left the family early and the mother, in converting to Catholicism, may have ensured that her son George received at least some instruction in the religion, especially since George's brother also became a devout Catholic. As well, Connolly surmises that "Nathan's own insecurity and desperate desire to be a 'genuine' aristocrat caused him to go to such lengths to disguise his true background." After all, he "spent his entire life in a society that cheerfully excluded Jews from hotels, apartment houses, clubs, and neighborhoods." With a side glance at Winslow, one might say that Nathan was as determined to "make it" in America as those early immigrants fresh off the boat from Lithuania, though he himself came from a privileged background. Like the Rosenheimers' Ross descendants, Nathan's notion of success was expressed in terms of sophistication, cosmopolitanism, and "cleverness" (as the *Smart Set* described itself), as one of the city's smart set with the best tables at the Stork Club and "21." In Connolly's wry summation, "that a cultural commentator of Nathan's status had such difficulty with his own identity remains as troubling as it is instructive."[35]

Nathan's own question, "Why all the race consciousness?", opens itself to interpretations and applications beyond the writer's intention. Nathan wished to forget he was born a Jew and wanted others to forget it too, no matter their race, religion, or creed. His succeeding statement—"The sooner all Jews forget it, the better it will be"—suggests with that vague second "it" that he thought life would be improved for all, Jews and non-Jews, if Jews would only let this self-identifier float away. For himself, he "forgot" about his Jewish heritage by obscuring it at first, and then making the final renunciation through conversion. But "Why all the race consciousness?" is also the question he might have asked when avoiding the risk of openly seeking an apartment in a ritzy Park Avenue building or revealing himself to his antisemitic actress girlfriend. With his aspirations and achievements, Nathan did not feel he could advance in society or his profession as an uncloseted Jew. This is what is both troubling and instructive about his case. "Why all this race consciousness?" was the question also asked by Jewish applicants to undergraduate and professional schools, and for jobs and homes, in the 1920s and beyond who had to answer questions about race and religion that they knew would keep them out. Why all this race conscious, indeed! It is the question of Jews who were openly Jewish and Jews who checked off the box that said Christian, especially if they didn't have the "Jewish look" and could thus pass successfully. And it is a question that many in 2018 America are still asking, not only Jews but African Americans, Latinos, Muslims, and other citizens and would-be citizens affected by the discrepancy between this country's open arms and its closed doors.

Notes

1. Dinnerstein, *Antisemitism in America*, xiii. Dinnerstein rehearses the Christian heritage of antisemitism in his prologue (xix–xxviii). Subsequent references in the text to this work are to this edition.

2. Obviously, such sentiments and practices were applied over the course of American history to a variety of groups considered racially undesirable. Chinese immigration had been restricted forty years before the anti-immigration agitation against the influx of southern and eastern Europeans culminated in several legislative acts of the 1920s that limited the numbers and set quotas for different nationalities. Prejudice against Catholics by Protestants also had a racial component since the Irish in particular, who came over in large numbers in the nineteenth century, were considered racially inferior to those of English stock. The Japanese were interned during World War II. African Americans, of course, did not immigrate at all—they were forcibly brought to the United States as slaves, and the discrimination they have experienced throughout American history, including long-lasting legalized and de facto segregation, is the prime reason that many light-skinned blacks opted for passing as white.

3. Philip Roth's "Defender of the Faith" would be well taught in the context of the military environment explicated by Dinnerstein in *Antisemitism in America* (138–39), in which—as but one example—a base commander ordered all the recruits to participate in the Easter Service, and the Catholic chaplain said to the Jewish chaplain who complained, "Why shouldn't all men regardless of creed or race pay homage to our Savior?" Given Grossbart's crass exploitation of his Jewishness to avoid military responsibilities, students today might

privilege his self-serving strategizing in their interpretation of the story and minimize the underlying issue of antisemitism, much as Grossbart refers to it; as one rabbi stated in his record of his life in the military during the war, "The reader will not be blamed if he reads of these experiences incredulously. I myself find it hard to believe them now, nearly two years after they occurred." It is harder for the reader three quarters of a century later.

4. Kestenbaum, "'Alt-Right' Sees 'Jewish Coup,'" 4.
5. Judaken, "Between Philosemitism and Antisemitism," 23–24, 40.
6. Aarons, Patt, and Shechner, introduction, 1, 3.
7. Pollack, "Bris," 86–87. Subsequent references in the text to this story are to this edition.
8. Aarons, Patt, and Shechner, introduction, 3.
9. Prose, "Electricity," 286, 285, 289, 288.
10. Steven J. Rubin, *Writing Our Lives*, 40, quoted in Browder, *Slippery Characters*, 165. See also Davidson and Wagner-Martin, *Oxford Companion to Women's Writing*, 435, 443. Goldstein's brief discussion of "Leah Morton" (he does not refer to her as Elizabeth Stern) in *Price of Whiteness* (168) reveals that he accepts her novel as an "autobiographical" work by a Jew.
11. Stern, *Secret Family*, 1, quoted in Browder, *Slippery Characters*, 166.
12. Umansky, "Representations of Jewish Women," 167.
13. Stern, *Secret Family*, 186, quoted in Browder, *Slippery Characters*, 167.
14. Dinnerstein mentions this letter housed in the Hobson collection at Columbia University (146).
15. Hobson, *Gentleman's Agreement*, 10, 9, 11. Subsequent references in the text to this novel are to this edition. As Dinnerstein reports, "Throughout the 1950s and into the 1960s, homeowners in prosperous Grosse Pointe, Michigan, calculatedly enforced discriminatory policies. . . . The Grosse Pointe Property Owners Association hired private detectives to secretly investigate prospective buyers" (157). The association analyzed the data and assigned points based on several categories, including complexion, religion, and ethnic background. WASPS needed fifty points to be accepted, Jews eighty-five. Needless to say, "Negroes" are not included on the list of prospects.
16. Quoted in Dreisinger, *Near Black*, 59. Another commentator on *Gentleman's Agreement*, Weber, also deals with unconscious stereotypes of Jews as inadvertently revealed in the film but also the novel. See his "Limits of Empathy," 91–104.
17. Macgregor, *Transformation and Identity*, 102–3.
18. *Black Like Me*, 156, quoted in Browder, *Slippery Characters*, 214–15.
19. Dinnerstein, *Antisemitism in America*, 153.
20. Jacobson, *Whiteness of a Different Color*, 189. Jacobson examines the novel over ten pages, 188–98.
21. Miller, *Focus*, 66, 117. Subsequent references in the text to this novel are to this edition.
22. Jacobson, *Whiteness of a Different Color*, 189. Jacobson comments that Hobson's Phil Green also looks Jewish, but it seems to me that the novelist takes great pains to assert that he does not.
23. Field and Field, "Interview," 11.
24. Gates, "White Like Me," 78. In Englander's *Ministry of Special Cases*, of course, Pato Poznan's documents constitute his existence in the most extreme sort of way; when they are "disappeared," so is he.
25. A brouhaha was created in the summer of 2015 by the remark of Israel's Minister for Religious Services, David Azoulay, in a radio interview; he said that he "cannot allow"

himself to say that a Reform Jew is Jewish. A follow-up speech in the Knesset did little to convey the impression that he had been misunderstood: "It is too bad that my words were removed from their context. . . . The correction was made in the course of the interview but they ignored that. It is obvious to all that as Our Sages of Blessed Memory determined, Jews are Jews, even if they are sinners. . . . No one has a monopoly for determining who is a better Jew. And yet, we see with great pain the danger of the Reformation in Judaism, which brought the greatest danger to the Jewish nation: assimilation. . . . We pray that sins will be purged from the land—sins, not sinners. We will continue to pray for the entire nation of Israel to repent, while we ourselves will do everything possible to be a beacon of light and values for everyone. To sum up: the Nation of Israel has a long history of sticking to Judaism even during difficult times; we must continue to uphold the Jewish heritage" (Gil Ronen, "Minister Claims 'Reform Aren't Jewish' Comment Misundersood," August 7, 2015, http:// www.israelnationalnews.com/News/News.aspx/197852#.Vu25o-YW4-g). More recently, Rabbi Yigal Levenstein, head of a modern Orthodox military academy in Israel, termed Reform Judaism "Christianity" (see Rosner, "How Israel's Modern Orthodox Jews Came Out of the Closet").

26. Heller, *Good as Gold*, 87, 111–112.

27. Metzker, *Bintel Brief*, 160.

28. Gold, *Jews without Money*, 78–80.

29. Nathan, "Hopkins," 135, 134. Having read *A Gentile Wife* for myself, looking for the reasons why Nathan took such umbrage at the purported Jewish influence on its demise, I find insufficient support for his view that it must have overly distressed a Jewish audience. True, the play contains antisemitic remarks, and it is also true that the main character, David Davis, falls in love with and marries a gentile. But the overall weight of the play is on pride in being a Jew—indeed, on reclaiming a Jewish identity—as well as on the perils of a mis-marriage (because in this play it is more than a *mixed* marriage). Both David the Jew and his gentile wife come to realize that one must be true to one's people—that this may be even more important than love. It seems to me that the play actually ran for only a few performances because it wasn't particularly good, plain and simple.

30. Connolly, *George Jean Nathan*, 23, 27.

31. Ibid., 28–29. Lillian Gish starred in the 1915 film *The Birth of a Nation*. This "nation," as Laura Browder remarks (144), is "a nation explicitly composed of white native-born Protestants, united in opposition to the threat posed by immigrants and African-Americans." Effectively, this movie revived the Ku Klux Klan.

32. Connolly, *George Jean Nathan*, 29–31.

33. Goldberg, *Theatre of George Jean Nathan*, 9. Goldberg is here quoting an anonymous source with the pseudonym Owen Hatteras, no reference provided. However, as we know, "Owen Hatteras" was a pen name for Mencken and Nathan working either together or separately, which adds a dollop of further irony to this supposed third-party description.

34. Hobbs, *Chosen Exile*, 16.

35. Connolly, *George Jean Nathan*, 32.

7 Racial Crossings between Jews and Blacks

"That You Might See Your Shadow"

WALTER WHITE, THE author, civil rights activist, and great-grandson of President William Henry Harrison through one of Harrison's liaisons with his slaves, was light skinned and fair haired enough to pass as white but chose to identify as black. In "Why I Remain a Negro," a 1947 essay in the *Saturday Review of Literature,* he remarked, "I am white and I am black, and know that there is no difference. Each one casts a shadow, and all shadows are dark."[1] White's explanation for choosing one race over another is true in one sense, since there is no biological difference between the races, but he knew only too well that in terms of society's attitudes, there was a great difference indeed—hence his special pleading. When we add Jewishness to the mix to complicate the black-white binary, and examine works in which all three components of identity come into play, we extend racial passing beyond its customarily understood meaning; in the process, we embrace a variety of interpretations of the shadows cast: by those who choose either to remain "Negroes" or to renounce that identity for one that is not only white but Jewish; by those who choose to be Jewish *and* black; and by others still whose adoption of blackness requires a renunciation of Jewishness.

In a different sense from Walter White's assertion, race theorists of the past considered Jews and blacks to be of the same ilk, each casting a dark shadow over the white race. In yet a third perspective on likeness—that of Edward Shapiro in his study of American Jewish identity in a chapter called "Blacks and Jews Entangled"—a kinship between Jews and blacks "revolving around a common victimhood status" (yet another kind of shadow) has been assumed by liberal Jews to the point of mythologizing the connection and erasing crucial differences.[2] Jews, after all, eventually "became white folks," to quote Karen Brodkin's title of her 1998 study of race in America, even if the process was and still is complex and problematic—as Eric Goldstein exhaustively delineates in his own work on the subject, *The Price of Whiteness.*[3] Whatever the relationships may be "in reality," whether in a biological, cultural, or political sense, and however entangled they may be, the fact remains that for personal and societal reasons, some Jews and blacks have chosen to exchange identities or opt for both, and these choices have consequences, resulting in confusion and dislocation for some, a sense of homecoming for others, and mixed reactions from the public at large.

Blacks into Jews

Philip Roth takes up the subject of racial crossings in his novel *The Human Stain* (2000), for which Shakespeare's *Julius Caesar* provides the inspiration (and from which my chapter subtitle derives). The "best memorized" play of the father in this work, considered by this cultured gentleman to be "English literature's high point," it is the source of the middle names given to his three children: Antony, Brutus, and Calpurnia. For Roth's purposes, the novel's protagonist, second child Coleman Silk, must have the middle name of Brutus in validation of the father's belief that *Julius Caesar* is "the most educational study of treason ever written."[4] Shakespeare's Cassius may cunningly flatter Brutus by referring in act 1, scene 2, to the long shadow that his heroic stature casts—"And it is very much lamented, Brutus, / That you have no such mirrors as will turn / Your hidden worthiness into your eye / That you might see your shadow"—but Coleman Brutus Silk has what many would call hidden unworthiness: an inflated sense of his individual worth and justifiable ambition that leads him to cut himself off from family and heritage. Roth's novel entertains the possibility that Silk's creation of a shadow self constitutes a betrayal against himself and against the African American people.

Roth purposely underlines the elocution of Coleman's father, so excellent that even in everyday conversation he seems to be "reciting Marc Antony's speech over the body of Caesar" (92), for that speech gradually announces the treachery and treason of Brutus in Shakespeare's play.[5] In Roth's version, the light-skinned Silk, who abandons his racial past and assumes a white and Jewish identity, imagines but refuses to heed his dead father's recrimination: "What else grandiose are you planning, Coleman Brutus? Whom next are you going to mislead and betray?" (183). Roth thus implies that the shadow Coleman possesses is not his larger-than-life presence but rather the darkness he bears within, exacerbated by his denial of the "darkness" he bears without, camouflaged by his light skin. That shadow is Coleman's stain. Roth is not subtle about drawing the reader's attention to classic literature, the name Athena College being only one further example of the signposts along the way. Although Silk, the classics professor, believes that he "does not have to live like a tragic character in his courses" (170), in fact he has determined his own destiny like some Greek or Shakespearean tragedian, by asserting his "precious singularity" and engaging in a "revolt of one against the Negro fate" (170). The Roman leader Julius Caesar is said to have uttered the words "the die is cast" when "crossing the Rubicon"—thereby providing two expressions that have come down to us as meaning a point of no return.

Such a point is reached in *The Human Stain*, when Coleman Silk first determines to leave his black heritage behind.

That Silk is not who he pretends to be is a secret whose full disclosure the author withholds until a quarter of the way into the novel, well after the precipitating factor in Silk's fall has been established: his use of the word "spooks"—meaning ghosts—in reference to two undergraduates on his class list who, weeks into the semester, have never appeared. These students happen to be African Americans, though Silk could not have known, and they take offense at what they consider to be a racial disparagement, leading to widespread condemnation and ostracism of Silk and his consequent enraged resignation from the college.[6] Silk had earlier made enemies during his deanship by his ambitious elevation of the college through strategic maneuvers, leading many to grumble, that's "what Jews do" (9). Silk believes that he has been forced out of Athena for being "a white Jew of the sort those ignorant bastards call the enemy" (16). In fact, Silk is described by Nathan Zuckerman as "one of those crimped-haired Jews of a light yellowish skin pigmentation who possess something of the ambiguous aura of the pale blacks who are sometimes taken for white" (15–16). Silk may have the skin color of (raw) silk, elsewhere described by a liberal white mother as "a very pleasing shade, rather like eggnog" (122), but the pale hue of his skin is not the issue for either the family that he abandons or the society that would label him a coal man no matter how "pleasing" his shade.

Self-identified as white when joining the navy, Silk is thrown out of a whites-only brothel in Norfolk as "a nigger trying to pass," and Roth brings up the issue of passing at a few points in the novel. Silk's girlfriend in New York, herself a light-skinned black, recognizes immediately that he is one of her own, eliciting a disquisition on passing, and some of Coleman's relatives have also crossed the line into whiteness. It is all well and good for Baz Dreisinger to assert that with his light skin Coleman is passing as much for black as he is for white and that "passing makes no sense" the more we accept that race is a constructed category.[7] True enough, but in a society in which racial politics play a strong role even until the present, it is reasonable that in the 1940s Coleman and several of his kin before and after would see the distinct advantages of crossing the color line, especially given the rise in violence against blacks during and after the World War II.[8] For obvious reasons, Langston Hughes's poem "Passing," referring to the Harlemites "who've crossed the line / to live downtown," has been inspirational to scholars on the subject, including Allyson Hobbs, who uses this poem as frontispiece for her study of blacks passing as white, *A Chosen Exile*, and Gayle Wald, whose book on the same subject is titled *Crossing the Line*.

If not exactly sui generis as a line crosser, Coleman Silk is certainly a member of a small subset: blacks who pass not only as white but as Jewish. The surname Silk would not be an untenable name for a Jew—some of Fannie Hurst's Jews in

"The Gold in Fish" are named Silk, after all—and besides, Coleman provides the plausible story that the name was changed at Ellis Island from Silberzweig (130).[9] Roth, in "Goodbye, Columbus," made a point of linking the outsider status of blacks and working-class Jews like Neil Klugman: the connection is brought up almost immediately, when Brenda Patimkin asks Neil if he is a Negro, and it is reinforced throughout the novella with the identification between Neil and both Carlota the maid (each of them "wooed and won on Patimkin fruit") and the little black boy in the library. The boy yearns to live in the lush "ree-*sort*" of Tahiti as portrayed by Gauguin in the art book he pores over, while Neil feels out of place during his summer residence on the Patimkin "ree-*sort*" in suburbia.[10] In *The Human Stain*, however, a black person is not a mere foil for the Jewish protagonist; the black person *is* the Jewish protagonist. Roth stands with another celebrated Jewish writer in making this connection: in the mid-twentieth century, Bernard Malamud created his own black Jew in "The Angel Levine," a fable about faith in the face of tribulation, and even his story about a persecuted blackbird, "The Jewbird," can be read as an allegory of the outsider status of blacks as well as of Jews, especially since it was published in the same year (1963) as Malamud's overt story about black-Jewish relations, "Black Is My Favorite Color." The fact that it was not uncommon for Jews in Malamud's day to use the Yiddish term *schwartze* to refer to a black person, especially an employee, also supports this unconventional interpretation of "The Jewbird."

Of course, blacks who practice Judaism have become more familiar in American society over time, even if they are still considered exotic by some and unwelcome by others. Essays, memoirs, and scholarly studies on the subject of such individuals have appeared for many years, and the phenomenon has been mainstreamed more recently in popular culture magazines like *Family Circle*, where an article's title, "Modern Life," says it all.[11] Black Jews in the United States comprise, among many others, the Hebrew Israelites whom Michael Gold included in *Jews without Money* decades ago and who trace their ancestry to ancient times; well-known converts like the entertainer Sammy Davis Jr., the academic Julius Lester, and the rabbi Capers Funnye (cousin to former first lady Michele Obama), currently serving as the chief rabbi of the International Israelite Board of Rabbis; countless blacks unknown outside their communities, some with names like Olufunmike Adeyemi that have become more prominent and are even taken for granted on synagogue rolls; and biracial children who adopt the Jewish faith of a parent.[12] All of them are "both/and" instead of "either/or," even if it is hard at times to reconcile both sides of the double identity.[13]

Writing a decade ago, Lori Harrison-Kahan remarked that "Jews are now 'almost ethnic, but not quite,'" yet in our times the proliferation of Jews of color calls for an update of that statement: Jews are increasingly "quite."[14] Melanie Kaye/Kantrowitz's *The Colors of Jews* noted in 2007 that "a number of innovative organizations and projects have emerged that are focused front and center on Jewish racial and ethnic diversity."[15] One such project, a Jews of Color National Convening, took place in May 2016; as the *Forward* duly reported, "Presented by the Jewish Multiracial Network and by Jews for Racial & Economic Justice, the event included African Americans and Latinos and Asians alongside Sephardic and Mizrahi Jews."[16] Indeed, so significant is the growth in the United States of those Jews who consider themselves nonwhite that the journal *American Jewish History* dedicated a recent issue to the matter, noting in the introduction that the next generation of Jews may contain upward of 20 percent persons of color.[17]

In Coleman Silk's youth and early manhood, in contrast, the phenomenon of a black Jew was uncommon, and the option to be "both/and" was less readily available than it is today. (It was not until the 2000 US census, after all, that a respondent could even check off both African American and white in the government's formal if belated and incomplete recognition of the complexity of identity.) If, for understandable reasons, light-skinned people like Silk might choose to pass as white, why Silk chooses to take on the second identity of Jew is a logical question, especially given the discrimination and exclusion that Jews in the United States in his time also experienced. Nathan Zuckerman, the narrator of the story, says that Silk "makes sense" as a "heretofore unknown amalgam of the most unalike of America's historic undesirables" (132); yet blacks and Jews were not exactly "the most unalike," given the historic linking of the two groups by race theorists, Ku Klux Kan members, hotel owners, and so forth, as a work like Dinnerstein's *Antisemitism in America* details. In fact, Silk's adopted Jewish identity will figure into his downfall: his troubles at Athena are stimulated in part by his antisemitic colleagues, and at the novel's dénouement, Coleman—who wears a blue tattoo inscribed on his body against his will in the navy, reminiscent of Holocaust tattooing—will be killed in part because he is a Jew, by the antisemite Les Farley.

A more salient reason why Coleman Silk's taking on of a Jewish identity is puzzling is the long history of negative attitudes by blacks toward Jews. Black Americans who grew up in the Christian tradition absorbed an adverse impression of Jews from church teachings as far back as the days of slavery. To supplement the sermons and tracts about the Jews killing Jesus, black folklore and humor were replete with stereotypical portrayals of the Jew as fixated on money and unscrupulous in business transactions. Over the years, Jewish employers, whether of restaurant workers or domestic help, were disproportionally blamed for unfair practices, whether or not backed up by actual data. Shopkeepers and landlords in the urban ghettos were assumed to be Jewish and denigrated as such. In the 1940s, at the height of American antisemitism, Ralph Bunche, then chair of the Political Science Department at Howard University (and later the recipient of both the Presidential Medal of Freedom and the Nobel Peace Prize), addressed and admonished this culture-specific version of a widespread attitude:

> In the home, the school, the church, and in Negro society at large, the Negro child is exposed to disparaging images of the Jew. . . . Negro parents, teachers, professors, preachers, and business men, who would be the first to deny that there is such a thing as "the Negro," or that there are "Negro traits," generalize loosely about "the Jew," his disagreeable "racial traits," his "sharp business practices," his "aggressiveness," "clannishness" and his prejudices against Negroes. . . . The Jew is not disliked by Negroes because he is "white," but because he is a "Jew," as the Negro conceives the Jew.[18]

Given these widespread opinions about Jews in the black community, along with the discrimination against Jews from white Christians, what would make sense of Silk's decision to assume a Jewish identity? The novel entertains a few possibilities. Certainly it is not the case, as Dreisinger implies, that Coleman's mother is Jewish,[19] for the mother has no Jewish heritage in either the novel or the film. So the ultimate reason for Coleman's adoption of a Jewish identity must be other than a reclaimed Jewish lineage. Coleman's first thought after passing into whiteness—that perhaps he will marry a Jewish woman, Iris Gittelman, because she has wild and kinky hair, so a child of theirs with similar looks could be taken as a Jew and not a black—does not translate into his needing to be a Jew himself in order to marry this woman; after all, liberal Iris would not have been at all fazed by Coleman's secret: being "two men instead of one," "two colors instead of one," even being "possessed of a double or triple or quadruple personality" (130). It seems that one push in the direction of a Jewish identity is the cultural ascendancy "among the Washington Square intellectual avant-garde" in the postwar New York City that Silk enters (131). Most important, though, is the fact that the Jews in Coleman's earlier experience have achieved success—they have become white, and in the process they are models for Coleman.[20]

From the late nineteenth century through the best part of the twentieth, black leaders gave advice to their constituents that mingled a customary linking of Jews and wealth with encouragement to look to the Jews for inspiration. In 1900, one black attorney stated that blacks needed to become like the "despised Jew, the representative of business and money." An editorial in *New York Age* in 1905 acknowledged whites' prejudice against Jews as second only to that against African Americans, "but it is displayed less, because the Jews are among the wealthy people of the country and know how to advance themselves by properly directing their wealth against those who offend them." NAACP leader James Weldon Johnson, in his 1918 *New York Age* essay "The Jew and the Negro," promulgated the notion that "two million Jews have a controlling interest in the finances of the nation," yet at the same time he held the "experiences of modern Jews" as a model for advancement among the "Negro" people.[21]

In this atmosphere, and with this kind of encouragement, it is logical that successful Jews as defined by their money, power, and influence would play the critical role in Coleman Silk's eventual decision to pass as one of their own. The Jewish surgeon from the hospital at which Mrs. Silk works tries to buy Coleman's acquiescence in relinquishing his valedictorian status so that the doctor's own son has a better chance of being one of a small Jewish quota gaining acceptance into medical schools. Coleman's parents refuse, out of pride, but the teenage Coleman sees only the opportunities lost in rejecting this bribe. (Incidentally, becoming one of the tribe, so to speak, would be a "score-settling joke" on the conniving Dr. Fensterman [131].) Another professional Jew occupies an equally large but affirmative presence in his life: the dentist Doc Chizner, who runs a boxing school populated largely by Jewish boys.[22] This Jewish professional works to develop Coleman's talents and to push Coleman forward instead of asking him to diminish himself and take second place. Even for Coleman's father, "the Jews, even audaciously unsavory Jews like Dr. Fensterman, were like Indian Scouts, shrewd people showing the outsider his way in" (97). But Mr. Silk is optimistic or naive in believing that this "social possibility" is open to a "colored family" (97). His son is not so optimistic. Both Fensterman and Chizner are influential for the power and ambition they display, and thus are of utility to Coleman as positive examples in contrast to his father's negative example of downward mobility; in fact, his decision to pass as white in the first place was no doubt informed by what he saw of his father's fate: a well-educated optician reduced in the Depression to waiting tables in a Pullman dining car, addressed as "boy." By declaring himself Jewish, Coleman becomes the symbolic sons of both Fensterman and Chizner and deliberately disinherits himself from his biological father, as this dinner table Q&A of years before suggests: "So who then is your father, if I may ask?" / "You know. You are. You are, Dad," / "I am? Yes?" / "No!" Coleman shouted. "No, you're not!" (92).

Coleman will become doubly disinherited because of his passing when he renounces his mother in addition to his father. His break with her means that he is now displaced as well as cut off, as much so as Delphine Roux, the French professor and current dean at the college, who has moved to this isolated northeastern US community from Paris and is thus "*dépaysée . . .* a displaced person, a *misplaced* person" (276). Delphine does not appear in the film, but in the novel she functions as a double (as well as a nemesis) for Coleman in that she is "exactly nowhere, in the middle, neither there nor here . . . [a] foreigner." In fact, what Delphine thinks about herself is what Coleman Silk's mother thinks about him; change the gender in the following thought and it applies to Coleman: "She's in exile in, of all things, a stupid-making, self-imposed anguishing exile from her mother" (277). Delphine lives, that is, in the "chosen exile" with which Allyson Hobbs has titled her book on black-white passing. Roth refers often to the "shadow" that Delphine's mother has cast on her daughter—the shadow of her accomplishments and her lineage—and of Delphine's desire to get out from under it and make herself anew in America.[23] Coleman Silk is likewise self-exiled from his mother's shadow. But his announcement to her that they will never meet again, once he has crossed the color line, is tantamount to murder—in the film, Gladys Silk actually calls him a murderer, though in the novel it is Nathan Zuckerman, imagining Coleman's thoughts, who acknowledges that the son is murdering his mother "on behalf of his exhilarating notion of freedom." To reinforce the Shakespearean subtext, Zuckerman/Roth writes of Coleman, "If, in the service of honing himself, he is out to do the hardest thing imaginable, this is it, short of stabbing [his mother]." To put a fine point on it (if I may pun), the author in this scene has Gladys Silk call her son by his full name, Coleman Brutus (138–39). To Gladys, her son's disinheritance of/from his mother is truly "the most unkindest [*sic*] cut of all."[24]

Daniel Itzkovitz has written persuasively on passing as it pertains to both blacks and Jews and the intersections thereof. He quotes a passage from James Weldon Johnson's 1933 autobiography that can be applied to Coleman Silk's transmutation: "All of us [blacks] have at some time toyed with the Arabian Nights–like thought of the magical change of race. . . . If the jinny should say, 'I have come to carry out an inexorable command to change you into a member of another race; make your choice!' I should answer, probably, 'Make me a Jew.'" Itzkovitz remarks that these musings occurred at a time of "explosive collision between the ideologies of social mobility and racial stasis. . . . If Johnson's oriental fantasy bespeaks a sense that, for Black Americans, racial change could happen only through the invention of a magical 'jinny,' it also draws a striking association between magical race-shifting and Jews."[25] The Jews in the Silks' world of Roth's novel may be "racially" distinct from White Anglo Saxon Protestants and blacks alike, but they have achieved upward mobility in large part because of their whiteness. James Baldwin famously remarked that "the Jews came here from countries where they were not white, and they came here in part because they were not white; and incontestably—in the eyes of the Black American (and not only in those eyes) American Jews have opted to become white."[26] Although Baldwin does not here acknowledge the fact that Jews were often considered to be only slightly less *not* white than blacks in the first part of the twentieth century, and even today in the eyes of some, the gist of the remark is undisputable, in part because of the Jews' chameleon-like adaptability to their surroundings.

Woody Allen exploited this trope of Jews as arch chameleons in his 1983 film *Zelig*, in which the Jewish protagonist of the 1920s and 1930s, nicknamed "The Human Chameleon," metamorphoses into a variety of personages. He takes on the coloration of his environment, whether that means becoming a socialite on Long Island, a baseball player, an "oriental" in Chinatown, or a "colored guy playing the trumpet" in a speakeasy band. Zelig is of endless fascination to the American public: a headline blares, "Human Who Transforms Self Discovered," a dance craze "The Chameleon" sweeps the nation, and sheet music about his amazing ability is placed on every piano. The underlying reason for his changing identities is articulated by Zelig himself under hypnosis by his psychiatrist: "It's safe to be like others. I want to be liked." The trope gives Woody Allen many opportunities for jokes, both verbal plays and sight gags. For example, again under hypnosis, Zelig looks back to the first time he changed identities: "I wandered into a bar. I wasn't wearing green. I turned into Irish." This self-diagnosis of the need for—indeed, the safety of—blending in is reinforced by the narrator of the mockumentary, who calls Zelig a "cipher, a nonperson who wanted only to fit in, to belong, to be liked, to not stand out." None other than Bruno Bettelheim (playing himself) calls Zelig "the ultimate conformist." Most of the real-life commentators whom Allen trots out to provide serious analyses of the Zelig phenomenon are, in fact, Jewish: Susan Sontag, Saul Bellow, and Irving Howe in addition to Bettelheim. Especially noteworthy is the interpretation of Howe, well-known author of *World of Our Fathers*, the encyclopedic analysis of Ashkenazi Jews in the United States from the late 1800s to the time of publication (1976). Howe remarks that Leonard Zelig's "story reflects the Jewish experience in America. . . . He wanted to assimilate like crazy."[27]

In effect, Philip Roth's Coleman Silk becomes his own genie, transforming himself into a Jew, marrying a Jewish woman, and having Jewish children. Several questions come to mind about his transition. Does he become a "cipher" in the process of this assimilation, like Zelig? Does Coleman miss Newark the way the passers in Langston Hughes's poem miss the Harlem of a Sunday afternoon? Does he experience "pangs of nostalgia for lost origins," as Allyson Hobbs notes of those light-skinned blacks whom she has interviewed in their "chosen exile"? Anna Deavere Smith, who played Coleman's mother in the film, gave her own opinion about his passing: "Lying about your identity is very disturbing to many of us. I don't think he should have done what he did. He needed a black community."[28] Did Coleman in fact need "a black community"? Silk's extended family, at their reunions, lament the loss of each relative who has passed for white and vanished without a trace—"Lost himself to all his people" is how they put it (144), and exactly how Coleman's sister, Ernestine, puts it to Zuckerman after her brother's death (324).

In his zeal to be a "self-freedom fighter" (130), to "take the future into his own hands" and determine his fate by "his own resolve" (120–21), Coleman Silk seems not to look back. The only clue that he still identifies somewhere deep down as black is when he shouts at his lawyer about that man's "lily-white face" (81), recapitulating what his brother, Walt, had shouted at *him* when he permanently ousted Coleman from the family because of his betrayal (145). In the film,

Coleman's fighting his black self is made very clear when, in a boxing match with an opponent whom he finishes off in the first round, he says, "I ain't holdin' up no nigger"; in the novel, the words are slightly different—"I don't carry no nigger" (117)—but the symbolism is the same.[29] What remains in Coleman's heart after pushing away his family in his chosen exile from his origins is a secret hidden from readers until the novel's end; as Zuckerman says at Silk's graveside, "There really is no bottom to what is not known" (315). That secret, as telling as the secret of his racial heritage, is that he has not in fact cut himself off completely. One hint of this early on is that Coleman has to suppress an impulse to visit his mother with his first child, in spite of his brother's diatribe (180). The ever-observant Zuckerman senses that there is in Coleman "a blotting out, an excision" (213), yet after the funeral Coleman's sister reveals to Zuckerman not only of what that excision consisted but also that she had kept up with her brother all those years in surreptitious phone calls from both sides, at significant family events. The family tie had not been completely broken after all, although the racial tie was disavowed.[30]

The words that Herb Keble uses to characterize Silk in his eulogy—that Silk was an "American individualist *par excellence*" (311)—present the other side of the story, a counter argument to the suggestion that, like a tragic hero, Coleman Silk is a hubristic striver with overweening ambition. True, this is precisely what Walt Silk hates about Coleman, that his brother was "in it for himself" (324), as opposed to Walt, a freedom fighter of another sort, invested in the struggle for school integration and civil rights in general. But the struggle between the "I" and the "we" is the tension at the heart of the novel and of America itself. Zuckerman wonders if Coleman wasn't just "being another American and, in the great frontier tradition, accepting the democratic invitation to throw your origins overboard" (334). He also believes that Coleman was a man undone by his particular historical moment, a moment of what the entire novel characterizes as political correctness writ large, used against President Bill Clinton in his sexual improprieties with the intern Monica Lewinsky as well as against Coleman Silk with his use of the word "spooks" and his liaison with a woman decades his junior. Ultimately it seems to this reader that *The Human Stain*, through its Rothian narrator, comes down on the side of a protagonist who wants to live life on his own terms, no matter the sacrifices and consequences. But the counter argument is also persuasive, as it so often is with Roth; as Debra Shostak remarks, "Roth's compulsion to contradict and counterimagine drives the logic within each narrative as well as the juxtaposition of one novel to the next or some previous works in his career."[31] The open question in *The Human Stain*, along with being a hallmark of this author's work, is what makes the novel a compelling exploration of the times.

The Human Stain, as it happens, bears a passing resemblance, in two senses, to Danzy Senna's *Caucasia*, which is also a compelling exploration of its own earlier time and setting: within the interethnic conflict and rising Black Power movement in Boston in the 1970s. From this milieu, the protagonist, Birdie Lee, "disappears," as she tells the reader on page 1. This is both a literal and figurative term: the mother is on the run northward to avoid what she fears is pursuit by the FBI for her revolutionary activities, and in the process, she removes her daughter from her black identity, turning her not only into a white girl but also into a Jew. Birdie's mother, Sandy, is white, and her African American husband, Deck Lee, like Coleman Silk, is a professor of classics teaching Plato and Aristotle (27). And like Coleman Silk, described by Zuckerman as "one of those crimped-haired Jews," Deck Lee's hair, from the perspective of the woman who will become his wife and Birdie's mother, "wasn't so woolly. . . . It was more like that of some of the Jews she had seen who had afros—black ringlets pleasantly curling into his scalp" (29)

Birdie is especially close to her older sister, Cole, with whom she communicates in their own made-up language that they call Elemeno and with whom she puts on costumes from the trunk in the attic. The performativity of identity is foregrounded in both cases. The language is a camouflage, because those who speak it, says the sister, are "a shifting people. . . . The Elemenos could turn deep green in the bushes, beige in the sand, or blank white in the snow, and their power lay precisely in the ability to disappear into any surroundings" (7). Then they do disappear into new surroundings, for the family splits up and goes their separate ways. Birdie's sister, Cole, whose skin tone is "cinnamon" (5), has become ever more black-identified, learning her father's language of racial politics—which her mother disparages as "Papaspeak, the art of bombastic and iconoclastic racial tomfoolery" (64)—and no longer figuratively speaking the language of Elemeno, the medium of communication with her sister. Cole, whose name may well be symbolic of her blackness, as Lori Harrison-Kahan suggests, has always been Deck Lee's favorite because she looks like she belongs to him; in contrast, in a painful scene with Deck and Birdie in a park, white onlookers assume that Birdie has been kidnapped by a black man (50–52).[32] Cole is taken by her father to Brazil, where Deck believes they will find a more hospitable home, and she disappears from the novel until the end. Sandy takes Birdie, whose complexion and hair texture are more like hers, first to upstate New York and then on to New Hampshire, where at age twelve Birdie in effect turns "blank white in the snow." In the land of "Caucasia," which the two enter a third of the way into the novel, the story now belongs wholly to Birdie.

Birdie's appearance has always been hard for onlookers to interpret. In Boston, at the Nkrumah School in the Roxbury section, where Black Power is the sustaining ideology, the students puzzle over her fitness for inclusion: she is perceived by them to be Puerto Rican, perhaps, or white (36). The situation is the same for the light-skinned Irene Redfield in Nella's Larsen's novel *Passing*, first published seventy years earlier: Redfield is always taken for "an Italian, a Spaniard, a Mexican, or a gipsy."[33] But in the 1970s, when the mantra is "black is beautiful," Birdie "must be ugly" (37). At this school, Birdie learns "the art of changing," a "skill that would later become second nature." She and Cole had always enjoyed play acting in costumes, but at the Black Power school it becomes "more than a game. There I learned how to do it for real—how to become some-one else, how to erase the person I was before" (53). Here she learns how to adapt in order to fit in, performing a black identity by sporting braided hair and gold hoop earrings like the other girls, adding Black English to the occasional use of Elemeno. With the popular crowd she has been "knighted" not only black but pretty (55), but Birdie feels it all as a tenuous identity that can be taken away from her at any moment. And taken away it is.

In the by now familiar observation, Sandy's patrician mother says of Birdie that, based on her looks, she "could be Italian. Or even French." (91) Sandy smiles and responds, "Yes, Mother, she could be." No wonder, then, that after Sandy escapes from Boston with Birdie and feels the need for reinvention, black is not one of the options in the list she provides to her daughter: "You've got a lot of choices, babe. You can be anything. Puerto Rican, Sicilian, Pakistani, Greek." Such versatility leads Sandy to a decision: "And, of course, you could always be Jewish. What do you think?" What Birdie thinks is that it is "a strange feeling to be such a blank slate." She shrugs, "I don't know. Italian, maybe? I like spa-ghetti—" Her mother cuts her off with, "Jewish is better, I think." "Does that mean I have to eat gefilte fish?" Birdie responds sarcastically. But the decision has been made, and immediately her mother schools her "on [her] Jewish self." (110)

The reason Sandy insists that Birdie pass as Jesse Goldman, the Jewish daughter of the fictitious David Goldman, is multifaceted. The name Jesse had belonged to Sandy's great-grandmother, whose cause was suffragism; by substi-tuting it for Birdie's real name, Patrice—after Patrice Lumumba, the Congolese opposition leader executed in 1961—Sandy in effect allies Birdie with the white, female side of the family, fighting for women's rights rather than black libera-tion. The Jewish-sounding last name is a further twist on reinvention, but it does not come out of nowhere. For one thing, Sandy is of the opinion that "Wasps were such a stupid race . . . experiencing the effects of too much interbreeding" (22). For another, because of her girth and her seriousness, Sandy had not fit into the environment of upper-crust schoolmates and debutantes that her privileged WASP background had afforded her. As an eighteen-year-old, she had interests in "literature, existentialism, and the Holocaust. She was obsessed by the footage she had seen of the Jews being liberated from Treblinka, and often found herself crying over photographs of the sad-eyed skeletons of the camps." (27) Perhaps identifying with outsiders provided the impetus to apply to a Jewishly identified university, Brandeis, where she was admitted but didn't attend (26). Even before her decision to turn Birdie into a half Jew, she employs Yiddish words or locutions on occasion: *tush* for rear end (69); "Papa Shmappa!" to disparage her husband (83). There is enough material from Sandy's past inclinations in combination with Birdie's looks to create a new, plausible (to her mind) identity for her daughter.

Many readers and critics attending to *Caucasia* are most interested in Senna's re-visioning of the "tragic mulatta" theme of earlier times, or the racial politics of the 1970s in which the novel is set, or the relevance to the issues posed in recent years by the increasing number of interracial relationships and bi-racial children; understandably, their essays underplay even if they mention the significance of Jewishness in the novel.[34] A few critics, like Michele Elam and Lori Harrison-Kahan, do explore the issue of Jewish identity in relationship to racial passing. In the context of a body of recent works in which characters pass for Jewish, Harrison-Kahan's interpretation is instructive:

> The theme of "passing for Jewish" calls into question existing notions of mixed race identity that tend to rely on binary configurations. Drawing attention to the multivalence of whiteness, texts in which characters pass for Jewish, instead of passing for white, present alternative theories of double consciousness by de-emphasizing "twoness." Jewishness becomes the chosen identity because of its status as a model minority—its capacity for assimilation, its closeness to whiteness—but it also functions as a figure for multiplicity due to its contradictions and because it is one of the many racial and ethnic identities that offer themselves as viable alternatives.[35]

The "schooling" Sandy imparts to Birdie about a faux Jewish history includes a deceased dad who (like Sandy's father) was "an esteemed classics professor." In the novel's second reference to stereotypically Jewish hair, the imaginary David Goldman has "a mop of curly black hair, an afro, the way Jews have sometimes"— a flashback to the evening she first met Deck Lee, her father's student, whose afro could have been that of a Jew. (The "Jewfro" will be referenced a third time [166–67].) Sandy dubs "Jesse" with her idiosyncratic Yiddish terms of affection, calling her a "*meshugga* [crazy] one" (111) and a "*meshugga nebbish* [crazy nothing of a person]" (119). So now Birdie becomes a hybrid of a second sort, not only half black, half white, but also half Jewish, half gentile. Transformed into Jesse Goldman, she wears an imitation-gold Star of David purchased from a pawnshop and later keeps it even when not wearing it. The necklace is one of the "artifacts of her life" (325) and also an artifice, just another disguise from the mother's seemingly inexhaustible trove of costumes: it is costume jewelry in two senses. Like Coleman Silk with his blue tattoo, Birdie Lee becomes marked by the Star of David when it leaves a tint on her body. Perhaps a Holocaust reference is implied, since Sandy, now renamed Sheila, brings her daughter *The Diary of Anne Frank* (again, a throwback to her own youth, when the Holocaust had fascinated her), and Birdie fears that a townsman is "a Nazi and had glimpsed the star around [her] neck" (169).[36] Sandy/Sheila tells people that Jesse inherited her "dark looks from [Jesse's] Semitic side," but privately she tells Birdie, using another familiar trope, that she "wasn't really passing because Jews weren't really white, more like an off-white [shades of Coleman Silk's "eggnog"!]. She said they were the closest I was going to get to black and still stay white. 'Tragic history, kinky hair, good politics,' she explained. 'It's all there'" (119). This new identity is not one chosen by Birdie herself; understandably, then, Birdie reminisces, "mostly my Jewishness was like a performance we put on together for the public" (119).

Being half Jewish feels like a game at first, but eventually the name Jesse Goldman "no longer [feels] so funny, . . . so make-believe." The box of "negro-bilia" that Deck Lee gave her when he left with Cole, so she would not forget her black heritage, has come to seem only like objects rather than meaningful parts of her identity: "They seemed like remnants from the life of some other girl whom I barely knew anymore, anthropological artifacts of some ancient, extinct people, rather than pieces of my past." At the same time, she feels detached from herself, watching herself live a life to which she does not belong—yet another way in which she has lost her integrity in the root sense of wholeness (160–62). She actually feels like an artifact, "someone who has been kept in a box" (187), an object rather than a subject, as well as a person confined in a constricting identity, boxed in as it were. The only way she can reveal her true self is to speak Elemeno to her horse and tell it about her real father and sister, "as if to convince [herself] that they had existed" (162), and also to whisper her secret to her boyfriend when she knows he is asleep: "I'm not who I say I am. I'm someone else. . . . The Jewish thing. It's a lie." (176). In fact, after another boy throws pennies at her and calls her a kike, and after her best friends ask if she is *really* Jewish, she says "not really" and puts the Star of David away (209–10). Her denial of Jewishness here and later is not so much a repudiation of Jewishness per se but rather a renunciation of a wholly white identity and the start of the retrieval of her black selfhood.

In the concluding section of the novel, Birdie has put Jesse aside and fled her mother's home in New Hampshire to try to find her father's people in Boston. Reunited at last, after six years, Birdie and Cole resume their sisterhood, even resurrecting Elemeno as their private means of communication. Deck finally, if halfway, acknowledges Birdie's kinship to him when he says that she looks a little like his mother, which he had never before noticed (337). And when Birdie glimpses her sister after the passage of several years, she notices some resemblance to their white mother (342). The binaries may not break down entirely, but their vulnerability is shown.

There is a good deal of Danzy Senna herself in this work of fiction, including the assumption of a Jewish identity; however, the *assumption*, or taking on, is not Senna's but instead the presupposition of those with whom she comes in contact. When asked why she identifies with Jews (though she is not a Jew), Senna responded,

> Because all of my life, people thought I was Jewish, and particularly Israeli. I grew up in Brookline, Massachusetts, which has a large Jewish population. My boyfriend in high school was Israeli, and we looked alike in a funny way. I've always been aware of the identity that I've worn into the world: this mask of being Jewish. In New York, I've also commonly been thought of as Arab. In cabs, the drivers think I'm whatever they are. Also, because I'm biracial, but people assume I'm white, I have a hidden identity. And I think a lot of Jewish people walk around with a hidden minority identity. They've come up to me on my book tour and said, "I identified with Birdie feeling like a spy, because I've been in a room full of non-Jews, and felt uncomfortable when the conversation turned to a certain topic, and felt I had to come out as Jewish, in that moment." There are a lot of parallels.[37]

Senna's photograph on the back flap of her 2009 "personal history," *Where Did You Sleep Last Night?*, reveals that she could, like Birdie Lee, pass as one of several ethnicities, including white and Jewish. This work also reveals other autobiographical elements in *Caucasia*: Danzy Senna's black professor father (though not of classics), who is an activist; the white mother from a Boston Brahmin family; their hippie marriage and lifestyle in the 1960s; the older sister, favored by the father; the subsequent divorce and strained relations between the parents. The vexing identity issues of growing up biracial pervade the history as they do the novel. However, in the decade between the publication dates of *Caucasia* and *Where Did You Sleep Last Night?*, the author gained additional knowledge about her history that presents almost a coda to the novel. The hitherto secret aspects of the family of Senna's father—complex interracial mixings, including the father's several half siblings sired by an Irish Catholic priest—uncovers a far more complicated series of personal and societal issues than she wrote of in the work of fiction. In addition, as she says near the end of her personal history, "My family is today, through blood and marriage, African American, Mexican, Polish Jew, Pakistani Muslim, Cuban, Chinese, Japanese, English, and Irish. We are wandering, spreading, splintering apart, all the time. We are trying to reinvent ourselves with each new generation. We are blending new races with each union."[38] The varied real-life ethnicities of her siblings, their partners, and their children not only indicate the rich diversity within the United States today; they also call into question the continuing relevance of the concept of "passing."

Caucasia provides one response to that issue of relevance when Birdie's mother tells her, "It doesn't matter what your color is or what you're born into, you know? It matters who you choose to call your own" (74). When Birdie finally meets up again with her father, in California, Deck insists, "There's no such thing as passing. We're all just pretending. Race is a complete illusion, make-believe. It's costume. We all wear one. You just switched yours at some point. That's just the absurdity of the whole race game" (334). Yet when Birdie tells Cole that their father had said "there's no such thing as race," Cole responds, "He's right, you know. About it all being constructed. But . . . that doesn't mean it doesn't exist." And there are consequences to allying with one race versus another (348, 349).

That it *can* still matter a great deal "who you choose to call your own" is highlighted by the recent case of Rachel Doležal, president of the Spokane chapter of the NAACP, part-time professor of African Studies, and civil rights activist, who assumed a black identity for over a decade. When it was discovered and publicized in 2015 that she is not black as she had claimed, her decision to pass as such was excoriated by many and defended by others. A great deal of ink was expended over this case, and with it a great deal of conversation over the water cooler. Was Doležal's black identity a charade, a masquerade, even a theft—yet another example of white appropriation of the black experience? As expressed in an essay called "Background Checks," by a biracial author on the issues of being biracial in the United States today, "Dolezal got to indulge in the myth of the self-made American, of choosing whom she wanted to be. But unlike actual black people, she could discard her putative blackness at any time, which made her performance all the more offensive and absurd."[39] Even before that essay appeared, seven letters to the *New York Times*, published together under the heading "On Racial Identity," showed the varied and sometimes very personal takes on the situation. One writer stated that Doležal's case has pointed out that racial identity is less biological than cultural and political, and yet her secrecy amounted to exploitation; another asked whether we shouldn't be as inclusive of those who identify as a different race as we are of those who identify as their nonbiological gender; a third understood Doležal as refusing to participate in the assumed shared racism of whites against blacks; and the remaining four letters contained different approaches still.[40] The *New York Times* magazine section continued the conversation by placing the Doležal case in a much wider context, with two essays several months later, one provocatively called "Takeover" and the other, longer essay subtitled with a double entendre, "Who Do You Think You Are?" As the former piece noted, "The line between cultural appropriation and cultural exchange is always going to be blurred."[41] As for the NAACP, its northwestern conference stood by Doležal's record with the chapter and stood true to its history by pointing out that racial identity itself neither qualifies nor disqualifies one to be a leader of the organization. (Neither does religious identity, since a Jew, Kivie Kaplan, was president of the national board of the NAACP from 1966 to 1975, and currently a Jew is a chapter head in Arizona.)[42]

The question "Who Do You Think You Are?" had earlier been turned into a definitive statement by journalist Brooke Kroeger for her book *Passing: When*

People Can't Be Who They Are. One of the several kinds of "passers" interviewed by Kroeger, David Matthews has made a choice of whom to call his own. Like the fictional Coleman Silk, real-life Matthews has a black father; unlike Coleman Silk, he actually did have a Jewish mother, an Israeli who was drawn more to the 1967 war than she was to the imminent birth of her child. She left her husband and son fairly soon thereafter and, except for a few cards in the succeeding months, was not heard from again. David did not even learn her name until he was nineteen. Nonetheless, although he was brought up to identify with his father as a black man, Matthews presented himself as white, usually Jewish, on and off for the better part of two decades. One influence in that decision was Matthews's grandmother on his father's side, who was not only very light skinned but, with an "us" and "them" attitude, differentiated between people like herself and the "darkies" (her term) who brought shame to the race. In this attitude, of course, she is reminiscent of the many assimilated Jews in nineteenth- and early twentieth-century America who looked down on the hordes arriving from eastern Europe and, later, of those "refined" Jews like Miss Wales in *Gentleman's Agreement*, who might be embarrassed by "vulgar" Jews and even use the epithet *kike* to differentiate between "us" and "them."

Matthews's passing began with a gravitation toward Jewish schoolmates— "To me, it was not even a conscious choice. It was an easy choice. Our sensibilities were similar, our sense of humor, our music." In his high school, he reports, a student could not have friends in both the black groups and the white circles, so he now made a conscious choice to pass, not only as fully white but as Jewish as well. Kroeger notes the irony that, of course, Matthews was already Jewish by matrilineal descent, whether or not he ever studied or practiced the faith. She draws the parallel with Henry Louis Gates's remark at the death of Anatole Broyard, the famous literary critic who passed as white all his life: "In a system where whiteness is the default, racelessness is never a possibility. You cannot opt out; you can only opt in."[43] Given that David Matthews was born in 1967, thirteen years after *Brown v. Board of Education*, his opting out of blackness seems "more like cultural treason," to use Kroeger's words, than like the "stuff of cultural tragedy" of the earlier generation in which Coleman Silk came of age. But Matthews's father did not disown him, and Matthews's black self was never totally obliterated. When he read a review of Danzy Senna's *Caucasia* in 1999, he saw enough of himself in that novel to start speaking out against racist comments instead of remaining silent.[44] Kroeger's interview with David Matthews was completed in 2002, however, at which point he still had white friends only and the latest in a string of Jewish girlfriends. His story is not a novel with a conclusion but a life in progress. And so, sixteen years later, this reader wonders where he now stands in terms of his racial and ethnic identifications. Does he identify as a white Jew, a black Jew, or something else entirely?

Jews into Blacks

In Nella Larsen's *Passing*, Irene Redfield, who identifies as black (though on occasion, when it suits her, she passes for white), says to a white friend, "It's easy for a Negro to 'pass' for white. But I don't think it would be so simple for a white person to 'pass' for colored."[45] Simple it may not be, but in American history and literature it has occurred, most famously, perhaps, in *Black Like Me*, John Griffin's stint (many have called it a stunt), via skin dye, as a black man in the later 1950s. What I want to concentrate on here is the passage not only from white to black but from white and Jewish to black. As Susan Gubar has commented about Malamud's "The Angel Levine," "if blacks are Jews then Jews can be blacks, and after such knowledge, who can keep the categories sequestered?"[46]

Ordinary American Jews in both the North and South blurred the categories by staging blackface minstrel shows in their social clubs and organizations for decades starting in the late nineteenth century; Eric Goldstein includes a poster for one in New York in 1914 and a photograph of another in Atlanta in 1925. Under the latter he captions, "While Jews of Eastern European background saw minstrelsy as an avenue to Americanization, they also frequently embraced black culture as a temporary escape from the pressures of conformity in white America."[47] On the national stage a well-known example of Jews in blackface is provided by Al Jolson in the 1927 movie *The Jazz Singer*, considered, not quite correctly, as the first talkie. Many critics have analyzed the scenes in which Jolson gradually transforms himself into a black man in his dressing room and then sings "Mammy" on stage to his adoring mother in the audience (the stereotypical Yiddishe Mama).[48] From one perspective, the Jew and the black are herein allied as persecuted groups, especially because Jolson (Jack Robin, né Jakie Rabinowitz) looks at himself in the mirror, in effect twinning himself. On the other hand, as has been said about Rachel Doležal, this jazz singer can and does remove his makeup and hence his black identity when it suits him, whereas the racial other cannot. (Just as Birdie Lee can remove her Star of David and hence her Jewish identity.)

One is reminded in this context of Fannie Hurst's first story with racial overtones, in this case literal ones, because in "The Smudge," published in 1922, a white woman performs in black makeup that leaves a smudge on her daughter when she bends down to kiss her. Lori Harrison-Kahan remarks of this story, in her book *White Negress*, "Although Hurst did not specify the ethnicity of her blackface protagonist, in the early decades of the twentieth century some of the best-known female performers to draw on black culture for their material came from Jewish backgrounds. The list includes singers and comediennes Sophie Tucker, Stella Mayhew, Nora Bayes, and Fanny Brice, who all blacked up—or, slightly more subtly, 'tanned up'—at some point in their careers and whose style of music was often referred to as 'coon shouting' because it was modeled on black song (or at least white perceptions of black song)."[49] In titling her book *White Negress*, Harrison-Kahan contests rather than adapts Norman Mailer's 1957 use of the term "white negro" to designate (in her words) "the post–World War II hipster whose nonconformity is conveyed by enacting the myths of black masculinity." In contrast to the "white negro," the "white negress," although she may at times succumb to stereotypes of black femaleness, "reveals how the unconventionality of the modern woman was viewed as an affront to ideals of white femininity and thus initiated a critique of whiteness as well as gender norms."[50]

In an interesting parallel, Jo Sinclair's *Wasteland* may be said to perform a similar function because of its insistence on foregrounding the lesbianism of Jake's sister Debby. In fact, *Wasteland* conflates Jewishness, blackness, and lesbianism as outsider status. Debby does not literally perform in blackface, but along with accepting her Jewish and lesbian identities she is strongly identified with her black women friends and becomes a "white negress" with the same motivation foregrounded by Harrison-Kahan in her study of Jewish women on the stage. Using the term *Negro* as opposed to her immigrant mother's denigrating "nigger," Debby places the family's move from Hillside Avenue in the context of white flight: "Was it really the Negroes? Or was it fear: and of course we pinned the word Negro to the fear, didn't we? Did we really think the Negro would contaminate us, or was it some old, secret nightmare we could name nigger now? And run from? It's easier to run away from something with a name, isn't it?"[51] Debby has just published her first story in *New Masses*, and her brother describes it as "about colored people" (29); true to form, her mother asks why Debby has "to write about colored people. Maybe that's why they didn't pay you anything for it." Debby says to her brother what she could not say to her mother: "Negroes are very important to people like us. She wouldn't have understood" (30). The phrase "people like us" is not defined but understood to mean Jews. Jake's emotional development in this novel, centered on retrieval of a religious heritage, relatedly results in acceptance of his sister's sexual identity, the redefinition of appropriate female behavior that she lives every day, and her embrace of black culture.

A fuller treatment of the subject of men and women in blackface is beyond the scope of my study. But I would spend a few more moments on the "jazz age" in which many of the figures noted above performed. Several authors on racial identity in general, and passing in particular, have remarked on jazz musician Mezz Mezzrow (given name originally Milton), described by Allyson Hobbs as "a 'white Negro hipster' born to Russian-Jewish immigrants, [who] passed as black to shore up his musical bona fides."[52] Mezzrow seems to be a touchstone for commentary on the subject of Jews passing into blackness: Baz Dreisinger and Gayle Wald also elaborate on Mezzrow's self-transformation. Dreisinger quotes from Mezzrow's memoir that in Harlem he finally, really "became a Negro." At Rikers Island for drug possession, he was accepted for black by the warden because of his "nappy head" and the Jewish musicians wondered "how come a colored guy understands their [Jewish] music so good." A profile in *Ebony* was called "Case History of an ex-White Man." But he did not discount his heritage, because, as Dreisinger says, "forging a link between Jews and Blacks is another way in which Mezz authenticates his passing: his heritage, he implies, already 'blackens' him in some way."[53] Interestingly but not surprisingly, the brouhaha over Rachel Doležal's passing as black—darkening her skin, marrying a black man, insisting she is black, becoming head of the Seattle branch of the NAACP—brought up a reference to Mezzrow yet again, in a letter to the editor in the *New York Times*:

> Racial fluidity is nothing new. Of course we know that some African-Americans have attempted to pass as white because of the racism in the United States. Less well known, however, is the case of Mezz Mezzrow, a jazz saxophonist, who lived in Harlem with his African-American wife.
>
> He wrote a book published in 1946 called "Really the Blues" in which he insisted he was a "voluntary Negro." His belief that he was black extended to persuading the warden of a prison where he was serving time for drug possession that he should be listed as "Negro" and placed in the blacks-only unit of the prison. He said he was more comfortable there than in the whites-only units.[54]

Mezzrow's era was "when the Negro was in vogue," as Langston Hughes titled his essay on the Harlem Renaissance, and as Larsen portrays in *Passing*. At this time the Jewish writer Waldo Frank traveled with Jean Toomer to Spartanburg, South Carolina, because both were writing novels about black life. As Hobbs puts it, "Frank's dark complexion and his association with Toomer allowed him to pass as black and to pose as Toomer's 'blood brother.'"[55] (Toomer's light skin made him racially ambiguous as well.) The issue of the Jew's complexion comes up again in the case of George Jean Nathan. Isaac Goldberg, Nathan's biographer, quotes a description from the pseudonymous commentator named Owen Hatteras: "'Fifteen minutes in the sun,' avers Hatteras, 'gives his complexion the shade of mahogany; twenty minutes, the shade of Booker T. Washington.' In proof of this [says Goldberg] I possess the only joint photograph of [H. L.] Mencken and Nathan ever taken, in which Nathan plainly looks like a graduate of Howard University."[56] Goldberg does not mention that "Hatteras" was a pseudonym for either H. L. Mencken or George Nathan himself or the two writing together. But even if the description is facetious, the important point is that Nathan is likened to a black in three ways: a generic description of skin color that codes for a black person, a reference to an actual (and famous) light-skinned black man, and a university founded for and attended largely by persons of color. The authors of these statements, of course, and Goldberg as well, knew that Nathan was a Jew by birth on both sides of the family, which only made the likening to black a natural comparison. In *Caucasia*, too, Birdie's white boyfriend, who doesn't know her true heritage and thinks she is Jewish, tells her, "Shit, maybe you could be colored in the right light. Better stay out of the sun" (173).

The racial haziness about a Jew's skin tone is at the center of the real-life situation recounted in James McBride's *The Color of Water*—a fascinating and complex story because it involves several self-transformations. Ruth McBride's passing was actually fourfold: in addition to becoming, in effect, black, she became an ardent Christian; more, she renounced the South and claimed a northern identity, as well as taking on a fully American self, rejecting her eastern European birth and background with their associations of restrictive Orthodoxy and a domineering, abusive, self-proclaimed rabbi father. It is appropriate that no photos from her obliterated past are included in her son's memoir except for his grandmother's passport picture from Poland, with her two children in her arms—the only memento that Ruth kept. In erasing her past and reinventing herself, Ruth moved beyond every Jewish relative except for this beloved, suffering mother. Among her several transformations, the particular emphasis of James McBride's work is on Ruth McBride's passage from white to black, as his subtitle—*A Black Man's Tribute to His White Mother*—implies. It is also appropriate that the montages of family photographs included as a frontispiece and at the end are all in a faded gray, neither starkly black nor white, but no doubt intentionally the "color of water," calling into question the notion of an assigned race.

In this context Baz Dreisinger usefully highlights Ruth's birth religion, noting that "much of what makes Ruth nonwhite is her Jewishness, which is fundamental to the memoir's plot and structure." This plot and structure "underscore the parallel between the discrimination faced by Ruth as a Jew—she is called 'Christ killer' and attends neither the black nor the white school in her Virginia hometown—and by James as an African American." James writes that his mother never spoke about Jewish people as white but instead as Jews, as if in a separate category. Dreisinger's summation is cogent: "Ruth's persona as the almighty matriarch evokes both Jewish lore and African American tradition; it is one way in which McBride merges the two cultures in his work. Jewishness thus acts as a kind of third race in *The Color of Water*; it is that which makes Ruth not quite white, not quite black, although she is also not quite Jewish. At the same time, because it is equated with blackness, Jewishness blackens Ruth. It is Al Jolson's burnt cork in *The Jazz Singer*, which darkens him on the one hand and whitens him on the other."[57]

Laura Browder, in her study of "ethnic impersonators," notes the similarity in Ruth McBride's story to that of Elizabeth Stern in that they were both molested by their rabbi father (in Elizabeth's case, foster father), but she also remarks on the difference that Elizabeth takes on the rabbi's identity and Ruth rejects that of her father: "In striking contrast to *Secret Family*, the memoir written by Elizabeth Stern's son Thomas, *The Color of Water* is a celebration of McBride's choice to enter a new ethnic and racial identity. While Stern's memoir excoriated his mother for lying, McBride's book is a warm celebration of his mother's choice and of her creative path to survival."[58] We recall John Brown's aversion to his father in *Wasteland*, and consequently his avoidance of the Passover seder; Ruth's memory of *her* father's seder is, like John Brown's, an unpleasant one, but whereas John retakes his father's identity and finds a comfortable place at the seder table—an inward movement or return rather than an exodus—Ruth does truly escape.[59] When, many years later, she attends the wedding of her son's Jewish friend, she looks the part of a Jew—"her long nose and dark eyes seeming to blend in perfectly with the mostly eastern European faces surrounding her"— but she is truly only a "guest" in the deepest sense (284). She is a "black woman in white skin," as James calls her (260); in her own words, she "stayed on the black side because that was the only place [she] could stay," and for the rest of her life she "never veered from the black side" (232).

Some might look upon Ruth McBride as an ethnic impersonator because she was "really" Ruchel or Rachel Shilsky, who abandoned Judaism only because of bad examples from her childhood and then the death of her mother, who was her last tie to the religion. Or one might say that she stayed on the black side only because in her day and time her white relatives would not have countenanced her two marriages to black men and her production of twelve black children. Or one might complain that she danced around the question of race, telling James when he asked if she was white that she was "light-skinned" (21). But the truth is that she gained greater fulfillment as a Christian in a black world than she ever had as a white Jew. Her passing was not a fancy in the sense of a fantasy, whim, or illusion, as we learn not only from the portions of the book that constitute her life story but also from her son's take on that story. Browder calls *The Color of Water* one of a group of modern autobiographies that "open up the national conversation about race. They cannot properly be called autobiographies of racial impersonation. Rather, they are autobiographies that, by questioning the existence of race as an essential category, resist the idea that impersonation is possible. Perhaps a more appropriate term would be 'autobiographies of racial recategorization.' . . . These new autobiographers write themselves out of the trap of racial identity by questioning the meaning of race itself."[60] Perhaps Rachel Shilsky pulled off the "recategorization" that Rachel Doležal could not because she remained in her private, domestic sphere; until her son created her memoir, she simply lived her life in a black community and seemingly did not feel a compulsion to dwell on or publicize who she "really" was or wasn't.

One cannot forget that *The Color of Water* is only in part Ruth's "autobiography," in the sections in italics; it is also James's memoir of growing up puzzled and confused. Given Ruth McBride's deflections and obfuscations when the young James asked about her history, it is not totally surprising that McBride did not probe his mother about her past until he was a college student and needed to know her maiden name. At the same time as Ruth becomes black and Christian in her memoir, her son in a sense becomes a Jew; this is because, through his tribute, James McBride to some small extent reappropriates what his mother had abandoned. When he visits the Jews of Suffolk, Virginia, he finds that most of the Jews "treated me very kindly, truly warm and welcoming, as if I were one of them, which in an odd way I suppose I was. . . . It said a lot about this religion—Judaism—that some of its followers, old southern crackers who talked with southern twangs and wore straw hats, seemed to believe that its covenants went beyond the color of one's skin. . . . They talked to me in person and by letter in a manner and tone that, in essence, said 'Don't forget us. We have survived here. Your mother was part of this.'" (224). In short, McBride's story is a search for his own identity through investigating his mother's. He comes to the conclusion that "all Jews are not like my grandfather and that part of me is Jewish too" (262). This is an aspect of racial crossing that, in my estimation, has been underplayed in the reception to McBride's book.

The real-life case of Ruth McBride is provocative in its own right, but a recent work of fiction takes the subject one step further: Jess Row's novel *Your Face in Mine*. In the context of passing from Jewish to black, it merits analysis in conversation with *The Human Stain*, in tandem with which it reads like a kind of "counter life." Row's novel is narrated by a friend, Kelly Thorndike—a technique similar to that of *The Human Stain*, in which Coleman Silk's story is related by Nathan Zuckerman. In both works, the main character enlists a writer to tell his story, which in Roth's case is about the Clinton years and sex and in Row's case about the Obama years and race. The protagonists of these two novels crisscross, as it were: Coleman Silk is a black man who becomes a Jew, and Martin Lipkin is a half Jew who becomes a black man named Martin Wilkinson (because Lipkin isn't a name for a "brother").[61] Both men lie to their wives and children about their origins, but Silk risks having identifiably black children with his white wife, whereas Wilkinson has a secret vasectomy so his genes will "stay put," adopting black children instead (33). Both Roth and Row play with the questions of what constitutes an authentic identity and to what lengths one will go to reinvent oneself. *Your Face in Mine* draws on and extends a phenomenon very much in currency today: surgery to correct identity dysphoria.

Key to Row's novel is that Martin Wilkinson has undergone racial reassignment, a term introduced early (7) and likened to sexual reassignment. The famous case of Christine Jorgensen, a transgender woman of the 1950s whose memoir publicized her surgical sex change, is a reference point for Martin: as he tells Kelly Thorndike, "I'm the Christine Jorgensen of the twenty-first century" (34). Wilkinson's self-diagnosis is that his "long history of psychological problems . . . was the result of being born in the wrong physical body. I term this 'racial identity dysphoria' because I believe it is in many ways similar to the gender dysphoria that is so commonly reported in the news" (41). If the inferiority complex was the psychological problem to be corrected in the earlier era of cosmetic surgery, racial identity dysphoria is the term of the day in Wilkinson's world. Wilkinson's childhood environment had reinforced what he now thinks of as his innate identification with blacks. At the commune in which he lived with his hippie parents, a black woman with a big smile left a strongly favorable impression, and he attended El-Hajj Malik El-Shabazz Elementary School as one of the only white students (the first in eight years), adopted as an ersatz family member by the mother of his black classmate, who saw the neediness in a little white boy more or less abandoned by his own people. After he is moved to Roland Park Elementary because of a drive-by shooting in the black section of Baltimore, he speaks "black English" out of habit; his father reassures the new teacher using a term we have seen in *Caucasia*, *Zelig*, and the Itzkovitz essay: his "little chameleon" will change colors soon enough (151). And so it happens that Martin Lipkin becomes white to adapt to his new surroundings, just like Birdie Lee in New Hampshire.

When Kelly Thorndike looks up the term *racial reassignment* he finds only "articles on passing, on Michael Jackson, on Jewish nose jobs, on eyelid surgery in Korea" (25). He will soon find out that the technology has developed light years from Jacques Joseph's first modern rhinoplasty in the nineteenth century, an operation that Row references from his reading of Sander Gilman (263–64). According to Row, the idea for this novel came to him after he picked up Gilman's *Creating Beauty to Cure the Soul* in a bookstore:

> The idea just sort of came to me as I read that book: What if there was something called racial reassignment surgery? Not unlike gender reassignment surgery, someone determines that they are of a different race on the inside and they wish to surgically correct that. The idea was a bolt from the blue. It didn't take me too long to interweave that idea with experiences I had in high school. A few friends of mine were these white kids who were obsessed with hip-hop culture and who were practicing a sort of racial masking. They weren't passing, but masking. They were creating a sort of self-camouflage without articulating it as racial. It was very clearly a form of escape, a form of self-abnegation. So the novel started as a theory that then connected with something from my own experience that I'd always wanted to write about but for which I'd never found the correct frame.[62]

As Row elaborated to an interviewer, those white kids who were obsessed with black culture included him: "I'd been writing about racial and ethnic difference [in his early stories collected as *The Train to Lo Wu*], and I went to high school in Baltimore and was haunted by the racial stratification there. As a white teen I was very drawn to hip-hop culture, almost to the point of disappearing in it—there was a sense of having no sense of authenticity except this one that wasn't mine. I kept coming back to the question of what would happen if that disappearance became permanent."[63]

One might ask why Jess Row's protagonist is half-Jewish, and thus why Jewishness is the identity renounced for blackness. There is more at work here than the fact that the rhinoplasty on assimilating German Jews was a prime impetus for *Your Face in Mine*; the author's exposure to and investment in Jewish culture also plays a part. Although Row is not Jewish on either side—raised as a Unitarian by Protestant parents, he is a practicing Buddhist—his wife is Jewish (and Indian), they belong to a Reconstructionist synagogue, and his children attend Hebrew school. In addition, as Row has related, he "attended a progressive private high school, the Park School, which is the model for the Willow School in YFIM. At the time [he] attended, Park was mostly Jewish (it was founded by secular German Jews) though this is no longer the case. Many of [his] closest friends in high school were Jewish or had one Jewish parent." And many of those Jewish teens, leaning politically left, felt alienated from their parents.[64] Alienation may explain, at least partially, why Lipkin abandons his Jewishness as he transforms to black. His Jewish father has left his religion behind, since it means nothing to him (129), and Martin himself has never gone to a synagogue much less had a bar mitzvah (182). The religio-cultural substratum is thus too weak to hold him up as he makes his racial identity change.

In fact, Jewishness seems more incidental to this novel than to both Roth's *The Human Stain*, where it stands in for making it in America post–World War II, and Danzy Senna's *Caucasia*, where it is a kind of halfway house between blackness and whiteness, thereby permitting Birdie Lee to hang onto at least a shred of her preferred identity even when she wears a Star of David after her mother takes her on the lam to "Caucasia." Other than an important but brief mention of a Bruno Schulz story about the temptation to create life out of matter that has "infinite possibilities," which Martin reads in a Jewish professor's class and learns is akin to Jewish mysticism (181–82), Jewishness in *Your Face in Mine* rather cursorily appears in Martin Wilkinson's abandoned family name and in token allusions to Jewish culture in Kelly Thorndike's reminiscences of his high school friends in Baltimore and girlfriend at college (56, 206). Row's usage of passing from Jewishness to blackness updates the versions of the phenomenon I have been discussing in this chapter. His Martin Wilkinson, arch entrepreneur, has as his ambitious goal the regeneration of Baltimore through making it a center of racial reassignment surgery—especially to transform whites into persons of color. The Jew in this novel, once emblematic as the dark other, the assimilated white, or both, is passé as a figure to be either emulated or excoriated. Dark others are in and mere passers are out. The malleability of identity has morphed into the total freedom to become whomever one wishes or considers oneself to be. "I'm not on a mission to destroy racism, [Wilkinson] says, and I'm not on a mission to destroy races. What *I* think is that people should have options. I believe in free choice. That's the American way, right?" (220). To Wilkinson's mind, being Jewish and black is not an option—we note his refusal to be a Black Hebrew (36)—because they are very different cultures. This is in spite of the fact that in his progressive high school, Wilkinson had classmates who were Hinjews, Mexijews, and a biracial African American Jew with a rabbi for a father, who could have passed for any of those dark others, including "Sephardi ex-kibbutzniks" (56). Thus, we are back to either/or, at least in this protagonist's terms. We are back, that is, to the choice that Coleman Silk makes in the 1940s, to be one or the other, but in the opposite direction: from Jewish to black.

With its emphasis on identity as a choice, Row's novel is appropriately placed in connection not only with Roth's but also with the Rachel Doležal case and the far wider cultural matrix of which that case is one part. As revealed in Doležal's 2017 memoir, in the firestorm of publicity she actually did have to resign from her NAACP position under pressure, along with being ousted from her various part-time jobs. After all, she had lied about her "race," an inexcusable breach of integrity. Yet her life story as she details it in this work is much more than an apologia for presenting herself as black when she was born of white parents, or her revenge against the people who treated her badly in her lifetime; it goes a long way toward explaining how she arrived at and interprets her choice, what the costs were for her and her family even before she was outed, and why her decision has elicited strong and contradictory reactions but at the same time has raised important questions about identity, race, and American society.

In her prologue to *In Full Color: Finding My Place in a Black and White World*, Doležal repudiates the view that blackness was, for her, "just a costume [she] had put on to amuse [her]self or acquire some sort of benefits."[65] Brought up in lily-white northwest Montana, she nonetheless thought of herself as black from an early age, as evidenced by her self-portrait with dark skin when she was four years old. Her succeeding years were devoted to developing her "true identity" (a phrase she repeats [1, 2]). One could psychologize on the basis of her horrific childhood in a home with verbal, physical, and sexual abuse that whiteness was something to run from, but that would be a layperson's speculation; of more import is the fact that her parents, for dubious reasons, adopted four black babies in quick succession, and Rachel was left to care for them and to try to ameliorate the unequal treatment her parents accorded the adoptees based on who had lighter or darker skin. Whatever the contributing factors, Rachel more and more identified with blacks as she grew and left home for a small college in Mississippi, where she agitated for observance of the Martin Luther King holiday as a day of service, painted black figures in art class, and began to assume an "Afrocentric way" of styling her hair and dress. A frequent question from her classmates was, "So, what are you?"

(84). She was thought of as a light-skinned black or mixed-race woman, and she began to check the box for black on application forms. The transformation was not so much a covering as a revealing in Doležal's estimation: it happened "not by wearing a disguise or being deceitful, but simply by being myself. It felt less like I was adopting a new identity and more like I was unveiling one that had been there all along. Finally able to embrace my true identity, I allowed the little girl I'd colored with brown crayon so long ago to emerge" (90–91). To quote the slogan on T-shirts sported by some Doležal supporters, she was "TransRachel" (246), a pun on transracial that Row's Martin Wilkinson would appreciate. To use Laura Browder's phrase, Doležal underwent a "racial recategorization."

Doležal notes that when a black friend reassured her that "to copy is to compliment," she took this opinion as approval to style herself so that her exterior accorded with her interior, so to speak: her looks expressed her sense of who she was deep inside. In addition, as she reveals in her epilogue, she changed her name in October 2016 because "Rachel Doležal" was by then too controversial: she adopted a name bestowed on her by an Igbo from Nigeria because he considered her a "'twin soul.' Born with a white veneer but living as a true Nubian in order to fight for justice for the Black family and culture" (273). She does not give the new name there, but the internet discloses it as Nkechi Amare Diallo—and that revelation elicited more outrage, including the remark on Twitter that she "can change her name to Kunte Kinte Abdul-Jabbar and she'll still be white" (a powerful reference since Kunte Kinte is a recovery of a lost African name in Alex Haley's influential *Roots* and Kareem Abdul-Jabbar is the name taken on by famed black basketball player Lew Alcindor when he converted to Islam). No matter the extent of the negative reactions to her decisions, with reference to cultural appropriation Doležal firmly sets herself apart from sports teams adopting Native American images or whites rapping about the black experience. Using an expression historically applied to blacks passing as white, but in a different if related sense, she mulls that it is important to determine which acts "cross the line": "not everything that's called appropriation is false or inauthentic" (91–92). When, in the media frenzy about her case, one of her adoptive brothers told a reporter that her "dark makeup" applied every morning (which she insists was nothing more than a suntan and a bronzer) is "basically blackface," she was saddened by the implication that she had been "wearing a costume and making fun of Black women instead of simply being myself. Wearing blackface is the opposite of being pro-Black, of celebrating 'Black is beautiful,' of working for racial justice, and of trying to undo white supremacy—all the things to which I had dedicated my life" (230). The bottom line is that in Doležal's assessment, she was not "passing":

> Passing has existed in the United States as long as white people have oppressed people of color, which is to say for its entire history. Typically, it's been

light-skinned black people who have passed for white in an attempt to accrue the same advantages white people enjoyed: to acquire gainful employment, avoid discrimination, and preclude the possibility of being lynched, But why would a white person want to pass for Black when doing so would involve losing social and economic benefits? . . . . Just as a transgender person might be born male but identify as female, I wasn't pretending to be something I wasn't but expressing something I already was. I wasn't passing as Black; I *was* Black, and there was no going back. (148)

In Allyson Hobbs's assessment, in contrast, the likeness to passing is central; as she wrote in a *New York Times* opinion piece quoted by Doležal, "As a historian who has spent the last twelve years studying 'passing,' I am disheartened that there is so little sympathy for Ms. Doležal. . . . The harsh criticism of her sounds frighteningly similar to the way African-Americans were treated when it was discovered that they had passed as white. They were vilified, accused of deception and condemned for trying to gain membership to a group to which they did not and could never belong" (244). For her own part, in the prologue to her memoir, Doležal insists that she and everyone else has a "right to self-determination"—to throw one's origins overboard, as Zuckerman says about Coleman Silk. In fact, she says, "one of the few silver linings of the media firestorm that followed [her] 'exposure' is that it sparked an international debate about race and racial identity" (1).

As part of that debate, in Wesley Morris's October 2015 essay in the *New York Times* Sunday magazine section, "The Self in the Age of Anything Goes: Who Do you Think You Are?," published four months after the Doležal story broke, the commentator reflected on the many recent developments in American culture over recent years—"but especially in 2015"—focusing on the fluidity of identity. As he wrote of Doležal, "Some people called her 'transracial.' Others found insult in her masquerade, particularly when the country's attention was being drawn, day after day, to how dangerous it can be to have black skin. . . . But there was something oddly compelling about Dolezal, too. She represented—dementedly but also earnestly—a longing to transcend our historical past and racialized present. . . . It was as if she had arrived in a future that hadn't caught up to her yet." Jess Row's novel comes back into focus in this context, when Morris comments on the four new "satirical novels of race" that he read that year—the number is another marker of America's fascination with identity issues. One of these novels is *Your Face in Mine*, which Morris sums up as an "eerily calm" work revealing that the white author "takes guilt to an astounding allegorical extreme: The surest cure for white oppression [of blacks] is to eliminate whiteness."[66] I think there is more at stake here. Not only does Row's Martin Wilkinson explicitly disavow such a motive (41–42), but Morris's summary statement to my mind does not do full justice to Row's intention and achievement in his novel; it ignores the equally important story of the narrator, Kelly Thorndike. In *The Human Stain*, Roth provides hints about Zuckerman's background but the focus is firmly on Coleman Silk. In Row's novel, Kelly Thorndike is on his own search to find a skin in which to feel comfortable: in his case, an Asian skin. Having lost his Chinese wife and daughter in a car crash, and his job to a merger, Thorndike experiences what Row has called, in an interview, an "existential crisis. I wanted him to be stripped of all his other options and looking for a way to redefine himself."[67]

A white man fully invested in Chinese culture—for he taught in China and met his wife there—Thorndike through Wilkinson eventually sees the possibility of becoming Chinese through his own racial reassignment surgery. As the reader eventually finds out, Wilkinson enlisted his friend in his project in the first place precisely, but surreptitiously, in order to get him to agree to undergo the surgery to be racially reassigned as Asian and thus to become a marketing tool for expanding the business into that continent and enlisting Asians to surgically appear Western. In the end, Kelly Thorndike does undergo the transformation, adopting the name Curtis Wang and going "home" to China as his father-in-law had urged him to do after Wendy and Meimei's deaths (18). Perhaps he is fleeing from his complicity in the death of another high school friend (a death that Wilkinson uses to enlist—that is, blackmail—Thorndike); perhaps he is merely fulfilling the terms of his contract with Wilkinson. Whatever the case, Kelly is no longer a *laowai*, or noncitizen foreigner. He dies to his old self and passes into the new more successfully than others who will go under the knife for racial realignment surgery, because his appearance now matches his knowledge of the Chinese culture in Wudeng: its dialect, food, and mores. The final line of the novel, "I'm home," marks a true fulfillment.

I have trouble categorizing *Your Face in Mine* as "satirical," in spite of the extreme and ethically dubious nature of the enterprise depicted therein. It is true that Wilkinson is more of an opportunist and even a con man than a social theorist or do-gooder. But in this novel the author, in taking the option of reinvention seriously, is very in tune with the times in which we live, in which the fluidity of identity has not lessened intolerance, and in which having had a biracial president who identifies as black could not mean that the country is "post-*race as an issue*," as a friend of Martin's asserts (208)—quite the contrary. I prefer the assessment of Josh Lambert, reviewing the novel for the Israeli newspaper *Haaretz*. As he put it, "The novel's lasting impression is of a fascinating irony: If the latest developments in trans awareness are any indicator, the book's sci-fi vision of racial reassignment sounds less like the future than do the novel's briefly mentioned biracial Jews who know how to be more than one thing at once."[68]

Knowing "how to be more than one thing at once" is the note sounded in a work in a different genre, by a woman with quadruple identities. Lisa Bloom, discussing the autobiographical nature of much contemporary visual art, uses the 1998 installation piece *Quadroon*, by Danielle Abrams, as a prime example of today's possibilities. Abrams is the grandchild of a paternal black grandmother and a maternal Jewish grandmother. Like Anna Deavere Smith, she can "play" it white or black, Jewish or Christian, and she does so in *Quadroon*, composed of four videos of herself in different roles telling each character's story: her southern black grandmother, Janie Bell; her immigrant Jewish grandmother, whom everyone called Dew Drop Lady; herself as a teenager in Queens, New York, confused about her biracial identity and wishing to pass herself off as Greek; and the older Abrams, represented as Butch in the Kitchen. As Bloom notes, the mature Abrams "is a light-skinned black as well as a dark-skinned Jew in a predominantly white gay and lesbian community and thus straddles multiple social and racial groups." The voices emanating from the four monitors, one in each corner of the gallery, "intersect, overlap, co-join, and talk over one another," as the artist herself described them in a 2002 talk at the Jewish Museum, transcribed by Bloom. Bloom then adds her own commentary: "In this way [Abrams] complicates reductionist understanding of what a Jewish/black/lesbian identity might be. Such a strategy allows her to assert the diversity and complexity of US Jewish/black/queer identities while at the same time refusing a celebratory stance in which all the tensions between these multiple identities are easily resolved."[69]

Abrams's strategy might complicate a "reductionist understanding," but it begs the question of who has a "right" to own an identity if that ownership is more tenuous than Abrams's. What about the increasing popularity of Passover seders held by evangelical Christians, for example? The title of an article in the *Forward* captures the issue: "Evangelicals Retool the Passover seder: Spoiler, It's Now a Feast about Jesus' Sacrifice." Televangelist Jim Bakker in 2013 enthused, "It's not a Jewish holiday, it is a fantastic Christian time. I mean, every detail of Jesus is in the Passover." Some Christians have pushed back against the idea that celebrating a seder within this framework is either legitimate or appropriate. One writer termed such seders "theologically dangerous and culturally insensitive": "One of the privileges [he wrote] that comes with being part of the majority culture is that nobody is likely to call you out on your cultural appropriation. So call yourself out. Don't host a seder."[70] And what about the black "tribes" in New Orleans who adopt Indian names and attire for their Mardi Gras parades?[71] In both these examples, as in the Rachel Doležal case, reactions run strong in various directions. May a person who believes herself to "be" black (and argues that we all trace our roots back to Africa anyway) present herself as black? If Christians view what they call the Old Testament as laying the groundwork for the New, and predicting the New, may they in good conscience hold a seder that revolves around Jesus as the sacrificial lamb? If the practice of blacks dressing and parading as Indians has its origins in respect for the Native Americans who harbored runaway slaves, does that make it culturally appreciative and not appropriative? Or will the future as depicted in Jess Row's novel one day eliminate the need to pose such questions, much less take offense or be on the defensive about such practices? That question is of necessity left hanging.

Notes

1. White, "Why I Remain a Negro," 52.
2. Shapiro, *We Are Many*, 246. These "crucial differences" are outside the realm of my book. Dinnerstein rehearses them in the context of the civil rights movement in his *Antisemitism in America* (208–11). Dinnerstein's entire chapter on "African-American Attitudes (1830–1990s)" is informative on the subject of black-Jewish relations.
3. Brodkin, *How Jews Became White Folks*; Goldstein, *Price of Whiteness*.
4. Roth, *Human Stain*, 92. Subsequent references in the text to this novel are to this edition.
5. The 2003 film version of the novel uses that speech for a different purpose: the minister at the funeral of Coleman's father recites part of it to emphasize the valor of the deceased.
6. Shostak surmises in *Philip Roth* (156) that Silk's use of this word "seems not at all accidental but an admission of his need to punish himself for his deceptions." I would be convinced by her interesting interpretation if I knew that Silk customarily had black students in his classes, but I am willing to entertain the possibility she suggests.
7. Dreisinger, *Near Black*, 124.
8. See Brodkin, *How Jews Became White Folks* (43), for some of the details of racial discrimination and violence during and after World War II.
9. Hurst, "Gold in Fish," 255.
10. Roth, "Goodbye, Columbus," 7, 37. Harrison-Kahan notes a similar feeling of kinship that Rebecca Walker expresses in her memoir *Black, White, and Jewish*: "When she is at the home of a Jewish friend . . . Walker describes feeling drawn to Maria, the Hoffmans' Latina maid in her black and white uniform: 'I feel closer to Maria than I do to Allison, like I should call her Mrs. Somebody and I should go with her to the kitchen or wherever she's walking to, and not stay back here in the fancy front rooms'" (quoted in Harrison-Kahan, "Passing for White, Passing for Jewish," 37). The quotation is from Walker, *Black, White, and Jewish: Autobiography of a Shifting Self*, 208.
11. See Rust, "Modern Life," 53–54. As the sidebar to this article reads, "The world is becoming more and more aware that Judaism is a religion, not a race, and one that comes in different flavors and colors."
12. Gold, *Jews without Money*, 176–77. An "Abyssinian Jew, descended from the mating of King Solomon and the Queen of Sheba," this visitor to the Gold home declares himself to have a pure faith unlike those who have been corrupted by "wander[ing] among the Gentiles." As the narrator says, "By his manner one could see he despised us as backsliders, as mere pretenders to the proud title of Jew." Mr. Adeyemi, a major in the US Marine Corps, is of Nigerian descent; he nominated his rabbi as one of America's most inspiring rabbis (see Tannenbaum, "America's Most Inspiring Rabbis," 15–16). In sub-Saharan Africa, significant rabbinical conversions in the last decade or so have occurred in Madagascar and Uganda, part of the "increased visibility and interest in emerging or Judai[ci]zing groups worldwide" (see Kestenbaum, "Madagascar Natives Convert En Masse," 10–11).

13. The Black Lives Matter movement is a current example, but its involvement by black Jews is multidimensional, as explored by Kestenbaum in "Black Jews Stand with Black Lives Matter amid Turmoil." The subtitle "but 'God Comes First'" indicates that for the century-old Hebrew Israelite movement, absence from social justice causes has to do with the prophetic interpretation of Jewish suffering. Kestenbaum's short piece helpfully provides background on the Hebrew Israelites. A longer piece by the same author in the same journal, a year earlier, provides even more context (see "Working Their Way in From the Margins," 8, 10–11).

14. Harrison-Kahan, "Passing for White, Passing for Jewish," 23. The statement is repeated in Harrison-Kahan's later work, *White Negress*, 178.

15. Kaye/Kantrowitz, *Colors of Jews*, 139.

16. Samuel, "Jews of Color," 18.

17. See Alexander and Haynes, "Color Issue: An Introduction," two unnumbered pages before 1.

18. Dinnerstein, *Antisemitism in America*, 197–207.

19. Dreisinger, *Near Black*, 123.

20. An interesting sidelight is provided by Michelle Cliff's novel set in Jamaica, *Abeng*; the author relates how black Americans "said that the West Indies were too uppity and didn't know their place. They called them Black Jews—half in admiration, . . . half in scorn. . . . The Americans said the West Indians were too intent on status. Too concerned with achievement" (see *Abeng*, 86).

21. Dinnerstein, *Antisemitism in America*, 201.

22. From the 1920s to the 1940s, Jews were prominent in the sport of boxing. See Bodner, "Boxing: A Jewish Sport."

23. Elam, in "Passing in the Post-Race Era," does not deal overtly with the function of this character in Roth's novel, but she no doubt has Delphine Roux in mind when she concludes her discussion of *The Human Stain* with this rather damning assessment of Roth's achievement: "Roth's use of passing ends up being largely an occasion to explore white male social and physical impotency, and given the narrative space devoted to both the castrating effects of prostate cancer (36) and feminist scholars (273), the performance of race starts to look more like performance anxiety" (see 761). I am not in disagreement with Elam's view of the sexual aspects of Coleman Silk's (and Roth's) story, but I do credit Roth's novel as a bona fide passing narrative, one that cleverly if subtly uses a woman as a double for the protagonist.

24. Anna Deavere Smith had a great-aunt who passed for white "to get ahead." See Clary, "Passing for White."

25. Itzkovitz, "Passing Like Me," 41. Itzkovitz provides an example of the Jews being termed chameleon-like in an editorial in an 1895 magazine (see 52n9).

26. James Baldwin, "On Being White," quoted in Kaye/Kantrowitz, *Colors of Jews*, as one epigraph to her first chapter "Are Jews White?" (1). Gilman includes the same question, "Are Jews White?," in the title of an essay on the "Jewish nose."

27. Not surprisingly, when Leonard falls out of favor with the public, one Christian commentator advises others to "lynch the little Hebe." Also not surprisingly, when society rejects him after he is supposedly cured, he begins to change identities again, metamorphosing into any group in power, even the Nazis. Yet at the end of the film, Zelig saves both himself and the doctor by "becoming" a pilot and safely landing a plane. Perhaps the ability to "merge," as Bellow puts it, is "salvation" after all.

28. Quoted in Clary, "Passing for White," 3.

29. Elam, "Passing in the Post-Race Era" (755–58) instructively discusses Roth's use of boxing, though not the prominence of Jews in the sport.

30. Here I take issue with Elam's assertion (761) that Silk "dismisses the aphorism ['Lost himself to all his people'] as mere nostalgia, the 'imprisonment' of the family history and 'ancestor worship.'" I see more ambivalence, more nuance, in Silk's relationship to his black roots.

31. Shostak, *Philip Roth*, 4.

32. Harrison-Kahan, "Passing for White, Passing for Jewish," 26.

33. Larsen, *Passing*, 16.

34. Two examples are Leverette's "Re-Visions of Difference," 110–27, 149, and Grassian's "Passing into Post-Ethnicity," 317–35. Grassian mistakenly states that Sandy Lee takes on a Jewish identity. She does not.

35. Harrison-Kahan, "Passing for White, Passing for Jewish," 34–35.

36. Harrison-Kahan, in "Passing for White, Passing for Jewish," 27, has a different take on the mark left on Birdie by the Star of David: since it is greenish in tint, this critic interprets the mark as a connection to her "fake immigrant past" because Birdie is a "'greenhorn' in her white New Hampshire environs."

37. Senna, "Coat of Many Colors."

38. Senna, *Where Did You Sleep Last Night?*, 196.

39. Holmes, "Background Checks," 15.

40. Respectively, the authors of those three letters are Mark Burford, Jess Coleman, and Gwen Davis-Feldman.

41. Sehgal, "Takeover," 14.

42. See the Duke University Archives website on its Kivie Kaplan collection and *The Daily Beast* for information about the Phoenix chapter head: http://library.duke.edu/rubenstein/findingaids/kaplankivie/ and http://www.thedailybeast.com/articles/2015/06/15/watch-out-rachel-dolezal-there-s-another-white-naacp-leader.html.

43. Clary, in his "Passing for White," states that Coleman Silk "was loosely modeled on the late Anatole Broyard, for many years a prominent literary critic for the *New York Times*" (2). But Philip Roth strongly denied this connection, stating that the character was in fact modeled on a friend of his, a Princeton University professor (see "Open Letter to Wikipedia").

44. Kroeger, *Passing*. David Matthews's story is related in chapter 1, "Not Some Social Agenda Struggle," 11–41. Kroeger prefaces this chapter with the quotation from James Weldon Johnson that Daniel Itzkovitz also references, about the wish for a "jinnee" to make one a Jew. (Kroeger remarks on Itzkovitz's chameleon theory in the body of the chapter.) The quotations in my text from the Kroeger chapter are from 20, 25, 35. The quotation from Henry Louis Gates is from his essay "White Like Me," 78.

45. Larsen, *Passing*, 118.

46. Gubar, *Racechanges*, 260.

47. Goldstein, *Price of Whiteness*, 58, 67–68, 156–57.

48. In addition to Gubar's study, see Rogin, *Blackface, White Noise*; Alexander, *Jazz Age Jews*; Jacobson, *Whiteness of a Different Color*, 119–22; and Goldstein, *Price of Whiteness*, 154–55. For an interesting take on the opposite phenomenon, a black musician's affinity with Jews, see Melnick, "Black Man in Jewface."

49. Harrison-Kahan, *White Negress*, 16. This author deals at some length with Hurst's story—indeed, the impetus for her book derives from it—and helpfully addresses the previous gender gap in discussions of minstrelsy. She summarizes various works on the meaning of Jews in blackface, and the various views they contain, on 3–6.

50. Ibid., 11.

51. Sinclair, *Wasteland*, 193. Subsequent references in the text to this novel are to this edition.

52. Hobbs, *Chosen Exile*, 20.

53. Dreisinger, *Near Black*, 104, 105, 112. Dreisinger also notes on 118, "The Jews' role in early hip-hop, in fact, intriguingly parallels their role in early jazz and ragtime."

54. Dougard, "To the Editor," 10.

55. Hobbs, *Chosen Exile*, 191.

56. Goldberg, *Theatre of George Jean Nathan*, 8.

57. Dreisinger, *Near Black*, 132–133.

58. Browder, *Slippery Characters*, 276.

59. McBride, *Color of Water*, 43. Subsequent references in the text to this memoir are to this edition.

60. Browder, *Slippery Characters*, 275.

61. Row, *Your Face in Mine*, 8. Subsequent references in the text to this novel are to this edition.

62. Row, "We Wear the Mask."

63. Schulman, "When Race Breaks Out," 46.

64. Personal email correspondence from Jess Row to Judith Ruderman, June 13, 2016.

65. Doležal, *In Full Color*, 1. Subsequent references in the text to this memoir are to this edition.

66. Morris, "Self in the Age of Anything Goes," 52, 53. The other three novels are Nell Zink's *Mislaid*, Paul Beatty's *The Sellout*, and Mat Johnson's *Loving Day*.

67. Row, "We Wear the Mask."

68. Lambert, "It All Begins with the Jewish Nose." Lambert also notes that "the novel, disappointingly, skims over [the] behavioral aspects of racial transition." However, Wilkinson's early steeping in black culture, and especially Kelly Thorndike's immersion in Chinese culture, seem to me to represent the author's subtle underlining of these necessary prerequisites for a successful transitioning—prerequisites that Wilkinson's marketing materials do not contain.

69. Bloom, *Jewish Identities*, 126, 128.

70. Kestenbaum, "Evangelicals Retool the Passover Seder," 10–11.

71. For a brief discussion of this phenomenon, see my *Race and Identity*, 252–53n53. The blog Racialicious.com, which hosted intense and contradictory opinions about the practice in 2010, is no longer available.

8   The Use of Clothing in Jewish Passing
Narratives

*"The Fashion Wears Out More Apparel
Than the Man"*

SHAKESPEARE'S APHORISM FROM *Much Ado About Nothing*—that for those who would keep up with the latest styles, the whims of fashion necessitate a replacement of clothes before they wear out—lends itself to an appraisal of apparel switches in passing narratives. Dr. Silpa, the plastic surgeon in Jess Row's *Your Face in Mine*, likens racial reassignment to a mere change of clothes: "Nobody has to wear the clothes they came in with. Nobody has to be stuck in one body."[1] Likewise, as we have seen, Birdie Lee's father, in the 1970s of Danzy Senna's *Caucasia*, argues that race is "a costume. We all wear one. You just switched yours at some point. That's the absurdity of the whole race game."[2] For both of these men—the devotee and enabler of cultural transitions, the passionate writer on race—a change of identity seems as easy as a change of clothes, much ado about nothing, if you will. Interrogating the connection that Dr. Silpa and Professor Lee make between clothes and identity requires a focus on works of art across the decades in which literal and figurative changes in clothing reveal personal and societal searches for identity. As it turns out, a change of clothes is quite often much ado about something.

Karen Brodkin, in *How Jews Became White Folks*, argues that the assimilation of Jews into American society has required a buying into "the practices and meanings of whiteness, of the dominant culture and values," which in turn requires a deliberate othering of the culture and values of blacks (and other racial minorities).[3] What happens when one makes a swerve and takes on the unfashionable (as it were) coloration of that Other? Sinclair Lewis's *Kingsblood Royal* (1947) offers an instructive analogy to *Gentleman's Agreement* of the same year: as the Christian Phil Green becomes at least "part Jewish" by pretending to be a Jew and raising his consciousness about WASP privilege in the process, so does Neil Kingsblood become part black by discovering a black ancestor and taking on the cause of rebellion against the mores of his community. Lewis's novel can also serve as an apt comparison point to another work of Jewish fiction: a broader way of thinking about Philip Roth's short story "Eli, the Fanatic," collected in the *Goodbye, Columbus* volume, and the clothing images therein.

The Kingsblood home in Grand Republic, Minnesota, is homogeneous and hence considered by its inhabitants to be idyllic; as the former mayor says, it is "free of Jews, Italians, Negroes and the exasperatingly poor."[4] But when Neil Kingsblood engages in some genealogical research, hoping to find a distinguished ancestry, he discovers that he is in fact a Negro in hiding. His first reaction is to keep this revelation to himself: "What's this about colored people 'passing,' if they're light enough. I certainly shall. Why should I be so conceited as to imagine that God has specially called me to be a martyr? And pretty vicious kind of martyr that would sacrifice his mother and his daughter. . . . Everything can be just as it was. It *has* to be, for Biddy's [daughter's] sake" (69). Yet Neil remains troubled by his discovery, so he visits his pastor, the reverend Dr. Shelley Buncer of the Sylvan Park Baptist Church. The seemingly incidental details that this clergyman has "an Episcopal voice" and dresses in tweeds, not to mention that he is "a companionable golfer . . . and a dependable extemporaneous speaker at bond drives" (130, 129), firmly encode him as a member of the town's white establishment. Neil presents his discovery of Negro ancestry under the guise of another man's problem, asking for wise counsel that he can pass along. The ever practical pastor, after exposing his own ignorance and prejudices about blacks, advises that the anonymous third party "play the game" of passing (132).

As Neil begins to associate with black citizens of his community, and to become their trusted friend, he learns a great deal about the trials they live with daily under segregation and second-class citizenship. In tandem, he develops a new consciousness about Jews: when his wife remarks, a propos of an appliance salesman, "I think you can jew him down five dollars on the price," Neil thinks, "I wonder if a Jew likes that phrase, 'jew him down,' any better than my people like 'sweating like a nigger'?" (163). The phrase "my people" is operative, for rather quickly Neil Kingsblood accepts his new identity—although he discovers he is only 1/32 black, he announces before the city fathers, "I'm very cheerful about being a Negro, gentlemen, and about the future of our race" (229). Neil will suffer the consequences of his decision: not to pass as white but to pass as black. In effect, he becomes just what the black woman Sophie Concord calls him, in a different context: a schlemiel (286). Neil Kingsblood's conversion experience on the road to blackness allies him with Philip Roth's Eli Peck, another schlemiel who flies against the norms of his society, looking foolish by some lights and heroic by others.

Laura Browder comments on *Kingsblood Royal* in terms that could also fit "Eli, the Fanatic": Lewis's novel, she says, "blends two models of postwar blackface: blackness as an escape from conformity (the more Neil learns about what it is like to be black in America, the more appallingly narrow-minded and dull he finds the suburban neighbors he once enjoyed), and blackness as spiritual odyssey."[5] "Eli, the Fanatic" can profitably be read in similar terms of blackness as both an escape from conformity and a spiritual odyssey, and also of race (black and white) as well as the more obvious interpretation of religion and culture (traditional versus assimilated Jew).

Hat Tricks

A common expression to refer to the ultra-Orthodox in America is "the black hats." This catchall phrase does not capture the variety of those hats, a variety that in and of itself emblematizes the differences and often the rifts among Orthodox denominations or sects. Samuel Freedman—in his chapter "Who Owns Orthodoxy?"—provides a partial list of such head coverings: "a small *kippa seruga*, or knitted yarmulke, for the Modern; a larger *kippa seruga* for the militant religious Zionists; a black velvet *kippa* for non-Hasidic *haredim*; a black fedora or fur *shtreimel* for Hasidim."[6] In "Eli, the Fanatic," the rift in question is between the Orthodox and the assimilated Jews. Eli Peck, the "fanatic" of the story's title, is the lawyer for the aptly named town of Woodenton who has been delegated by his "modern community" to inform the Jewish refugees from Europe that they cannot establish a Jewish school nearby, since the area is zoned residential.[7] The assimilated Jews of suburbia, at ease with their Christian neighbors in a community formerly restricted against Jews, do not want to have the tenuous rapprochement upset by these traditional Jews with their Yiddish accents and their black clothes. Those black clothes, specifically the black hats, function as synecdoche for the entire way of life of Jews who hold on to the traditional elements of Jewish culture, including a Yeshiva education for their children. The black hat worn by one of the refugees on his shopping expedition in town is in fact "the very cause of Eli's mission" to the head of the Yeshiva, to use the law as a tool for preventing "Brownsville" (a section of Brooklyn heavily populated by Jews and itself a synecdoche) from encroaching on Woodenton, that "modern" community—the characterization "modern" reiterated for emphasis (256, 277).

After his first in-person visit to the Yeshiva's rabbi, symbolically named Tzuref, a word close to *tsuris* (troubles) in Yiddish, Eli writes a letter that clarifies the issue: "Woodenton is a progressive suburban community whose members, both Jewish and Gentile, are anxious that their families live in comfort and beauty and serenity. This is, after all, the twentieth century, and we do not think it too much to ask that the members of our community dress in a manner appropriate to the time and place." Rather audaciously, not to mention naively, he proposes that if before the war these Orthodox Jews had given up "some of their more extreme practices in order not to threaten or offend the other," the persecution of the Jews might have been prevented. The letter concludes with the seeming concession that Yeshiva personnel are welcome in Woodenton "provided they are attired in clothing usually associated with American life in the 20th century" (262). Such clothing is neatly summarized in the title of Sloan Wilson's novel

The Man in the Gray Flannel Suit (1956), published only three years before Roth's story appeared in *Commentary*; in fact, one of the articles of clothing that Eli will give to the refugee is his gray flannel suit (272). As is true for all eras, the clothing in fashion in the 1950s made statements about the time period; in the case of the Eisenhower years (1953–1961), the time has been characterized as one of conformity in dress and behavior, a period of calm between World War II and the turbulent 1960s. For the Jews in the United States, it was the era of the move from "shtetl to suburbia," to appropriate the title of Sol Gittleman's study of "the family in Jewish literary imagination."[8]

A one-sentence reply from Rabbi Tzuref to Eli Peck's letter comes two days later: "The suit the gentleman wears is all he's got" (263). Understandably, Eli interprets the response to mean that the refugee has only one suit of clothing; but the rabbi means something deeper: that this clothing is all that the man has of his past life—a wife and baby and a "village full of friends," all of whom were annihilated by the Nazis (264). Tzuref presses Eli to affirm an identity with the suffering Jews rather than with the complacent ones: "I am them, they are me, Mr. Tzuref," says Eli of his community, standing his ground. "Aach [*sic*]! You are us, we are you!" responds the rabbi (265). Soon enough, what Eli terms the rabbi's "double-talk" (267) becomes actualized in Roth's presentation of Eli's identification with the man in black. At first Peck wishes only to give his own high-quality clothes to that man—"the guy in the hat" (271)—which he packs up, appropriately enough, in his wife's Bonwit Teller box, yet another marker of the suburban life of ease and access. Another missive must be sent, this time a note in the box, which informs the rabbi that the clothes are for "the gentleman in the hat": "All we say to this man is change your clothes." The replacement hat, the one that Eli had worn that day, is emphasized, as if it is especially important (274). When Eli assures his neighbor Ted Heller that the matter has now been resolved because the man is changing his clothes, Heller replies, "Yeah, to what? Another funeral suit?" (275). This allusion to one kind of passing symbolically portends another kind: that Eli Peck will die to his familiar and socially acceptable identity when he passes into the identity of the man in the black hat. Indeed, when his wife, Miriam, later sees him in the greenhorn's clothes, she whimpers, "Eli, Eli, you look like you're going to your own funeral" (296).

Eli's transformation has probably begun long before the story itself begins, since he has always been troubled by his life of moderation and rationality (a life in which painting rocks pink is considered rational). The visits to the Yeshiva only set something in motion that was already embryonic: a birth, so Roth has it. Miriam is nine months pregnant with their first child and goes to the hospital in labor right before Eli delivers the clothes to the Yeshiva; her story is a foil to Eli's, so it is fitting that the nurse tells him to go home because "he looked like *he* was having the baby" (279). At the Yeshiva Eli observes the greenhorn beating his breast and moaning, which stimulates Eli to try out the moaning himself. After this act of identification, the man in the hat that was once Eli's delivers his old clothes at Eli's doorstep, perhaps sensing Eli's receptivity for change. Opening the box is like turning a light onto darkness: "Inside the box was an eclipse. But black soon sorted itself from black, and shortly there was the glossy black of the lining, the coarse black of trousers, the dead black of fraying threads, and in the center a mountain of black: the hat. He picked the box from the doorstep and carried it inside. For the first time in his life he *smelled* the color of blackness: a little stale, a little sour, a little old, but nothing that could overwhelm you" (285). The first article that Eli dons is the mountainous hat; shedding the rest of his clothes, he observes himself "naked in a hat" and then, feeling "tempted," he puts on the rest of the greenie's castoffs (285–86). At first, he conceptualizes himself as "Eli, in costume" (287), but the questions the story is asking are, first, what is a costume and what is an authentic identity, and, second, can a new identity be assumed (in both senses of taken on and understood as) if the owner is devoid of its cultural context?

At Eli's transformation into a black-hatted Jew, the town of Woodenton decides that he is having a nervous breakdown; after all, he had been diagnosed previously with two such episodes. Eli, in contrast, "knew what he did was not insane, though he felt every inch of its strangeness. He felt those black clothes as if they were the skin of his skin" (293). Observing his newborn son through the nursery window, Eli is determined to hand off his black clothing to the child eventually and "make the kid wear it. . . . whether the kid liked it or not!" (297). Earlier Roth had referenced the story of Abraham and Isaac, in Ted Heller's complaint about the Bible stories his daughter is forced to listen to in Sunday school: "This Abraham in the Bible was going to kill his own kid for a sacrifice. . . . You call that religion? Today a guy like that they'd lock him up. This is an age of science, Eli" (277). Now, in the final scene, Ted stands by his friend at the nursery window but cannot "stand by" him in any deeper sense; he says to Eli, "You're not thinking of doing something you'll be sorry for. . . . I mean you know you're still Eli, don't you?" (297). Calling Eli "rabbi" the doctors lead him away from the window and inject him with a sedative. The last line reads, "The drug calmed his soul, but did not touch it down where the blackness had reached" (298).

In terms of its symbols, "Eli, the Fanatic" is not subtle: consider the names Woodenton, Tzuref, and also Eli, the high priest of Israel, whose name means "ascent" or "God is most high," along with the motif of child sacrifice, highlighted by the reference to Abraham and Isaac. But in terms of its meaning, the story does not reveal its secrets so openly. Philip Roth engages here in "double-talk." Given the story's proximity to the novella "Goodbye, Columbus," one would logically assume that Woodenton is a wooden town indeed and that assimilation has come at a very steep price: the shedding of a rich tradition and culture and the taking on of a bland conformity with modern American values. After all, Roth's novella is a biting satire of the consumerist, ostentatious Patimkins, even as it simultaneously shows understanding of and even sympathy for their situation. From the perspective of Tzuref in the short story, Eli has found himself in identification with the suffering of his people, but from the perspective of the townspeople, Eli's passing fancy is a sign of his mental instability. Both views are operative—the story has it both ways.

Neil Kingsblood's responses to finding out that he has a "Negro" ancestor rather than a "royal" one bear recalling in reference to Eli's sacrifices: at first Neil decides to "pass" as white in order not to be a "martyr" who would sacrifice his family if he acknowledged a black identity, but he eventually does become a martyr, hauled away to jail at the end of Lewis's novel, sacrificing his child for the cause. So, too, does Eli Peck—dressed in blackness now "the skin of his skin"—wish to sacrifice his own child in order to pass along a deep and meaningful heritage. Each of these protagonists is a "guy like that," as Ted Heller complains of the Bible's Abraham, who should be, and is, locked up: one in jail and the other presumably in a sanitarium. What is the "blackness" that the sedative cannot reach in the case of Eli, in the story's concluding line? Laura Browder, in discussing the Black Power movement, states that at its basis the movement was "a reconception of African American identity. Black Power advocates encouraged African Americans to undergo the 'Negro-to-Black conversion process,' as the psychological model was described, in order to 'discover the blackness within themselves.'"[9] In Roth's account, the blackness is that of the clothing yanked from his body—and all it stands for, now perhaps permanently his own possession nonetheless (unless he will be "cured" and whitened again)—and also the blackness of despair and suffering that he learns to emphasize with and now must experience as an outcast, and perhaps as well the blackness he has endured in leading an inauthentic life. One might also say that the blackness is akin to that advocated by the Black Power movement, a pride in racial otherness and unwillingness to act the "Negro"—in this case, the assimilated Jew who gets along in what Ted Heller calls "a good healthy relationship" with the town's Protestants (277).

A viable alternative interpretation, in Timothy Parrish's words, is that "Eli is less recovering his true cultural identity than performing what an 'authentic' identity might look and feel like."[10] In the same vein, Ken Koltun-Fromm argues, in his *Material Culture and Jewish Thought in America*, that the clothing is nothing more than material to Eli because he "lacks the cultural and religious knowledge to accept" it as symbolic of a "robust Jewish identity." As a clear example of this lack, the critic points to Eli's ignorance about the white garment in the "greenie's" box, which thus "fails as a meaningful religious signifier" for him as the "*tallit katan* [undergarment with fringes] worn by observant Jews."[11] In Jess Row's *Your Face in Mine*, in contrast, it is precisely Kelly Thorndike's cultural knowledge that leads me to imagine he will actually pass effectively into a new identity as Chinese, in the brave new world of Martin Wilkinson's fancy.

"Eli, the Fanatic," like *Kingsblood Royal*, also resonates with aspects of Hobson's *Gentleman's Agreement*. Using a clothing image that Roth will literalize, Phil Green's sister Mary writes him a letter about his proposed series, saying that "it's such a *sweet* thing for you to do, Phil, sort of trying it on to see if it fits." Of course, it is hardly a "sweet" endeavor at all, but Mary is correct in assuming that even if "it doesn't make a good series, it'll be something inside you for the rest of your life." Her brother has already recognized this: "He had changed. Once you change about things like this, you never unchange." On another point, his son, Tommy, being enlisted into the "game" of pretense—what Phil will later call the Game of Identification—makes sense of it by remembering a Danny Kaye movie they had seen about a dead brother's ghost who inhabits his twin's body. Tommy asks, "You mean you're not Jewish but just as if you had a twin brother's ghost in *you*, like the movie, and *that* one is Jewish?" Anne Dettrey also remarks on the duplicity—the doubling—in similar terms: "This must have been dizzy, though, kind of mirror-within-mirror stuff. Watching yourself as Jewish but at the same time watching yourself as Christian-watching-Jew."[12]

Werner Sollors has noted that the recognition of passing in American literature emerged not only with the passing as white of runaway slaves but also in connection with the literature of "masquerading and with traditional social satire upon the upstart; hence passing has not infrequently remained allied with such themes as the *parvenu*, cross-dressing, double, rebel and victim." He elaborates on the concept of the double in a footnote, commenting, "Since 'passing' suggests a person who is both one thing and another, it is logical that the motif sometimes occurs in conjunction with that of the double." Sollors references a 1908 work by Ray Stannard Baker, *Following the Color Line: American Negro Citizenship in the Progressive Era*, in which a black passing as white explains his double life in terms of Robert Louis Stevenson's *Dr. Jekyll and Mr. Hyde*. Says Sollors, the "literature of passing includes stories in which two persons change places, encounter each other as mirror images of themselves, or recognize their interior doubleness." He also remarks that "the camouflaging of aspects of one's identity is probably a human universal."[13] Roth's story is certainly social satire, but his Eli Peck may be seen as both rebel and victim, both a danger to stable society (Mr. Hyde) and a member of that society (Dr. Jekyll). The confusion lies in the fact that all perspectives are offered: "kind of mirror-within-mirror stuff," to echo Hobson's Anne Dettrey. Interpretation, like Eli himself, is doubled: Is Roth's protagonist camouflaging his Jewish identity when dressed in his gray flannel suit, or camouflaging his modern identity when dressed in the garments of an Orthodox Jew? The answer seems to be not either/or but both/and. Yet his closed society has forced him to make a choice of one or the other, which is actually no choice because opting for Otherness means that one is mentally unbalanced. Ultimately, whether Eli's new identity is "authentic" or not, the prominent motif of fathers-and-sons in this story suggests that the protagonist does stand in "for the line of Jewish fathers, or elders, his neighbors have forgotten or denied," as Parrish puts it.[14] As such, Eli's passing fancy comments on the vacuity of the alternative choices of Woodenton's assimilated Jews.

Because of its emphasis on the refugee's hat, "Eli, the Fanatic" could have been titled "On Account of a Hat"—except for the fact that Sholom Aleichem had already written a story by that name.[15] The use of the hat as a transformational medium in both stories invites a comparison between them in order to indicate how passing by means of an exchange of clothing reveals the environment for Jews in different settings and periods and the obstacles those environments present for identity formation and stability.

"On Account of a Hat" is a tale within a tale, an anecdote told to Mr. Sholom Aleichem by a stationery merchant from Kasrilevke in eastern Europe about a third party, a man named Sholem Shachnah, whom the unnamed informant considers a "rattlebrain." Deciding that this story must be true, because the gossiper is a merchant and "no *litterateur*," the narrator Mr. Aleichem—created by the author, of course, who *is* a bona fide *litterateur*—proceeds to relate the anecdote in the merchant's own words. The bare-bones of it is that Sholem Shachnah has been out of town brokering a real estate deal and must hurry home for Passover. He cables his wife that he will arrive home in time for the seder, without fail. The last train is not leaving for a while, so he finds the single unoccupied spot on a bench on which some sort of official in a uniform full of buttons is snoring away. The teller of this tale relates to Mr. Aleichem, "It's not such a bad life to be a Gentile, and an official one at that, with buttons, thinks he—Sholem Shachnah, that is—and he wonders, dare he sit next to this Buttons, or hadn't he better keep his distance? Nowadays you can never tell whom you're sitting next to."[16] Before resting his eyes, Sholem Shachnah gives the porter a coin to wake him up in case he falls asleep, to ensure that he will not miss the train.

When he awakes with a start he grabs the nearest hat, puts it on his head, and races for the train. Astonishingly, people treat him with the utmost deference, calling him Your Excellency, clearing his path, and insisting that he belongs in first class and not third. Thinking he must be dreaming, because why else would gentiles be so respectful of him, Sholem Shachnah happens to look in a mirror and discovers that the person staring back at him is wearing the hat of a minor official, not that of a Jewish real estate broker. Immediately he "realizes" that the porter has awakened the wrong man: "Twenty times I tell him to wake me and I even give him a tip, and what does he do, that dumb ox, may he catch cholera in his face, but wake the official instead!" (108). So Shachnah the Rattlebrain rushes off the train in order to locate himself sleeping on the bench and shake himself awake. Meanwhile, of course, the train leaves the station and our hero the schlemiel does not get home in time for Passover after all.

Readers (and the author) have great fun with this story of doubles and mistaken identity, but underlying the humor is a very serious point, which Gerald Shapiro sums up in his introduction to an anthology of short fiction, in a reference to "On Account of a Hat": "A hundred years later, the absurd humor of Sholem Aleichem's story remains, but the bitter, painful reality behind the story's comedy has faded. It's difficult for us now to grasp the fact that in the Pale of Settlement, our great-grandparents really did ride in third-class and live their lives as non-citizens, unwelcome guests of the state, in constant dread, fearful of anyone, anyone at all, in a uniform. Outside the study-house, away from the *shul*, a Jew's sense of identity was a tenuous, fragile thing, trembling on the verge of disintegration at any moment."[17] Sholem Shachnah had cabled his wife that he would be home for Passover "without fail"; the story asks, "How dare a human being say 'without fail' in the first place" (109). The implied reason is not so much that some impediments are in God's hands but rather that many impediments are in the hands of the hostile gentile, who can sabotage a Jew's plans at will and on a whim. Irving Howe and Ruth Wisse also entertain the deeper meanings of Sholom Aleichem's stories in a conversation with each other. Howe remarks, "Perhaps the ferocious undercurrent in Sholom Aleichem's humor has never been fully seen, or perhaps Jewish readers have been intent on domesticating him in order to distract attention from the fact that, like all great writers, he can be very disturbing." Ruth Wisse agrees: "Nowadays his name has become such a byword for folksy good humor, innocent 'laughter through tears' [because, in great part, of *Fiddler on the Roof*, the ever-popular musical based on the author's Tevye stories] that we're surprised to rediscover the undertone of threat in his work."[18]

In terms of threats to identity, there are similarities between "On Account of a Hat" and "Eli, the Fanatic," set in different times and circumstances. Eli Peck's identity is also fragile, and a change of hat tops off his identification with religious Jews that is almost like a calling, even though it is disorienting not only to him but also to his wife and his neighbors; the change of hat shakes up their entire world, and thus the hat must be removed and Eli neutralized. Sholem Shachnah's change of hat is arguably more frightening because the change of identity, though transient, is in effect a passing into a powerful Christian world where he doesn't belong and isn't wanted. Pretending to be what he is not, even if inadvertently, poses dangers to life and limb, potentially worse even than institutionalization. When Ted Heller pleads with his black-hatted friend, "You know you're still Eli, right?" Roth raises the question of who is the "real" Eli. When Sholom Aleichem has Sholem Shachnah mistake himself for Buttons, in a society where the choice to be whoever one wishes is not available, the consequences are grave indeed.

Just as "Eli, the Fanatic" conjures up a connection between one narrative about Jews and another, *Kingsblood Royal*, about a white man passing into black-nesss, so does Sholom Aleichem's story lend itself to comparison with a passing narrative of a light-skinned black woman into whiteness. Allyson Hobbs tells of a semiautobiographical story published in the December 1926 issue of *Opportunity* by anthropologist Caroline Bond Day. Once the protagonist, a "Negro woman of mixed blood," puts on a pink hat her life changes dramatically because the hat conceals her hair texture and brightens her face. Though plain and made of straw, the hat becomes a "magic carpet" that whisks her into hitherto forbidden territory. As described by Hobbs,

> A gentleman offered her a seat on the train, a young man helped her off of a railway car and retrieved her lost gloves, and a salesgirl addressed her as "Mrs.," a respectful title reserved for white women only. "Lo! The world was reversed." . . . For a few fleeting moments, Sarah glimpsed the pleasures of life beyond the limits of her Jim Crow world—a cold drink at a soda fountain, a pair of shoes purchased in the town's best shop, a comfortable seat in a movie theater, a stroll through an art gallery, a clean ladies' room—all on account of a pink straw hat.

On account of a hat, both Sarah and Sholem are treated with the respect that they deserve as who they already are but do not get unless they pass, on purpose or by accident, as someone they are not—someone they are not allowed to be in their societies. Sarah, like Sholem Shachnah, is not discovered as an imposter during her forays into a world of privilege, but when she breaks her ankle, no white physician will treat her and she returns to the bosom of her black family for care. As Hobbs puts it, "As her ankle healed, so did her fractured identity": Sarah realizes that with everything good in her life that is supplied by her family and her neighborhood, "Who'd want a hat?"[19] The reader of Sholom Aleichem's story may not be quite as sanguine that the "Rattlebrain" will find both joy and security in his own familiar environment even after putting on the hat that is rightfully his: he has an angry wife to greet him at the doorstep, after all, and a vulnerable existence in the Russian czar's domain.

Perhaps it is because a hat is easily donned and doffed, and sits so close to the face, that it serves as a convenient motif for a focus on identity. We find it again in the context of immigration to America, in Abraham Cahan's "Yekl," as well as in Joan Micklin Silver's film adaptation of Cahan's story, *Hester Street*. In the novella, at the neighbor Mrs. Kavarsky's insistence, Jake buys his newly arrived wife a cheap hat and a corset, both of which she tries on in her second week in the New World. Cahan spends two full pages on these items and Gitl's eventual willingness to put them on.[20] Looking into the mirror, she thinks herself quite a *panenke*, or young noblewoman, and is "all aglow with excitement," even pardoning the corset for the discomfort it causes (40). Silver's film, of the feminist era in the 1970s, plays a different note on this scene. Persuaded by Mrs. Kavarsky to modernize her look in order to keep her husband, whom Gitl already suspects of not loving her, Gitl puts on a corset to rein in her waist and an enormous feathered hat to replace her modest kerchief; as she gazes at herself in the mirror in this incongruous garb, she feels rather ridiculous and takes both items off with a sigh of relief. She will never be (nor will she want to be) like Jake's modern lover, Mamie, who looks, as Gitl says in the film and the novella, like a "veritable *panenke*" (52), but she has a glimpse of the new self that she will soon become: in her own hair, wearing fashionable though not fancy dress (83), accommodating to American norms while retaining traditional values.

The film in particular makes much use of hats as indicators of either greenness or acculturation, religiosity or secularism. The Russian immigrant fresh off the boat is confused and discomfited when Jake and his cronies laugh at his old-world head covering and remove it, playfully but disrespectfully, from his head, preventing him from starting the Hebrew blessing before eating; Jake's purchase of a bowler is a prominent sign of his becoming a "regular Yankee." And in the divorce scene, Gitl sports a tasteful, modern hat over her own hair. As for Mr. Bernstein the boarder—who will eventually become Gitl's much more suitable husband—he wears a yarmulke under his street hat and places a yarmulke on Joey's head to instruct him in Hebrew, in contrast to Joey's father, Jake, who places his own bowler on the boy's head before teaching him baseball. Bernstein is comfortable, and all indications suggest he will become more so, with two hats, two roles: American and Jewish at the same time. In fact, in the opening paragraph of the novella the as-yet-unnamed Bernstein, a "rabbinical-looking man," is struggling over an English newspaper with a dictionary on his lap; and in the film, he is giving English lessons to immigrants for twenty-five cents a session. At the close of both novella and movie, Bernstein and Gitl will open a grocery store with the money Gitl secured from Jake's lawyer; that she will run it so he can study in the back is an addition by the filmmaker, who looked back nostalgically at that option precisely at a time when it was no longer a viable division of labor for most Jews.

The use of the hat as a signifier of "passing" can thus be traced over many decades and different milieus. "On Account of a Hat" is set in the early twentieth-century Pale of Settlement and written with the author's firsthand experience of Russian pogroms. "Yekl" takes place in the Jewish ghetto of New York City, as its subtitle makes clear, during the mass immigration of eastern European Jews who are eager to forge an American identity and "make it" in the Golden Land of opportunity. "Eli, the Fanatic" is set in mid-twentieth-century American suburbia, where Jews, now living in largely gentile communities, are anxious to get along with their Christian neighbors and not rock the boat. Taking the motif even further, Dara Horn's *In the Image* is set a generation later, in the early twenty-first century, when more options are open for finding the "real" self and hence meaning in one's life. In Horn's novel, a change of hat is once again symbolic of a change of identity.

In this work, Leora's college boyfriend, known for his prowess on the soccer field, must reinvent himself when an injury obliterates his identity as Jason the Soccer Player. Influenced by an Orthodox Jew in his dorm, the Jason who had known next to nothing about his religious heritage, and who had considered the Hasidic Jews at his father's zoo to be little different from the exotic animals caged therein, steadily turns to orthodoxy himself. Leora, gazing wistfully at a photo taken of them at the zoo not long before, notes the difference between Jason in his customary baseball cap and Jason in his adopted head covering, a yarmulke: she "could scarcely believe how different a person could look, through nothing more than the choice of hats."[21] Unlike the negative portrayal of Orthodox Judaism and cheder (Jewish elementary school) instruction in such immigrant novels as *Bread Givers*, *Jews without Money*, and *Call It Sleep*, Horn portrays in Jason's born-again experience a fulfilling source of identity. It may not be Leora's source of identity, or the reader's, but one cannot gainsay the sympathetic treatment offered by the author in yet another of her efforts to retrieve Jewish history. Whereas "Eli, the Fanatic" leaves the passing into Orthodoxy open to interpretation, *In the Image*, through its elaboration of Jason's fulfillment in its later chapters, insists on its validity.

There is more to be said about hat changes in the context of the Mizrahi experience in the Old World and the New. Consistent with the salient differences between the stimuli for Ashkenazi Jews to leave eastern Europe and the Jews from Arab countries to make a similar journey from their own lands, a hat change may have a contrasting significance in Mizrahi literature from what we tend to find in works by Ashkenazi Jews. Lucette Lagnado, in her memoir concentrating largely on her father, the "man in the white sharkskin suit" of her title, recovers the meaning of hats in Egypt that she was too young to recognize at the time of her family's changed situation after Nasser's revolution in the 1950s. As she writes of the hat customarily worn by pashas and schoolboys alike, the edict of the new regime "banishing the tarboosh was perhaps the most telling sign of the ruthlessness of the new order. My father was no longer allowed to wear the red fez he favored above all other hats. To the revolutionary colonels, the cone-shaped hat was a small but potent symbol of the ancient regime. . . . By ruling against the tarboosh, the generals were taking action against an icon whose origin was Turkish but which was now as Egyptian as the Pyramids or the Sphinx." Leon Lagnado, once a dashing boulevardier consorting with the British and even, on occasion, King Farouk, had to put his collection of hats into a closet, "next to his treasured British regulation pith helmet. He never wore a tarboosh out on the street again, though he was determined to hold on to them, and enjoyed simply fingering their soft velvety contours and playing with the tassels."[22] That the author titles her chapter "The Last Days of Tarboosh" underscores that a hat is not just a hat: the removal of this hat is emblematic of the removal of Jews from the country and, more particularly, from a way of life wholly enjoyed and always longed for in the subsequent reduced circumstances of this father's American experience.

Clothing and Upward Mobility

Leon Lagnado leaves behind his favorite clothes when he sets sail for Paris and eventually the United States: not just his "secret stash of red tarboosh," but also his white sharkskin suits and jackets, which seem "superfluous, a relic of a life that was ending." The brocade robes that he had custom-made in the last days of that life are packed into one of the twenty-six suitcases that the family lugs around the world and never opens again. Gone is the privileged existence in which the wealthy Jews of Egypt and other Arab countries dressed opulently and as they wished; Leon now wears a faded and battered raincoat, becoming like so many others who went "overnight from riches to rags."[23] This story of downward mobility is the opposite of what one encounters in so much literature about Ashkenazi Jewish immigrants, for many of whom the new land served as a launch pad for economic success.

In fact, for Jewish immigrants, and others as well, clothes and the garment industry that produced them provided a mechanism for passing into a desired American way of life. Allyson Hobbs, writing of nineteenth century America and "anxieties of racial imperceptibility," particularly with regard to the indeterminate status of free blacks, notes the following: "Opportunities for self-fashioning and re-fashioning abounded in a society where both people and goods circulated widely. Clothing, perhaps the most essential commodity in the process of self-making for the poor and the genteel alike, became increasingly accessible, transportable, and resalable beginning in the mid-eighteenth century."[24] New outfits also enabled immigrant Jews to circulate more widely and to pass as assimilated Americans. But Jews were the producers as well as the consumers of this clothing, and their prominent role in the garment industry enabled this process of self-making for themselves and others.

In the mid-nineteenth century, German Jews were often peddlers of clothing and other goods into the hinterlands of the country; some of these immigrants eventually founded many of the department stores whose names are familiar even today. Later in the century, most eastern European immigrants in New York City found their first employment in the needle trades, whether they had worked at such a job in the old country or not: over half of the Russian Jewish men, and more than two-thirds of the women, were working in the New York garment industry in the first decade of the twentieth century. Annie Polland and

Daniel Soyer explain the system in their study of New York's Jews in the age of immigration:

> Weaving through the pushcarts, boys carried bundles of fabric already cut to pattern to tenement contractor shops throughout the neighborhood, where they were assembled into garments. The contracting system prevailed in the garment industry, relieving manufacturers of the responsibility of managing the workforce. Manufacturers hired skilled workers to design the garments and cut the cloth, this they then farmed out for assembly to an army of small contractors. The contractors hired the sewing-machine operators, pressers, basters, and finishers and organized the assembly of the garments, which were then returned to the manufacturer. This flexible system expanded during the busy season and contracted during slack season, leaving both workers and contractors bereft of work and pay but insulating manufacturers from any wasted expenditures for overhead and wages. Although the contracting system put relentless downward pressure on wages and conditions, it allowed workers to become "bosses" by opening their own shops with little capital. All that was needed to do so were a sewing machine, a pressing table, and a stove for the irons. Sewing machines could be purchased on installment, and one could use a tenement apartment for space. Immigrants also needed a strong will to compete. At the turn of the century, a third of contractors went out of business each year.[25]

Given the large presence of eastern European Jews as sweatshop workers, it is not surprising that Jews were also at the forefront of the clothing labor unions. An excerpt from the *Forverts* from a century ago provides but one indication of their prominence, along with a strong hint as to the significant size of the garment industry: "New York City's cloak makers have responded with a massive strike after bosses locked organizing workers out of their factories last week. When the clock struck 11 on a Wednesday morning, tens of thousands of cloak makers stood up, left their machines and walked out of their factories. With so many on the picket line, the Cloakmakers Union leaders, Benjamin Schlesinger, Jacob Halpern and Saul Metz, along with others, addressed the workers while a roll call was made of the striking shops. All told, 2,317 shops were counted among those that the strikers shut down."[26] Abraham Cahan, the immigrant socialist who cofounded the popular daily Yiddish newspaper that printed the above notice in 1916, was also the first Russian-speaking immigrant Jew in America to write a novel (albeit a short one) in English. Although his "Yekl" focuses on the assimilationist strivings of Jake Podkovsky, and their consequences, it not incidentally portrays aspects of the clothing industry in the late nineteenth century: the role of already assimilated and successful German bosses (the *shisters* [shoemakers] who become misters [25]), the slack work periods, the different aspects of clothing construction to which different workers were assigned, even the differences between the clothing trade in New York City and that in Boston.[27]

"Yekl" mirrors in fictional form the actual circumstances of the labor system, though only as background matter: it is in Cahan's newspaper and his labor union oratory that we get a better sense of the long hours in crowded, unsanitary, and often stifling conditions that existed in many of the tenement factories and the various ways in which, all along the chain beneath the manufacturers, workers were "sweated" of profits. (Dara Horn's *In the Image* also provides such details, in the section about Leah.) Elaboration of this aspect of the garment industry is beyond the scope of my study: with my focus on clothing change as a passing strategy, I return to Thyra Samter Winslow's novelette "A Cycle of Manhattan" to provide more relevant detail than "Yekl" on the Jews' role in the industry, as well as on clothing as a means of passing as a bona fide American. This novelette does more than offer a compelling example of naming practices among acculturating Jews in America, as I have detailed earlier; it also affirms what social historians have said about the importance of clothing to immigrants and succeeding generations. Thus the Rosenheimers' trajectory bears reexamination with this focus.

As Polland and Soyer comment, "One of the first things an immigrant did after arriving in the neighborhood was to transform him- or herself from a greenhorn into an American via the acquisition of a new suit of clothes, often with the aid of already-settled friends or family." The task completed, the freshly attired would set off for the photographer's studio to record the transformation in a picture to send back to the relatives in Europe. American clothing was not only assumed to be superior in quality to that made in Europe, it was thought to convey social status—as being "in fashion" often does, whatever the era. Mass production—in which Jewish manufacturers and workers played a prominent part—created opportunities for purchase hitherto available only to higher classes, as Hobbs remarks in relation to free blacks integrating into society. Here in America, a woman could wear a hat, for example, whereas back in the old country she might have been relegated to a shawl. As Cahan's narrator in his novel *The Rise of David Levinsky* (1917) writes of his first days as an immigrant in New York, gawking at the passersby, "The great thing was that these people were better dressed than the inhabitants of my town [in Russia]. The poorest-looking man wore a hat (instead of a cap), a stiff collar and a necktie, and the poorest woman wore a hat or bonnet."[28] Of course, there were always cynics who disparaged such democratization of clothing and the attempts at passing oneself off as a member of a higher social stratum. In 1904, one such observer of the fashion scene called it "Purposeless imitation!" when shops on Fourth Avenue copied styles from those on tony Fifth Avenue, and then Third Avenue shops offered imitations for lower prices, on down to the pushcarts on Hester Street, where the copy sold for thirty-nine cents. Nonetheless, as Polland and Soyer remark, "Self-reinvention—whether by means of a new suit of clothes or a piano—was another promise held open by America and New York.["29] Thyra Samter Winslow delivers both the piano and the new suit(s) of clothes in "A Cycle of Manhattan."

The Rosenheimer paterfamilias, a clothing cutter in Lithuania, comes over to this country with his family all dressed in their "foreign clothes."[30] Within three days, through his already assimilated distant cousin, a clothing trimmer by trade, Abraham Rosenheimer finds a job as a pants cutter (101). His wife, Minnie, in her forays within their new city, sees people "in fine clothes, people of her own race, too" (104). Soon enough, Winslow begins to focus on clothing, to mirror the Rosenheimers' newfound obsession:

> Each week the Rosenheimers' clothes changed nearer to the prevailing styles of MacDougal Street. Only a few weeks after they arrived Mrs. Rosenheimer, overcome by her new surroundings, bought, daringly, a lace sailor collar, which she fastened around the neck of her old world costume. As the months passed, even this failed to satisfy. The dress itself finally disappeared, reappearing as a school frock for Yetta, and Mrs. Rosenheimer wore a modest creation of red plaid worsted which Grandma and she had made, huge sleeves, bell skirt and all, after one they had seen in Washington Square on a "society lady." (106)

In addition, son Ike "had a new suit, bought ready-made, his first bought suit. . . . They couldn't call him a 'greenhorn' now" (106). Winslow emphasizes the new clothes in the context of the new curtains and furniture, all of them a sign not only of Americanization but also of upward mobility—the two concepts to be understood as synonyms. A third leg of this stool is, of course, consumerism. As the family leaves MacDougal Street for East Seventy-Seventh Street, Minnie Rosenheimer begins "to pay more attention to herself, buying clothes that were not absolutely necessary, cheap things that looked fine to her" (117).

Seven years later, the Rosenheim and Abrams men (for they have shortened their names by now) become partners in the Acme Pants Company, Men's and Boys' Pants (120), a good idea because "people liked ready-made pants" (121). Since Mr. Rosenheim runs a factory, once again it is time for the family to move: "They decided on the Bronx, new and good enough for any manufacturer's family. They had friends there and there were lots of stores. It was a nice neighbourhood, Yetta thought, with lots of young people who wore good clothes" (123). Good clothes are the sine qua non of a good neighborhood.

In the Bronx, Yetta has no need for school because she doesn't intend to be a teacher: "She preferred putting on her best clothes, her hat an exaggerated copy of something she had seen in Broadway and had made after the description at a neighborhood shop, a cheap fur round her neck, high-heeled shoes" (126). New clothes, new furniture, and again a new name: Rosen. And, as the piéce de resistance, a piano![31] There is a downside to living in the Bronx, thinks Minnie Rosen, with her new address and new name: "Here in the Bronx you had to be 'dressed' all the time. In Seventy-seventh Street you could go out in your house-dress." Nevertheless, it was "nice, having a lot of rooms and new clothes and all that" (128). Meanwhile, teenage Carrie "liked to spend money, . . . buying unnec-essarily expensive ribbons and purse. . . . Carrie liked expensive clothes and she liked putting them on and taking long walks" (129). As the family associates with tonier people, Minnie Rosen buys "a fine black silk dress, with revers [trimmings] of green satin, lace covered," and a similar dress for Grandma (still wearing her orthodox wig) for when company is coming; and Yetta, now Yvette, wears out her clothes with all her party going (131).

Not surprisingly, the Bronx will no longer suffice, and because Harlem "sounds more stylish" to Yvette (133), the Rosens move yet again, to West 116th Street. Minnie goes to a beauty parlor for the first time, at the age of forty-four, and considers going on a diet; she also buys a fur coat (137). In 1907, the Acme Pants Company, Men's and Boys' Pants, merges with the Rex Suit Company, Gentleman's Ready-Tailored Suits, for "ready-tailored suits, it seemed, were more in demand each day" (138). The owners hire a man to advertise the newly named "King's Suits for the Kings of America" in magazines and on billboards, branding their product and themselves at the same time (138–39). The Rosens, Abrams, and their ilk have made it in America—they have tailored themselves in the pattern of the American ideal of success—and they make the promise via advertising that by wearing their clothes, others can be kings as well. In 1909, these families Americanize their names to Rose and Adams, and first names continue to evolve accordingly. Carrie, now Carolyn, continues to be fixated on clothes, which the author describes again in detail: "She added a bit of 'elegance' to whatever fash-ion had dared to ask for. She liked smooth broadcloth suits, much tailored, for day wear, and elaborate chiffon evening gowns" (140). Even her speaking voice becomes upper class when she remembers to talk with a British accent, thus mim-icking the Anglo-Saxon elite, who in turn are emulating British aristocracy.[32] At the same time she is critical of her parents, who in her eyes lack the good taste of genteel America: her mother, with her Yiddish-inflected English, her father, who removes his work attire when he returns from the office instead of wearing a smoking jacket (which she eventually buys for him) as men of the smart set do (129, 130, 138). It is all well and good for Minnie Rosen to look "as good as anyone in her crowd" (137), but Carolyn wants the family to look and sound and act like those *outside* their crowd of Jews. Yvette's crowd is "loudly vulgar," and Carolyn disparages her sister's 'terrible taste in clothes" (144).[33]

The Rex Suit Company becomes so successful that the annual catalogue of King styles has sections for Prep Youth, the College Man, the Younger Set, and the Older Fellow. Merchants around the country feature the brand (153). The family's increasing prosperity affords more and more acquisitions of better-quality things and addresses. When Yvette gets engaged to MacDougal Adams, her trousseau takes several weeks to acquire. Carolyn, moving to the position of senior daughter after Yvette's marriage, plumps for a more fashionable address, and the move to Riverside Drive is accompanied by a more stylish name, Ross. Carolyn progresses to becoming not just a fashion plate but a trend setter:

> Always gowned a bit ahead of fashion, perfectly groomed, silky, smooth, crisp, she went to the theatre, evenings and matinées, to luncheons and to parties. . . . You could see Carolyn almost any fair afternoon on the Avenue with Eloise or Helen or Mary Louise, stopping in at one little shop for a bit of lingerie, at another for flowers. They spent money with no thought of its value. . . . There was always a car waiting and they wore low pumps or slippers and the thinnest of stockings even when snow was on the ground. (159)

Sister Dorothea, née Dorothy, has her own style, also described by the author in detail. In contrast to Carolyn, who "wore things that 'looked expensive,' rich broadcloth, elaborate furs—Dorothea preferred rough tweeds. She paid extraordinary sums for little suits that Mrs. Ross thought looked as if she'd got them for twenty dollars in Third Avenue. They were of mixed weaves, in grey or tan, and she wore big tailored collars over her coats, not mannish looking or freakish, just plain. She paid fifty dollars for her little round velour hats. . . . Dorothea paid huge prices for plain little evening frocks which she bought at exclusive little places" (161–62). It follows that the next move, to East Sixty-Fifth Street, requires the services of a professional decorator (165). Decorating the body and the home are of a piece in the consumer society that the Rosses literally and figuratively buy into. All signs of the old-world lifestyle, as manifested in modes of furniture and clothing, not to mention accents, are superseded, like the Patimkins' Newark couch gathering dust in the attic in Short Hills. The only sign of assimilation missing from the Ross story is the nose job.

Along with names and addresses, then, "A Cycle of Manhattan" utilizes clothing, especially women's clothing, as a prime marker of social advancement. Read in tandem with a work of the same period, Anzia Yezierska's novel *Bread Givers*, it both reinforces the clothing motif in Yezierska's novel and provides context for it. Yezierska's focus in *Bread Givers* is on breaking free from the patriarchy of Orthodox Judaism and finding the space to become one's own person; for Yezierska's semiautobiographical protagonist, Sara Smolinsky, clothing is but one means of effecting this transformation. But the author also uses clothing images more broadly, in order to address other issues of importance to her, such as the search for beauty in a sordid environment, the differences that gender roles play in making a living and making a life, and fashion as a means to, and trumpeting of, status (this last point being the sole focus of Winslow's novelette).[34]

Anzia Yezierska herself rose from poverty on the Lower East Side of New York to fame and privilege (albeit fleeting) in Hollywood as a script writer for the movies, including a screenplay for a film based on her short story collection *Hungry Hearts*. She became known in the Sunday magazine sections as the "Rags to Riches" girl,[35] which in her case may be a literal description, given the sordid living conditions we glimpse in *Bread Givers*, where the immigrant family has "rags to dress [them]selves" (38). In Book I, "Hester Street," Yezierska immediately introduces a scene reminiscent of the other works we have been considering, in which a character looks into the mirror to admire (or be horrified by) a hat. Mashah, the second of four daughters, is intent on beautifying and elevating herself, and so buys pink roses with which to festoon her hat; as she says, "Like a lady from Fifth Avenue I look, and for only ten cents, from a pushcart on Hester Street" (2). While her sisters have been out on the streets looking for work, Mashah has been walking through stores looking for hat trim to match her pink calico dress, in order to make her look "just like the picture on the magazine cover" (3). Fifth Avenue and popular magazines like *Ladies' Home Journal* (founded in 1883) are Mashah's twin standards of fashion, and she has used her lunch money not only to create beauty in the midst of poverty, excess in the midst of want, but also to align herself with American standards of dress. As the title of the novel suggests, earning a life for which one hungers is a paramount theme; in Mashah's case, beauty is what she hungers for, and her purchases are why she does not starve (4). Window shopping on the way home from work gives her a sense of "the prettiest and latest styles" (35). Sara, the youngest sister and the novel's narrator, remarks that somehow Mashah is able to transform even her everyday clothes so that she looks like "the dressed-up doll lady from the show window of the grandest department store" (4, 18). Thus, Yezierska implies that Mashah has turned herself into a mannequin, as doll-like as those in the windows.

The oldest sister, Bessie, is the workhorse in the family, taking bundles home for night work to contribute to the family's coffers since the father spends all his days studying the Talmud and praying. To Bessie, as well as to Mashah, the pink calico dress that Mashah hangs high and covers with a sheet is "like a holy thing" (40), as holy to these women as Reb Smolinsky's scriptures are to him. But Bessie does not have Mashah's ideal American shape, "straight up and down" (30), and when she surreptitiously tries on the dress to look beautiful for her suitor, Beryl Bernstein, she is too fat for it and it rips. Given that Bernstein would not pay a dowry to Bessie's father, the point is moot; to marry her off to Zalmon the fishmonger, who *will* buy her hand in marriage, Bessie's father buys her "a new velvet dress, richer than anything she had seen. It looked like a fifty-dollar dress from Fifth Avenue. Father had spent all afternoon, bargaining for the $20 Zalmon had given him, the finest dress in the Grand Street show window" (98). With her wooden demeanor (100), Bessie too looks like a mannequin in a store window. More, to make the purchase of Bessie even more attractive, Reb Smolinsky lies that she had sewn the dress herself. What she does actually sew is a garter for

Zalmon's youngest child, who has stolen her heart, and she also sews up a rip in his sleeve—his poor clothes, and the need for a mother's care that they symbolize, are what clinch the deal.

Meanwhile, the husbands in *Bread Givers* come off rather poorly in the main, and clothes make the point. It is all well and good for Reb Smolinsky to wear the threadbare long frock coat and skullcap of the Orthodox Jew (except for when he, as a widower, needs a wife to look after him, and thus wears his Sabbath clothes for show [260]); but his adherence to old-world religious practice comes at the expense of his family. He cares for his daughters' emotional welfare only to the extent that their suitors will literally enrich his life. Zalmon transforms himself into "a dressed-up American man" in his new clothes, eliciting Reb Smolinsky's warning to Bessie that he "dressed himself up all in your honour, and you got to do him the honour back" (103). Zalmon's offering his dead wife's fur coat even woos Mrs. Smolinsky, who exclaims, from her own station of poverty, "Red-silk lining and sealskin fur. What more do you want from a man?" (105). As it turns out, there is a lot more to want from a man. Mashah, after being snubbed by her lover's wealthy father, whose "riches of his grand clothes" (58) say all there needs to be said, is set up with a putative diamond salesman, Moe Mirsky, who spends all his money on clothes and restaurant meals while at home with their three children Mashah can't even pay for the gas to light their meager rooms. Sara runs into Mirsky on the street, wearing "a new checked suit, with a carefully folded, blue-bordered handkerchief sticking out of his breast pocket. His freshly ironed trousers were turned up at the bottom, showing his silk socks and new patent-leather shoes. Such a grand gentleman!" (144, 146). His once-beautiful wife, in contrast, is struggling at home and berated by her husband for having lost her looks.

The third daughter, Fania, is set up with Abe Schmukler, in the cloaks-and-suits business in Los Angeles. Fania agrees to marry him only to get away, and the night before her wedding she stamps on the black dress trimmed with gold that Abe had given her; at Bessie's envy (for Bessie is now a poor fish seller covered in scales rather than velvet and sealskin), Fania cries, "What do you envy? The shine of these gilded rags with which I choke my emptiness?" (80). Although she returns to New York for a visit "shining with silks" (174), she confesses her unhappiness with a gambler for a husband and a boring, inauthentic life playing cards to fill the time. She dresses in finery only because her husband wants her "dressed in the latest style" to brag that he is a "cloaks-and-suits millionaire" (176). As for Bessie, she is stepmother to several children, one of whom is as fixated on style as the young Mashah was, and who offers no gratitude for Bessie's efforts to sew her a dress for her first dance: as Bessie explains, "I bought her a grand piece of silk for a dress. I stayed up half the night sewing, but before it was half done, she said I didn't have any style. She had to take it to an uptown dressmaker" (177).

Yezierska devotes over half the book to Sara's sisters and their fates; they constitute the prolegomena to Sara's story, the motivation for her choice of a different course. Not long after the beginning of Book II, "Between Two Worlds," Sara Smolinsky and her own journey come to the fore. Again, clothes have significance in detailing Sara's upward mobility and the terms in which she conceives it. Before Fania confesses her empty life she asks Sara, picking at "the patched elbow of [her] worn-out serge," "Why don't you put on a little style?" Sara, whose life is now dedicated to studying so she can go to college, responds, "I haven't time or money for outside show" (174). In contrast to Fania, Sara wears drab clothing that she comes to lament as the outward manifestation of her lonely life: "a black shirt-waist, high up to the neck. Not a breath of colour. Everything about me was gray, drab, dead. I was only twenty-three and I dressed myself like a lady in mourning" (181). Yet when she buys a lace collar and red roses to trim her hat (182), reminiscent of Mashah's former efforts, Sara feels "like a dolled-up dummy" (183). A suiter sent by Fania from California, Max Goldstein, says that he likes her "style," her refusal to "doll [herself] up for men"—he relates to her humble beginnings since he began as a worker for a pushcart peddler selling secondhand clothes on Hester Street, though he has risen to be a department store owner in California. But Max is more interested in himself than in Sara, praising himself "as if he were goods for sale" (199), and she regretfully lets him slip out of her life.

Sara finds "the beauty for which [she] had always longed" (211) at college, in an unnamed town somewhere a train ride from New York City. The beauty is represented, in part, by women's clothes of the sort that the Rex Suit Company produces for Prep Youth and the College Man in Winslow's novelette. Sara relates, "What a sight I was in my gray pushcart clothes against the beautiful gay colours and the fine things those young girls wore. I had seen cheap, fancy style, Five- and Ten-Cent Store finery. But never had I seen such plain beautifulness. The simple skirts and sweaters, the stockings and shoes to match. The neat finished quietness of their tailored suits. There was no show-off in their clothes, and yet how much more pulling to the eyes and all the senses than the Grand Street riches I knew" (212). Perhaps the most poignant passage in *Bread Givers* soon follows: "I looked at these children of joy with a million eyes. I looked at them with my hands, my feet, with the thinnest nerves of my hair. . . . They pulled me out of my senses to them. And they didn't even know I was there" (213). Feeling like she doesn't belong in such a place, Sara decides to "tear [her]self out of [her] loneliness" and attend a freshman dance, putting "a fresh collar over [her] old serge dress" (218). But the dance is a disaster for her, and it seems so unfair that neither character nor brains count, only "youth and beauty and clothes"—things she "never had and never would have" (220). Bit by bit, through her ironing job, Sara earns enough to purchase items with which to dress up, but the effort to do so robs her of study time and she fails a course (221). With renewed devotion to her studies, unlike the "wooden dummies" (224) among her fellow students, and the fellow ironers at work who think only of dresses and beaux, she successfully completes her college education.

At the start of Book III, "The New World," Sara is on the train again in the opposite direction, back to New York. This time she is wearing kid gloves and having dinner in the dining car. Even her food is now Americanized: "No more herring and pickle over dry bread, I ordered chops and spinach and salad" (237). She has come a long way since the family served unfamiliar "American" food to Jacob Novack's wealthy father, only to be spurned in return.

Fine clothing, not just kid gloves, becomes an important component of Sara Smolinsky's rise out of the lower class. As soon as she arrives in New York she browses on Fifth Avenue for the first time in her life, "devouring with [her] eyes the wonderful shop windows." Sara has hungered for an education, with the goal of becoming a teacher and her own bread giver; that status attained, she also hungers for the appropriate accoutrements, just as Mashah did but in Sara's own way. With a thousand dollars in her pocket from winning the college's essay contest she can buy whatever she wants: not a pink ball gown, not furs, not pearls. "Here's the Sport Shop—that's where the college girls get their college clothes. How I had dreamed of them and despaired of ever having them. What fine suits in that window. There! There! That graceful quietness. That's what a teacher ought to wear" (238–39). With joy she watches as "quality clothes" are modeled for her, choosing a dark-blue serge suit with "more style in its plainness than the richest velvet" (239). Having moved beyond that cracked mirror in the tenement on Hester Street, Sara tries on the suit in a "beautiful fitting room lined with mirrors." In the store's other departments she buys a hat, "shoes, stockings, new underwear, gloves, and fine handkerchiefs" (240): "When my things came, I tried them on again before the big mirror in my hotel room—hat, coat, shoes, the whole outfit, even the new handkerchief. For the first time in my life I was perfect from head to foot. Now I laughed aloud in my pleasure. There was no saleslady around whom I had to act as though I were used to it always. No prima donna dressed up for the opera ever felt grander than I, ready to be a teacher in the schools" (240). Whereas Yetta Rosen's clothes announce her consumerist lifestyle (*she* would never be a teacher, she proclaims), Sara's clothing literally suits her to be a model for immigrant children in the public schools. She is actually modeling (contradictory) American norms: hard work and determination to enable the rise out of one's class, coupled with an ever-present class system that belies the democratic ideal of classlessness; self-expression in an individual's choice of job and attire, coupled with adherence to standards of aesthetics and beauty.[36] The new clothes and the room of her own give her the sense of power and self-determination she has always craved. Sara has achieved what Gitl in Cahan's "Yekl" could only dream of when *she* first tried on a new hat before her tenement mirror.

After six years away, Sara finally returns to her parents' apartment, where her ailing mother exclaims over her clothes, "You shine like a princess" (244). Her sisters had long ago used the same term for her because she wanted to be alone in peace and quiet (156). Of course, to Fania, Sara is not a "new-found stylish lady," as the mother calls her; "Some style! [Fania scoffs]. Like a regular old maid. Any one can see a mile off Sara's a school teacher" (247).[37] Fania's attire, as we know, is that of a nouveau riche trophy wife of the sort that Thorsten Veblen disparaged, in his *The Theory of the Leisure Class* (1899), as exhibiting conspicuous consumption. As Meredith Goldsmith has remarked, because Sara's serge suit is made "from a traditional working-class fabric, . . . [it] initially serves as a metaphor of the reconciliation of her immigrant past with her Americanized present." However, when the mother dies, and the undertaker cuts the garments of the family members "according to the Biblical law and ages of tradition," Sara refuses to have her new clothes torn: "It's my only suit, and I need it for work" (255). All the mourners disparage her refusal: "Look at her, the *Americanerin!*" (255). Goldsmith argues that the unwillingness to have her new suit cut actually betokens "the failure and incompleteness, of Sara Smolinsky's Americanization. If Sara cannot allow her dress to be rent, she cannot mourn her mother, which would allow her to achieve closure on the past."[38] But in my estimation, Sara does in fact mourn her mother deeply, out of love as well as guilt, and eschewing such traditional Jewish rituals actually supports her "Americanization."

In fact, Sara will eventually find a man suited to her, the principal of her school, Hugo Selig; for him she dresses up, in elegant attire with the color she had craved years ago: "I threw off my dark school dress and put on my new challis. I turned to the mirror. How becoming was that soft green with that touch of rose embroidery. How well it suited my pale skin and dark hair that I learned to braid so becomingly around my head! I hope Hugo will like it" (283). Hugo does like it, and her, but the novel has no happy ending, in spite of Sara's attainments that include a husband-to-be of whom—miracle of miracles!—her father approves. The shadow of the Old World from which Sara hungered to escape hangs over her still, since Reb Smolinsky will now come to live with her and Hugo. Nonetheless, as Sara has progressed from poverty to the middle class, with clothing purchases as one sign of that passage, she has at least not had to leave her family and her background totally behind, as so many of the light-skinned blacks passing for white felt they had to do, as represented in Allyson Hobbs's case studies or Philip Roth's fictional Coleman Silk. Though melodramatic, the last line of the novel, about the weight of the generations still on her, is actually inconclusive. Everything that has led up to the conclusion of the third book leaves room for the reader to hope that, like Gitl, Sara with her supportive husband will find accommodation for the Old World as she plants herself firmly in the New.

It is a big leap from Sara Smolinsky to Barbra Streisand, to put it mildly, but the four decades between them permit us to look not only at changes in fashion, and who determines a style, but also at a woman in the later twentieth century who showed the will and determination of a Sara Smolinsky (or Anzia Yezierska) to make "of herself a person," a line repeated often in *Bread Givers*, on her own terms. These terms include her choices in dress. On the way up, Streisand made it part of her brand to avoid the typical accoutrements of the well-dressed woman, and in doing so, she flouted the conventional definition of beauty. I have taken the position that in reference to her nose, Neal Gabler has overstated the case with his assessment that Streisand "managed to change the entire definition of beauty." She may have been admired for her nose but she did not have significant actual influence on halting the rhinoplasties of Jewish girls from Queens (her home territory) and elsewhere. I would argue in the same vein about Streisand's taste in clothes, which was too idiosyncratic to become adopted as a widespread trend. Even as a teenager Streisand had her own style, wearing black stockings and sweaters. Soon she was introduced to thrift stores and began to purchase her clothing there; as she explained her predilection in 1964, "The salespeople in department stores are so mean, a haughty bunch. In thrift shops, nobody's mean." Streisand made deliberate reference to her style in at least one night club act in 1961, when she asked the audience how they liked the *schmatta* (rag) she was wearing. For an appearance on *The Tonight Show* in 1961, she wore a burgundy dress made of furniture upholstery, the fabric being more interesting to her than its provenance. On that show again the following year, she explained to host Johnny Carson how the big coat and hat she wore to auditions elicited the scornful reaction that she should wear high-heeled shoes and stockings when meeting people: they called her kooky, said Barbra, "but now they sort of look at me and say I'm a style-setter or something."[39]

The "sort of" and the "or something" belie Streisand's seeming confidence at this point, when she was barely twenty-two years old. It must have stung that in spite of her success as Miss Marmelstein in *I Can Get It for You Wholesale*, when she was all of nineteen—she was nominated for a Tony—she could not get the attention of the haughty salespeople at an upscale department store on Fifth Avenue because she did not resemble their customary chic clientele. "I'll be a success," she said, "when I'm famous enough to get waited on at Bergdorf Goodman." Streisand exacted her revenge on this iconic store in her very first television special, *My Name Is Barbra*, when she delivered several numbers from the floors of Bergdorf Goodman itself, each with an ironic title given the context: "Give Me the Simple Life," "I Got Plenty of Nothin'," "Brother, Can You Spare a Dime?," and "Nobody Knows You When You're Down and Out." Nobody recognized her in the fancy store when she was on her way up, but now that she was a star, she ruled the domain that once excluded her. Yet I think that there was more than payback at stake here; there was also the delicious fact, enjoyable for its own sake, that Barbra Streisand now had all the money and fame she needed to buy whatever she wanted. Even if her clothes were no longer made from upholstery fabric, she "upholstered" her penthouse duplex on Central Park West with the all the lush, over-the-top furnishings of an arriviste. She was still manifesting the Streisand style—it may not have been in conventionally defined good taste, but it was hers, and not for her the simple life once she had plenty of somethin'.[40]

Streisand would later explain to Nora Ephron in 1969 that she had moved on from thrift store purchases because she did not want to continue to be known as kooky or to have her "nutty clothes" distract from her voice. When another Tony nomination came her way for the Broadway musical *Funny Girl* in 1964, and a Grammy for *The Barbra Streisand Album*, and a $5 million contract with CBS to provide television specials, Streisand was all the rage. Shana Alexander burbled in *Life* magazine for May 22, 1964, "Hairdressers are being besieged with requests for Streisand wigs (Beatle, but kempt). Women's magazines are hastily assembling features on the Streisand fashion (threadbare) and the Streisand eye make-up (proto-Cleopatra). And it may only be a matter of time before plastic surgeons begin getting requests for the Streisand nose (long, Semitic and—most of all— like Everest, there.)" Alexander's over-the-top admiration to the contrary, Barbra Streisand did not become what could truly be called a "fashion icon," which is what Gabler terms her. The one term from his subtitle *Redefining Beauty, Femininity, and Power* that is most operative in my estimation is *power*. Her choice of attire for her performance at President Bill Clinton's inauguration in January 1993 exuded power. Gabler provides a description from a newspaper assessment: "That outfit, wrote Anne Taylor Fleming in the *New York Times*, 'sent a disturbing signal to—and about—American women.' It was a 'three-piece pin-striped male power suit, with a feminine touch'—that touch being a slit up the side and a 'definite hint of cleavage' in her vest. As she sang, Taylor noted a 'mixed metaphor,' which was a 'woman letting us know that underneath her peekaboo power suit, underneath all her bravado and accomplishments, she is still an accessible femme fatale.'" I very much agree with Gabler's determination, following Camille Paglia, that Streisand's choice of outfit did not exhibit ambivalence about conventional notions of appropriate dress for a woman but, rather, her boldness in asserting as a woman the prerogatives of a man. This, more than her fashion statements or the retention of her original nose, seems to me to be her most lasting impact on both women and men—second only to her magnificent singing voice, of course.[41]

Contemporary visual artist Beverly Naidus, whom Lisa Bloom includes as one of the feminist artists in her *Jewish Identities in American Feminist Art*, has also addressed fashion in the context of mainstream standards of beauty. Bloom reproduces Naidus's 1995 laser print on paper and mixed media called *Right Dress Size*, which superimposes text over part of an advertisement from the 1950s that shows a smiling and beautiful blond mother and daughter, each wearing the identical spiffy (for the time) outfit. The text reads: "The assimilation generation was brought up to conform, to look like the people in the magazines, to be better at being WASPs than the WASPs themselves. Both genetically and temperamentally she could not fit into the proper role or the right dress size." The text conveys the message that the clothing, and whether it "fits" or not, is a matter not only of dress but also of size—the "she" of this piece, presumably the artist herself, does not conform to WASP standards of beauty, whether those standards concern dress or weight ("straight up and down," as Mrs. Smolinsky describes the American look [30]).[42] Indeed, the ad's mother and daughter have incredibly small waists, and the daughter appears to be tightening her belt to make herself even thinner. As Bloom assesses the meaning and significance of this artist's body of work on Jewish themes, "Naidus deliberately distances herself from the assimilationist impulse and class narrative that have enabled a generation of Jewish-American artists to disidentify themselves from American class and racial struggles. As a dark-skinned Ashkenazi Jewish woman who is often mistaken for a non-white non-American, Naidus makes explicit and tangible in much of her work both the pitfalls of 'passing' and what it means to be unable to 'pass.'"[43]

Whether depicting rebellion against or buy-in to standards of fashion in clothing (or noses, for that matter), or an ambivalent stance in between, the artists discussed in this chapter have shown the many ways in which clothing choices make statements about who we think we are, who we want to be, or whom society takes us for. Hats ranging from wide-brimmed Hasidic hats to yarmulkes to derbies to ornate creations with feathers to military caps with red bands and visors—all play their parts in these stories of identities taken or mistaken. Outfits of blue serge or red plaid worsted or fine black silk with green satin and lace or even upholstery fabric take their turns in these fictional and real-life wardrobes, depending on the circumstances and the aspirations. Whether bought from a pushcart on the sidewalks of the Lower East Side or purchased from a counter in a posh uptown department store, clothing is always more than a literal body covering: it is a statement of our actual or fantasized place in the world and, as such, an optimal medium for narratives of passing.

One final story comes in for examination on this subject: Steve Stern's "The Tale of a Kite," originally published in 1997 but set in early twentieth-century Memphis, close to the time in which Cahan published his novella about New York Orthodox immigrants in the process of assimilating to American norms. Revolving around the threat posed by old-world Jews to American Jews feeling vulnerable in a majority Christian society, the story wrings a twist on both Roth's "Eli, the Fanatic" and Malamud's "The Jewbird" in that these Jews in Stern's tale send their children to a Talmud Torah (Jewish primary school) and retain many vestiges of Yiddishkeit in the foods they eat (and the stereotypical Jewish mother's preparation and serving of the meal), the klezmer music they play, and the locutions they employ in speech. However, although they are not painting rocks pink, like Woodenton's residents, they are "observant (within reason)," and that parenthetical qualifier, mentioned almost immediately on the first page, tells it all; in fact, they share the Woodenton Jews' antipathy toward the ultra-Orthodox, in this case the Hasidic rebbe who is luring the Memphis sons away to his *shtibl*, a little room over a feed store that he uses for teaching. The narrator of Stern's tale, Jacob Zipper, speaks for the others when he says, "We citizens of Hebrew extraction set great store by our friendly relations with our gentile neighbors. One thing we don't need is religious zealots poisoning the peaceable atmosphere."[44] By that the townspeople mean that the mere existence of these zealots, heretics, and fanatics (all three terms are used) will give rise to antisemitic rumors—those old shibboleths about murdering children for Christian blood, for instance, or plotting a Jewish takeover of the world—and hence will "upset the delicate balance of the entire American enterprise" (11).

Stern's choice of the word *enterprise* is significant. The Jews of North Main Street are "foremost an enterprising bunch, proud of our contributions to the local economy" (5), proud of being "respected men of commerce" (6). As "progressive people" they keep their business enterprises open on the Jewish Sabbath and were even able to obtain permission from the ward bosses to do so on Sunday—after all, as those bosses say, in words repeated by Zipper with no sense of irony or shame at voicing a derogatory term for Jews, "Our sheenies are good sheenies!" (5) These Jews are defined, in fact, by their businesses, like "Benny Rosen of Rosen's Delicatessen" (7). In contrast, Rabbi Shmelke and his disciples from the eastern European town of Shpink seem to live "mostly on air" (5), "praying instead of being gainfully employed," as Zipper says (11). Shmelke is the author's incarnation of the Yiddish figure of the *luftmensch*, or "man of air," existing without any practical source of income. That this rabbi is said to actually fly literalizes the concept of being an air man and is reminiscent of Malamud's Schwartz, who is not only a bird, but also (according to Harry Cohen) a freeloader and a loser, not to mention "too Jewish."

Another strategy that Stern employs to differentiate the Jews of North Main Street from the Hasids over the feed store is to emphasize their clothing. That the Hasids are "frankly insane" is evidenced in part by their "questionable attire" (6). The rabbi wears a belted caftan and fur hat, and his stockinged legs are "spindly as the handles on a scroll," a simile that equates him with the Torah he teaches, which Zipper calls "back-numbered lore" (10). As the merchants' sons begin to come under the influence of the rebbe, they take on an overtly Jewish look, growing facial hair and adopting the clothes of their fathers that had been put away after the "greenhorn days": a homburg hat and Prince Albert coat, considered by their fathers at first to be only "outward signs of eccentricity" (8). Later, when the boys become bolder, Zipper reports that for them, "rebellion is a costume party. They revel in the anomalous touch, some adopting muskrat caps (out of season) to approximate the Hasid's fur shtreimel. Milton Rosen wears a mackintosh that doubles as a caftan, the dumb Herman Wolf uses alphabet blocks for phylacteries. My own Ziggy has taken to picking his shirttails into ritual tassels" (13). To Jacob and his cohort, all of this is costume, not authentic. Appropriately the so-called Improvement Committee of these merchants meets in the "tasteful showroom" of the chairman, "Irving Ostrow of Ostrow's Men's Furnishings" (9), where all the items displayed are no doubt in season as well as in good taste (which means fitting into gentile society).

In a scene reminiscent of "Eli, the Fanatic," but related in a Yiddishized manner of speech from which Roth's Woodenton bunch has long been *oysgreened*, Ostrow submits a resolution to the committee "to dispatch to the Shpinkers a delegatz, with the ultimatum they should stop making a nuisance, which it's degrading already to decent citizens, or face a forcible outkicking from the neighborhood. All in agreement say oy" (10). When the delegation arrives their outrage is "compounded with interest" because they see that their children are present among the disciples. The lesson they interrupt happens to be about the Akidah, or the story of Abraham's impending sacrifice of Isaac on the mountain, again an echo of "Eli, the Fanatic." Stern's tale revolves largely around fathers and sons, like Roth's and like Malamud's too: central questions are how to be a father, what sacrifices to make, and the relation of those questions to what Irving Howe called "the world of our fathers." The jewbird is more of a father to Maury than Harry Cohen is, by taking the time with him as his *melamed*, or teacher. (In this the author himself is well named.) Likewise, the flying rabbi satisfies a spiritual need in Ziggy Zipper that Jacob Zipper is oblivious to or downright dismissive of. If it isn't "compounded with interest," it isn't a legitimate transaction. To apply a familiar phrase from immigrant fiction like *Bread Givers*, Zipper works hard so that his son "can be a person"; he cannot understand how Rabbi Shmelke offers anything else of utility: "What did I do wrong that he should chase after motheaten yiddisher swamis? Did he ever want for anything? Didn't I take him on high holidays to a sensible synagogue, where I showed him how to mouth the prayers nobody remembers the meaning of? Haven't I guaranteed him the life the good Lord intends him for?" (12) "Who's your father anyway, that feebleminded old scarecrow or me?" shouts Jacob, shaking and cuffing his son before in essence disinheriting him: "I don't know him anymore. He's not my son" (15). In "The Jewbird," Schwartz is the scary crow that Cohen abuses and ultimately kills, thereby reasserting his parental prerogatives over Maury.

Zipper's equation of Shmelke with his clothing, both moth-eaten, is a way to disparage Jewish history, teachings, and culture as old hat, figuratively speaking. Ted Heller in Roth's work is outraged that the children are taught such a horrible story about blood sacrifice; it is an antiquated, outdated, unacceptable story for the modern era and assimilated Jews in America. But Eli Peck finds in such material—the clothes, the culture—not so much a turning backward as a turning inward, to a part of him that needed nourishment. The rebbe's interpretation of this text in Stern's tale is that Isaac's soul separated from his body while he was under his father's knife, and this interpretation reinforces dichotomies that underpin the story: between body and soul, rationality and mysticism, commerce and religion, secularity and spirituality. Whereas Shmelke, light as air, flies toward the heavens tied to a rope, the North Main Street Jews keep their "noses to the ground" (14). The bellies of the fathers are "protuberant" (16) with the good life of meat and dumplings, but the children of those fathers feel unfed, no matter how much brisket and knaidel is available to fill their stomachs; the rabbi over the feed store is the one who nourishes the soul because he exemplifies the holy, the sacred, and the miraculous (14). At the climax of the story, Jacob Zipper, attempting to rid the town of the flying rabbi once and for all, cuts the rope that serves to tether the rebbe to the earth and bring him back down from the heavens when he has finished praying. What Zipper has not anticipated is, first, that all the children including Ziggy will grab onto the rabbi's feet and each other to form "the tail of the human kite," rising with him rather than staying with their own noses to the ground/grindstone. And second, that Zipper himself will for a moment imagine himself grabbing hold and ascending as well, before remembering that he is "a stout man with no match for gravity" (18).

In "Eli, the Fanatic," the Displaced Persons, refugees from World War II, have escaped one persecution only to encounter another in the reputed land of liberty. In "The Jewbird," Schwartz experiences a pogrom of a new-world kind, repudiated and killed by a fellow Jew. In "The Tale of a Kite," right before Zipper takes his drastic action to get rid of the rebbe, he mentions without any specific details several troubling cases of antisemitism in the Old Country and the New: the Beilis trial for blood libel then occurring in Kiev (incidentally the basis of Malamud's 1966 novel *The Fixer*); the nativists' backlash against the influx of eastern European immigrants; even the suspicion that the Guggenheims had something to do with the wreck of the *Titanic*—these events, noted without dates, set the story in 1913, during the Beilis trial. And in the final line, the sunset into which the flying rabbi ascends is "all the brighter as it's soon to be extinguished by dark clouds swollen with history rolling in from the east" (18). This ominous note suggests persecutions to come, whether from more pogroms or, further down the line, from the Holocaust. Neither Malamud nor Roth nor Stern is suggesting that all Jews should become ultra-Orthodox like Rebbe Shmelke— that his is by definition the only nourishing Jewish identity for American Jews. Each of these authors actually underscores the circumstances that might make a Jew wish to blend into the majority culture and be safe, something that Sholem

Shachnah cannot achieve in the Old World. At the same time, each portrays the compromises involved in such a wish and such an achievement, the precariousness of the security attained, and the costs of ignoring Jewish peoplehood in an effort to "be a person" in American society.

Notes

1. Row, *Your Face in Mine*, 329.
2. Senna, *Caucasia*, 334.
3. Brodkin, *How Jews Became White Folks*, 178.
4. Lewis, *Kingsblood Royal*, 10. Subsequent references in the text to this novel are to this edition.
5. Browder, *Slippery Characters*, 211.
6. Freedman, *Jew vs. Jew*, 218.
7. Roth, "Eli, the Fanatic," 250. Subsequent references in the text to this story are to this edition.
8. Gittleman, *From Shtetl to Suburbia*. Gittleman discusses "Eli, the Fanatic" on 151–56.
9. Browder, *Slippery Characters*, 216, quoting William Van Deburg, *New Day in Babylon: The Black Power Movement and American Culture, 1965–1975*, 53.
10. Parrish, "Comic Crisis of Faith," 33.
11. Koltun-Fromm, *Material Culture*, 197.
12. Hobson, *Gentleman's Agreement*, 257, 232, 270, 163, 251.
13. Sollors, *Neither Black nor White yet Both*, 258; f. 59, 499; 247.
14. Parrish, "Comic Crisis of Faith," 33.
15. The pen name of the author of the Tevye stories popularized in the musical *Fiddler on the Roof* is sometimes referred to in print as Sholom Aleichem and at other times as Sholem Aleichem. I have chosen to follow the former spelling because it is the one used by the editors and commentators I reference.
16. Rabinovich (Sholom Aleichem), "On Account of a Hat," 105. Subsequent references in the text to this story are to this edition.
17. Shapiro, "Group Portrait," xiii.
18. Howe and Wisse, introduction, viii, ix.
19. Hobbs, *Chosen Exile*, 124–25.
20. Cahan, "Yekl," 39–40. Subsequent references in the text to this work are to this edition.
21. Horn, *In the Image*, 59.
22. Lagnado, *Man in the White Sharkskin Suit*, 68–69.
23. Ibid., 153, 172.
24. Hobbs, *Chosen Exile*, 33.
25. Polland and Soyer, *Emerging Metropolis*, 118–119.
26. Reprinted in the *Forward* of May 6, 2016 (33), as part of the journal's featuring of excerpts from its pages published one hundred years ago, seventy-five years ago, and fifty years ago.
27. Cahan's second, lengthy (at almost six hundred pages), and ambitious novel, *The Rise of David Levinsky*, narrated by a rags-to-riches clothing manufacturer, gives a great deal

more detail than "Yekl" on the ready-made garment industry itself and on the spiritual and ethical losses attendant on material success.

28. Cahan, *Rise of David Levinsky*, 93.

29. See Polland and Soyer, *Emerging Metropolis* (116–18), for the details in this paragraph (other than the quotation from Cahan's novel).

30. Winslow, "Cycle of Manhattan," 99. Subsequent references in the text to this work are to this edition.

31. Acquiring a piano was a common aspirational undertaking for immigrants looking to Americanize. Polland and Soyer, in *Emerging Metropolis* (116), provide an interesting paragraph on the importance of the piano for attaining social status. In fact, like the nose job, learning to play the piano was one tool that unmarried young women employed to make them more marriageable.

32. See Dinnerstein, *Antisemitism in America*, 39.

33. Romeyn discusses "taste as an important marker of class" in "Eros and Americanization" (28–34). The quotation is on 28.

34. Stubbs discusses Yezierska's autobiographical writings, two early stories, and first novel, *Salome of the Tenements*, in relation to clothing and the ambivalence of garment workers who made the ready-wear. Stubbs is very instructive as well in her analyses of class and gender (see her "Reading Material," 157–72).

35. Harris, introduction, x. Subsequent references in the text to this novel are to this edition.

36. Catherine Rottenberg discusses such competing norms in her analysis of Yezierska's *Salome of the Tenements*, in *Performing Americanness* (67–69).

37. Indeed, the public schools were a prime venue for acculturating Jews and other immigrants. One example of how "Jewish schoolchildren learned to identify as white as they came to see American history as their own" is found in the 1928 Colonial Day pageant in Annapolis, in which the children dressed in colonial garb to enact key historical scenes in the state's founding. Here, costuming is used as a passing strategy (see Goldstein, *Price of Whiteness*, 139–40).

38. Goldsmith, "Dressing, Passing," 43, 44.

39. Gabler, *Barbra Streisand*, 116, 46, 48, 50, 52, 54.

40. The details in this paragraph are again from Gabler, who quotes various sources for his information (see Gabler, *Barbra Streisand*, 59, 96, 95).

41. Ibid., 54, 95, 147–48. For a trend setter with a similar motive, see Harrison-Kahan's discussion in *White Negress* (50–51) of an earlier icon, Sophie Tucker. Tucker's styles "were intended to push boundaries of feminine respectability rather than adhere to them"; with her tight sheath skirts and her trousers, she "celebrate[d] consumerism not because it leads to assimilation but because, for her, it is couched in an adamant refusal of patriarchal dependence."

42. Weight goes hand in hand with dress style (and noses) when considering passing strategies to look less Jewish and more "American." In "Cycle of Manhattan," Minnie tries unsuccessfully to diet when moving up socially and accommodating to American ideals of beauty. Winslow published a weight reduction guide and articles on beauty, and Fannie Hurst also published a book on diet and nutrition. Hurst may have been against the face lift, but she struggled with her weight for much of her life and went on drastic diets to the point of near starvation. Kroeger, in *Fannie*, deals with Fannie's obsession with food deprivation and

exercise in order to look stylishly thin; see 135–38 for Fannie's efforts to attain the ideal body of the flappers in the 1920s. In contrast, Sophie Tucker, singing the blues, challenged notions of the American valuation of a trim body in such songs as "I Don't Want to Get Thin": "Why should I when I'm all right as I am? . . . If you want to keep your husband styraight [*sic*] / Show him a lot of curves" (see Harrison-Kahan, *White Negress*, 48–49).

43. Bloom, *Jewish Identities in American Feminist Art*, 138–39

44. Stern, "Tale of a Kite," 5. Subsequent references in the text to this story are to this edition.

9 In Search of an "Authentic" Jewish American Identity

"Who Is It Who Can Tell Me Who I Am?"

THE NOVELIST HARRY Lesser, in Bernard Malamud's *The Tenants* (1971), chooses the above quotation from Shakespeare's *King Lear* as the epigraph for his book-in-progress; the title of that work, *The Promised End*, comes from *Lear* as well. Malamud's novel ends not in promise but in tragedy, with the white Jewish protagonist, Harry Lesser, coming to lethal blows with the black antagonist, "Willie Shakespear [*sic*]" (one pen name of Willie Spearmint), in the racial conflagration of the United States in the late 1960s and early 1970s.[1] That novel shows the impossibility of the white Jew identifying with a black man, and vice versa. Malamud's figurative "black and white" conclusion about this subject actually has a complicated back story in American history, one that includes the basic issue of Jewish identity itself. Probing that issue across its racial and religious dimensions places the debates about what defines a Jewish American in the wider context of the very human desire for self-understanding and the commonly assumed imperative to prescribe that understanding for others.

In many countries and eras, the non-Jewish majority has struggled with what was often called "the Jewish question"—a question of what to make of, and do about, the Jews in their midst. But the Jews, too, have asked a "Jewish question," as posed in the title of a 1910 lecture by historian Max Margolis: "Who Are We?" Eric Goldstein engages and elaborates on Margolis's question in his study of "Jews, Race, and American Identity"—the subtitle of *The Price of Whiteness*—and even appropriates Margolis's lecture title for his chapter "'Who Are We?' Jewishness between Race and Religion." American Jews in the first part of the twentieth century were unable, in Goldstein's words, "to find stable, emotionally satisfying terms for self-definition in a society insistent on dividing the world into black and white." Jews were just as prone as anyone else to calling the Jewish people a race, a term with the dual connotations of apartness from society and cohesiveness within the group. When categorization (actual or threatened) as nonwhite put their status as Americans in jeopardy time and again, Jews put on a public face as a religious denomination while privately maintaining their emotional attachment to the notion of a Jewish race. No wonder that Max Margolis concluded his 1910 lecture by throwing up his hands, as it were: as Goldstein quotes him, Jews constituted "a great anomaly which cannot be classified according to accepted rules of definition." The hope at that time, in the Progressive era, was that a more stable identity for Jews as Jews, accepted by all Americans, could eventually be reached.[2]

Allegiance to the norms of the "group" or to the norms of the larger society characterizes the tension experienced by American Jews over time. Post–World War II, Jews adopted such other labels as *ethnicity, peoplehood, civilization,* and *community* in the hopes that one or another of these words would capture both Jewish distinctiveness and Jewish integration: as Goldstein says, each term was "largely a linguistic strategy designed to recast [Jews'] continual attachment to a racial self-understanding in terms more acceptable to the non-Jewish world." By the 1950s, religious pluralism was an American value touted in popular culture and not viewed as an impediment to full integration into society; thus, religion became an accepted marker of Jewish identity. With the rise of black nationalist movements in the mid-1960s, however, many Jews once again felt the need to distinguish themselves from the white majority by asserting a group identity. Disconcertingly, increasing intermarriage rates and dis-affiliation from synagogue Judaism caused—and still cause—much hand-wringing about the future of American Jews.[3] As a character in the "Judea" chapter of Philip Roth's *The Counterlife* laments, referring to the Holocaust and to intermarriage in the same breath, "First there was the hard extermination, now there is the soft extermination."[4]

In *The Human Stain*, Roth takes up the "I" versus the "we" in the context of black culture, and in *The Counterlife* he addresses the individual versus the collective in a Jewish context by engaging the questions of what place Israel holds in Jewish identity and who is more authentic, the Jew in Israel facing danger on all sides or the comfortable, often detached Jew in America. (As journalist Samuel Freedman adds, "far from unifying American Jews, Israel now divides them on both political and religious grounds."[5]) Mostly, though, by riffing on the counter selves of the two Zuckerman brothers, *The Counterlife* refutes the very notion of "authentic" identity by defining identity as role play: "The human gift for playacting. . . . may be the only authentic thing that we *ever* do," Nathan says to Henry (138), now named Hanoch since making his passage to Israel, Zionism, and Orthodoxy. A persona is a literal sounding through (*per sona*), harking back to Greek tragedy, in which the actors spoke through masks; the novel thus suggests that the donning and doffing of masks are signs of authenticity—very unlike the use of masks in the stories by Englander and Winslow, where they signify just the opposite. Identity, Roth posits, is unstable by its nature. Transformations, counter lives, are the order of the day.

Modern open societies certainly support this conception, affording options for self-determination unimaginable in other environments and eras. The subtitle

of Wesley Morris's essay in the *Times*—"Who Do You Think You Are?"—emphasizes the freedom of the subject to choose as opposed to the prerogative of the
society to confer. This freedom is complicated by the fact that Morris's subtitle
is actually a double entendre, since the question can be read with two meanings
that are not mutually exclusive: Who is it that you perceive yourself to be? (Who
do *you* think you are?) How do you have the audacity to choose? (Who do you
think you *are*?) Set off in bold colors at the bottom of one page of Morris's essay
are lines from the text: "Gender roles are merging. Races are being shed. In the
last six years or so, but especially in 2015, we've been made to see how trans and
bi and poly-ambi-omni we are." Morris explains what has led up to this situation:

> For more than a decade, we've lived with personal technologies—video games
> and social-media platforms—that have helped us create alternative or auxil-
> iary personae. We've also spent a dozen years in the daily grip of makeover
> shows, in which a team of experts transforms your personal style, your home,
> your body, your spouse. There are TV competitions for the best fashion design,
> body painting, drag queen. Some forms of cosmetic alteration have become
> perfectly normal, and there are shows for that, too. Our reinventions feel glee-
> ful and liberating—and tied to an essentially American optimism. After cen-
> turies of women living alongside men, and of the races living adjacent to one
> another, even if only notionally, our rigidly enforced gender and racial lines
> are finally breaking down. There's a sense of fluidity and permissiveness and
> a smashing of binaries. We're all becoming one another. Well, we are. And
> we're not.[6]

In terms of the "smashing of binaries," Jess Row's *Your Face in Mine* includes
a scene in which Martin Wilkinson—a self-described "convert" to blackness"—
discusses President Obama with his friends, "interpreting *the meaning of
Obama*" as one friend puts it. Another remarks that we are not in a postracial
era but rather a time of "post-*race as an issue*." Wilkinson calls Obama "a hybrid.
A mongrel. A cobbled-together person who's *chosen* his categories all the way
along"; a "master of the mask," adds another, using a phrase that Nathan Zuckerman would approve.[7] Row's novel as a whole, however, belies the assumption that
America is either "post-race" or "post-race as an issue." Michele Elam interrogates
that assumption in her essay "Passing in the Post-Race Era," where she argues
convincingly that we are not, in fact, "post-racial," and that in "millennial passing
novels, racial identity and its transgressions are not outdated abstractions; rather,
these works foreground the capacity of racial passing to challenge the enduring
canards of identity formation itself." She concludes by reiterating that the novels
she discusses "make relevant a literary form assumed unfit for racial postmoder-
nity; they find in passing a particularly timely medium to explore the ongoing relevance of race amidst the recent rise in anti-identitarianism and post-racialism."[8] Just
as Row's novel, published seven years after Elam's essay, reinforces the continued

and in some ways enhanced import of race in America, so too does Wesley Morris end his essay with the point that races are *not* being shed. Morris, an African American, wonders "if being black in America is the one identity that won't ever mutate. . . . I live with two identities: mine and others' perceptions of it. So much of blackness evolving has been limited to whiteness allowing it to evolve."[9] In response to one interpretation of Morris's subtitle—Who do you perceive yourself to be?—Morris would say that he, like other blacks, lives with *double* perceptions at all times.

In the United States of today, with the rise of antisemitic rhetoric and actions, Jews in this country—as in many places abroad—are finding those double perceptions more applicable to their own lives than they would have thought possible only a few years ago. Just a month after the 2016 presidential election, with good reason as it turns out, Karen Brodkin entitled a piece in the *Forward* "How Jews Became White Folks—and May Become Nonwhite under Trump." She summarized the thesis of her well-known book—how, after World War II, Jews became "white" in the sense of beginning to enjoy the benefits of acceptance as real Americans—and noted the distinct possibility that these benefits are not permanent since "the closet of bigotry" has been opened. She ended by wondering if the new regime "will 'unwhiten' and mark Jews racially on a national scale."[10] True, the perceptions of putative racial characteristics that Matthew Frye Jacobson delineates in his chapter "Looking Jewish, Seeing Jews," in *Whiteness of a Different Color*, are not as stubbornly held as in the past, especially in relationship to the negative traits and tendencies associated with them.[11] Nonetheless, so many of the works I have discussed, products of various time periods, either covertly or overtly raise the issue of what "a Jew" looks like, often in reference to a "Jewish nose" (whether the person in question has one or not, and if not, by a quirk of genetics or a fix through rhinoplasty), but also in regard to speech, manners, and taste. In society at large there is still a propensity to pinpoint a person's racial or ethnic identity on the basis of appearance, as demonstrated by a presidential candidate's insistence on his ability to tell and hence to dictate who is (or is not) a Native American by looking at that person. Even more salient than a question of a Jew's appearance is the underlying question Brodkin poses, of whether Jewish assimilation is in fact a done deal. Perhaps, like a black identity, a Jewish identity "won't ever mutate," to use Morris's phrase, even if one has only one Jewish ancestor or converts to Christianity: as the former book critic for the *New York Times*, John Gross, is alleged to have remarked, "To be Jewish is to belong to a club from which no one is allowed to resign."[12]

Visual artist Beverly Naidus responds to this issue in her laser print on paper and mixed media called *Neat, Blonde Wife* (2001). Whereas her *Right Dress Size* centers on the Jews' attempts to assimilate, to be "right," this corollary work comments on the Jews' inability to become totally integrated into mainstream society. As reproduced in Lisa Bloom's study of Jewish feminist art, Naidus's print shows a dark-haired man sitting on a white wicker chair in a garden setting, with his back to the viewer. Although the man is impeccably dressed, the large bowler-type hat sitting askew on the chair knob and the bottle of kosher wine on the table not only indicate his Jewishness but also, in being foregrounded and facing the onlooker, suggest that his Jewishness is what everyone sees first, even without the man's face. Like *Right Dress Size*, this work seems to be a take on an actual advertisement, in this case for wine, since underneath the photo, to the right, the banner reads "When dining out enjoy WINE. It's nice to have some at home, too." But to the left, the real caption of the picture undercuts the bland enticement of the ad: "No one could tell he was Jewish from his name or his looks, but he felt that there was something impalpable that gave it away. Even his neat, blonde wife could not erase it." No wife is in the picture, neat, blonde, or otherwise—she is erased, as it were, presumably because he is not at home but "out." Perhaps he has married "out," to the blonde shiksa of his dreams. Whatever the man's passing fancies, Lisa Bloom's commentary on this art work is apt: "The text suggests that even with the most elaborate performative efforts, a Jew trying to obtain upward social mobility and to make his Jewishness disappear through radical assimilation was often doomed to fail." [13] That is, this man is "outed" as a Jew, as if it were impossible to rid himself of Jewish accoutrements and traits through nose jobs, name changes, speech lessons, chic attire, WINE at dinner, gentile wives at home. We might not be able to ascertain for sure whether the man's feelings are justified, for they are presented by the text as his feelings alone; yet we sense that his insecurity has been earned.

This insecurity is in spite of the fact that, in the fervent desire to assimilate, many Jewish immigrants and their progeny abandoned aspects of their identities that they deemed to be strictures of the Old World, out of keeping in the New. In the late nineteenth and early twentieth centuries, passing by a Jew in the United States often meant throwing one's tefillin overboard, whether literally as Dara Horn depicts or, in typical cases, figuratively. Cahan's Yekl, in his ardent desire to be "an *American* feller, a *Yankee*," leaves his "former self" behind by becoming Jake, riding a streetcar on the Sabbath, shaving his beard, and frequenting the dancing academy rather than the synagogue. When his eastern European wife comes to America, and Jake must resume his role as husband and father, he feels himself to be "an innocent exile from a world to which he belonged by right"— that world is the American one. [14] Sara Smolinsky refuses to be married off by her father or to be relegated to second-class status as a woman: she strikes out on her own for a college education, a blue serge suit, and a career as a teacher helping other young immigrants to become acculturated to America. The Ross family puts their Rosenheimer self behind them, leaving the grandmother in her wig and her loneliness. Bruce Gold's sister Joannie, like Sara's sister Fania, opts for the California lifestyle; social climbing trumps religious observance in Heller's novel as in Roth's "Goodbye, Columbus."

The newest world of Jews in America, that of the present time, is one in which the polarity or binary (to use Morris's term) has widened between the segment of the Jewish population identifying as cultural/secular and those who identify as Orthodox. Across the range of Jewish allegiance and practice, as Samuel Freedman says with sad irony, "nowhere more than in the United States, with its unparalleled climate of tolerance and modernity, have Jews struggled to unite their competing and often contradictory strains."[15] According to the 2013 Pew Foundation survey of Jews in the United States, Jews are marrying outside the faith at the highest rate ever—58 percent for all Jews, and an unprecedented 71 percent for non-Orthodox Jews[16]—and two-thirds of the self-identified Jews do not belong to a synagogue. Moreover, 32 percent of respondents born after 1980 say they have no religion. Although the Orthodox, at 10 percent, constitute the second-lowest percentage of respondents identifying as Jewish, they tend to have large families, and the retention rate in this branch is growing. Thus, the *New York Times* summary of the Pew survey quotes Steven M. Cohen, a sociologist of American Jewry at Hebrew Union College–Jewish Institute of Religion in New York, in predicting "a sharply declining non-Orthodox population in the second half of the 21st century, and a rising fraction of Jews who are Orthodox."[17] This is the fraction I would like to examine next.

The path to acculturation is usually a gradual one, as evidenced, for instance, by the Rosenheimers' multiyear loosening of ties as they advance toward their goal of indistinguishability from WASP society; their "cycle" shows only that tenement apartments can also slowly shed their former identities in the process of becoming hip and chic. Other works record a different kind of cycle: a reclaiming of tefillin as it were. From Shakespeare we get the now-familiar term *sea change*, when Ariel sings in Act I of *The Tempest* about the presumed drowning of Ferdinand's father in the tempest that sank their ship: "Nothing of him that doth fade, / But doth suffer a sea-change / Into something rich and strange." Rich and strange, indeed, is the transformation in this song, in which pearls replace the eyes and coral forms the bones, but many of the real-life and fictional personages whom I have discussed in the preceding chapters have experienced only slightly less dramatic sea changes. Jason in Dara Horn's *In the Image* undergoes a metamorphosis that he could hardly have imagined for himself when he was a college soccer player gazing with fascination verging on repugnance at the Hasids visiting the zoo. No pearls and coral for him—only the diamonds that he will eventually sell in his father-in-law's business. In fact his passing into ultra-Orthodoxy finishes him in two senses, forming his once-malleable clay into hard diamond, confining him to a narrow world but at the same time providing him a fulfilling sense of self—a placement in "a world where people knew who they were and didn't spend years on end deciding it."[18] He does not have to ask any longer, in the words from *King Lear*, "Who is it who can tell me who I am?" God and tradition have told him. Jason may be said to exemplify a trait of American society today that Wesley Morris identifies as a counterweight to the loosening of binds and boundaries: "our comfort with fixed, established identity and our distress over its unfixed or unstable counterpart."[19]

Although the Jason story in *In the Image* seems to play a secondary role to that of Bill Landsmann, Leora, and even Jake, in terms of passing into a new identity it takes center stage. The road Jason travels basically starts out from nowhere in terms of his religious and cultural knowledge and practice: As he explains to Leora when they are college sweethearts, "My family's Jewish, but just barely, and, I mean, we don't go to synagogue or anything" (43). When he and Leora are at the zoo and the group of Hasidim arrives, he snidely remarks that he hopes this is not "a permanent massive Jewish invasion." Leora remarks that he seems "really uncomfortable around religious Jews" and he responds, "I guess I just don't understand how I'm supposed to feel about them. . . . I mean, I see one of these guys on a bus with a hat and a nice, long beard, and I know I'm supposed to be thinking to myself, Yes, you are my brother, we stood at Mt. Sinai together. . . . But it doesn't work that way. Instead I just think to myself, Why are you dressed like you're Amish?"(47). But after a moment he asks, "And why . . . do they make me feel, since I'm Jewish and they're Jewish, but I'm not Super-Duper Jew like they are, that everything I'm doing in my life is totally wrong?" (48) After his soccer accident, "as he sank into the depths, he called out and was rescued" by the campus Orthodox Movement, becoming one of the "born-agains," in the words of the novel (103). Now he is what his nursing home patient always asked of him: the deep-sea diver who symbolically brings the tossed tefillin up again from the depths and who, by becoming a man, lays tefillin in prayer. A religious Jew literally binds tefillin, but religious artifacts and rituals also bind one as a community. So Jason transmogrifies from barely Jewish Jason into Super-Duper Jew Yehudah. The same is the case with the father in Francine Prose's story "Electricity." On the other hand, Philip Roth's Eli, making a similar passage, is disoriented by his transformation; viewed by his assimilated neighbors as having gone off his rocker in becoming a "fanatic," meaning an Orthodox Jew, he loses his place in his family and community, perhaps forever. One can imagine Eli asking in bewilderment, as he is carried away by the interns, "Who is it who can tell me who I am?" Like Shakespeare's king, who utters this question on the heath, Peck's situation is so disorienting that his very identity is in doubt.

The important difference is that Horn's Jason has undergone his transformation a half century after Eli became a "fanatic." Unlike Beverley Naidus's unnamed modern Jew, uncomfortable with being taken for a Jew in spite of his best efforts at assimilation, Jason would be happy to be recognized as an ultra-Orthodox Jew by any passerby—recognized immediately by clothing and facial hair, no matter that distinctions between Hasidic sects such as Satmar and Lubavitch are beyond the knowledge base of the general public. He would be happy to be credited with diving down into eastern European culture as part of the rescue team for the language of that culture: Yiddish. Before his transformation, Jason knew no Yiddish, not even terms in popular culture like *mentsh* (43). When the Hasids speak Yiddish to their children as well as English, the author seizes the opportunity to differentiate between the Yiddish that Leora had studied in college—"the Yiddish that Jewish writers [in Europe] once used to free themselves from the religiousness of Hebrew, to prove that they were modern men"—and Yiddish as an everyday language whose purpose among these Hasids in America is the polar opposite: "the language of ultraorthodox American Jews, a hybrid of dialects that they used to avoid speaking Gentile English" (46).

We have come a long way in presentations of Yiddish from "Yekl" to *In the Image*. Yekl's fervid desire to assimilate is depicted in part by the fractured English that Cahan puts in his mouth; since the novella was published specifically for the American reading public, Yiddish is presented in Standard English with helpful footnotes to explain those Yiddish terms inserted here and there for the sake of realism. Cahan provides a hint of the language's variations along with its own evidence of assimilation with a telling description of Yiddish in the mouth of Yekl's love interest: When Mamie visits the home of Jake and the wife of whom Mamie had been unaware, Jake insists that she speak Yiddish so that Gitl will not think anything is amiss, but Mamie speaks "with an overdone American accent in the dialect of the Polish Jews, affectedly Germanized and profusely interspersed with English, so that Gitl, whose mother tongue was Lithuanian Yiddish, could scarcely catch the meaning of one half of her flood of garrulity."[20] In *Bread Givers*, Sara Smolinsky's family speaks Yiddish in the home, rendered by Anzia Yezierska in English with an occasional inverted word order and a real Yiddish word (usually a curse) thrown in as a reminder. *Jews without Money* is written almost totally in Standard English (again, a few Yiddish words are sprinkled in like seasoning), but the reader understands that the immigrant Jews are speaking Yiddish, especially after being told that the father has been in America for a decade and "can't speak a word" of English, and the mother curses in "Elizabethan Yiddish." Harry the Pimp, the "pattern of American success" among the tenement dwellers, advises all the youngsters that "America is a wonderful country. . . . One can make much money here, but first one must learn to speak English. . . . Learn English; become an American. . . . Look at me; if I hadn't learned English I myself would still be buried in a shop. But I struggled—I fought—I learned English." It is Harry who gives Mikey Gold his first book in English so he can study the language.[21]

Henry Roth's *Call It Sleep* utilizes extremely poetic English for Yiddish, especially when spoken by the mother, and presents a variety of muddled English pronunciations not only of the Jewish boys in the study house or on the street but also of the Italian street sweeper, Irish cops, and assorted other ethnics in early twentieth-century New York.[22] In *Good as Gold*, Joseph Heller reserves Yiddish mainly for a hilarious bombardment of Henry Kissinger with disparaging terms, since Kissinger (like Gold himself) has "forgotten" that he is a Jew and needs to be reminded.[23] In contrast, *In the Image* presents Yiddishkeit alive in the close-knit Hasidim of New Jersey, who hold on to their old-world customs in language along with dress and religious practices. (Perhaps they are among the tens of thousands of ultra-Orthodox who would never subscribe to the liberal *Forverts* but who do read the weekly paper *Der Yid*, put out by the Satmar Hasids.)[24] From learning English as a passing strategy to incorporating Yiddish terms into American speech so integrally that most non-Jews don't even know they are Yiddish (or Yiddishized), Jewish American literature has presented language as a marker of assimilation as well as its opposite, a marker of a close(d) society. Even though the reader of *In the Image* is merely told that the Hasids speak Yiddish, here the use of Yiddish as the *mamaloshn*, the mother tongue of Ashkenazi Jews, indicates the antithesis of assimilation: a continuance of a form of community that relies for its existence on the eschewing of many aspects of modern American life, including allegiance to the American vernacular.

As David Sax said in a *Vanity Fair* essay on "the new Yiddishists," a group including Dara Horn, this younger generation is "vastly more comfortable in their Jewish skin than previous generations of American Jewish writers ever were, and their stories reflect that." Horn herself remarks that contrary to the pattern often depicted in Philip Roth's fiction, many of her generational peers have become more outwardly Jewish as they have gotten older: "When Jews came to this country, the way to piss off your parents was to eat pork and marry a *shiksa*," Horn says. "Now the best way to piss off your parents is to go to Chabad, marry at 18, have 10 kids, and refuse to eat in their house because they're not kosher enough." Sax subtitles this section of his essay "Reverse Assimilation," and he quotes a former vice president of the National Yiddish Book Center as saying, "Our generation is secure enough in their Americanism to be hungry for a more clearly defined sense of self."[25]

That clearly defined sense of self, however, may also be a seemingly paradoxical hybrid of pride in being Jewish combined with total secularism—the reverse of reverse assimilation, in a sense. After all, the vast majority of those in the Pew survey who said they had no religion also said they were proud to be Jewish. The magazine *Heeb*, titling itself with a term historically employed to disparage Jews, is one example of the foregrounding of Jewishness by such proud but secular Jews; here in full is the magazine's defiant declaration on the website, speaking of itself in the third person: "Its audience (frequently referred to as the 'unaffiliated'), feel little connection with organized Jewish life, but search for ways to express their

Jewish identities that are relevant and meaningful to their lifestyle. Heeb is not an institutional arm and it has no hidden agenda. Live with it."[26] Eric Goldstein, in the final chapter of his study of the relationship of Jews to whiteness, includes *Heeb* among other examples that, in his words, "tell us something about the pain and resentment that has resulted from a system that often predicated full acceptance in white America on the abandonment of cultural distinctiveness and the disavowal of deeply held group ties, once expressed in the language of 'race.'"[27] In these cases, cultural distinctiveness is strongly asserted even if divorced from religious practice. It is expressed in the language of ethnicity, but a nonessentialist concept of ethnicity that insists on authenticity that is not antithetical to assimilation and change.[28]

Whether one abandons Judaism and Jewish culture entirely or adopts a new form, rejection of one identity for another seems to encourage a need to denounce as well as to renounce, in counterpoint to (in some cases as internalization of) mainstream society's attitudes toward Jews that encouraged passing in the first place. George Jean Nathan's obfuscations about his cultural heritage, for instance, go hand in hand with his antisemitic statements. But even among those who retain a Jewish identity, "othering" is common. Factionalism and rival interpretations of Judaism occur within Orthodoxy itself: As Michael Gold relates in *Jews without Money*, the Hasidic Jews of the early twentieth century "look[ed] down on other orthodox Jews, and call[ed] them the '*Misnagdem*,' the worldly ones, the outsiders. And these others sneer[ed] in turn."[29] Among the non-Orthodox we have seen how Miss Wales in *Gentleman's Agreement* differentiates herself from the kind of Jew she considers vulgar and terms a "kike." According to the biographer of author Fannie Hurst, Hurst's mother also disparaged her daughter's two college boyfriends with this term because neither was "Unserer Leute"—our people. She meant more by "our people" than simply Jewish people: the Hursts were assimilated midwestern German Jews, and one of the suitors was of eastern European descent and hence a "kike." In the words of Fannie's biographer, the wrong kind of Jews was "even less desirable, in her world, than a non-Jew."[30] The origin of the term *kike* is uncertain, says Goldstein; "it was most likely coined by acculturated Central European Jews as a term of reproach for their less cultivated Eastern European cousins, whose surnames often ended in 'ki.'"[31] Matthew Frye Jacobson quotes a comment from the *American Hebrew* of 1894, as eastern European Jews flocked to the United States in increasing numbers: "The acculturated German Jew is closer to christian [*sic*] sentiment around him than to the Judaism of these miserable darkened Hebrews."[32] By the 1920s, "kike" had spread into the population of non-Jews, "most often to refer to the Jews as members of a distinct race who were dangerously powerful and influential, rather than marginal, in the white world."[33] Birdie Lee in *Caucasia* certainly feels completely marginalized and endangered when she is called kike, and thus to play it safe she removes her Star of David, passing out of her new Jewish identity.

Such disparaging terms as *kike* reveal the extent to which adaptation to the American values of reinvention, entrepreneurialism, and individualism can reside side by side with a tenuous sense of fitting in, being accepted by society and even by one's own people. What Werner Sollors says about blacks passing as white applies as well to the Jews: "The paradoxical coexistence of the cult of the social upstart as 'self-made man' and the permanent racial identification and moral condemnation of the racial passer as 'imposter' constitute the frame within which the phenomenon of passing took place."[34] For Coleman Silk, who leaves behind his heritage in order to become white and Jewish, upward mobility means he refuses to "carry the Negro," as he says about his black boxing opponent. Likewise, in "Eli, the Fanatic" Roth offers a vivid picture of those Jews who, in their perceived need to mollify their Christian neighbors in Woodenton, become intolerant of those who would threaten their peaceful existence in suburbia, including and especially the Jewish refugees and their emissary in the black hat. Steve Stern relates a similar message in his "Tale of a Kite." Metaphorically, these Jews don't want to "carry the Negro." In Horn's novel, too, Jake regards Yehudah as a Mad Hatter (202–3), recapitulating, if less stridently, the way in which Jason himself had formerly regarded Hasidic Jews. And Samuel Freedman, in his book tellingly called *Jew vs. Jew,* begins his study with the case of the Marcus family in Great Neck, Long Island, who felt the need in the early 1990s to move away when their next-door neighbors the Guilors became "fanatics," "flaunting" their new-found orthodoxy (to use the Marcus's terms). From the opposite perspective, that of the Guilors, they had done nothing more than find a meaningful community, and Edna Guilor even wondered whether Janet Marcus was "really Jewish." Freedman sums up the dueling philosophies of Jewish identity: "'I am what I feel' versus 'I feel what I am.' I am what I feel: I define the terms of my Jewish identity. I feel what I am: Judaism defines the terms of my Jewish identity. I am what I feel: Jewish ethnicity exists independently of Jewish religion. I feel what I am: Jewish ethnicity arises from Jewish religion."[35]

"Othering" of Jews by Jews can be found everywhere, leading to the fractured environments captured in Samuel Freedman's title and detailed throughout his book. In fact, Freedman reminds or informs the reader that the Jewish people's fractiousness is as ancient and long-standing as the Jews themselves, as he briefly rehearses the history of Jewish civilizations from the golden calf of the Book of Exodus through the partitioning of Jewish land into southern Judea and northern Israel, through the fragmentation into competing sects eight hundred years later, to the dawn of Christianity, and on and on into the modern era.[36] In some ways it has always been Jew versus Jew. Though America offered the promise of freedom to be a Jew in any way, including culturally, whether as Labor Zionist or Yiddish theatergoer, it also offered refugees arriving during and after World War II the "freedom to segregate themselves and preserve their ways," as

Freedman puts it. And these days, "othering" of Jew by Jew seems to be particularly salient among those born into or "born again" into Orthodoxy, who have asserted the right to set limits on, and boundaries around, Jewish authenticity: the one true way to be Jewish is to be religiously observant as commanded by God and recorded in the Torah.

The newly religious Hanoch Zuckerman makes his brother Nathan wonder, "Is this the role he has decided to play—the good Jew to my bad Jew?" (125). With the added investment in Israel at the center of his identity, Hanoch (following his mentor, Lippmann) considers himself the only kind of authentic Jew. Before his own passage into Orthodoxy, Dara Horn's Jason had held the same attitude toward the Super-Duper Jews who made him feel that everything about his life was wrong. Roth's novel, replete with statement and counterstatement, entertains all ideologies and opinions; the reader's challenge (along with the fun) is to sift through the verbiage and bombast to find the nuggets of truth on both sides. Fiction is "playful hypothesis and serious supposition, an imaginative form of inquiry," as Nathan's editor says at Nathan's funeral (210), in a eulogy we later discover was written by Nathan himself. Horn and Francine Prose are better positioned to treat the passage into Orthodoxy with unalloyed respect because it is unmixed with nationalism in their work. The downside in their treatment from this reader's perspective is that their characters' newfound religiosity seems to require a disparagement of less traditional forms of Judaism, typically but not exclusively the Reform movement. In Prose's story, the father makes negative remarks about "church"; in Horn's novel, the narrator comments that Leora attends a more traditional synagogue "than she would have liked it to be, but she continued attending nonetheless, because no one under the age of 35 attended the more liberal ones" (105). The suggestion is that Orthodoxy is gaining in numbers, while the "liberal" synagogues decline because the more "American" branches of Judaism cannot satisfy a Jew's search for spiritual meaning.

The same proposition is made in a contemporary British novel, *The Believers*, by Zoë Heller. In this novel the family is ardently socialist and the protagonist, Rosa, finds herself in opposition to her parents when she becomes attracted to Orthodox Judaism; her father rails out in protest about her buying into "this kind of fairy tale," just the kind of response to which Dara Horn referred in the *Vanity Fair* piece. Rosa sees how strange it is for her to have "wandere[ed] into synagogue one day and [found] her inner Jew. But there it was. Something had happened to her, something she could not ignore or deny." Perhaps it is not strange at all to find her praying in the balcony with the women, when she had been raised to avoid any celebration of Jewish holidays or attendance at synagogue services—"even the bar mitzvahs of their friends' children—loosey-goosey reform affairs, at which nothing more solemnly religious occurred than the unveiling of the chocolate fountain at the after-party."[37] Reform Jews in this view (not even permitted the grace of a capital letter), with their shallow values and little knowledge, are barely Jews at all.

I need not present an apologia for Reform Judaism, but a few points are pertinent. As Eric Goldstein says, the Reform movement is "one of the longest established institutions of the acculturated Jewish community"; reform rabbis' advocacy in civil rights for African Americans in the 1920s and 1930s, for one example, was a result in great part of ecumenical cooperation, itself a mark of acculturation. As early as 1859, eminent Reform rabbi Isaac Mayer Wise said, "We are Jews in the synagogue and Americans everywhere."[38] Even as the number of Jews who affiliate with Reform and Conservative synagogues is dropping, the fact that the Reform branch has more self-identifying Jews than any other today—at 35 percent, nearly twice as high as the next most populated, the Conservative movement—need not mean only that there is a liberalization (or attenuation, as some would have it) of religious identity as formerly observant Jews become less so; it can also mean that the adaptability, inclusivity, and social action emphases of the Reform movement are compelling attractions, in tandem with the fact that Reform synagogues since World War II have moved toward reincorporating traditional elements that had been abandoned in the nineteenth-century rejection of Orthodoxy by Classical Reform. Nonetheless, Dara Horn's Leora disparages "liberal synagogues," and Jason-soon-to-become-Yehudah rejects Leora as an unfit wife for a religious man and later prejudges Jake as "one of these Jews who could care less about Judaism, who probably thought it was some outdated code with nothing of value left in it, the type who hadn't celebrated a single holiday since childhood—a heretic, why not come out and say it?" (210).

Not only is Yehudah's premature evaluation of Jake incorrect, but Jake has views about religion with which the author is as sympathetic as she is with those of her Orthodox characters. Jake "knew that the people who had changed Jewish life for the good hadn't been the ones who didn't question life as it was, but those who did and who therefore demanded better": topping his list of such people—a list containing a biblical prophet and a secular Zionist alike—are "the brotherless daughters in the Book of Numbers who had demanded their father's inheritance despite their gender" (211). Jake is surely a "liberal" Jew, a questioning Jew, a feminist Jew who no doubt fully resonates with liberal prayer books' use of gender neutral language.[39] Yet what strikes me as most important about these two men is that in spite of their differences, the academic historian Jake and the diamond salesman Yehudah are actually alike in valuing sincerity, love, and the holy moments in life. Both are secure in their identities, not needing to ask who it is who can tell them who they are. Both are Jews, and both are given a voice by Dara Horn.

In the world today, in fact, many boundaries between sects and factions of Jews are actually blurring, and labels separating these groups may not give the whole picture. Samuel Freedman's analysis of Jewish factionalism led to his prognostication in his 2000 book that in America we are moving toward a different set of demarcations, which he labels Haredi (an alliance among all forms of ultra-Orthodoxy), Conservadox, Reformative, and the secular Jews he calls "Just Jews."[40] Jay Michaelson asks in the title of a 2015 opinion piece in the *Forward*, "Do Our Denominational Turf Wars Even Matter Anymore?" He argues that "the artificial map of American Jewry obscures a much more interesting set of designations hiding underneath," by which he means that, with some exceptions, diverse movements within Judaism are cross-fertilizing. The result is that "divisions and denominations used to matter in a way they don't now." Some Orthodox rabbinic bodies still patrol "the boundaries of legitimacy," to be sure, but the fluidity of identities of which Wesley Morris writes with regard to race and gender are apparent within the branches of Judaism and those who affiliate (or not) with one or another of them. The graphic accompanying Michaelson's essay shows a Star of David constructed as a tag, each point with its own string; the points can be pulled away from each other, but the names on the tag cross the fissures, tumbling into each other. Even "Russian" gets a space on the star, because, as Michaelson says, the Russian-speaking community in the United States today "defies all the categories that American Jews try to throw at it. If you ask many Russian-speaking Jews, they'll define themselves as a race."[41] Whether the sense of community *within* factions, however we label them, precludes a sense of unity among them—and whether there is any possibility of the continued viability of a cultural, secular Jewishness (Freedman's "Just Jews")—remains to be seen.

Over the course of my study of passing "fancies" in Jewish American literature and culture, in my discussions of Jewish literature and life from the late nineteenth century to the present day, I have explored definitions of "Jew" and "American," and the interactions between them. My concentration has been on how Jews in America have accommodated to perceived or actual American values over time: how they have acquiesced to cultural norms or resisted acquiescence; and how they have struggled to respond to the question "Who Are We?" I have considered literature and visual art of all kinds, and faces as well, as texts for analysis. Although I have addressed some of the most common strategies, including changes of names, noses, and clothing, I would consider two additional strategies before I conclude, one of them a key aspect of popular culture, the sport of baseball, and the other a key liturgical text, the Haggadah.

It is not surprising that two of our best-known Jewish American authors, Bernard Malamud and Philip Roth, each wrote a novel about baseball: Malamud's *The Natural* (1952) and Roth's *The Great American Novel* (1973). As Malamud's daughter has written about her father's first novel, "he'd found a baseball story, a good choice . . . for a Jew intent on becoming an American."[42] Roth also wrote an op-ed piece for the *New York Times* the year his novel came out, for publication on opening day of the baseball season: called "My Baseball Years," the essay surely speaks for Malamud's love for the game as well, when Roth remembers that the game for him had a "mythic and aesthetic dimension that it gave an American boy's life—particularly to one whose grandparents [in Malamud's case, parents] could hardly speak English. For someone whose roots in America were strong but only inches deep . . . baseball was a kind of secular church that reached into every class and region of the nation and bound millions upon millions of us together in common concerns, loyalties, rituals, enthusiasms, and antagonisms. Baseball made me understand what patriotism was about, at its best."[43] For the view of those immigrant ancestors themselves, one need only look to "Yekl." At our first glimpse of Jake, he is regaling his sweatshop compatriots with his knowledge of American boxing (another kind of passing strategy, for both Jews and blacks), but soon enough, after being taunted for lauding uneducated fighters, he switches to challenging his co-workers about baseball: "*Alla right*, let it be as you say; the fighters are not *ejecate* . . . . But what will you say to *baseball*? All *college boys* and *tony peoplesh* play it." Continuing in his Yiddish punctuated by broken English, Jake presses on about the knowledge necessary to play the sport; and when one of the workers scoffs that only children play ball, and "yet people say America is a *smart country. I don't see it,*" Jake scorns him as "a bedraggled *greenhorn*, afraid to budge out of Hester Street." For his part, Jake wants "to know that I live in America. *Dot'sh a' kin' a man I am!*"[44] The film based on Cahan's novella makes baseball even more central to Jake's life, and more symbolic, when Jake teaches his son how to play the sport (the joy in play highlighted by the playfulness of the background music) while Mr. Bernstein reads his holy book and prays on the sideline. The contrast between the passions of the two "fathers" (one actual, one potential), and their secular and sacred approaches to life, is thereby underscored. In addition, the two men exemplify the different gender norms of the Old World and the New: Jake is performing an American male body and identity—active, dominant, and strong—whereas Bernstein sits on the ground, head bowed over his book, like the valued Talmudic scholar of eastern Europe that he wishes he could be.[45]

Annie Polland and Daniel Soyer, in their study of immigrant Jews, reproduce a 1914 cartoon from a Yiddish humor magazine that pictures the struggle faced by Jewish parents in weaning their sons' interest from baseball to Jewish education. As the authors describe and interpret the cartoon, "the artist pokes fun at the separation of generations and the perceived friction between religious orthodoxy and orthodoxy of quite another kind—the secular worship of baseball, America's game. . . . Instead of a *Yidisher kop* (an intelligent head), the young boy's head is swelled up into an oversized baseball on which a sporting cap perches. The old rabbi, recoiling at the young boy's power and height, literally cowers in his shadow. The American religion of sports challenged Judaism."[46] In spite of Mr. Bernstein's nurturing religiosity, as pictured in *Hester Street*, it seems quite possible that if there were a sequel to this film, with Mr. Bernstein now married to Gitl and raising Joey, the stepfather might be wringing his hands over his inability to have the boy pick the cheder over the homer. On the other hand, a scenario further down the line could reflect an accommodation to both worlds: if at the turn of the twentieth century Bernstein wears a yarmulke in the house and a bowler on the street, his modern Orthodox grandson in the 1950s might well "honor the mitzvoth without sticking out by wearing a *kippa* [skull-cap] inside school and a baseball cap on the street," as Samuel Freedman reports on a common practice by students in an Orthodox high school of that period.[47] Even today, a song by popular Orthodox children's performer Uncle Moishy emphasizes the unity of Orthodox Jews in one of its verses by reference to hats: "Yitzi wears a different *kipah*. / His father's hat is tall and round. / Baseball caps are Yossi's favorite. / Yet both can go hand in hand."[48]

Authors Chaim Potok in *The Chosen* and Joseph Heller in *Good as Gold* picture Orthodox Jews choosing the homer *and* the cheder, at different points in the mid- to late twentieth century. In several respects it would be hard to name two more different authors than Potok and Heller, but they both elected to feature baseball in its connection to Jewish identity. *The Chosen*, set during World War II, begins with a ball game between modern Orthodox and Hasidic Jews whose significance the narrator explains: "To the rabbis who taught in the Jewish parochial schools, baseball was an evil waste of time, a spawn of the potentially assimilationist English portion of the yeshiva day. But to the students of most of the parochial schools, an inter-league baseball victory had come to take on only a shade less significance than a top grade in Talmud, for it was an unquestioned mark of one's Americanism, and to be counted a loyal American had become increasingly important to us during these last years of the war." Heller ends his novel with Jewish boys in a yeshiva schoolyard, one of them—"a muscular, red-headed youth with freckles and sidelocks and a face as Irish or Scottish or Polish as any Gold had ever laid eyes upon"—screaming at the pitcher, "*Varf* [throw] the fucking ball!"[49] The incident may seem, even be, improbable, but clearly the author wishes to make a final statement about the Jewish experience in America: that it encompasses many improbable appearances and situations, and thus obviates easy or narrow generalizations.

Another way that Jewish religion has aligned itself with American values is demonstrated within Jewish practice itself. In the context of Jewish ritual in an American setting, and as a coda to my discussion of religious difference vis-à-vis assimilation, I turn now to the Jewish holiday of Passover and the liturgical text used for its home observance—a text that both reflects and facilitates passing, a text that has evolved to become more "American" over the decades.

The Passover seder plays an important role in Jo Sinclair's *Wasteland* and provides the title and frame for Dara Horn's *All Other Nights*. As well, Sholem

Shachnah is rushing home for the first night seder in "On Account of a Hat." In Philip Roth's "Defender of the Faith," Sheldon Grossbart's strategic use of Jewish observance, in this case to fraudulently get a pass from the US base during World War II (a literal passing strategy), supposedly to attend a seder at his aunt's house, provides another of Roth's examinations of Jewish identity in his *Goodbye, Columbus* collection.[50] Woody Allen has seder scenes in at least two of his films, *Crimes and Misdemeanors* (1989) and *Café Society* (2016). The title story of Thane Rosenbaum's collection, "Elijah Visible," centers on a seder that is a "far cry from the family's origins in Poland. Rabbinic grandfathers, observant fathers—now a new generation of fragmented legacies, American torchbearers skilled in the art of cultural compromise." As a "typical Posner family Seder," it has reduced to a carnival the once "solemn and sanctified event." Cousin-in-law Angelo literalizes Adam Posner's complaint that the family gathered around that table is "not even Jewish" when he reveals that when he underwent conversion and the rabbi told him he was now a Jew, he kept his fingers crossed behind his back[51]—a reversal of Michael Gold's Mendel, who had been baptized only in order to procure a free meal, and who, under his breath, had repudiated the act and declared himself "Mendel still, a Jew among Jews!" Even the seder led for a few chimpanzees and one gorilla by Calvin (né Seymour) Cohn—the only human survivor of God's second destruction of the world in Bernard Malamud's dystopian novel *God's Grace*—is part and parcel of that author's questioning of what kind of animal humans are, and vice versa. Cohn of necessity makes the few members of the ape kingdom his colleagues, even children and, in his desire to repopulate the world, his wife; in fantasizing that he can get inside the head of chimpanzees, imagining that the answer to "who they think they are" is *humans*, he makes a fatal (mis)calculation.[52]

Given such featuring of the seder in works by Jewish American writers, and the popularity of this ritual and its adaptations to modernity in the lives of Jews of all stripes, the text at the core of the seder, the Haggadah, is constructively seen as a passing strategy in and of itself. Nathan Englander, who cowrote a Haggadah with Jonathan Safran Foer, said as much when he remarked that "out of all the traditional Jewish documents, it's the one that's most living."[53] Joel Gereboff's essay "One Nation, with Liberty and Haggadahs for All" displays the extensive research that reveals how changes in this key text—over three hundred editions in America from 1837 until today—disclose the movement toward reconciling Jewish and American identities. As Gereboff summarizes, the alteration "in nearly every one of [the Haggadah's] aspects, including wording, layout, language, and sponsorship, indicates that it is a significant site of cultural negotiations and Jewish acts of self-definition."[54] The ultimate point of Gereboff's detailed account is that in most branches of Judaism, and within unaffiliated but Jewishly identified segments of society as well, modifications of the Haggadah over time provide evidence of the impact of American culture on this central Jewish text.

In the 1920s, to give one example, a traditional Haggadah noted in its introduction, "The ideal of liberty borrowed from the Israelites of old, encouraged the American Revolution against the British unjust rule which culminated in American Independence in 1776." Other Haggadahs contained the score for "The Star-Spangled Banner" and additional quintessentially American music. During World War II, Haggadahs designed for those in military service deliberately stressed the compatibility of the American valuation of liberty, for which these soldiers were fighting, with the Passover story's emphasis on freedom. In the 1950s and 1960s, new commentaries and foci accompanied traditional ritual elements to appeal to various sectors of American society, and that trend has continued: "What is important about nearly all the recent Haggadot [says Gereboff] is that, except for the Orthodox publications, the authors take for granted the harmony between Jewish and American values and proceed to present Judaism as relevant to contemporary issues. Jews are so at home in America that they can combine recovered elements of Jewish learning with the insights of non-Jewish thinkers, while simultaneously affirming their Jewishness and motivating Jews to deal with a host of issues facing America and the world." Even the Orthodox Haggadahs, grounded in Torah and eschewing topical references, can be said to make a statement about American identity because, as Gereboff puts it, "for these authors America, with its guarantee of religious freedoms, provides a good context in which to construct their largely separatist life." All in all, Gereboff has compellingly demonstrated how the Haggadah is truly a key text for negotiating an identity both Jewish and American.[55]

The central message of the Haggadah—*In every generation the story must be told*—can thus serve as a motto for the various editions of this text over the decades, which tell their own stories of Jews' adaptations to the Promised Land of America. The permutations of the Haggadah, that is, provide a distinctive example of the reconciliations between religious, cultural, and national identities that many Jewish authors and editors in America have sought to portray in their texts. Contemporary works of literature support the proposition that this subject matter is not outdated and no doubt never will be, Irving Howe's famous prediction in 1977 to the contrary. In Howe's introduction to an anthology of Jewish American stories he pondered the demise of American Jewish literature because he thought the subject matters of such literature would very soon be depleted: the immigrant experience, making it in America, struggling with Jewish identity.[56] By at least the 1990s, editors of story collections of Jewish American writers were referencing Irving Howe in their own introductions, in order to point up his shortsightedness. Said Gerald Shapiro, for instance, "If you buy Howe's basic premise—that Jewish-American fiction arose from and was tied to a specific place, a particular time, a temporary state of affairs—then . . . by now the whole enterprise must be as stale as a sixty-year-old loaf of pumpernickel."[57]

That Jewish American fiction is both fresh and plentiful is evidenced by the number of published works continuing to fill the library and bookstore shelves, not to mention the readers' hunger for such literature. One contributing factor that Howe did not imagine in the 1970s is the ensuing influx of Jews into America from other countries, and the consequent wrestling of these new immigrants with their trifold identities as Jew, American, and fill-in-the-blank nationality of their birth. Jewish American fiction writers with Russian roots, such as Gary Shteyngart, have reached particular acclaim for their works in English; another from the impressive list of Russian-born writers is Lara Vapnyar. The author of three novels and a collection of short stories, Vapnyar has also written an informative essay "On Becoming a Russian Jewish American." In the Soviet Union, where "nobody practiced any kind of religion," she was often considered first and foremost a Jew, not a real Russian like everybody else. A six-year-old classmate's taunt, "I know something about you. You're a Jewess," was her first inkling of difference. "Even though I had no idea what Jewish or Jewess was [she muses in this essay], from the tone in which my classmate spoke, I knew that it meant to be something different, and most definitely something inferior." The worst part was that "Jewish" was the nationality printed on all her identification documents: "It was required on all application forms, and on the class roster in school, so that even if you didn't have distinctly Jewish features or character traits, you still couldn't conceal your nationality from your teachers or classmates." In love with Russian literature, Vapnyar cringed to see the multitudinous antisemitic sentiments from her favorite authors. Thus, in the Soviet Union it was a constant struggle for Vapnyar to cope with her twofold identity.[58]

Once in the United States, after Perestroika, her identity issues became more pronounced. Labeled a Jew in her former country, Vapnyar now felt she had no right to be called a Jew in America. After all, with her atheistic upbringing she knew nothing of Jewish history and culture, not to mention religion. Nor could she consider herself an American, ignorant as she was about the language, history, and culture of the United States. So Russian was the default identity, bestowed on her by Americans and received ambivalently, since it had been denied her in the Soviet Union: "I couldn't possibly accept the identity of a people who had called me a dirty Jew." The way she came to reconcile all three identities was by becoming a writer (her fourth major identity). With some delight, she notes that her book of short stories, *There Are Jews in My House*, is listed in all three categories: Russian, Jewish, American; and in reviews, she's "now called a Russian American, a Jewish American, a Russian Jew, or—if the reviewer is not afraid of excess—a Russian Jewish American writer."[59] I would add that the *New York Times* book review of her latest novel, *Still Here* (2016), doesn't refer to her by those identities—perhaps by this stage in her career her reviewers do not feel quite the need to do so.[60]

Significantly, Vapnyar conceived her title story "There Are Jews in My House" when in Washington, DC, at the Holocaust Museum. "That moment I knew with the utmost certainty that I was Jewish, whatever that meant [she says]. I also knew that one day I would have to write a story about the Holocaust." Two stories about antisemitism followed, both created "as a Russian, greatly influenced by Russian writers, who are still my painful favorites. I wrote them in English, the language I feel most comfortable with, even though I often struggle with grammar and vocabulary. I would even say that I wrote in American, which for me became the language of immigrants, who come from all over the world bringing their stories, their cultures, and their pain."[61] The editors of the anthology *The New Diaspora* include several stories about the Holocaust in addition to the large number by contemporary immigrant writers. As those editors state, "The literary preoccupation with the Holocaust among Jewish writers, especially in the decades surrounding the turn of the twenty-first century, has taken on considerable momentum."[62] This "literary preoccupation" includes fiction by writers who are descendants of Holocaust survivors. In "The Day the Brooklyn Dodgers Finally Died," one of this cohort, Thane Rosenbaum, tells of a group of Holocaust survivors who take on the mantle of their beloved but lost (to Los Angeles) Dodgers when the police fail to catch the hoodlums who have marked swastikas throughout the Jewish sections of Brooklyn. Wearing Dodgers' caps, they literally leave their own mark—their concentration camp numbers—all over the borough: "It was not an act of defacement, but defiance." Yet, in the act of writing stories about the Holocaust, Rosenbaum is also capable of interrogating the very preoccupation with it, notably in "An Act of Defiance": an "act of defiance" in itself, one might say, to the central role played by the Holocaust in the identity of many Jews, and a mark of a contemporary author's nuanced approach to the subject.[63]

As the Holocaust survivors die out, and with them the firsthand recollections, many Jewish American writers feel the need to look back to that defining historical moment. To put this into a wider context, Americans of all backgrounds have been obsessed for many decades with filling in the gaps in their personal and racial/national identities. Alex Haley's book *Roots* became a television phenomenon in 1977, in the miniseries by that title about black history from Africa to the United States—both a reflection of and instigation for finding oneself by uncovering the past. We are all deep-sea divers, it seems, looking to recover something lost that will make us feel complete, even the horrors of our racial/ethnic histories like slavery and the mass extermination of European Jews. We are like Dara Horn's Leora, that "conservation-minded" girl who never wanted "to throw anything of hers away." The subtitle of Wesley Morris's piece— "Who do you think you are?"—is also the title of a television show on The Learning Channel (TLC), airing first in March 2010 and continuing today; it features celebrities discovering their roots, among them Lisa Kudrow, who first produced the show, and Lea Michele, who learned more about her Sephardic ancestors on her father's side in the May 1, 2016, episode. Henry Louis Gates's PBS show "Finding Your Roots" is another example. The popularity of these television programs along with such websites as ancestry.com (sponsor of the Gates show), instructional DVDs, and in-class or online adult education courses hosted by libraries and colleges indicates that famous and ordinary citizens alike want to understand where they came from so that they can be more rooted, more placed, in the present. DNA sampling is but the latest development in facilitating this quest, not just to identify the rightful heritage of babies stolen during the Dirty War, but to put everyday folks in touch with their histories (and hitherto unknown relatives) as well. At a time when identities are more fluid than ever, if neither uniformly nor uncontestably so, Americans are avid for vehicles that help answer the burning question posed by Shakespeare's Lear: Who is it who can tell me who I am?

Notes

1. Malamud, *Tenants*, 193, 192, 219.
2. Goldstein, *Price of Whiteness*, 115.
3. Ibid., 204–11.
4. Roth, *Counterlife*, 103. Subsequent references in the text to this novel are to this edition. The whole "Judea" chapter pertains to Israel, but see especially 103–6. The insistence on identity as performance is found at the novel's conclusion (319–21), but the entire novel revolves around this subject. With a focus on the rite of circumcision, Budick provides an insightful discussion of this novel in relation to a history-centered adherence to Jewish identity (see "Performing Jewish Identity," 75–88).
5. Freedman, *Jew vs. Jew*, 27. Israeli policies toward the Palestinians have also complicated the allegiances of black Jews in the United States.
6. Morris, "Self in the Age of Anything Goes," 52.
7. Row, *Your Face in Mine*, 36, 208, 209, 211. The italics are the author's.
8. Elam, "Passing in the Post-Race Era," 750, 764. Elam provides an instructive analysis of racial passing in this essay but incorrectly employs the term *Judaism* on a few occasions when she means "Jewishness" or "Jewish culture." The term for a set of religious beliefs and practices is particularly inaccurate when used about Iris Gittleman's family, confirmed socialist atheists.
9. Morris, "Self in the Age of Anything Goes," 55.
10. Brodkin, "How Jews Became White Folks." After the 2016 election, sales of George Orwell's 1949 novel *1984* skyrocketed, but Philip Roth's own alternative history, *The Plot against America*, portrays a hypothetical situation more directly relevant to the Jews' situation in this country.
11. Jacobson, *Whiteness of a Different Color*, 171–99.
12. A letter to the editor by one Ira Sohn, published in the *New York Times* Book Review for March 13, 2016, p. 6, contains this reference.
13. Bloom, *Jewish Identities*, 140.

14. Cahan, "Yekl," 70, 12, 44.

15. Freedman, *Jew vs. Jew*, 275.

16. Between 1908 and 1912, Jews married out at a rate of 1.17 percent. Though this is low compared to the rate of Italian and non-Jewish German intermarriages at the time (nearly 17 percent and 33 percent, respectively), even this comparatively small rate for Jews occasioned much discussion, mainly because of the American pressure to assimilate and "the increased difficulty American Jews faced in justifying their preference for endogamy" (see Goldstein, *Price of Whiteness*, 98–99).

17. Goodstein, "Poll Shows Major Shift."

18. Horn, *In the Image*, 212. Subsequent references in the text to this novel are to this edition.

19. Morris, "Self in the Age of Anything Goes," 55.

20. Cahan, "Yekl," 49–50.

21. Gold, *Jews without Money*, 120, 158, 29.

22. Wirth-Nesher provides an in-depth analysis of Roth's use of language in this novel in "Between Mother Tongue and Native Language" (443–62).

23. Heller, *Good as Gold*, 350–62.

24. Baker, *Jew*, 63. Outside of the ultra-Orthodox world, Yiddish and Yiddishkeit are experiencing something of a revival. As a recent review of a comprehensive English-Yiddish dictionary states, "Today, after decades of linguistic assimilation, a growing number of Ashkenazi Jews are reclaiming Yiddish as a heritage language. They are taking Yiddish classes; singing and performing Yiddish songs; and attending cultural events like Yiddish concerts, films and theater. Some are even raising their children in the *mameloshn*, the mother tongue" (see Schaechter, "Want to Say 'Panic Attack' in Yiddish?," 30). In summer 2018, the National Yiddish Theatre Folksbiene (meaning People's Stage), founded in 1915, put on a production of *Fiddler on the Roof* in Yiddish (*Fidler Afn Dakh*), the first time the show had appeared in Sholom Aleichem's native language in fifty years. In addition, Yiddish Farm provides immersion in the language and culture along with organic farming (see https://yiddishfarm.org/).

25. Sax, "Rise of the New Yiddishists," 3.

26. "About Heeb," Heeb, http://heebmagazine.com/about.

27. Goldstein, *Price of Whiteness*, 236.

28. Sollors, "Introduction," xiv–xvi.

29. Gold, *Jews without Money*, 192.

30. Kroeger, *Fannie*, 7.

31. Goldstein, *Price of Whiteness*, 127. Goldstein cites Mencken's history of the English language, along with Eric Partridge, as his source (see 270n33).

32. Jacobson, *Whiteness of a Different Color*, 175.

33. Goldstein, *Price of Whiteness*, 127.

34. Sollors, *Neither Black nor White Yet Both*, 250.

35. Freedman, *Jew vs. Jew*, 14–17, 26.

36. Ibid., 29–30.

37. Heller, *Believers*, 62–63. These bar mitzvahs are reminiscent of Ron Patimkin's wedding in "Goodbye, Columbus"—most notably in the film, with its lavish ice sculptures—although the Patimkins are not Reform Jews, and Mrs. Patimkin is piqued at the thought that Neil or anyone else would be "reformed" (88).

38. Goldstein, *Price of Whiteness*, 93, 148, 12. In the name of full disclosure, I must mention that Rabbi Wise's daughter married a Christian in 1878, an early example of what would become even more prevalent in the open society of America (see 15).

39. For example, the Reform prayer book for the Sabbath and, later, weekdays as well (*Gates of Prayer*), evolved over the twenty years from 1974 to 1994 to incorporate gender neutral language wherever possible; all three editions during that period bore the tag line "A gender sensitive prayer book." By the time of the latest edition (2007, now called *Mishkan T'filah*, which loosely translates as a dwelling place for prayer), the tag line was no longer needed; not only is gender-neutral language a given by this time, but the introduction to the book also lists feminism as one of the themes of Reform Judaism and Life and stresses inclusivity in general as a byword (see Stern, *Gates of Prayer*, iv, and Frishman, *Mishkan T'filah*, ix). The use of a Hebrew title for the latest prayer book is another example of how the Reform movement has adopted more Hebrew into its service over time.

40. Freedman, *Jew vs. Jew*, 354–58.

41. Michaelson, "Do Our Denominational Turf Wars Even Matter Anymore?," 22–23.

42. Smith, *My Father Is a Book*, 122.

43. Roth, "My Baseball Years," 180.

44. Cahan, "Yekl," 5–6.

45. Rottenberg discusses gender identity and "performing Americanness" in her chapter on David Levinsky's competing ideals in Cahan's *The Rise of David Levinsky* (1917) (see 20–21). I would point out that in *Hester Street*, the 1975 film based on "Yekl," Gitl grows into an assertive womanhood as she assimilates, one that, paradoxically, recapitulates the assertive and strong Jewish ideal of womanhood in the Old Country. She not only takes the lead in her relationship with Bernstein, she will work in the grocery store they will soon own so that her new husband can study in the back. Director Joan Micklin Silver thus combines her 1970s feminist sensibility with a nostalgic view of an old-world conception of a wife's role.

46. Polland and Soyer, *Emerging Metropolis*, 282–83. These authors pose the question "*Kheyders* or homers?" on 282.

47. Freedman, *Jew vs. Jew*, 232.

48. Benor, *Becoming Frum*, 6–7.

49. Potok, *Chosen*, 12; Heller, *Good as Gold*, 447.

50. Roth, "Defender of the Faith," 186–97. This final deceit by Grossbart in the name of religion is the straw that breaks Sergeant Marx's back, causing him to "defend the faith" in his own way.

51. Rosenbaum, "Elijah Visible," 89, 91, 93.

52. Malamud, *God's Grace*, 163.

53. Englander, "Stories of Faith, Family and the Holocaust."

54. Gereboff, "One Nation, with Liberty and Haggadahs for All," 275. The Rubenstein Rare Book and Manuscript Library at Duke University contains a variety of Haggadot illustrating the adaptations of this central text to American interests at any given time. Among my favorites are the 1970 *The Freedom Seder: A New Haggadah for Passover*, picturing Martin Luther King on the cover; *Like an Orange on a Seder Plate: Our Lesbian Haggadah* (1999); and *Haggadah for a Liberated Lamb*, a 1988 "vegetarian manifesto." Rachel Ariel, Duke University subject librarian for Jewish Studies, created an exhibit of Haggadot throughout the ages for display in Duke's Perkins Library in the spring of 2017.

55. Gereboff, 280, 285, 287, 288, 289.

56. Howe, introduction, 16–17.

57. Shapiro, "Group Portrait," viii. Shapiro quotes the message of the Passover Haggadah at the end of his introduction, to lead into the stories to follow.

58. Vapnyar, "On Becoming a Russian Jewish American," 293, 294–95.

59. Ibid., 297, 298.

60. Bock, "Russian Midlife Crisis Handbook," 15. The only mention of any one of Vapnyar's identifiers comes in a single phrase of a four-column, full-page review: "combining Vapnyar's tragic Russian sensibility with her modernist aesthetic."

61. Vapnyar, "On Becoming a Russian Jewish American," 299.

62. Aarons, Patt, and Shechner, introduction, 6.

63. Rosenbaum, "Day the Brooklyn Dodgers Finally Died," 205; "Act of Defiance" is one of the stories in his interconnecting stories called *Elijah Visible*. Nathan Englander's "What We Talk about When We Talk about Anne Frank" (8) has a character who does seem to have the "unhealthy obsession" with the Holocaust that her husband accuses her of. Neither Englander nor Rosenbaum takes the extreme position of Philip Roth's Jimmy Lustig from West Orange, New Jersey, in *Counterlife* (165–67), who argues in his manifesto that Jews must "forget remembering" the Holocaust. But they would no doubt agree with Samuel Freedman's resistance, in *Jew vs. Jew*, to the outsize role that the Holocaust plays in many Jews' lives as "the basis of an identity built on victimization" (344).

Bibliography

Aarons, Victoria. "Philip Roth's Comic Realism in *Goodbye, Columbus*." In *Playful and Serious: Philip Roth as a Comic Writer*, edited by Ben Siegel and Jay L. Halio, 35–46. Newark: University of Delaware Press, 2010.

Aarons, Victoria, Avinoam J. Patt, and Mark Shechner. Introduction to *The New Diaspora: The Changing Landscape of American Jewish Fiction*, edited by Victoria Aarons, Avinoam J. Patt, and Mark Shechner, 1–18. Detroit: Wayne State University Press, 2015.

Ackerman, Diane. *The Zookeeper's Wife: A War Story*. New York: W. W. Norton, 2007.

Alexander, Michael. *Jazz Age Jews*. Princeton, NJ: Princeton University Press, 2001.

Alexander, Michael, and Bruce D. Haynes. "The Color Issue: An Introduction." In *American Jewish History* 100, no. 1 (January 2016): two unnumbered pages before page 1.

American Society of Plastic Surgeons. "Plastic Surgery Statistics 2017." https://www.plasticsurgery.org/news/plastic-surgery-statistics/

Austerlitz, Saul. "The Hidden One of N. J.: Why Dara Horn Is the Best of the New Breed of Jewish Novelists." *Tablet*, September 9, 2013. http://www.tabletmag.com/jewish-arts-and-culture/books/143707/dara-horn-profile.

Baker, Cynthia M. *Jew*. New Brunswick, NJ: Rutgers University Press, 2017.

Barkan, Elazar. *The Retreat of Scientific Racism: Changing Concepts of Race in Britain and the United States between the World Wars*. Cambridge: Cambridge University Press, 1992.

Baum, Charlotte, Paula Hyman, and Sonya Michel. *The Jewish Woman in America*. New York: Dial Press, 1976.

Bell, Vikki. "Mimesis as Cultural Survival." In *Performativity and Belonging*, edited by Vikki Bell, 133–62. London: SAGE Publications, 1999.

———. "Performativity and Belonging: An Introduction." In *Performativity and Belonging*, edited by Vikki Bell, 1–10. London: SAGE Publications, 1999.

Belzer, Tobin. "On Being a Jewish Feminist Valley Girl." In *Yentl's Revenge: The Next Wave of Jewish Feminism*, edited by Danya Ruttenberg, 181–88. Seattle: Seal Press, 2001.

Benor, Sarah Bunin. *Becoming Frum: How Newcomers Learn the Language and Culture of Orthodox Judaism*. New Brunswick, NJ: Rutgers University Press, 2012.

Bloom, Lisa E. *Jewish Identities in American Feminist Art: Ghosts of Ethnicity*. New York: Routledge, 2006.

Blum, Virginia L. *Flesh Wounds: The Culture of Cosmetic Surgery*. Berkeley: University of California Press, 2003.

Blyth, Myrna. *Cousin Suzanne*. New York: Mason/Charter, 1975.

———. *Spin Sisters: How the Women of the Media Sell Unhappiness—and Liberalism—to the Women of America*. New York: St. Martin's Press, 2004.

Blythe, Will. "Innocents Lost." Review of *The Ministry of Special Cases*, by Nathan Englander. *New York Times*, June 3, 2007. Book Review. www.nytimes.com/2007/06/03/books/review/Blythe-t.html?_r=2&.

Bock, Charles. "The Russian Midlife Crisis Handbook." *New York Times*, August 14, 2016, 15. Book Review.

Bodner, Allen. "Boxing: A Jewish Sport." *My Jewish Learning*. http://www.myjewishlearning .com/article/boxing-a-jewish-sport/.

Bolton-Fasman, Judy. "The Original Jewish Princess and I." *Forward*, June 5, 2015, 46.

Briquelet, Kate. "Watch Out, Rachel Dolezal. There's Another White NAACP Leader." *The Daily Beast*, June 15, 2015. http://www.thedailybeast.com/articles/2015/06/15/watch-out -rachel-dolezal-there-s-another-white-naacp-leader.html.

Bristow, Edward J. *Prostitution and Prejudice: The Jewish Fight against White Slavery 1870–1939*. New York: Schocken Books, 1983.

Brodesser-Akner, Taffy. "Apostates Anonymous." *New York Times Magazine*, April 2, 2017, 36–41.

Brodkin, Karen. "How Jews Became White Folks—and May Become Nonwhite under Trump." *Forward*, December 6, 2016. http://forward.com/opinion/356166/how-jews -became-white-folks-and-may-become-nonwhite-under-trump/.

———. *How Jews Became White Folks and What That Says about Race in America*. New Brunswick: Rutgers University Press, 1998.

Broom, Leonard, Helen P. Beem, and Virginia Harris. "Characteristics of 1,107 Petitioners for Change of Name." *American Sociological Review* 20, no. 1 (February 1955): 33–39.

Browder, Laura. *Slippery Characters: Ethnic Impersonators and American Identities*. Chapel Hill: University of North Carolina Press, 2000.

Brown, Corinne Joy. "Raquel: A Marked Woman." *Hadassah Magazine*, August/September 2014, 60.

Budick, Emily Miller. "Performing Jewish Identity in Philip Roth's *Counterlife*." In *Key Texts in American Jewish Culture*, edited by Jack Kugelmass, 75–88. New Brunswick, NJ: Rutgers University Press, 2003.

Burford, Mark, Jess Coleman, and Gwen Davis-Feldman. "On Racial Identity, Readers Discuss Issues Raised by a White Woman's Efforts to Pass as Black." *New York Times*, June 21, 2015, 10. Sunday Review.

Burrell, Angus and Bennett Cerf, editors. *An Anthology of Famous American Stories*. New York: Modern Library, 1953.

Café Society. Dir. Woody Allen. Perf. Jeannie Berlin, Steve Carell, Jesse Eisenberg, Blake Lively, Parker Posey, Kristen Stewart, Corey Stoll, Ken Stott. Gravier Productions, New York, NY, 2016. DVD.

Cahan, Abraham. "A Providential Match." In *Yekl and The Imported Bridegroom and Other Stories of the New York Ghetto*, 163–87. New York: Dover Publications, 1970.

———. *The Rise of David Levinsky*. New York: Penguin Books, 1993.

———. "Yekl: A Tale of the New York Ghetto." In *Yekl and The Imported Bridegroom and Other Stories of the New York Ghetto*, 1–89. New York: Dover Publications, 1970.

Cain, Susan. *Quiet: The Power of Introverts in a World That Can't Stop Talking*. New York: Random House, 2012.

Calisher, Hortense. "Old Stock." In *The Collected Stories of Hortense Calisher*, 263–75. New York: Arbor House Publishing, 1975.

Canales, Gustavo Sánchez. "'The Benevolent Self Was a Disgrace beyond Measure for Every Argentine Jew': Between the Need to Remember and the Desire to Forget in Nathan Englander's *The Ministry of Special Cases*." *Partial Answers: Journal of Literature and the History of Ideas* 13, no. 1 (January 2015): 57–71.

Chute, Hillary L. *Graphic Women: Life Narrative & Contemporary Comics*. New York: Columbia University Press, 2010.

Clary, David. "Passing for White." *South Florida Sun-Sentinel*, 2003. http://www.racematters .org/passingforwhite.htm.

Cliff, Michelle. *Abeng*. Trumansburg, NY: Crossing Press, 1984.

Connolly, Thomas F. *George Jean Nathan and the Making of Modern American Drama Criticism*. Madison, WI: Fairleigh Dickinson University Press, 2000.

Crimes and Misdemeanors. Dir. Woody Allen. Perf. Martin Landau, Anjelica Huston, Woody Allen, Mia Farrow, Jerry Orbach, Alan Alda, Sam Waterston, Claire Bloom, Joanna Gleason. Orion Pictures, Los Angeles, CA, 1989. DVD.

Dahl, Julia. *Invisible City*. New York: Minotaur Books, 2014.

Davidson, Cathy N., and Linda Wagner-Martin, eds. *The Oxford Companion to Women's Writing in the United States*. New York: Oxford University Press, 1995.

Davis, Kathy. *Dubious Equalities and Embodied Differences: Cultural Studies on Cosmetic Surgery*. Lanham, MD: Rowman & Littlefield Publishers, 2003.

Dellheim, Charles. "Is It Good for the Jews?" In *Key Texts in American Jewish Culture*, edited by Jack Kugelmass, 57–74. New Brunswick, NJ: Rutgers University Press, 2003.

Deresiewicz, William. "The Imaginary Jew." Review of *The Ministry of Special Cases*, by Nathan Englander. *The Nation*, May 28, 2007, 44–48. http://www.thenation.com /article/imaginary-jew?page=0,2.

Dinnerstein, Leonard. *Antisemitism in America*. New York: Oxford University Press, 1996.

Doležal, Rachel, with Storms Reback. *In Full Color: Finding My Place in a Black and White World*. Dallas, TX: BenBella Books, 2017.

Dougard, John. "To the Editor." "On Racial Identity, Readers Discuss Issues Raised by a White Woman's Efforts to Pass as Black." *New York Times*, June 21, 2015, 10. Sunday Review.

Dreisinger, Baz. *Near Black: White to Black Passing in American Culture*. Amherst: University of Massachusetts Press, 2008.

Edut, Ophira. "Bubbe Got Back: Tales of a Jewess with Caboose." In *Yentl's Revenge: The Next Wave of Jewish Feminism*, edited by Danya Ruttenberg, 24–30. Seattle: Seal Press, 2001.

Eggenberger, Nicole. "I Got 'Life-Altering' Nose Job at Age 16, Was 'Hideous' Before." *US Magazine* (October 28, 2013). https://www.usmagazine.com/stylish/news/lisa-kudrow -i-got-life-altering-nose-job-at-age-16-was-hideous-before-20132810/.

Eisner, Jane. "Three Rules for Changing Identities. *Forward*, June 26, 2015, 18.

Elam, Michele. "Passing in the Post-Race Era: Danzy Senna, Philip Roth, and Colson Whitehead." *African American Review* 41, no. 4 (2007): 749–68.

Englander, Nathan. Interview, BookBrowse, 2007. www.bookbrowsw.com/author_interviews /full/.../nathan-englander.

———. Interview 2 with Drew Nellins, Bookslut, 2007. www.bookslut.com/features/2007_05 _011077.php.

———. *The Ministry of Special Cases*. New York: Vintage Books, 2007.

———. "Stories of Faith, Family and the Holocaust." Interview. *Fresh Air*. NPR. Aired February 15, 2012, transcript March 22, 2013. www.npr.org/2013/03/174964910/nathan -englander-stories-of-faith-family-and-the-Holocaust.

———. "What We Talk About When We Talk About Anne Frank." In *What We Talk about When We Talk about Anne Frank*, 1–32. New York: Alfred A. Knopf, 2012.

Faber, Eli. *A Time for Planting: The First Migration 1654–1820.* Baltimore, MD: Johns Hopkins University Press, 1992.

Felsenstein, Frank. *Anti-Semitic Stereotypes: A Paradigm of Otherness in English Popular Culture 1660–1830.* Baltimore: Johns Hopkins University Press, 1995.

Field, Leslie A., and Joyce W. Field. "An Interview with Bernard Malamud." In *Bernard Malamud: A Collection of Critical Essays,* edited by Leslie A. Field and Joyce W. Field, 8–17. London: Prentice-Hall, 1975.

Franklin, Ruth. "Kaddish's Nose," *New Republic,* May 31, 2007. www.newrepublic.com /article/kaddishs-nose.

Freedman, Jonathan. "'Who's Jewish'? Some Asian-American Writers and the Jewish-American Literary Canon." In *Jewish in America,* edited by Sara Blair and Jonathan Freedman, 214–38. Ann Arbor: University of Michigan Press, 2004.

Freedman, Jonathan, and Sara Blair. Introduction to *Jewish in America,* edited by Sara Blair and Jonathan Freedman, 1–10. Ann Arbor: University of Michigan press, 2004.

Freedman, Samuel G. *Jew vs. Jew: The Struggle for the Soul of American Jewry.* New York: Simon & Schuster, 2000.

———. "When Solidarity Turns to Slumming." *Forward,* June 26, 2015, 20.

Friedman, Lester D. *The Jewish Image in American Film.* Secaucus, NJ: Citadel Press, 1987.

Frishman, Elyse D., ed. *Mishkan T'filah: A Reform Siddur.* New York: CCAR Press, 2007

Funny Girl. Dir. William Wyler. Perf. Barbra Streisand, Omar Sharif, Kay Medford, Anne Francis, Walter Pidgeon. Warner Brothers, Burbank, CA, 1968. DVD.

Gabler, Neal. *Barbra Streisand: Redefining Beauty, Femininity, and Power.* New Haven: Yale University Press, 2016.

Gates, Henry Louis, Jr. "White Like Me." *New Yorker,* June 17, 1996, 68–81.

Geller, Jay. "The Aromatics of Jewish Difference; or, Benjamin's Allegory of Aura." In *Jews and Other Differences: The New Jewish Cultural Studies,* edited by Jonathan Boyarin and Daniel Boyarin, 203–56. Minneapolis: University of Minnesota Press, 1997.

———. "(G)nos(e)ology: The Cultural Construction of the Other." In *People of the Body: Jews and Judaism from an Embodied Perspective,* edited by Howard Eilberg-Schwartz, 243–82. Albany, NY: State University of New York Press, 1992.

Gentleman's Agreement. Dir. Elia Kazan. Perf. Gregory Peck, Dorothy McGuire, Celeste Holm, John Garfield. Twentieth Century Fox Film Corporation, Los Angeles, CA, 1947. DVD.

Gereboff, Joel. "One Nation, with Liberty and Haggadahs for All." In *Key Texts in American Jewish Culture,* edited by Jack Kugelmass, 275–92. New Brunswick and London: Rutgers University Press, 2003.

Gilman, Sander L. *Creating Beauty to Cure the Soul: Race and Psychology in the Shaping of Aesthetic Surgery.* Durham, NC: Duke University Press, 1998.

———. *The Jew's Body.* New York: Routledge, 1991.

———. "The Jewish Nose: Are Jews White? Or, the History of the Nose Job." In *The Other in Jewish Thought and History: Constructions of Jewish Culture and Identity,* edited by Laurence J. Silberstein and Robert L. Cohn, 364–401. New York: New York University Pres, 1994.

———. *Making the Body Beautiful: A Cultural History of Aesthetic Surgery.* Princeton, NJ: Princeton University Press, 1999.

———. *Picturing Health and Illness: Images of Identity and Difference.* Baltimore: Johns Hopkins University Press, 1995.

———. "R. B. Kitaj's 'Good Bad' Diasporism." In *Absence/Presence: Critical Essays on the Artistic Memory of the Holocaust,* edited by Stephen C. Feinstein, 167–93. Syracuse: Syracuse University Press, 2005.

Gittleman, Sol. *From Shtetl to Suburbia: The Family in Jewish Literary Imagination.* Boston: Beacon Press, 1978.

Go-i, Uki. "Jews Targeted in Argentina's Dirty War." *The Guardian,* March 23, 1999. www.theguardian.com.

Gold, Michael. *Jews without Money.* New York: Carroll & Graf Publishers, 1984.

Goldberg, Isaac. *The Theatre of George Jean Nathan: Chapters and Documents Toward a History of the New American Drama.* New York: Simon & Schuster, 1926.

Goldenberg, Shifra. "What's in a Name: Erasing the Past and Losing the Memory." Review of *The Ministry of Special Cases,* by Nathan Englander. *Currents: A Journal of Politics, Culture, and Jewish Affairs* (Fall 2007). http://www.columbia-current.org/whats-in-a-name-erasing-the-past-and-losing-the-memory.html.

Goldstein, Eric L. *The Price of Whiteness: Jews, Race, and American Identity.* Princeton, NJ: Princeton University Press, 2006.

Goldenstein, Cheryl. "Every Individual Should Feel *As If*: Exilic Memory and Third Generation Holocaust Writing." *International Journal of Humanities and Social Science* 3, no. 8 (April 2013): 67–75.

Goldsmith, Meredith. "Dressing, Passing, and Americanizing: Anzia Yezierska's Sartorial Fictions." *Studies in American Jewish Literature* 16: *A Significant Pattern* (1997): 34–45.

Goodman, Allegra. Review of *"The Ministry of Special Cases." Publishers Weekly,* March 19, 2007, 36. http://www.publishersweekly.com/978-0-375-40493-1.

Goodstein, Laurie. "Poll Shows Major Shift in Identity of U. S. Jews." *New York Times,* October 1, 2013. http://www.nytimes.com/2013/10/01/us/poll-shows-major-shift-in-identity-of-us-jews.html?_r=1.

Gordon, Sarah. *Hitler, Germans and the "Jewish Question."* Princeton, NJ: Princeton University Press, 1984.

Grassian, Daniel. "Passing into Post-Ethnicity: A Study of Danzy Senna's *Caucasia*." *Midwest Quarterly* 47, no. 4 (2006): 317–35. http://go.galegroup.com.proxy.lib.duke.edu/ps/i.do?p=ITOF&u=duke_perkins&id=GALE|A149985148&v=2.1&it=r&sid=summon&userGroup=duke_perkins&authCount=1.

Graziano, Frank. *Divine Violence: Spectacle, Psychosexuality, & Radical Christianity in the Argentine "Dirty War."* Boulder: Westview Press, 1992.

Gubar, Susan. *Racechanges: White Skin, Black Face in American Culture.* New York: Oxford University Press, 1997.

Haiken, Elizabeth. *Venus Envy: A History of Cosmetic Surgery.* Baltimore: Johns Hopkins University Press, 1997.

Hanson, Philip. "Horror and Identity in 'The Jewbird.'" *Studies in Short Fiction* 30, no. 3 (Summer 1993): 359–66.

Harris, Alice Kessler. Introduction to *Bread Givers,* by Anzia Yezierska, v–xviii. New York: Persea Books, 1975.

Harrison-Kahan, Lori. "Passing for White, Passing for Jewish: Mixed Race Identity in Danzy Senna and Rebecca Walker." *MELUS* 30, no. 1 (Spring 2005): 19–48.

———. *The White Negress: Literature, Minstrelsy, and the Black-Jewish Imaginary.* New Brunswick, NJ: Rutgers University Press, 2010.

Heller, Joseph. *Good as Gold*. New York: Simon & Schuster, 1979.

Heller, Zoë. *The Believers*. New York: Harper Perennial, 2008.

Hester Street. Dir. Joan Micklin Silver. Perf. Carol Kane, Steven Keats. Midwest Film Productions Inc., New York, NY, 1975. DVD.

Hobbs, Allyson. *A Chosen Exile: A History of Racial Passing in American Life*. Cambridge, MA: Harvard University Press, 2014.

Hobson, Laura Z. *Gentleman's Agreement*. New York: Simon & Schuster, 1947.

Holmes, Anna. "Background Checks." *New York Times Magazine*, July 5, 2015, 13–15.

Horn, Dara. *All Other Nights*. New York: W. W. Norton & Co., 2009.

———. "Articles of Faith." *New York Times*, August 29, 2013. Book Review. http://www.nytimes.com/2013/09/01/books/review/articles-of-faith.html?emc=eta1&_r=0.

———. *Eternal Life: A Novel*. New York: W. W. Norton, 2018.

———. *A Guide for the Perplexed*. New York: W. W. Norton, 2013.

———. *In the Image*. New York: W. W. Norton, 2002.

———. "Shtetl World." *Commentary*, September 1, 2010. https://www.commentarymagazine.com/articles/shtetl-world/.

———. *The World to Come*. New York: W. W. Norton, 2006.

Howe, Irving. Introduction to *Jewish American Stories*, edited by Irving Howe, 1–17. New York: Mentor Book/New American Library, 1977.

Howe, Irving, and Ruth R. Wisse. Introduction to *The Best of Sholom Aleichem*, edited by Irving Howe and Ruth R. Wisse, vii–xxvii. Washington, DC: New Republic Books, 1979.

Human Stain, The. Dir. Robert Benton. Perf. Anthony Hopkins, Nicole Kidman, Ed Harris, Gary Sinise. Miramax Films, Los Angeles, CA, 2003. DVD.

Hurst, Fannie. "The Gold in Fish." In *The Stories of Fannie Hurst*, edited by Susan Koppelman, 254–81. New York: Feminist Press at City College of New York, 2004.

Iny, Julie. "Ashkenazi Eyes." In *The Flying Camel: Essays on Identity by Women of North African and Middle Eastern Jewish Heritage*, edited by Loolwa Khazzoom, 81–100. New York: Seal Press, 2003.

Itzkovitz, Daniel. "Passing Like Me." *South Atlantic Quarterly* 98, nos. 1 and 2 (Winter/Spring 1999): 35–57.

Jacobson, Matthew Frye. *Whiteness of a Different Color: European Immigrants and the Alchemy of Race*. Cambridge, MA: Harvard University Press, 1998.

Jervis, Lisa. "My Jewish Nose." In *Body Outlaws: Rewriting the Rules of Beauty and Body Image*, edited by Ophira Edut, 62–67. Emeryville, CA: Seal Press, 2003.

Judah, Sophie. *Dropped from Heaven*. New York: Schocken Books, 2007.

Judaken, Jonathan. "Between Philosemitism and Antisemitism: The Frankfurt School's Anti-Antisemitism." In *Antisemitism and Philosemitism in the Twentieth and Twenty-First Centuries: Representing Jews, Jewishness, and Modern Culture*, edited by Phyllis Lassner and Lara Trubowitz, 23–46. Newark: University of Delaware Press, 2008.

Kaganoff, Benzion C. *A Dictionary of Jewish Names and Their History*. New York: Schocken Books, 1977.

Kaye/Kantrowitz, Melanie. *The Colors of Jews: Racial Politics and Racial Diasporism*. Bloomington: University of Indiana Press, 2007.

———. "Jews in the U.S.: The Rising Costs of Whiteness." In *Names We Call Home: Autobiography on Racial Identity*, edited by Becky Thompson and Sangeeta Tyagi, 121–138. New York: Routledge, 1996.

Katz, Paul. "A New 'Normal': Political Complicity, Exclusionary Violence and the Delegation of Argentine Jewish Associations during the Argentine Dirty War." *International Journal of Transitional Justice* 5 (2011): 368–89.

Kestenbaum, Sam. "'Alt-Right' Sees 'Jewish Coup' in Trump Policy Flips." *Forward*, April 28, 2017, 4.

———. "Black Jews Stand with Black Lives Matter amid Turmoil: But 'God Comes First." *Forward*, July 29, 2016, 3–5.

———. "Evangelicals Retool the Passover Seder." *Forward*, April 14 and 21, 2017, 10–11.

———. "Madagascar Natives Convert en Masse." *Forward*, June 3, 2016, 10–11.

Khazzoom, Loolwa. "United Jewish Feminist Front." In *Yentl's Revenge: The Next Wave of Jewish Feminism*, edited by Danya Ruttenberg, 168–80. Seattle: Seal Press, 2001.

———. "Working Their Way in From the Margins: With the Ascent of a New Chief Rabbi, the Hebrew Israelites Seem Poised to Reach Out to Mainstream Jewry." *Forward*, July 10, 2015, 8, 10–11.

Kirchheimer, Gloria DeVidas. "Goodbye, Evil Eye." In *Goodbye, Evil Eye: Stories*, 91–120. New York: Holmes & Meier, 2000.

Kirschenbaum, Gayle. "Look at Us Now, Mother!" http://lookatusnowmother .com/#&panel1-4.

———. *My Nose*. www.kirschenbaumproductions.com/mynose/index3gk.htm.

Kolatch, Alfred J. *The Name Dictionary: Modern English and Hebrew Names*. New York: Jonathan David, 1967.

Koltun-Fromm, Ken. *Material Culture and Jewish Thought in America*. Bloomington: Indiana University Press, 2010.

Kominsky-Crumb, Aline. "The Nose Job." www.adambaumgoldgallery.com/Kominsky Crumb_Aline-Nose_Job1WB.jpg.Dahl, Julia. *Invisible City*. New York: Minotaur Books, 2014.

Koppelman, Susan. "Introduction: Rediscovering Fannie Hurst." In *The Stories of Fannie Hurst*, edited by Susan Koppelman, ix–xxvii. New York: The Feminist Press at The City College of New York, 2004.

———. "The Naming of Katz: Who Am I? Who Am I Supposed to Be? Who Can I Be? Passing, Assimilation, and Embodiment in Short Fiction by Fannie Hurst and Thyra Samter Winslow with a Few Jokes Thrown in and Various References to Other Others." In *Ethnicity and the American Short Story*, edited by Julie Brown, 229–52. New York: Garland Publishing, 1997.

Kostelanetz, Richard. "Sephardic Culture and Me." In *Jewish in America*, edited by Sara Blair and Jonathan Freedman, 23–29. Ann Arbor: University of Michigan Press, 2004.

Kroeger, Brooke. *Fannie: The Talent for Success of Writer Fannie Hurst*. New York: Random House/Times Books, 1999.

———. *Passing: When People Can't Be Who They Are*. New York: Public Affairs, 2003.

Lagnado, Lucette. *The Man in the White Sharkskin Suit: A Jewish Family's Exodus from Old Cairo to the New World*. New York: Harper Perennial, 2007.

Lambert, Josh. "It All Begins with the Jewish Nose." *Haaretz.com*, August 15, 2014. http://www.haaretz.com/misc/article-print-page/.premium-1.610746?.

Larsen, Nella. *Passing*. New York, Modern Library, 2000.

Leverette, Tru. "Re-Visions of Difference in Danzy Senna's *Caucasia*." *Obsidian* 12, no.1 (Spring 2011): 110–27, 149.

Lewis, Sinclair. *Kingsblood Royal*. New York: Random House, 1947.

Lippman, Gary. "Pynchonicity." *The Paris Review*, Arts & Culture section, September 5, 2013. http://www.theparisreview.org/blog/2013/09/05/pynchonicity.

Lipton, Sara. *Dark Mirror: The Medieval Origins of Anti-Jewish Iconography*. New York: Metropolitan Books/Henry Holt and Company, 2014.

———. "The Invention of the Jewish Nose." *New York Review of Books*, November 14, 2014. http://www.nybooks.com/daily/2014/11/14/invention-jewish-nose/.

Macgregor, Frances Cooke. *Transformation and Identity: The Face and Plastic Surgery*. New York: Quadrangle/The New York Times Book Company, 1974.

Malamud, Bernard. "The Angel Levine." In *The Stories of Bernard Malamud*, 277–89. New York: New American Library, 1983.

———. *The Assistant*. New York: Farrar, Straus and Giroux, 1957.

———. "Black Is My Favorite Color." In *The Stories of Bernard Malamud*, 73–84. New York: New American Library, 1983.

———. *God's Grace*. New York: Farrar, Straus and Giroux, 1982.

———. "The Jewbird." In *The Stories of Bernard Malamud*, 144–54. New York: New American Library, 1983.

———. "The Lady of the Lake." In *Bernard Malamud: The Complete Stories*, edited by Robert Giroux, 221–40. New York: Farrar, Straus and Giroux, 1997.

———. *The Natural*. Harcourt, Brace, and Company, 1952.

———. *The Tenants*. New York: Farrar, Straus and Giroux, 1971.

Mann, William. *Hello, Gorgeous: Becoming Barbra Streisand*. Boston: Houghton Mifflin Harcourt, 2012.

Marcus, Lisa. "'May Jews Go to College?' Fictions of Jewishness in the 1920s." In *Antisemitism and Philosemitism in the Twentieth and Twenty-First Centuries: Representing Jews, Jewishness, and Modern Culture*, edited by Phyllis Lassner and Lara Trubowitz, 138–53. Newark: University of Delaware Press, 2008.

Marks, Copeland. "Jewish Indian Cuisine." *My Jewish Learning*, 2010. http://www.myjewishlearning.com/article/jewish-indian-cuisine/.

Marshall, Jack. *From Baghdad to Brooklyn: Growing Up in a Jewish-Arabic Family in Midcentury America*. Minneapolis: Coffee House Press, 2005.

Mason, Wyatt. "Disappearances: Nathan Englander's Novel of Political Terror." Review of *The Ministry of Special Cases*, by Nathan Englander. *New Yorker*, May 14, 2007. www.newyorker.com/magazine/2007/05/21/disappearances.

Matza, Diane. Introduction to *Sephardic-American Voices: Two Hundred Years of a Literary Legacy*, 1–19. Hanover, NH: University Press of New England, 1997.

McBride, James. *The Color of Water: A Black Man's Tribute to His White Mother*. New York: Riverhead Books, 1996.

Meerlo, Joost A. M. "The Fate of One's Face: With Some Remarks on the Implications of Plastic Surgery." *Psychiatric Quarterly* 30, no. 1 (January 1956): 31–43.

Melnick, Jeffrey. "A Black Man in Jewface." In *Race and the Modern Artist*, edited by Heather Hathaway, Josef Jařáb, and Jeffery Melnick, 126–39. Oxford: Oxford University Press, 2003.

Mencken, H. L. *The American Language: An Inquiry into the Development of English in the United States. The Fourth Edition and the Two Supplements, Abridged, with Annotation and New Material, by Raven I. McDavid, Jr.* New York: Alfred A. Knopf, 1963.

Merwin, Ted. *Pastrami on Rye: An Overstuffed History of the Jewish Deli*. New York: New York University Press, 2015.

Metzker, Isaac, ed. *A Bintel Brief: Sixty Years of Letters from the Lower East Side to the Jewish Daily Forward*. New York: Behrman House, 1971.

Michaelson, Jay. "Do Our Denominational Turf Wars Even Matter Anymore?" *Forward*, November 20, 2015, 22–23.

Michele, Lea. *Brunette Ambition*. New York: Crown Archetype, 2014.

Miller, Arthur. *Focus*. New York: Reynal & Hitchcock, 1945.

Morris, Wesley. "The Self in the Age of Anything Goes: Who Do You Think You Are?" *New York Times Magazine*, October 11, 2015, 47–55.

Nathan, George Jean. "Hopkins." In *The Smart Set: A Magazine of Cleverness* 58, no. 3 (March, 1919): 131–37.

Nellins, Drew. "The Ministry of Special Cases by Nathan Englander." *Bookslut*, May 2007. www.bookslut.com/fiction/2007_05_011059.ph.

Noomin, Diane. "The Agony and the Ecstasy of a *Shayna Madel*: The Epitome of a Perfectly Pretty Jewish Girl." In *Wimmen's Comix* No. 3, edited by Sharon Rudahl. Berkeley, CA: Last Gasp Eco Femmes, 1973. Comic Book and Graphic Novel Collection, David M. Rubenstein Rare Book & Manuscript Library, Duke University.

Oksman, Tahneer. *How Come Boys Get to Keep Their Noses? Women and Jewish American Identity in Contemporary Graphic Memoirs*. New York: Columbia University Press, 2016.

Ozick, Cynthia. "Envy; or, Yiddish in America." In *A Cynthia Ozick Reader*, edited by Elaine M. Kauvar, 20–63. Bloomington: Indiana University Press, 1996.

Parrish, Timothy. "A Comic Crisis of Faith: Philip Roth's 'Conversion of the Jews' and 'Eli, the Fanatic.'" In *Playful and Serious: Philip Roth as a Comic Writer*, edited by Ben Siegel and Jay L. Halio, 25–34. Newark: University of Delaware Press, 2010.

Pellegrini, Ann. "Whiteface Performances: 'Race,' Gender, and Jewish Bodies." In *Jews and Other Differences: The New Jewish Cultural Studies*, edited by Jonathan Boyarin and Daniel Boyarin, 108–49. Minneapolis: University of Minnesota Press, 1997.

Phillips, Bruce A. "Not Quite White: The Emergence of Jewish 'Ethnoburbs' in Los Angeles, 1920–2010." *American Jewish History* 100, no. 1 (January 2016): 73–104.

Pinsker, Sanford. *The Schlemiel as Metaphor: Studies in Yiddish and American Jewish Fiction*. Carbondale: Southern Illinois University Press, 1991.

Pollack, Eileen. "The Bris." In *The New Diaspora: The Changing Landscape of American Jewish Fiction*, edited by Victoria Aarons, Avinoam J. Patt, and Mark Shechner, 85–110. Detroit: Wayne State University Press, 2015.

Polland, Annie, and Daniel Soyer. *Emerging Metropolis: New York Jews in the Age of Immigration, 1840–1920*. New York: New York University Press, 2013.

"A Portrait of Jewish Americans: Findings from a Pew Research Center Survey of U. S. Jews." Pew Research Center. October 1, 2103. http://www.pewforum.org/files/2013/10/jewish -american-full-report-for-web.pdf.

Potok, Chaim. *The Chosen*. New York: Fawcett Crest, 1967.

Prell, Riv-Ellen. "Cinderellas Who (Almost) Never Become Princesses: Subversive Representations of Jewish Women in Postwar Popular Novels." In *Talking Back: Images of Jewish Women in American Popular Culture*, edited by Joyce Antler, 123–38. Hanover: University Press of New England, 1998.

———. "Why Jewish Princesses Don't Sweat: Desire and Consumption in Postwar American Jewish Culture." In *People of the Body: Jews and Judaism from an Embodied Perspective*, edited by Howard Eilberg-Schwartz, 329–59. Albany: State University of New York Press, 1992.

Preminger, Beth Aviva. "Plastic Surgery, Aesthetics, and Medical Professionalism: Beauty and the Eye of the Beholder." *Annals of Plastic Surgery* 64, no. 4 (April 2009): 340–43.

———. "The Jew and the Nose: Plastic Surgery and Popular Culture." In *Jews and American Popular Culture*, vol. 3, edited by Paul Buhle. Westport, CT: Praeger Perspectives, 2006.

———. "The 'Jewish Nose' and Plastic Surgery: Origins and Implications." *JAMA* 286, no. 17 (November 7, 2001): 2161.

Propst, Lisa. 2011. "'Making One Story'? Forms of Reconciliation in Jonathan Safran Foer's *Everything Is Illuminated* and Nathan Englander's *The Ministry of Special Cases*." *MELUS: Multi-Ethnic Literature of the United States* 36, no.1 (Spring): 37–60.

Prose, Francine. "Electricity." In *The New Diaspora: The Changing Landscape of American Jewish Fiction*, edited by Victoria Aarons, Avinoam J. Patt, and Mark Shechner, 283–98. Detroit: Wayne State University Press, 2015.

Pynchon, Thomas. *V.* Philadelphia: J. B. Lippincott Company, 1963.

Rabinovich, Solomon Naumovich (Sholom Aleichem). "The Man from Buenos Aires." In *Tevye the Dairyman and the Railroad Stories, by Sholem Aleichem*, translated and introduction by Hillel Halkin, 166–77. New York: Schocken Books, 1987.

———. "On Account of a Hat." In *The Best of Sholom Aleichem*, edited by Irving Howe and Ruth R. Wisse, 103–110. Washington, DC: New Republic Books, 1979.

Roback, A. A. *A Dictionary of International Slurs (Ethnophaulisms)*. Cambridge, MA: Sci-Art Publishers, 1944.

Rogin, Michael. *Blackface, White Noise: Jewish Immigrants in the Hollywood Melting Pot*. Berkeley: University of California Press, 1996.

Rogovoy, Seth. "The Original Rachel Dolezal Was a Jew Named Mezz Mezzrow." *Forward*, June 26, 2015, 16.

Romeyn, Esther. "Eros and Americanization: David Levinsky and the Etiquette of Race." In *Key Texts in American Jewish Culture*, edited by Jack Kugelmass, 25–45. New Brunswick, NJ: Rutgers University Press, 2003.

Rosenbaum, Thane. "An Act of Defiance." In *Elijah Visible*, 55–86. New York: St. Martin's Press, 1996.

———. "The Day the Brooklyn Dodgers Finally Died." In *The New Diaspora: The Changing Landscape of American Jewish Fiction*, edited by Victoria Aarons, Avinoam J. Patt, and Mark Shechner, 195–208. Detroit: Wayne State University Press, 2015.

———. "Elijah Visible." In *Elijah Visible*, 87–103. New York: St. Martin's Press, 1996.

———. "Lost, in a Sense." In *Elijah Visible*, 157–88. New York: St. Martin's Press, 1996.

Rosenthal, Gilbert S. *The Many Faces of Judaism: Orthodox, Conservative, Reconstructionist & Reform*. New York: Behrman House, 1978.

Rosner, Shmuel. "How Israel's Modern Orthodox Jews Came Out of the Closet." *New York Times*, August 4, 2016. Opinion Pages. https://www.nytimes.com/2016/08/05/opinion/how-israels-modern-orthodox-jews-came-outofthecloset.html?emc=edit_ee_2016080 5&nl=todaysheadlineseurope&nlid=829114&r=1.

Roth, Henry. *Call It Sleep*. New York: Picador/Farrar, Straus and Giroux, 1991.

Roth, Philip. *The Counterlife*. New York: Farrar, Straus & Giroux, 1986.

———. "Defender of the Faith." In *Goodbye, Columbus, and Five Short Stories*, 161–200. New York: Vintage Books, 1987.

———. "Eli, the Fanatic." In *Goodbye, Columbus, and Five Short Stories*, 247–98. New York: Vintage Books, 1987.

———. "Goodbye, Columbus." In *Goodbye Columbus and Five Short Stories*, 1–136. New York: Vintage Books, 1987.

———. *The Great American Novel*. New York: Holt, Rinehart & Winston, 1973.

———. *The Human Stain*. New York: Vintage Books, 2003.

———. "My Baseball Years." In *Reading Myself and Others*, 179–84. New York: Farrar, Straus and Giroux, 1975.

———. "An Open Letter to Wikipedia." *New Yorker*. September 6, 2012. http://www .newyorker.com/books/page-turner/an-open-letter-to-wikipedia.

———. *The Plot against America*. New York: Houghton Mifflin, 2004.

———. *Portnoy's Complaint*. New York: Random House, 1969.

Rottenberg, Catherine. *Performing Americanness*. Hanover, NH: University Press of New England, 2008.

Row, Jess. *Your Face in Mine*. New York: Penguin-Riverhead Books, 2014.

———. "We Wear the Mask." Interview with Grace Bello, *Guernica*, October 15, 2014. https:// www.guernicamag.com/interviews/we-wear-the-mask.

Rubel, Nora L. *Doubting the Devout: The Ultra-Orthodox in the Jewish American Imagination*. New York: Columbia University Press, 2010.

Ruderman, Judith. *Joseph Heller*. New York: Continuum, 1991.

———. *Race and Identity in D. H. Lawrence: Indians, Gypsies, and Jews*. Basingstoke, UK: Palgrave Macmillan, 2014.

Rust, Susan. "Modern Life," *Family Circle*, April 2015, 53–54.

Samuel, Sigal. "I'm a Mizrahi Jew. Do I Count as a Person of Color?" *Forward*, August 10, 2015. http://forward.com/opinion/318667/im-a-mizrahi-jew-do-i-count-as-a-person-of-color/.

———. "Jews of Color Get Personal and Political at First-Ever National Convening." *Forward*, May 16, 2016, 18–19.

———. "Racist Israeli Hanukkah Video Mocks Sephardic and Mizrahi Jews." *Forward*, November 30, 2015. http://forward.com/opinion/325657/racist-israeli-hanukkah-video -mocks-sephardic-and-mizrahi-jews/.

Savitz, Leonard D. and Richard F. Tomasson, "The Identifiability of Jews." *American Journal of Sociology* 64, no. 5 (March 1959): 468–75.

Sax, David. "Rise of the New Yiddishists." *Vanity Fair*, April 8, 2009, 1–4. http://www .vanityfair.com/culture/features/2009/04/yiddishists2000904.

Schaechter, Rukhl. "Want to Say 'Panic Attack' in Yiddish? Help's on the Way!" *Forward*, July 29, 2016, 30.

Schiff, Stacy. "Camp Stories." *New York Times*, February 19, 2012, 1, 9. Book Review.

Schireson, Henry J., MD. *As Others See You: The Story of Plastic Surgery*. New York: Macaulay Company, 1938.

Schoen, Carol B. *Anzia Yezierska*. Boston: Twayne Publishers, 1982.

Schulman, Martha. "When Race Breaks Out: PW Talks with Jess Row." *Publishers Weekly*, July 14, 2014, 46. https://www.publishersweekly.com/pw/by-topic/authors/interviews /article/63269-when-race-breaks-out-pw-talks-with-jess-row.html

Scodel, Alvin, and Harvey Austrin. "The Perception of Jewish Photographs by Non-Jews and Jews." *Journal of Abnormal and Social Psychology* 54, no. 2 (March 1957): 278–80.

Sehgal, Parul. "Takeover." *New York Times Magazine*, October 4, 2015, 13–15.

Senna, Danzy. *Caucasia*. New York: Riverhead Books, 1998.

———. "Coat of Many Colors." Interview with Susan Comninos. *Tablet*. June 10, 2004. http://tabletmag.com/jewish-arts-and-culture/books/774/coat-of-many-colors.

———. *Where Did You Sleep Last Night? A Personal History*. New York: Farrar, Straus and Giroux, 2009.

Serero, David. "How to Tell 'Othello' the Sephardic Way." *Forward*, July 1, 2016, 32.

Shapiro, Edward S. *We Are Many: Reflections on American Jewish History and Identity*. Syracuse, NY: Syracuse University Press, 2005.

Shapiro, Gerald. "Group Portrait." Introduction to *American Jewish Fiction: A Century of Stories*, edited by Gerald Shapiro, vii–xv. Lincoln: University of Nebraska Press, 1998.

Shostak, Debra. *Philip Roth—Countertexts, Counterlives*. Columbia: University of South Carolina Press, 2004.

Shteyngart, Gary. *Absurdistan*. New York: Random House: 2006.

Sinclair, Jo. *Wasteland*. New York: Harper & Brothers, 1946.

Siner, Emily. "How I Moved from Chicago to Nashville and Found My Jewish Soul in Tennessee." *Forward*, March 3, 2017, 6–7.

Skibell, Joseph. *A Curable Romantic*. Chapel Hill, NC: Algonquin Press, 2010.

Smith, Jenna Malamud. *My Father Is a Book: A Memoir of Bernard Malamud*. Boston: Houghton Mifflin Company, 2006.

Sohn, Ira. "To the Editor." *New York Times*, March 13, 2016, 6. Book Review.

Sollors, Werner. "Introduction: The Invention of Ethnicity." In *The Invention of Ethnicity*, edited by Werner Sollors, ix–xx. New York and Oxford: Oxford University Press, 1989.

———. *Neither Black nor White yet Both: Thematic Explorations of Interracial Literature*. New York: Oxford University Press, 1997.

Spada, James. *Streisand: Her Life*. New York: Crown, 1995.

Starbuck, Margot. *Unsqueezed: Springing Free from Skinny Jeans, Nose Jobs, Highlights and Stilettos*. Downers Grove, IL: IVP Books, 2010.

Stavroulakis, Nicholas. *The Jews of Greece: An Essay*. 2nd ed. Athens: Talos Press, 1997.

Stern, Chaim, ed. *Gates of Prayer for Shabbat and Weekdays*. New York: Central Conference of American Rabbis, 1994.

Stern, Steve. "The Tale of a Kite." In *The Book of Mischief: New and Selected Stories*, 5–18. Minneapolis: Graywolf Press, 2012.

Strauss, Elissa. "The Prurient Male Gaze Is Alive and Well in 'Red Oaks,'" *Forward*, November 6, 2015, 23.

Stubbs, Katherine. "Reading Material: Contextualizing Clothing in the Work of Anzia Yezierska." *MELUS* 23, no. 2 (Summer 1998): 157–72.

Sullivan, Deborah A. *Cosmetic Surgery: The Cutting Edge of Commercial Medicine in America*. New Brunswick, NJ: Rutgers University Press, 2001.

Susman, Gary. "Here's what the cast of 'Friends' were up to this week," *Entertainment Weekly*, October 23, 2002. http://ew.com/article/2002/10/23/heres-what-cast-friends-were-this-week-2.

Tabachnick, Stephen Ely. *The Quest for Jewish Belief and Identity in the Graphic Novel*. Tuscaloosa: University of Alabama Press, 2014.

Tannenbaum, Abby, ed. "America's Most Inspiring Rabbis, 2016: 32 Men & Women Who Move Us Most." *Forward*, May 20, 2016, 14–24.

Taylor, Sydney. *All-of-a-Kind Family*. New York: Taylor Productions, 1951.

——. *All-of-a-Kind Family Downtown.* New York: Taylor Productions, 1972.

——. *All-of-a-Kind Family Uptown.* New York: Taylor Productions, 1958.

——. *Ella of All-of-a-Kind Family.* New York: Taylor Productions, 1978.

——. *More All-of-a-Kind Family.* New York: Taylor Productions, 1954.

Terzian, Peter. Review of *The Ministry of Special Cases. Bookforum*, September 7, 2007. www .bookforum.com/inprint/014_01/223.

Tieck, Gustav. "New Intranasal Procedures for Correction of Deformities of the Nose Successfully Applied in Over 1,000 Cases During the Past Twelve Years." *American Journal of Surgery* 34, no. 5 (May 1920): 117–20.

Treglown, Jeremy. 2007. Review of *The Ministry of Special Cases. Financial Times*, August 18, 2007. www.FT.com.

Umansky, Ellen M. "Representations of Jewish Women in the Works and Life of Elizabeth Stern." *Modern Judaism* 13, no. 2 (May 1993): 165–76.

Vapnyar, Lara. "On Becoming a Russian Jewish American." In *Who We Are: On Being (and Not Being) a Jewish American Writer*, edited by Derek Rubin, 293–99. New York: Schocken Books, 2005.

Walker, Rebecca. *Black, White, and Jewish: Autobiography of a Shifting Self.* New York: Riverhead, 2001.

Weber, Donald. "The Limits of Empathy: Hollywood's Imagining of Jews circa 1947." In *Key Texts in American Jewish Culture*, edited by Jack Kugelmass, 91–104. New Brunswick, NJ: Rutgers University Press, 2003.

Wellman, Rita. *A Gentile Wife: A Play in Four Acts.* New York: Moffat, Yard, & Company, 1919.

White, Walter. "Why I Remain a Negro." *Saturday Review of Literature*, 30 (October 11, 1947): 13–14, 49–52.

Winegard, Richard Clarence. "Thyra Samter Winslow: A Critical Assessment." PhD diss., University of Arkansas, 1971.

Winslow, Thyra Samter. "A Cycle of Manhattan." In *Picture Frames*, 96–173. New York: Alfred Knopf, 1923.

——. "A Love Affair." In *Picture Frames*, 237–54. New York: Alfred Knopf, 1923.

——. "Amy's Story." In *Picture Frames*, 174–93. New York: Alfred Knopf, 1923.

——. "Birthday." In *Picture Frames*, 255–76. New York: Alfred Knopf, 1923.

——. "Corinna and Her Man." In *Picture Frames*, 277–97. New York: Alfred Knopf, 1923.

——. "The End of Anna." In *Picture Frames*, 298-324. New York: Alfred Knopf, 1923.

——. "Grandma." In *Picture Frames*, 21–49. New York: Alfred Knopf, 1923.

——. "Her Own Room." *Century*, 101 (January 1921), 363–74.

——. "Indian Summer." In *Picture Frames*, 213–36. New York: Alfred Knopf, 1923.

——. "Mamie." In *Picture Frames*, 50–95. New York: Alfred Knopf, 1923.

——. "Matt." *Chicago Tribune.* 29 June 1930, E4, E9.

——. "The Odd Old Lady." *New Yorker*, 3 (23 July 1927), 14-15.

Wirth-Nesher, Hana. "Between Mother Tongue and Native Language in *Call It Sleep*." Afterword to *Call It Sleep*, by Henry Roth, 443–62. New York: Picador/Farrar, Straus and Giroux, 1991.

Wisse, Ruth B. *The Schlemiel as Modern Hero.* Chicago: University of Chicago Press, 1971.

Wolff, Rachel. "Warhol Warhol Everywhere." ARTnews, September 2012. http://www .artnews.com/2012/09/04/warhol-warhol-everywhere/.

Wolitzer, Meg. *The Ten-Year Nap.* New York: Riverhead Books, 2008.

Wouk, Herman. *Marjorie Morningstar.* Garden City, NY: Doubleday, 1955.

Yehuda, Gil. Respondent on Quora website. https://www.quora.com/What-are-the-various-sects-within-Hasidic-or-ultra-Orthodox-Judaism.

Yezierska, Anzia. *Bread Givers.* New York: Persea Books, 1975.

Yiddish, the Mame-Loshn (*Yiddish, the Mother Tongue*). Writer/producer Pierre Sauvage for KCET-TN Los Angeles. Dir. Cordelia Stone. Waltham, MA: National Center for Jewish Film, 1991. DVD.

Zelig. Dir. Woody Allen. Perf. Woody Allen, Mia Farrow, Patrick Horgan. Warner Brothers, Burbank, CA, 1983. DVD.

Zeveloff, Naomi. "Cut to Fit: How the All-American Nose Job Got a Makeover." *Forward*, October 16, 2015, 24–27.

Zurawik, David. *The Jews of Prime Time.* Hanover: University Press of New England, 2003.

Index

JUDITH RUDERMAN is Visiting Scholar of English at Duke University. She is the winner of the 2017 Harry T. Moore Award for lifetime contributions to D. H. Lawrence studies and author of four previous books, including *Race and Identity in D. H. Lawrence: Indians, Gypsies, and Jews.*

CPSIA information can be obtained
at www.ICGtesting.com
Printed in the USA
LVHW090403160219
607781LV00001B/60/P

9 780253 036964